Musicianship-Focused Curriculum and Assessment

Musicianship-Focused Curriculum and Assessment

Colleen Conway, Editor

Contributing Authors:

Colleen Conway

Sommer Forrester

Heather Russell

Christina Hornbach

Ryan Shaw

Alison Reynolds

John Eros

Kristen Pellegrino

Chad West

Ryan Hourigan

Jill Reese

Shannan Hibbard

Heather Shouldice

Wendy Valerio

Jared Rawlings

Ann Marie Stanley

Scott Edgar

Johanna Siebert

Amy West

C. Michael Palmer

Cynthia Taggart

Linda Hartley

J. Si Millican

William Bauer

GIA Publications, Inc.
Chicago

G-8919
Musicianship-Focused Curriculum and Assessment
Colleen Conway, Editor

ISBN: 978-1-62277-270-4

TABLE OF CONTENTS

Part Three: Musical Development

Part Four: Specific Contexts for Learning and Future Directions

PREFACE

Musicianship-Focused Curriculum and Assessment is for music teachers working in P–12[1] settings who wish to align their curricula with the new core arts standards while continuing to focus on active music making in music classes. Each contributing author has focused his or her chapter on useful curriculum and assessment strategies for teachers. The text will also be helpful to those who are learning to teach and those who are teaching teachers in both preservice and inservice programs.

The book includes 21 chapters divided into four parts. Part I (Defining the Field) includes a chapter describing the fields of curriculum and assessment, a chapter on the intersection between curriculum, philosophy, and advocacy and a chapter that introduces readers to the characteristics of research in music curriculum. In the second part (Framework for Curriculum Development) authors examine various approaches to designing curricula including Understanding by Design, Universal Designs for Learning, and 21st Century Skills and the Common Core.

The authors for the middle section of the book (Musical Development) were charged with combining the ideas within the various approaches to music teaching including Orff, Kodály, Dalcroze, Suzuki, and Music Learning Theory as they sequenced instruction for music in the areas of: movement, rhythm, singing, creative music making, musical sensitivity and expression, music literacy, and music listening. The final section of the book (Specific Contexts for Learning and Future Directions) addresses curriculum and assessment within: (a) early childhood; (b) adult music learning; (c) English language

---

[1] P–12 is used throughout the book to include early childhood through 12th grade.

learners; (d) preparation for adjudicated events; (e) preservice education; (f) inservice education; and (g) technology. The final chapter examines the challenges to focusing on musicianship in music teaching.

Acknowledgments

Each chapter was reviewed by at least two reviewers. In most cases one reviewer was a P–12 educator and the other a higher education scholar. We wish to thank the following teachers and scholars who read and responded to early drafts of chapters: Chapter 1 - Carla Gannon and Bill Winters; Chapter 2 - Matthew Clauhs and Clint Randles; Chapter 3 - Carla Gannon and James Shouldice; Chapter 4-Paul Schapker and Jeri Hockensmith; Chapter 5 - Deborah Blair and Elizabeth Crabtree; Chapter 6 - Lynn Tuttle and Marcia McCaffrey; Chapter 7 - Herbert Marshall and Mary Kate Newell; Chapter 8- Hannah Picasso and Yael Rothfeld; Chapter 9 - Warren Henry and Denise Guilbault; Chapter 10 - Joanna Aldridge and Michele Kaschub ; Chapter 11 - Tim Cibor and Robert Woody; Chapter 12 - Julie Derges Kastner, Corynn Nordstrom and Holly Olszewski; Chapter 13 - Karen Salvador and Jenny Spurbeck; Chapter 14 - Stephanie Daniel and Joanne Rutkowski; Chapter 15 - William Dabback and Nathan Kruse; Chapter 16 - Carlos Abril and Justin Milota; Chapter 17 - Stephen Meyer and William Pitts; Chapter 18 - Kelly Parkes and Michael Raiber; Chapter 19 - Vicki Lind and Tim Nowak; Chapter 20 - Kimberly Walls; Chapter 21 - Daniel Albert and Chris Bulgren.

I would like to thank the students in the University of Michigan's summer master course MUSED 503 (Curriculum and Assessment) in the summer of 2014 who also read draft chapters and provided feedback: Kelsey Davidson, Jeri Hockensmith, Leeann Kuchta, Ashleigh Miller, Hannah Picasso, Aubrey Selaty, Ethan Shan, Amanda Thoms, and Olivia Zang.

Finally, as always, a big thank-you to my husband, Tom Hodgman and children Sarah Hodgman and Tommy Hodgman for putting up with the constant chatter about music education.

PART ONE:
DEFINING THE FIELD

CHAPTER 1

DEFINING MUSICIANSHIP-FOCUSED CURRICULUM AND ASSESSMENT

Colleen Conway
University of Michigan

This first chapter in *Musicianship-Focused Curriculum and Assessment* is devoted to defining the constructs of musicianship, curriculum, and assessment as they are considered in this book. I begin with the notion of musicianship and then continue with an examination of the terms *curriculum* and then *assessment*. I encourage readers throughout the chapter to think critically about their own personal experiences with musicianship-focused curriculum design, implementation, and assessment. Throughout this chapter I refer to other chapters in this text that will expand on the constructs defined.

Musicianship

Although this book represents diverse perspectives regarding curriculum and assessment, the authors hold a shared understanding that the development of musicianship is a key goal in P–12 music education. Authors agree that students in music classes need to be actively engaged in musical activities including moving, chanting, singing, playing instruments, reading, improvising, composing, and listening to music. This notion of musicianship is different from simply the ability to sing or play an instrument well. Good musicians have sensitivity to music, the ability to audiate both tonally and rhythmically, and the ability to perform, compose, and improvise with and without musical notation. All of the authors in this text have grappled with how to design curriculum and assessments in ways that best support growth of musicianship.

Curriculum

Curriculum scholars spend much of their time and energy trying to understand what a curriculum is. Historically, educators and music educators have disagreed regarding a working definition of curriculum. In her chapter entitled "Curriculum and Its Study" in the *Handbook of Research on Music Teaching and Learning*, Lizabeth Wing (1992) opened the discussion with the following:

> There is no "method" of curriculum discovery, any more than there is a method of exploring the jungle or falling in love. There is just understanding something about jungles, love, and school curricula, and the use of a motley collection of skills, disciplines of thought and ideas to make progress in them. There is no "conceptual system" to guide the decision-making (p. 2)

There is no one correct way to write a curriculum, and decisions about design depend on the teaching and learning context. In examining research studies on curricula that were available at the time in 1992 Wing determined that we needed to examine curricula at the local level:

> The profession [music education] knows itself largely from the standpoints of stated values and scientifically conducted quantitative inquiry into some of its curriculum efforts. Not much is known with any certainty about the past or what is really happening in music classrooms today. For example, what and how are teachers teaching? What and how are students learning? What are the primary influences on decisions related to who is taught what and how? What are the long-term outcomes of curricular experiences in music? These are questions central to curriculum. (p. 3)

Although there is certainly more research on local-level curricula now than back in the early 90s there is still relatively little known about what is happening in individual schools and classrooms. Chapter 3 in this book provides suggestions for ways in which music teachers may be more involved in the generation of research on curriculum.

In the curriculum chapter in *The New Handbook of Research on Music Teaching and Learning,* authors Betty Hanley and Janet Montgomery (2002) highlight the intersections of curriculum with educational concerns regarding student interaction, critical thinking, policy, gender and ethnicity, equality, and general assumptions about schools and schooling. I begin to address these concerns by first discussing the written document, what is taught, and what is learned. I then present a list of curriculum vocabulary concepts that need to be considered in order to address the bigger educational issues presented by Hanley and Montgomery. The most important element of curriculum is the notion that curriculum is a dialogue between teachers. So, although we often focus on the written document, what is taught, and what is learned, curriculum is really the process of working on those components.

The Written Document

Many music teachers think primarily about the written document when defining curriculum. They often do not consider how the written document relates to teaching and learning, how philosophical beliefs intersect with curriculum writing, how influences from a number of stakeholders can restrict curriculum, and how issues like scheduling, grouping of students in ensembles and classes, and choosing repertoire are all part of the big picture of curriculum. It is possible to get a doctorate in curriculum and the term itself encompasses all that exists in schools and schooling. When music teachers are working on the written document aspect of curriculum we must remember that a document that does not address what is taught and what is learned as well as many of the other issues brought forth in this section will not be useful for teachers and students. In my experience, some curriculum documents have so much educational jargon that it is difficult to determine what should be taught and what might be learned in relation to music.

In order to be useful to teachers, a music curriculum should include the following:

- overall music program philosophy (Chapter 2 provides more details regarding developing philosophy and advocacy statements)
- specific program goals and beliefs (early childhood music, elementary general music, band, marching band, orchestra, choir, etc.)
- lists of developmental skills or benchmarks (The chapters in Part III and Part IV provide these sequences for early childhood, movement, rhythm, singing, creative music making, musical sensitivity and expression, music literacy, music listening, and music in adult learning contexts.)
- required resources (teaching spaces, staffing needs, equipment, storage, and budget)
- sample teaching strategies/lesson plans (The chapters in Part III and Part IV provide lesson plan suggestions for early childhood, movement, rhythm, singing, creative music making, musical sensitivity and expression, music literacy, music listening, and music in adult learning contexts.)
- sample assessment strategies - checklists, rating scales, and rubrics (The chapters in Part III and Part IV provide sample assessment strategies for early childhood, movement, rhythm, singing, creative music making, musical sensitivity and expression, music literacy, music listening, and music in adult learning contexts.)
- suggested curricular resources (series books, method books, and ensemble literature)

Although many districts require specific formats for a written curriculum, if a music curriculum has the sections recommended here, it can most likely be formatted to meet district requirements.

What Is Taught?

One of the issues that must always be considered when writing curriculum is how to assure that it will be implemented by music teachers. Too often only a few teachers are involved in the curriculum writing process and then the document lacks "buy in" from other teachers. All teachers need to be involved in the curriculum writing process. If teachers are part of the development process, there will be healthy discussion regarding teaching, which will affect what is included in the document. There will be a disconnect between the written document and what is taught if teachers are not part of the curriculum development process and if they are not given adequate time and in-service education for trying new ideas suggested by the curriculum.

What Is Learned?

Most teachers have had the experience of thinking that they taught something very well only to realize during the next lesson that the students did not learn what the teacher thought was taught. In order for a curriculum document to be useful, ideas for assessing students' learning must be considered concurrently with curriculum development. I address assessment later in this chapter and all authors in the book have been charged with making sure that assessment is closely linked to curriculum in their work.

Personal Experiences

Before I proceed to other issues related to defining curriculum, readers are encouraged to consider the following regarding their own curriculum experiences:

1. Consider the notion of "method" of curriculum discovery as mentioned by Wing (1992). Think about the unpredictable nature of music teaching and learning and the interaction between planning and responding in music teaching.
2. What written document do you have in place in your school? What are the next steps for revision in that document?

3. How does your school address the need for all music teachers to be involved in curriculum development?

4. What is the balance between considerations of what is taught versus what is learned in your own lesson planning?

Curricular Influences and Stakeholders

There are many influences and a variety of stakeholders that affect curriculum writing for a music teacher. The chapters in Part II of this text address influences of Understanding by Design (Chapter 4), Universal Designs for Learning (Chapter 5); 21st Century Skills and the Common Core (Chapter 6). In addition to these national influences, music teachers must address the requirements set forth by state, district, building, and department stakeholders. Parent and community expectations also intersect with music teacher curricular planning. Curriculum is inherently political. Music teachers need to work to use that political nature of curriculum to support their programs. Chapter 17 addresses the balance of sequential curriculum with the expectations of various stakeholders with regard to performance and adjudicated events.

Curriculum Vocabulary

This section includes vocabulary of curriculum that helps us to understand how to tie the written document to what is taught and learned. Each of these words represents a complete field of study and readers are encouraged to explore these bodies of literature, if interested. I have had teachers tell me that they feel like educational words "fly by" in meetings and it is hard to know what is being said. This section is my effort to demystify these terms. The words or concepts listed here appear in some way in most curriculum documents. I present them here in alphabetical order. These terms will be used throughout the book and addressed in context.

Constructivism. This refers to the idea of meeting learners where they are in their development and modifying instruction so that students can construct their own understandings of content rather than be "delivered" that content from a teacher (as would be a more behaviorist model of teaching). Constructivist music curricula are very "hands on" and include many opportunities for creative music making. Chapter 10 (Creative Music Making) is particularly focused on elements of constructivism as is the Early Childhood chapter (14).

Culturally relevant teaching. Other terms along these conceptual lines include multiculturalism, culturally responsive teaching/pedagogy, and culturally relevant pedagogy. Authors in this text use these terms when considering how to respond to ethnic, racial, and cultural diversity within the learners in the music classroom. Authors also use these terms in considering what music is taught as well as how and why. Chapter 16 is particularly focused on this concept.

Curriculum alignment. General curriculum theorists consider matching what is taught to what is tested. Since in most states music is not a tested subject, music educators must consider what curriculum is aligning to. Is it the concert literature? State frameworks? National Standards?

Equal access to instruction. There is a great deal of research and scholarship on equity. Music educators intersect with these concepts in designing curricula that include a need for instruments, reeds, lessons, etc. Fees associated with travel and honor ensembles are a part of the concern for equal access. A curriculum document should address these issues of equity in some way.

Hidden curriculum. Hidden curriculum refers to those things experienced by students that are not planned for or anticipated. Hidden curriculum can be positive or negative. Students often leave our courses having learned things that we did not intend. It is important to consider what these things might be.

Interdisciplinary curriculum. The current focus on the Common Core encourages using music to teach other content areas. Chapter 6 on the Common Core and 21st Century Skills provides some insight in this area. Some teachers are asked to provide sequences for interdisciplinary curriculum by grade level.

Readiness. Readiness refers to a student exhibiting a particular behavior deemed a prerequisite for learning. It is important to consider the musical readiness for success in music. For example, students who come in to beginning band already able to sing on pitch and move to a steady beat will be much more "ready" to play a musical instrument than students without those skills. A curriculum should consider appropriate readiness for skills at the next levels.

Tracking. Tracking refers to organizing students into homogeneous groups (alike) according to musical achievement levels. Research has suggested that this practice of tracking is not helpful to strong and weak students in other academic areas. Making decisions about how many ensembles and how those ensembles are populated are essentially curricular questions of tracking.

Personal Experiences

1. How is your district addressing connection to Core Arts Standards and/or the Common Core?
2. What are the state, district, building, department, parent, and community influences on your curriculum?
3. Reflect on some of the challenges of constructivism in relation to class size, student past musical experience, performance expectations, etc.
4. Consider the demographics of your student population in relation to the notion of culturally relevant practice.
5. What is the communication in your district around the notion of vertical alignment? Are you required to connect to state or national standards, or some other criteria?
6. How does your district address issues of equity in relation to music instruction?
7. Reflect on the hidden curriculum, both positive and negative in your classroom.
8. How is music considered in an interdisciplinary way in your school?

9. What are the issues regarding musical readiness in your K–12 music program?

10. How are issues of tracking addressed within your music program?

Format of a Written Document

One of the greatest difficulties for many teachers writing a comprehensive music curriculum is sometimes deciding where to start. The first decision that music teachers may need to make is whether to work linearly from Kindergarten to first grade, to second, etc., or to do what I call a subject specific approach where there is an elementary general music curriculum, a middle school band, a middle school choir, etc. There is not one better way to begin; it depends on the context and who is involved in the writing process.

It is important to focus on what is learned as well as what is proposed to be taught as I have seen schools try the linear model (K, 1, 2, 3…) and by the time the document gets to seventh grade the content is similar to that expected of a college music major. It is also important to remember that for music we cannot depend on past instruction to bring all students to certain grade level expectation (i.e., we do not report whether or not children are at the fifth grade level in music reading). Thus, what one might call musical age (based on past experience) becomes more important than chronological age or grade level. Finally, when writing curriculum for courses that include multiple grade levels (i.e., 9–12 in a high school choir) teachers may need to consider levels (beginning, intermediate, advanced) even within the same curriculum to document the need for multiple years of instruction in a course.

Ultimately decisions regarding approaches must be made within a specific context. In this next section I outline four distinct starting points for music curriculum writing including objectives, repertoire, knowledge, and skills. A good written curriculum document needs attention to all four of these areas, but depending on the type of music course focus it might make sense to start with one or the other of these four. Part II of this text provides additional models for formatting the written document.

Objectives-Based Curriculum

The objectives-based approach to instructional design is common in all of education (Tyler, 1949). This is a four-phase process that begins with the development of objectives for the learner, objectives are then sequenced (often referred to as *scope* and *sequence*), activities are designed to meet the objectives (lesson plans), and evaluation tools are designed to assure that learning takes place (tests). Although this model has been pervasive in curriculum deign, many scholars have criticized this approach, suggesting that it is too linear and that real teaching does not occur in such a clear-cut line. Good teachers often mix up the phases of this design. For example, meaningful assessment of student learning does not occur at the end of a linear process, but must occur throughout the teaching and learning interaction. Good teachers do not follow a restrictive sequence, but adjust their teaching to the needs of a specific context. Real classrooms are multidimensional, and to force curriculum into such a linear model is a compromise. However, many school and district guidelines for curriculum will require an objectives-based model. Although this approach to curriculum may be the most common, teachers are encouraged to focus on the other approaches listed here as well as the objectives based approach so that curricula reflect the "messiness" of good teaching in music classes and not just the jargon of curriculum.

Repertoire-Based Curriculum

Some musicians have suggested that the music literature chosen for a course is the curriculum (Conway, 2002; Reynolds, 2000). In general curriculum theory there are scholars who suggest a curriculum based on the project-method (Kilpatrick, 1918) which I believe is similar to designing instruction around musical interaction with particular musical literature. In their 2004 overview of Kilpatrick's work, Walker and Soltis (2004) suggest the following about the "Project-Method":

> He [Kilpatrick] characterized the project method as one
> that combined three elements: wholehearted activity, laws of
> learning, and ethical conduct with his basic idea that "educa-
> tion is life." He sought a way to replace traditional teaching
> methods, which forced learning, with a method in which
> learning was achieved without compulsion. In daily life, he
> argued, we learn from the activities we engage in, from our
> experiences, not from memorizing or studying, but from doing
> things with a purpose. He believed that this form of "learning-
> by-living" and "acting with a purpose" should be brought into
> the school, thus making school and its curriculum not a prep-
> aration for life but an actual part of living and life itself. The
> means for doing this was the "project method." (p. 47).

In considering this idea for music, I think about the repertoire and
the musical engagement with the repertoire as "doing things with a
purpose" as stated by Kilpatrick. This literature-based approach works
very well for many types of music courses. Reflect on the specific
musical repertoire to be studied and then address the other approaches
(objectives, skills, and knowledge) through the lens of the repertoire. These approaches are meant to be starting places for thinking.
If a teacher were to focus only on the repertoire aspect, for example,
a middle school trombone student might experience a curriculum
based only on playing in the first position and this is certainly not what
any music teacher would consider a strong curriculum for the trombone. As mentioned above a solid curriculum will have elements of all
(objectives, repertoire, skill, and knowledge).

Skills-Based Curriculum

A skills-based approach in music courses refers to what students
will do musically. These skills should not be confused with what they
might be expected to know about music (knowledge-based curriculum). Skills include musical behaviors (singing, moving, playing on
instruments, creating sounds, improvising, composing, and listening)
as well as aural recognition of musical concepts (tonality, meter, form,

phrasing, etc.). The skills-based approach does not include attitudes or preferences towards music, but rather abilities of the student to interact (sing, move, create, listen, or play) within a specific musical context. This is the curriculum approach that teachers are encouraged to focus much thought on so that active strategies for interacting with music form the core of the approach in music courses.

Knowledge-Based Curriculum

Some music courses focus heavily on the knowledge base of curriculum (musical terms, knowledge of music theory and history, etc.). Since music is an active, aural art authors in this book will encourage teachers to include elements of skills-based and repertoire-based approaches even for courses that seem to be primarily "knowledge-based." Again, it is desirable for a music class curriculum to reflect all elements of these approaches (objectives, repertoire, skills, and knowledge). The knowledge-base is the easiest content to assess and so many teachers fall into the trap of including more knowledge than skill due to ease in measuring growth.

Assessment

One should not write curriculum without considering the assessment outcomes associated with the sequence. However, the linear nature of curriculum development often encourages teachers to write objectives, design a sequence for instruction, and then develop an evaluation or test of the content for the purpose of a grade. Wiggins (1998) refers to *backward design* in curriculum writing in which the writer begins with the notion of assessment. All of the chapters in Parts III and IV provide sample assessment strategies and tools such as checklists rating scales, and rubrics. Readers are encouraged to consider these assessment ideas up front as they draw sequences for their own students from the ones provided in the text. I begin now with a discussion of music aptitude and music achievement for clarity regarding what it is that music teachers are working to assess.

Music Aptitude and Music Achievement

Music teachers usually measure and assess musical achievement. Achievement refers to what a student has learned in music. Gordon (1997) defines aptitude as "a measure of a student's potential to learn music" (p. 41). There are a number of tests available for measuring music aptitude (Gordon, 1979, 1986, 1989). The chapters in Part III and Part IV of this text that provide sequences for Early Childhood (Chapter 14), Rhythm (Chapter 8), Singing and Tonal Audiation (Chapter 9), and Musical Sensitivity (Chapter 11) all address musical aptitude in relation to sequencing instruction.

We sometimes hear music colleagues talk about "talent" and often wonder whether talent refers to aptitude or achievement. Gordon suggests:

> Most of us have become accustomed to hearing and to using such words as *ability*, *talented*, *gifted*, and *musical*, but these words only confuse the issue by obscuring the important distinction that must be made between music aptitude and music achievement. Whereas music achievement is intellectual and primarily in the brain, music aptitude is spontaneous and primarily in the cells and genes, that is, in the entire body. (p. 42)

I share this information on aptitude primarily to encourage music teachers to accurately use the term *achievement* when referring to what is measured in music classes. In addition, I encourage teachers for music classes to recognize that musicianship and musical behaviors can, and should, be assessed. I find some music teachers who are somewhat opposed to thinking about assessment of musical skills in favor of a sort of "artistic" view that music is meant to be a communication of whatever the student feels they wish to communicate. Although there are times when this may be the case, in most instances a tool can be designed to document student musical growth.

Assessment versus Grading

As mentioned above, early on in the curricular planning process the teacher must plan assignments and criteria for grading. It is important to consider the relationship between grading and assessment in music courses. Kohn (1993) regularly criticizes the practice of grading and states:

> Grades cannot be justified on the grounds that they motivate students, because they actually undermine the sort of motivation that leads to excellence. Using them to sort students undercuts our efforts to educate. And to the extent that we want to offer students feedback about their performance— a goal that demands a certain amount of caution lest their involvement in the task itself be sacrificed—there are better ways to do this than by giving grades. (p. 203)

Kohn has written extensively on this topic and the reader is encouraged to consider his work and the work of others who examine the relationship between grading and motivation. Music students need to view learning as the goal and not "good grades." However, this is a difficult concept and one that is deeply rooted in experiences they may have had previous to your music class. Regardless of the philosophical concerns regarding grading, most schools require teachers to give a final grade to reflect the work of students. Good assessment goes beyond the mere reporting of student work and is used to provide feedback to students as well as information to the teacher regarding student learning. Authors throughout this text provide suggestions for ways to accomplish this in various music class contexts.

Criteria for Assessment

When designing assessments for music classes it is important to consider the reliability and validity of the test or tool. Reliability refers to the consistency of the tool. Multiple-choice tests that are provided by series textbook companies often report the reliability of individual test items. Researchers study the items on these tests and make changes to items based on the data they collect. Tests provided by textbook companies are often quite helpful as they typically include study guides for students as well as answer templates for the instructor. Validity refers to whether the tool is actually measuring what it is designed to measure. This is a particularly important criterion to consider when designing your own test. Sometimes we may think we are testing musical knowledge or skill but the test itself relies so heavily on some other content (for example ability to write) that the test is not a valid measure for music.

Other assessment criteria questions the teacher might ask include: How long will it take for students to complete the test? Is the test an authentic musical activity (i.e., something a musician might be asked to do)? How will students learn from taking the test? Can I provide timely feedback to students using this measure?

Personal Experiences

1. How might knowledge of music aptitude affect curricular planning?
2. How do you address the difference between grading and assessment in your classroom?
3. Think about ways to make assessments more reliable.
4. Consider issues of validity in relation to the music assessments you often use.

What is Unique to Musicianship-Focused Curriculum and Assessment?

Although all teachers have the task of planning, implementing, and assessing for diverse learners, the goal of this book is to highlight what is unique in curriculum and assessment for music teachers. In this final section of the chapter I examine some of the phenomena surrounding music teaching that create this uniqueness.

Teaching Music versus Teaching About Music

One of the key tenets of musicianship-focused curriculum as supported in this text is that classroom and rehearsal activities that utilize active music making (moving, chanting, singing, playing, reading, composing, improvising, and listening) should form the core of a music curriculum. To me, this reveals the difference between teaching music and teaching "about" music. It may just be semantics but I have seen many music curriculum documents that focus so much on teaching "about" music that any teacher in the building (musician or not) would be able to deliver that instruction. Chapter 2 in this text (Advocacy and Philosophy) will examine this phenomena more in depth.

Musical Curriculum Consistency and Alignment

All content areas must consider the notion of vertical alignment of the curricula: How do teachers work to provide the readiness for learning from one grade to the next? In music, decisions regarding solfege and rhythm syllables are just one area where music teachers in the same district often differ, and this lack of consistency inhibits the needed transfer of learning for students from one year of instruction to the next. Authors in Parts III and IV of this text have worked hard to address notions of consistency and highlight the areas where teachers need to work on consensus.

One Teacher Seeing All Students for Multiple Years

In many music teacher settings a single teacher has the opportunity to interact with students over multiple (i.e., K–5 or 9–12) years. The sequences addressed in Part III of this text will help music teachers to consider this challenge to curriculum. In addition, music teachers, particularly at the elementary level, often see all children in the school. Chapter 5 addressing students with learning differences and Chapter 16 discussing English language learners provide some insight into the music teacher responsibility in these areas.

School, Parent, and Community Performance Expectations

Music teaching has high visibility in the community due to the nature of concerts as well as adjudicated events. Chapter 18 addresses many of the issues involved in balancing sequential curriculum and assessment with school, parent, and community performance expectations. Chapter 18 considers how to prepare preservice teachers for this music teaching environment, and Chapter 19 examines how to support inservice teachers as they work to create musicianship-focused curriculum and assessment within the expectations of schools, parents, and communities.

Use of Technology for Music-Specific Instruction

Although all content areas are encouraged to incorporate up-to-date technology into teaching and learning, the music-specific ways in which technology is appropriate are unique to music. Chapter 20 examines technology as it is used for teaching music as well as how it can be used for management of curriculum and assessment.

Teacher Preparation and Professional Development

Preparing teachers for success in designing and implementing musicianship-focused curriculum and assessment is a challenge. Music students in undergraduate programs are working concurrently to become musicians and teachers and it is often difficult for them to focus on concepts such as curriculum and assessment that seem far removed from the every day experiences in a music school. Chapter 18 provides an examination of ways in which to engage preservice students in solid curricular thinking. Chapter 19 addresses the same issues in relation to in-service teacher professional development. As was stated in the "What is Taught" section of this chapter it is important for teachers to be empowered to consider, design, implement, and assess musicianship-focused curriculum and in-service professional development is where this occurs.

Music Teaching and Learning beyond the School Setting

Finally, I believe music is unique from many other school content areas in that there is a strong focus within music education on teaching and learning outside of the school setting. Many school music teachers work in church and community music settings in addition to their work in schools. Chapter 14 which focuses on early childhood music as well as Chapter 15 focusing on adult musical learning provide insight into this work of music teachers beyond the school.

Personal Experiences

1. What is the balance between teaching music and teaching about music represented in your current curriculum materials?

2. Think about issues of consistency across the K–12 continuum in your school.

3. Think about the opportunities related to the notion of working with students for multiple years. How do you address this in your big picture curriculum planning?

4. How do music teachers in your setting work to balance sequential curriculum with school, parent, and community performance expectations?

5. Think about how you and your colleagues are working with technology and media to further student musical experiences.

6. Reflect back on your teacher preparation experience in relation to designing musicianship focused curriculum and assessment.

7. How does your district work to support musicianship-focused curriculum and assessment through professional development?

8. Think about ways in which you and your colleagues provide music instruction in community and other outside of school settings. How do you design and assess this instruction?

References

Conway, C. M. (2002). Curriculum writing in music. *Music Educators Journal, 88* (6), 54–59.

Gordon, E. E. (1979). Primary measures of music audiation. Chicago: GIA Publications.

Gordon, E. E. (1986). Intermediate measures of music audiation. Chicago: GIA Publications.

Gordon, E. E. (1989). Advanced measures of music audiation. Chicago: GIA Publications.

Gordon, E. E. (1997). *Learning sequences in music.* Chicago: GIA Publications.

Hanley, B., & Montgomery, J. (2002). Contemporary curriculum practices and their theoretical bases. In R. Colwell & C. Richardson (Eds.). *The New Handbook of Music Teaching and Learning* (pp. 113–143). New York: Oxford University Press.

Kilpatrick, W. (1918). The project method. *Teachers College Record,* 19, 319–334.

Kohn, A. (1993). *Punished by rewards, the trouble with gold stars, incentive plans, A's, praise and other bribes.* New York: Houghton Mifflin.

Reynolds, R. (2000). Repertoire IS the curriculum. *Music Educators Journal, 87 (1),* 31–33.

Tyler, R. (1949). *Basic principles of curriculum and instruction.* Chicago: University of Chicago Press.

Walker, D., & Soltis, J. (2004). *Curriculum and aim (4th Ed.).* NewYork: Teachers College Press.

Wiggins, G. (1998). *Educative Assessment: Designing Assessments to Inform and Improve Student Performance.* San Francisco: Jossey-Bass.

Wing, L. (1992). Curriculum and its study. In R. Colwell (Ed.). *Handbook of research on music teaching and learning* (pp. 197–217). New York: Schirmer.

CHAPTER 2

PHILOSOPHIES IN CURRICULUM AND ASSESSMENT

Chad West

Ithaca College, Ithaca, New York

Philosophy is sometimes criticized as esoteric musings written by ivory towered professors completely disconnected from realities of the classroom; I will try to avoid making this chapter one of those. Instead, this chapter is designed to be a practical look at contemporary philosophical positions as they apply directly to curriculum and assessment within American school music education. For context, this chapter begins with a brief look at general education and music education philosophies that have guided and shaped much of the curriculum since the early 20th century. The next section suggests counter-arguments to certain micro-philosophical assumptions (both tacit and explicit) often revealed in our curricula. The third section is a discussion of philosophies that influence assessment. The chapter concludes with suggestions for aligning philosophy, curriculum, and assessment.

General Education Philosophies

It is important to note some general philosophies that have guided American education. At the risk of oversimplifying, but for clarity, consider two broad perspectives that have shaped our schools: the good of society and the good of the individual. Plato believed that people should be educated according to their abilities and strengths for the purpose of contributing to a well balanced and smoothly functioning society. Centuries later, Rousseau argued that education should allow each individual to develop naturally, unfettered by societal norms or doctrines, for the purpose of self-realization and personal under-standing. Most educational policy today is rooted, whether consciously or tacitly, in one of these two broad aims: society or the individual. (see Walker & Soltis, 2004).

Today, it is apparent that much of the American public has come to presume that the primary aim of education is to prepare students for the workforce, both global and local, but this has not always been the case in American education. Earlier in its history, the aims of public education were not as focused on workforce preparation as they were on preparing individuals to lead healthy and fulfilling lives and contribute as effective and responsible members of a democratic society. Since the last part of the 19th century, the pendulum has swung back and forth between essentialist approaches and progressive approaches to educa-tion. In 1893, for instance, the NEA formed a committee that recom-mended a nation-wide adoption of a curriculum consisting of subjects aimed at preparing students for college work. In 1918, the NEA orga-nized another committee to examine the high school curriculum. The committee recommended not a curriculum aimed at college prepara-tion, but one aimed at skills students needed to be successful in life outside of school. Their main objectives were health; command of the fundamental processes of writing, reading, math, and speaking; worthy home membership; vocation; citizenship; worthy use of leisure; and ethical character. In only 25 years, we saw the pendulum swing between concern for society and concern for the individual.

In 1957 the Soviet Union launched Sputnik and Americans became worried that the Soviets were winning the space race. Essentialists pointed to the need for America to use the public schools as a platform for preparing more students to enter college where their education in the sciences would better prepare them to compete globally. This call would be strengthened in the 1980s with the release of "A Nation at Risk" which once again suggested that American schools were falling behind globally and urged the country to get "back to the basics." With the reauthorization of the Elementary and Secondary Education Act in 2001, otherwise known as "No Child Left Behind" and most recently, the "Race to the Top," we see an ever-increasing focus on preparing all students for college and global workforce competitiveness. It seems that many policy makers today have come to view the public education system as a vehicle by which to increase math scores rather than happiness, develop global competitors rather than local contributors, and regurgitate facts rather than heighten personal understandings. The further we move toward concern for society over concern for the individual, the more likely we are to assume that the primary purpose of public education is that of college and workforce preparation. Once we assume this, it is difficult to justify a place in the curriculum for music, art, physical education, health, social studies, or any other subject that's purpose is other than to develop students as national economic commodities. But if American curriculum history tells us one thing, it is that the pendulum will swing back toward a more humanistic and liberal education; the question is only of timing (see Mark & Gary, 2007).

Music Curriculum Philosophies

As with general education, the music education philosophy literature is far too vast to discuss in detail here, but there exist some philosophical guideposts that are helpful in explaining how much of the music education curriculum and assessment has developed into what it is today and where it may be heading. Bennett Reimer is widely recognized as having provided the profession with a cogent, understandable, and relatable philosophy of music education, which united the profession unlike any previously. Reimer's (1970) book, *A Philosophy of Music Education*, changed measurably with each edition; one in 1989, and the last in 2003, but his underlying premise remained consistent: Music education is a form of aesthetic education whereby we know ourselves more fully through experiencing the feelings that music can evoke.

Reimer's notion of music education as aesthetic education was challenged in the 1980s when music education philosophers such as David Elliott (1995) began questioning whether the fundamental value of music, and by extension, music education, might lie in something other than the education of feeling. Elliott and others suggested that music is a diverse human practice and is experienced in ways that extend beyond Western European notions of aesthetic experience and musical works. Music's value, Elliott contended, lies not in contemplating, but in doing.

People conceive of music in fundamentally different ways, and it is easy to forget that our own assumptions about the nature of music are not necessarily universally shared, even within our own profession. For instance, if you were to ask a group of music teachers to define music, you might get very different responses. Some conceive of music as a musical work. Others define it as sound organized in time. Some conceive of music as notation. Others consider it a form of human interaction. The list could go on.

You would get a similar myriad of responses if you asked the same group of music teachers to explain why music education is important. Since our conception of the nature of music influences what we value about a music education, there exists a wide continuum of musical vs. utilitarian values. One who conceives of music as a musical work might highly value a music curriculum that includes a focus on listening, making connections between music and the other arts, and understanding music in historical and political contexts. One who conceives of music as sound organized in time might value a music curriculum that includes a focus on developing musical skills such as the ability to play and sing with good rhythm, intonation, technique, expression, and creativity. One who conceives of music as notation might deliver a music curriculum that focuses heavily on sight-reading, theory, form, and structure. One who conceives of music as a human interaction might advocate a music curriculum that includes music for functional purposes such as dancing, worshiping, celebrating, and other human interactions. Of course, most see the value in all of these things, but it is the *relative value* that we place on them that influences our curriculum.

Music as Affective

We see evidence of our assumptions about the essence of music—and the role of music education—by examining our curricula. For instance, a curriculum rooted in aesthetics might be one where students learn about music in historical and political contexts, and are taught to listen critically toward experiencing feelings and beauty within music. In these classes, teachers want students to contemplate, experience, and express beauty so that they may have a more intimate understanding of how sound, created in various political and historical contexts, can convey meaning and inspire feelings in audiences here and now. In a sense, it is knowing about music in a way that is more affective than cognitive. Similar to taking an art history class and learning about different art movements so that one could then attend an art museum with greater awareness, understanding, context, and appreciation, so do many curricula rooted in aesthetics aim to educate students in music.

Music as Kinesthetic

As with many performance-driven school music programs, contemporary music ensembles are good examples of a kinesthetic orientation to music. This orientation to music can be seen in non-academic settings such as rock bands, fiddling groups, mariachi bands, and all the myriad ways that humans perform music outside of school. In many of these ensembles, the focus is more on performing than appreciating, creating than experiencing, and skills than contemplation. Members of these ensembles may also be consumers, but their focus is primarily on being producers of music. Certainly, school ensemble curricula reflect a kinesthetic valuing of music; what separates many of these groups from school ensembles is their orientation toward music theory.

Music as Theoretical

As with many contemporary ensembles, the focus in school ensembles is largely skills-based; that is, the focus is more on performing music than appreciating it. School ensembles, though, often focus more heavily on notation and theory than do contemporary ensemble musicians. School-based ensemble teachers teach students to perform music by reading music notation, whereas contemporary ensemble musicians often perform music by ear. Thus, while school music ensemble curricula reflect a kinesthetic orientation to music, they also reflect a theoretical orientation. In these classes, value is placed not only on the ability to perform music, but also on the ability to theoretically understand how music is structured through notation. Another difference between contemporary ensemble musicians and school musicians is the orientation toward creativity. Whereas many contemporary ensemble musicians create their own music, school ensemble musicians generally have few opportunities to do this since the focus is more often on group performance than individual creativity. Individuals with a theoretical orientation to music value the knowing of music from a structural rather than kinesthetic or affective perspective.

Music as Social

Many music teachers want their students to experience musical affect, develop musical skills, and cognitively understand music from a theoretical perspective, but their main focus is on using music as a vehicle by which to socialize students. They conceive of music as a verb rather than a noun, whereby the focus is not as much on the product as the process. They value interaction over conformity, creation over re-creation, and transformation of self over perfection of the group. These teachers view music as a social interaction whereby people worship, dance, celebrate, mourn, form identities, and know different cultures. We see evidence of this conception of music every time we hear music in a movie, TV show, or at a patriotic or religious event; experience a different culture through its music; or identify with a particular culture based on mutual musical interests.

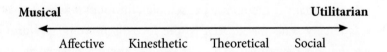

Questioning Micro-Philosophical Curricular Assumptions

The term *curriculum* is often used as a generic term when referring to teaching and learning. When people talk about curriculum, they may be referring to what is taught, what is learned, instructional content, instructional delivery, the music that is performed, educational benchmarks, goals and objectives, the sequence, the skills to be mastered, the knowledge to be acquired, the in-the-moment experiences between teacher and learner, or even the written document itself! Estelle Jorgensen (2002) goes even further by suggesting that curriculum can also be viewed as realms of meaning, practical applications of reason, and discourse. The point is that the term, as it is often used in American education, is imprecise and often used to mean many different things. It may seem like semantics, but how one conceives of curriculum reflects their philosophical orientation to teaching and learning, which influences the teaching and learning experience.

For instance, a teacher who considers the curriculum to be what the students learn will plan and interact with her students very differently than a teacher who conceives of curriculum as what the teacher teaches. A teacher who considers the curriculum to be the music that is performed will choose music differently than one who considers the curriculum to be a set of musical benchmarks. The better grasp teachers have of what they consider to be "the curriculum," the better chance they have of avoiding accepting what Elliott (2010) refers to as a "default philosophy";

> ...a default philosophy of something arises from lack of careful thinking and democratic dialogues. Default philosophies grow and feed on unexamined assumptions. We often fail to notice them because they sneak up on us; before we know it we are saluting rather than challenging. Thus, default philosophies morph into the "commonsense" of our societies, institutions, and professions. (p. 367)

It is fair to point out that there is no one correct way of conceptualizing music curriculum. Who would be the arbiter, anyway? There are, however, conceptualizations that are more developed and thought out than others. Below are some examples of positions and beliefs often heard by those within the profession, along with their counterarguments. Consider each position along with its counterargument to refine your own beliefs. This list is not exhaustive—you can play devil's advocate with an infinite number of positions not mentioned here to help you define and refine your beliefs about music so that your curriculum becomes conscious and intentional.

"Music is a big part of society, therefore it should be studied in schools." Many people would argue that is precisely why music is not valuable as an academic subject. Why do we need to teach a subject that is already so richly experienced outside of school? Think of all of the pop artists who make millions of dollars who have never taken a school music class. Many would argue that music in society would continue to thrive without music in schools and point to hundreds of years and multiple societies where this is true. The argument that music is a part of society and should thus be learned in schools might be stronger if music experienced in schools more closely resembled music experienced in society.

"Music develops creative and critical thinking skills." Music classes can theoretically help students develop critical thinking skills, but before making this claim, we should ask ourselves in a typical school music program how much time is actually spent honing critical thinking skills. Many would argue that the typical ensemble rehearsal involves the teacher providing directives on how to improve the performance. This is not necessarily a bad thing, but the argument that music can develop creative and critical thinking skills might be best made by music programs that include small student-led ensembles, and multiple opportunities for song writing, composition, and improvisation.

"Music educators should teach high quality music." What is *high quality music*? Who decides? The notion that we can objectify quality in something as personal as one's musical tastes and preferences is rooted in an idealist conception of beauty that exists independent of the individual. This conception has served to manufacture a distinction between "high-brow" and "low-brow" music, between opera halls and Broadway stages, between orchestras and garage bands, and between school music and music in society. There are those who would argue that quality exists not between genres, but within; that is, within any genre there exists music of varying degrees of quality. While this argument acknowledges that beauty is not specific to genre, it is nevertheless rooted in the assumption that beauty is objective. Some would argue that music educators hold the knowledge and expertise to objectify quality. Dissertations have even been written with the aim of identifying and codifying quality in music, but if we conceive of beauty as lying in "the eye of the beholder," then we must challenge the notion that music educators, or any other musical "experts" are the arbiters and teachers of an objectified quality music. Once challenged, we must acknowledge that students' musical tastes are no less and no more quality than our own. Imagine what a powerful experience school music could be if we facilitated experiences where students were free to explore their musical interests rather than to learn ours.

"Everyone should have a music education." We often hear this argument from the same music teachers who feel it is acceptable to kick a student out of their ensemble for poor behavior, lack of practice, or failure to attend an out-of-school performance. These are all acceptable if we conceive of school music as an extra-curricular activity, but if we make the claim that music is curricular or co-curricular, then such actions are not justified. Last, if we are to claim that every student should have a music education, we must ask ourselves whether our current offerings are valuable or even realistic for every student and how we might change our curricula to accommodate students whose musical interests lie outside our current model.

"Music is an essential part of a 'well-rounded' education." Many of us would agree with this statement, but in so doing we must also ask ourselves what other parts of a well-rounded education should students also experience. If our goal is that students have a well-rounded experience, we must also acknowledge the need for visual art, home economics, child rearing, conservation, philosophy, spirituality, ethics, responsibility, vocation, etc. Since there is no universally identifiable set of experiences that makes someone well-rounded, can we presume that music is an essential part of such an education? Even if we presume that it is, how do we determine which other experiences are not equally suitable for a well-rounded education?

"Notation reading ability is an essential part of musicianship." Why does one need to read notation to be musical? Think of all of the people in society who recreate and create music beautifully without the ability to read notation. Pop singers, garage bands, fiddle groups, drumming ensembles, Flamenco groups, blue grass ensembles, etc. Notation is not required to reproduce sound, and with the advent of sound recording technology, notation is not even required to preserve and pass on tunes from one generation to the next. A better argument would be that notation is an essential part of the kinds of musicianship that require it such as the orchestras, concert bands, and choruses generally found in schools. One might then ask why schools are teaching musicianship skills that are needed only by a small portion of the world's musicians.

"Music study leads to an appreciation of music." Why does one need to study music to appreciate it? There are instances where through learning about something, we develop a deeper understanding, which leads to a heightened appreciation. However, if we make this argument, we must ask ourselves why we are interested in developing students' appreciation for music in the first place. I have heard some argue that this is important because those students then go on to be consumers and supporters of music. But do we really believe that music consumption would dwindle if school music programs ceased to exist? If the study of music were a prerequisite for appreciating, valuing, supporting, and consuming music, the music industry would not be the multi-billion dollar industry that it is. Nearly every human being appreciates music of some kind or another. I imagine that the "appreciation" of music to which supporters of this argument refer, is appreciation of a certain type of music, namely Western art-music. When viewed in this light, I would agree that (a) many students enter school without an appreciation for or valuing of this music, (b) studying this music could potentially lead to an appreciation of it, and (c) many students would not come to an appreciation of this music on their own. I have even heard people say that they want students to appreciate art music so that they will one day become audience members, supporters, and advocates for this genre. If this is the case, it reveals a somewhat didactic and disturbing conception of the role of school music; we should not be in the business of manufacturing musical appreciation for the purposes of perpetuating our own musical tastes or securing our jobs.

"In music, students work toward a common goal." It is sometimes said that in music, students work together to accomplish a common goal, whereas in other classes their work is independent. Some point to the fact that the success of the ensemble relies entirely on the relative contribution of its members. But this argument does not acknowledge that students can work together in any subject to accomplish common goals. Think about students working together on a science project, the English department putting on a play, students working in groups in a social studies class to reenact the Virginia and New Jersey plan, math students working together to solve a complex word problem. Working together to accomplish a common goal is a constructivist way of engaging students in a task rather than an inherent trait to any particular subject. Other instances of mistakenly linking pedagogy with content include arguments such as, "Music can be taught cross-curricularly," "Music can be taught according to needs of diverse learners," and "Music utilizes the three major modes of learning: visual, aural, and kinesthetic." That these things can be true of music makes them neither inherent nor unique to the subject.

"Music is a 'universal language.'" While we learn music in ways similar to how we learn language, most linguists would not agree that music is a language. Language is a way of communicating something, and "universal" means that it is the same to everyone. Music is culturally bound and does not communicate the same thing to everyone; a Chinese opera communicates something entirely different to someone from China than someone from the U.S., for instance. Similarly, music notation is not the same across the world; Western music notation is different from Indian, Chinese, etc. Similar to the claim that music is a universal language is the claim that music develops one's aesthetic perception; the notion of musical aesthetics is familiar to many Westerners, but one that is entirely foreign to many cultures around the world.

"Multicultural music teaches students to be tolerant of other cultures." While many music teachers provide students with authentic musical experiences from other cultures, "multi-cultural" music often consists of a band arrangement of a tune from a different country, which could hardly be considered "multi-cultural" education. Further, that music classes sometimes study musics of other cultures does not mean that students learn anything about the unique characteristics of different cultures outside of whatever musical characteristics were learned. Last, there is no guarantee that because students might learn something about the musical characteristics of a certain culture, they have become more tolerant or appreciative of that culture.

"Music study contributes to academic achievement in other areas, such as math and reading." In addition to placing music in a subservient position to other subjects, much of the research purporting that music makes you smarter has been discredited, misrepresented, or inconclusive. While there may be correlations between music instruction and improved academic achievement in other areas, that does not mean that music instruction "contributes" to such areas. For instance, does music instruction improve test scores or do students with high test scores choose to participate in music? Such a claim puts one in the precarious position of hoping that researchers would not one day find another, less expensive, and less time consuming activity for which the same could be accomplished. Regardless of whether or not music causes increased performance in other areas, many would suggest that music is valuable for reasons that extend beyond such utilitarian purposes.

Music Assessment Philosophies

According to Shuler (2011) there are four primary purposes for assessment: (a) improving student learning, (b) improving teaching, (c) improving programs, and/or (d) informing stakeholders (students, parents, and policy makers). This portion of the chapter addresses some of the current philosophical issues associated with each form.

Formative Assessment

Formative assessment is something that teachers engage in every day; sometimes consciously, and other times subconsciously. Formative assessment is taking place when students perform a task and the music teacher determines how well it was performed. Then the teacher can provide the student feedback as well as determine where to go next in the teaching process. For instance, a band director might give the downbeat in a school rehearsal. Several measures in she notices that the clarinets are playing a rhythm incorrectly and decides to stop and teach the correct rhythm. These types of assessments are constant throughout our teaching day, so much so that they simply become woven into the fabric of teaching. Formative assessments are the moment-to-moment judgments, based on student performance, about what to teach next; Schön (1983) refers to this as *thinking in action*. Examples of this can be seen in nearly all of our everyday activities. Consider the act of driving a car. We ease down on the gas pedal, assess our speed in relation to the speed limit, and then readjust. If a car pulls in front of us and slows down we reassess our situation in the moment and again readjust our speed. Certainly, we do not conceive of these actions as assessments; they are simply actions that make up the process of safe driving. Similarly, we often do not conceive of our in-the-moment formative decisions about student understanding as assessments; they are simply actions that make up the process of good teaching.

Summative Assessment

Whereas the purpose of formative assessment is to guide teaching and learning, the purpose of summative assessment is to measure and report student achievement. Tests and grades are examples of summative assessments. Music teachers today are well aware of summative assessments. Summative assessment is used not only by parents to determine how well their children are doing in their classes, but also by policy makers to determine how well schools and/or teachers are performing.

When we consider summative grading practices in traditional classroom subjects such as math, English, and science, we often think of pencil and paper tests, worksheets, portfolios, experiments, etc., all aimed at getting students to demonstrate their knowledge of the content. Certainly on a math test, one would expect to see math problems for students to solve to demonstrate their knowledge of the math concepts previously taught. However, it is not uncommon for music classes to grade students on content other than music. Many times students' ensemble grades are based, in part, on extra-musical criteria such as attendance, behavior, whether they have a pencil on their stand, and how much they say they practiced the previous week. Imagine if the same grading practices were implemented in a math class; students could get an "A" for simply showing up with a good attitude and pencil and saying they did their homework. It seems absurd to grade math students in such a way, yet many band, orchestra, and choir students receive grades based on such criteria. Paul Lehman (1998) explains,

> The problem with these criteria is that they have nothing to do with music itself. Anyone reading a transcript has a right to assume that a good grade indicated knowledge and skill in the subject matter. A grade is not just misleading, it's dishonest if it means merely that the student has come to class, or tried hard—or, more accurately, given the appearance of trying hard. No student who does poorly in algebra or biology can expect a good grade solely because she tried hard or came to class. Why should music be any different? (p. 23)

Part of the problem with grading music students on musical criteria is that it is time-consuming, especially considering the large number of students in one ensemble class as compared to, say, a math class. Another problem is that ensemble directors want students to enjoy music and many believe that if music becomes a stringently graded subject similar to their academic classes, students will decide not to continue in music or take a different elective in which they can get an easy "A." Many music teachers would rather use grading as a means to encourage behavior that they want students to demonstrate (bringing a pencil, good behavior, participation, and practicing) rather than to assess students' musical achievement. However, if we are to be taken seriously as a curricular subject by administrators, parents, and students, we need to make sure that we are basing students' grades on musical, rather than extra-musical behaviors. How well does the student perform in tune, with steady time, and with proper technique? How well does the student improvise, compose, read notation, and perform in an ensemble?

Authentic Assessment

Many definitions exist for the term *authentic assessment* but what is generally meant by the term is assessment that flows naturally from the curriculum. Duke (2005) stated, "The distinction between the assessments and the substance of the instruction day to day should be diminished to the point that the day to day activities of instruction closely resemble the assessments themselves" (p. 71). For instance, if we spend time teaching our students to *perform* with good intonation, rhythm, and sound, then an authentic assessment would measure how well a student *performed* those tasks.. This seems obvious in theory, but many times we teach students to perform with good intonation, rhythm, and sound and then assess students using a pencil and paper test. In essence, we ask students to *talk about* the things we have taught them rather than to *perform* those things, which is not a natural outflow of the curriculum. Elliott (1995) describes this as the difference between formal knowledge and procedural knowledge. Formal knowledge he describes as cognitive knowledge about music, whereas procedural knowledge is musical actions:

A performer's musical understanding is exhibited not in what a performer says about what she does; a performer's musical understanding is exhibited in the quality of what she gets done in and through her actions of performing.... If I tell you that I know how to ski, and if I explain the why-what-and-how of down-hill skiing, will this convince you that I really know how to ski? No—the proof of my "skiership" lies in the effectiveness of my skiing actions (p. 56). While formal knowledge about music and music making is necessary to become a music teacher, critic, or musicologist, it is neither a necessary prerequisite, nor a sufficient corequisite for achieving competent, proficient, or expert levels of musicianship. (p. 62)

Certainly, we want our students to know about music in a theoretical sense, but many of us would agree that this is secondary to knowing music in a procedural sense. If we are teaching for procedural knowledge then our assessment should assess musical actions. To do this, we have to hear students individually as well as in an ensemble context. Too often we assess the ensemble as a whole, which provides only general feedback to students and does little to inform future plans for teaching individuals. However, while hearing students individually is crucial to assessing and improving students' procedural knowledge, it is insufficient in assessing what Elliott (1995) calls *informal knowledge*:

Informal music knowledge involves the ability to reflect critically in action. Reflecting critically depends, in turn, on knowing when and how to make musical judgments. And knowing how to make musical judgments depends on an understanding of the musical situation or context: the standards and traditions of practice that ground and surround a particular kind of music making and music listening (p. 63).... The process resembles the way a chess player learns; not by repeating moves over and over in isolation but by solving real chess problems in the context of playing real chess games. (p. 63)

If we apply the chess analogy to music, then the ability to perform musically in isolation is only part of what is required to be musical in an ensemble; performing musically in an ensemble requires critical adjustments in relation to what is unfolding in the moment. Thus, if individual assessment is taken too far out of the ensemble context, it can actually become an inauthentic assessment. Feldman & Contzius (2011) explain:

> Though we want students to perform musically on their own, the goal of the ensemble experience is not solely to develop high-achieving individuals. Indeed good ensembles embody a brand of music making that is more than the sum of their parts. Among other things, playing successfully in an ensemble involves listening for blend, balance, and intonation; the ability to interface one's individual playing into a small group (section) and then into a larger group (full ensemble); an understanding of how one's individual part fits into the whole, etc. If we indeed value the "task" of performing musically in a group, then authentic assessment of the group's performance is a legitimate goal. (p. 110)

Aligning Curriculum and Assessment

Educational curriculum theorist, Ralph Tyler (1949) argued that four fundamental questions must be answered in developing any curriculum and plan of instruction:

1. What educational purposes should the school seek to attain?
2. What educational experiences can be provided that are likely to attain these purposes?
3. How can these educational experiences be effectively organized?
4. How can we determine whether these purposes are being attained?

Many in the post-Sputnik education mindset embraced this seemingly efficient and mechanical approach to designing curriculum and aligning assessment. On some level, this approach does make sense;

we should have an idea about what we want to accomplish, how we will accomplish it, and how we will know if we have accomplished it. While this approach can be helpful when considering our philosophical values regarding curriculum and assessment, it is not as helpful in determining our practical day-to-day interactions with students. When using this approach to plan lessons, music teachers can find themselves designing behavioral objectives in a mechanical way that does not actually reflect the interdependent, contextual, and multi-dimensional ways people learn and interact with music. Experienced teachers know that it is not in the writing of objectives, but in the moment-by-moment interactions with the students, and what Schön (1983) calls *thinking in action*, that the curriculum is realized. Conceiving of the curriculum as a series of objectives and subsequent assessments can give those outside the profession the illusion of scientific process and efficiency, but really do little to reflect the actual process of teaching and learning. In fact, Elliott (1995) points out that research has shown that (a) expert teachers tend to not use objectives-based models of curriculum planning, (b) teachers' informal mental preparations tend to be far more complex and important to their professional practices than written plans, and (c) teaching expertise is fundamentally procedural and situational rather than mechanical and predetermined.

Philosophical Issues of Assessment

There are some who question whether music can or should be assessed. Critics of summative assessment in music argue that many elements of music such as creativity, personal aesthetics, and self-expression are subjective and do not lend themselves to the objective nature of summative assessment. If a student creates a composition that she is happy with, why would we then subject that composition to an assessment? And if it *is* to be assessed, by what standards would we do so? Assessing the student's composition according to its nature and intent (likely self-expression and creativity) has its own set of problems; why would we want to measure and evaluate someone else's musical aesthetic? Even if we did, how is it possible to put an objective label on a subjective piece of art? Fautley (2010) argues that this type of experience positions teaching in a top down and sterile experience that does not account for the personal curiosities or natural developmental paths of the students and suggests that we instead shift our focus from teacher assessment to student self-assessment. Such an approach would require a shift from attainment and toward progress and development, not to mention a significant shift in the way summative assessment is measured and reported.

Due to the educational climate in which we are forced to survive, we often find ourselves assessing things that have little to do with what we value, or even with what we teach! Most of us value life-long and life-wide music making, yet we do not assess this. We value self-expression and creativity, but we do not assess these. We value aesthetic experiences and happiness in making music, but we do not assess these. As the old saying goes, "Not everything that can be counted counts, and not everything that counts can be counted."

When it comes to summative assessment in music, it is less problematic to assess things such as correct notes, balance, blend, intonation, and other performance skills than it is to assess creativity or self-expression. Although somewhat subjective and unreliable, professional music educators can still make evaluations regarding how well students perform these skills. Festival evaluations are examples of summative evaluations. However, the subjective and unreliable nature of these types of assessments do not fit well within an educational climate that values objective right and wrong answers such as with multiple choice standardized tests. Thus, music teachers, in an attempt to simply survive in this climate, often resort to distilling their music assessments to music vocabulary, note-naming, theory, aural skills, and history rather than music performance, musical enjoyment, life-long participation, creativity, self-knowledge, self-growth, flow, or self-expression.

The problem is that the nature and value of music is not well suited for summative assessments. Sure, we can assess musical skills and musical knowledge, but we have not yet found a way to assess that which most of us value, and many would argue that that which we value should not be assessed even if it could be. As Wiliam (2001) put it, "We start out with the aim of making the important measurable and end up only making the measurable important" (p. 58).

Auditing. Some in education feel that we should stop summative assessments altogether (see books and articles by Alfie Kohn). Proponents argue that grades tend to diminish students' interest in what they are learning, create a preference for the easiest possible route, and reduce the quality of students' thinking. They argue that grades are one of the biggest barriers between students and learning:

> If we begin with a desire to assess more often, or to produce more data, or to improve the consistency of our grading, then certain prescriptions will follow. If, however, our point of departure isn't mostly about the grading, but about our desire for students to understand ideas from the inside out, or to get a kick out of playing with words and numbers, or to be in charge of their own learning, then we will likely end up elsewhere. We may come to see grading as a huge, noisy, fuel-guzzling, smoke-belching machine that constantly requires repairs and new parts, when what we should be doing is pulling the plug. (Kohn, 2011, p. 32)

So why are we trying to assess music in a summative fashion in the 21st century? It is because school music education lives within the general education world and the general education world values summative and objective evaluation. One must then ask why the general education world values objective and summative evaluation. I would argue it is that we have come to conceive of assessment not in terms of formative assessment for the purposes of guiding instruction and learning, but for the purposes of holding schools, teachers, and students accountable to predetermined and extemporaneous measures of achievement. Assessment is used as a means to punish schools and teachers whose students do not meet these measures. Funding is withheld to schools that do not show improvement indicated through rigorous testing requirements. We have come to value assessment not as a means of improving teaching and learning for student success and self-actualization, but as a means of measuring our teachers and institutions for punishment and reward. Fautley (2010) eloquently sums it up: "...there has been a shift away from learning, towards auditing. This shift becomes problematic when auditing *replaces* teaching and learning. As the old country saying goes, the pig doesn't get fatter by being weighed frequently!" (p. 62).

Music Standardized Tests. Many music teachers are familiar with standardized music tests such as Gordon's music aptitude, audiation, and achivement tests (see Gordon, 1986), the Watkins-Farnum Performance Scale (Watkins & Farnum, 1962), and other various tests that have been used as reliable, valid, and norm-referenced music assessments aimed at helping teachers identify strengths, weaknesses, and potential in their students. Typically these tests have been used as formative assessments aimed at improving teaching and learning rather than for high-stakes auditing purposes as seen delivered in the subjects for which schools are held accountable. While many music teachers, for myriad reasons, do not want to see music subjected to the same rigorous high-stakes standardized testing requirements as other subjects, there are some who argue that music should be held to the same testing requirements and standards as other core academic subjects:

> In essence, music educators want the benefits of being seen as equals to the other core subjects, but do not want to abide by the same rules. Music educators cannot have it both ways. Either music education should relinquish their status as a core curricular subject and focus solely on the artistic, subjective offerings of the arts, or be held accountable through standards and assessment just as other basic subjects. (Fisher, 2008, p. 5)

Proponents of this stance contend that accountability through standardized testing is required for music to be taken seriously as a core academic subject. And perhaps there is a grain of truth in that; schools tend to focus more on subjects for which they are held accountable. The tacit, and sometimes not so tacit, motivation behind many proponents of this stance is one of advocacy and perceived legitimacy rather than the improvement of teaching and learning. While this may seem to be the answer to music gaining a stronger foothold in public education, the consequences might far outweigh the benefits. Many people would argue that high-stakes testing is precisely the problem with American education. We must keep in mind that assessment serves its primary purpose when it informs teaching and learning. To use it as a tool for holding schools and teachers accountable, I would argue, is a misappropriation of educational time, effort, and resources. To use it as a tool with which to more firmly situate music within schools is simply academic fraud and abuse.

Aligning Philosophy, Curriculum, and Assessment

As music educators, we are in the difficult position of trying to articulate to various stakeholders the inherent value of a music education. We value music because we have experienced its value, but those experiences are difficult for us to label—how does one describe the essence of music without sounding grandiose? If our values guide our behaviors, and we advocate that which we value, then what we say about the importance of music to those outside the profession should reflect our beliefs. Sometimes, though, what we believe is valuable about music and what we say is valuable are different; that is, our advocacy arguments do not always align with our philosophical beliefs. West and Clauhs (in press) point out that there are several instances in history, such as at the Tanglewood and Housewright symposia, where the music education profession has declared its values. Music educators at Tanglewood declared music's value in the art of living, the building of personal identity, and the nurturing of creativity (Choate, 1968). Three decades later in Tallahassee, music education leaders affirmed their beliefs that music exalts the human spirit, enhances the quality of life, and is worth studying because it is one of the primary ways human beings create and share meanings (Madsen, 2000). Nowhere in either the Tanglewood Declaration or the Housewright Declaration is it suggested that the value of music lies in utilitarian purposes, yet music education advocates often try to convince others that its value lies in extra-musical outcomes such as increased performance in other areas. Bowman (2005) argues that advocacy should not dictate philosophy. In fact, to preserve intellectual honesty, our advocacy arguments must be derived from our philosophical beliefs, even if those beliefs are not perceived as the most expedient ways of preserving our programs.

All of us enter the profession with preconceived notions about why music education is important, what we want our students to know and be able to do, and how we want to structure our classrooms and our teaching. Often, these notions are not explicit or even fully formulated in our minds, yet they influence the type of experiences our students have. As professionals, it is important that we question our notions about what we value, make those values explicit, and align our teaching with those values. Situated at the intersection of that alignment is our philosophy.

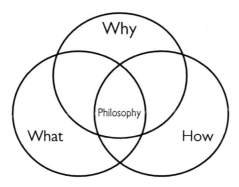

For example, let's consider that part of the reason why you value music education is so that you can develop students' musicianship. In this scenario, part of what you believe students should know and be able to do might include performing tonally and rhythmically in the context of different modes and meters with steady time and good intonation. Singing, moving, chanting, and audiating are all activities that might describe how your class would look to achieve these goals and, thus, reflect what you value in music education. Another example might be where a music teacher values music education for its ability to inspire affect and feeling within students. If this were the case, the teacher might want her students to develop the ability to play expressively and with passion. She might utilize metaphors, analogies, programmatic music, and stories in her teaching to help students play expressively so that they can experience musical affect and feeling. This model of "why" leading to "what" leading to "how" can be applied to an infinite number of different scenarios such as those described in the chart below.

Why	What	How
Learning a new symbol system	Accurately performing notated music	Sight reading and music theory
Connecting school music to music in society	Perform pop and contemporary music	Small group ensembles, playing by ear, composing original music
Character education	Develop discipline, leadership skills, and personal responsibility	Student-run sectionals, weekly individual playing tests, and practice reports
Creative thinking	Get students to make musical decisions	Improvisation, composition, arranging, song writing
Social development	Develop personal identity, emotional maturity, and democratic ideals	Provide time and space for group social interaction, problem solving, and peer mentoring

Certainly, most of us value all of these things to varying degrees and this list is by no means exhaustive. However, problems arise when our why, what, and how are not aligned. Many of us value musical creativity, but spend most of our instructional time drilling notation. Many of us want our students to be lifelong creators of music, but only give them the tools to do so in the presence of a conductor and a large ensemble. Many of us value character education and social development, but provide few spaces for students to explore and interact. Many of us value musical affect and feeling, but perform for ratings and competition. The list goes on. The point is that we determine why we believe music education is valuable, decide what students should know and be able to do to reflect those values, and align our activities to develop the required competencies.

When determining why music education is valuable to you, it is important to be honest with yourself; avoid answering the question according to what you have heard from others or what you feel should be important, and simply observe what is true to you. To help develop and refine why music education is valuable to you, consider the following questions:

- Recall one instance when music evoked a powerful emotional response in you. What were the circumstances? What was it like?
- Describe one instance when you experienced a powerful learning moment. What characteristics made this moment powerful?
- Can you recall how music evoked a sense of self in you? A sense of identity? When? What were the characteristics of that moment?
- Someone once said, "Music is good for students who may not be good for music." What does this statement mean, and how do you feel about this?
- Is it more important to you that your students become great musicians or great people? Why? How can you affect either outcome?

When deciding what is important for your students to know and be able to do in music, you might consider the following questions:

- Some define musicianship as the ability to decode notation. Others define it as the ability to keep a steady beat and discriminate pitch. Others define it as the ability to perform expressively. How do you define musicianship?
- Could school music education broaden itself to attract a higher number of students, and be more socially and culturally relevant to the way people experience music outside of school? *Should* it?
- Is it more important to you that your students *learn music* or learn *about music*? Why?
- In general, what are some appropriate benchmarks for elementary, middle, and high school? Put another way, if you were the middle school band/orchestra director, what skills, concepts, and dispositions would you want your students to come to you with? What if you were the high school band/ orchestra director?
- Where do you fall on the continuum of developing students' personal creativity vs. ensemble performance skills?
- What relative importance do you place on developing students' affective, kinesthetic, cognitive, and extra-musical skills? What is most important to you? What is least important? Why?

Finally, when deciding how you will structure experiences for your students, it is important to align them to what you want students to know and be able to do, in a way that reflects why you value music education. Consider the following questions:

- Recall one of your "best" teachers. What made this teacher great? What were some of the characteristics of this teacher? Did this teacher make learning easy and fun? Why was this teacher's class a great place to be?
- What is more important, the journey or the destination? The process or the product?

- Many teachers prefer to teach notation from the first day of instrument instruction. Other teachers advocate rote teaching as a preliminary exercise to teaching notation. Where do you fall on this continuum and why?
- Consider the 80 percent of students in our schools that are not interested in band, orchestra, and choir. Should you broaden your course offerings to accommodate them? Could you?
- Do you identify as a band/orchestra/choir director specifically or a music educator broadly?
- Some teachers are "respected." Other teachers are "loved." What kind of teacher do you want to be? Why?
- How will you assess students in ways that reflect your value of music education?

References

Choate, R. A. (1968). *Documentary Report of the Tanglewood Symposium.* Washington, D.C.: Music Educators National Conference.

Bowman, W. D. (2005). To what question(s) is music education advocacy the answer? *International Journal of Music Education, 23*(2), 125–129.

Duke, R. A. (2005). *Intelligent music teaching: Essays on the core principals of effective instruction.* Austin, TX: Learning and Behavior Resources.

Elliott, D. J. (1995). *Music matters: A new philosophy of music education.* New York: Oxford University Press.

Elliott, D. J. (2010). Assessing the concept of assessment; Some philosophical perspectives. In T. S. Brophy (Ed.), *Assessment in music education: Frameworks, models, and designs* (pp. 367–381). Chicago, IL: GIA Publications, Inc.

Fautley, M. (2010). *Assessment in music education.* New York, NY: Oxford University Press.

Feldman, E., & Contzius, I. (2010). *Instrumental music education: Teaching with the musical and practical in harmony.* NY: Routledge.

Fisher, R. (2008). Debating assessment in music education. *Research & Issues in Music Education*, 6(1), 1–10.

Gordon, E. E. (1986). *Music aptitude and related tests: An introduction.* Chicago, IL: GIA Publications, Inc.

Hoffer, C. R. (2011). Issues in the assessment of K–12 music instruction. In T. S. Brophy (Ed.), *Assessment in music education: Integrating curriculum, theory, and practice* (pp. 29–37). Chicago, IL: GIA Publications, Inc.

Jorgensen, E. R. (2002). Philosophical issues in curriculum. In R. Colwell & C. P. Richardson (Eds.), *The new handbook of research on music teaching and learning* (pp. 48–63). New York: Oxford University Press.

Kohn, A. (2011). The case against grades. *Educational Leadership, 69*(3), 28–33.

Lehman, P. R. (1998). Grading practices in music. *Music Educators Journal, 84*(5), 37–40.

Madsen, C. K. (Ed.). (2000). Vision 2020 : *The Housewright symposium on the future of music education.* Reston, VA: MENC.

Mark, M. L., & Gary, C. L. (2007). *A history of American music education* (3rd ed.). Lanham, MD: Rowman & Littlefield, Inc.

Reimer, B. (1970, 1989, 2003). *A philosophy of music education.* Englewood Cliffs, NJ: Prentice-Hall.

Schön, D. A. (1983). *The reflective practitioner: How professionals think in action.* London: Temple Smith.

Schuler, S. C. (2011). Music assessment, part 1: What and why. *Music Educators Journal, 98*(2), 10–13.

Tyler, R. W. (1949). *Basic principles of curriculum and instruction.* Chicago, IL: University of Chicago Press.

Walker, F. D., & Soltis, J. F., (2004). *Curriculum and aims* (4th ed.). New York: Teachers College Press.

Watkins, J. G., & Farnum, S. E. (1962). *The Watkins-Farnum performance scale: A standardized achievement test for all band instruments.* Winona, MN: Hal Leonard Music.

West, C., & Clauhs, M. (in press). Strengthening programs while
    avoiding advocacy pitfalls. *Arts Education Policy Review*.

Wiliam, D. (2001). What is wrong with our educational assessment and
    what can be done about it? *Education Review, 15*(1), 57–62.

CHAPTER 3

THE STUDY OF CURRICULUM AND ASSESSMENT

Colleen Conway
University of Michigan

Scott Edgar
Lake Forest College

Chad West
Ithaca College

"A rich confusion is the right state for curriculum writing."
–Decker Walker, 1980 (from Wing, 1992)

The "rich confusion" of curriculum makes it a difficult phenomenon to study. This chapter discusses issues with traditional research approaches in the study of curricula and assessment and introduces the reader to the notion of teachers studying their own curriculum and assessment strategies through teacher inquiry. We build the case that teachers studying their own students might help to contextualize the study of curriculum and assessment. Terms associated with teachers doing their own research including action research, teacher research, teacher inquiry, and practitioner inquiry are defined and explored.

The second section of the chapter presents the steps a teacher researcher might take to design, implement and complete a teacher research project. The end of the chapter includes worksheets for teachers interested in designing and implementing a teacher research project and a list of action research and teacher research examples in music education.

Issues in Music Education Curriculum Research?

Back in 1992 Edwards suggested: "Research is not viewed as being in the mainstream of either music or music education. Most musicians and music teachers have little interest in what music researchers do, how they do it, or the conclusions that they reach" (p. 5). Although we suggest that the work of the profession in the past 25 years may have improved upon this notion (the list of published action research and teacher research studies at the end of this chapter are a testament to this), it is still common for music teachers to feel as if they are disconnected from music education research. We begin this section by problematizing who does research and why. This is not meant to say that all higher education, graduate student, and industry-sponsored research should be ignored. It is just meant to get readers thinking about reasons for a research-to- practice disconnect which still seems apparent in our field.

Who Does Music Education Research and Why

It appears to us as if the large majority of published research in music education is generated from higher education. Although higher education faculty have research expertise and experience we worry sometimes about the potential disconnect of their work from the day-to-day issues in schools since these faculty are often no longer regularly involved in P–12 music education. Another concern about faculty researchers is that the motivation to conduct and publish research may be driven by the tenure and promotion process and the notion of "publish or perish." Within that environment there is often a lack of longitudinal work as well as little research on what might be perceived as controversial topics that might otherwise be relevant for P–12 teachers.

Closely related to the "publish or perish" climate in which researchers are required to operate is the question of quantity versus quality. There are often instances where a study might evolve not so much from a *need* to study a topic, but from an *opportunity* to study a topic. For instance, researchers might see a need to include school children in their study, but are dissuaded by the logistics involved with institutional review boards, school access, parent waivers, and teacher cooperation. The researcher might instead decide to study a topic that does not involve such lengthy and complex processes even though it may hold only marginal relevance to the profession.

Graduate student researchers are often more grounded in the inner workings of P–12 schools. However, their motivation is often to complete a course project, thesis, or dissertation, and the rules of these types of research projects set by committee members and other stakeholders can restrict the work of graduate students as well.

Finally, some research in music education comes from the music industry and although some of it may provide useful information, much of it is geared towards sales of products marketed by the same organizations funding the research.

Dissemination of Research

Music education research is disseminated largely through research journals. All of these journals require subscription fees and not all music teachers have access to these journals. Much of the research disseminated in music education uses highly technical research jargon which often makes the research unapproachable for teachers. Another concern is the time it takes for a research study to go from data collection to publication can be several years. Although this is necessary to ensure the rigor of blind peer review, for some topics (e.g., technology) this time frame is problematic. One journal that we find particularly friendly to teacher-researchers is the journal *Update: Applications of Research to Music Education* that is free to members of the National Association for Music Education and is focused on direct application of research to the school music classroom.

Authenticity of Musical Activity and the "So What" Factor

When we examine much of the research published in music education we worry about what we call the "authenticity of the musical activity" as well as the "So what?" factor. Too often researchers examine phenomena outside of the music classroom in what we would call an inauthentic environment. For example, if a researcher studying compositional practices of 3rd grade children collects data by pulling a few children out into the hallway and having them compose on keyboards and then suggests classroom activities to teach composition based on this work, we worry about whether the data collection is authentic to the suggested teaching practice. In some research studies the controls and procedures are so rigid that nothing about the situation remotely connects to real kids in real classrooms and we call this a problem of "So what?" Again, we wish to stress, it is not that these studies are not helpful to the profession in many ways, but the profession seems to lack research that captures the specific contextual issues in music classrooms. While research emerging from institutions of higher education may be problematic for practitioners, we believe in the value of research to inform classroom practice. This may take the form of teachers conducting their own research.

Contextualizing the Study of Curriculum and Assessment

All good teachers, whether they consciously carry out research or not, are researchers in the broadest sense of the word. This is because good teachers are also learners, and they recognize that they need to keep learning throughout their careers if they are to improve. They probe their subject matter, constantly searching for material that will excite and motivate their students; they explore pedagogy to create a learning environment that is both rigorous and supportive; they talk with their colleagues about difficult situations. Above all, they value the intellectual work that is at the core of teaching. (Nieto, 2003, p. 76–77)

Amidst all the different demands on music educators and their time, there must be a compelling argument to want to add something else to their schedule. Teachers conducting research in their own class-rooms can potentially require a great deal of time; however, much of the activity associated with conducting research in one's own class-room can be classified as what good teachers are already doing, only more formally. When teachers weave research into their daily routine and practices, the additional demands can be minimal. Questioning one's practice and seeking to improve teaching are practices the best teachers engage in regularly for the good of their students. Teacher research does nothing more than formalize these exemplary practices.

Teacher research is driven by teachers' need to improve student performance and understanding. A benefit of conducting teacher research in your classroom is that the topic being investigated origi-nates in the classroom, thus will be inherently relevant. Good research always starts out with a problem: "how can I make this better," "why is this happening," "I'm not happy with this result." These problem-based prompts are the foundation for self-reflection, an impetus for change, and a sign that the teacher is ready to question her practice and adjust for student benefit. The problem is whatever YOU want to change about YOUR classroom.

Often the questions teachers ponder have been empirically studied in other settings. Unfortunately, those other settings are not your classroom. The differences can be profound. No other teacher or researcher knows your classroom or your students better than you. While the existing research can help inform your change, the potential for successful change will be so much greater if the research is done in the setting where change is wanted.

On a daily basis, students give so much data regarding what they are learning, what they like, what they are confused about, what they need more of, and what teachers can do to better facilitate student performance and understanding. Often, this data is not realized or digested through no fault of the teachers; there is so much coming at teachers that it is difficult to focus unless they make a concerted effort. We suggest frameworks to formalize this data collection and encour-ages teachers to actively collaborate with their students to make the classroom a more positive educational environment. Quality teacher inquiry requires a teacher humble enough to know she has areas needing improvement, curious enough to try new teaching techniques, and caring enough to involve the students in the change process. The potential benefits include:

- better teaching
- improved student learning
- helping solve classroom problems
- encouraging change
- revitalizing and empowering teachers
- identifying what is and is not working
- promoting teacher reflection

It is professional development, it is viewed favorably by administration, and good teachers are already doing it whether they know it or not!

Teacher Research or Practitioner Inquiry

The concept of action research or teacher research requires a shift in the power structure of research—from a relationship between the researchers (typically university professors) and the researched (P–12 music teachers or students) to a collaboration between equal partners or work by the music teacher alone (Conway & Borst, 1999; Conway & Jeffers, 2004; Robbins, Burbank, & Dunkle, 2007; Robbins, 2014; West, 2012). The terms *action research* and *teacher research* are often used synonymously; however, action research refers specifically to a research design in which teaching practice will change immediately as a result of data collection, and that change will then lead to new research questions and a new research study in an ongoing spiraling process. For example, a teacher might conclude from research in her classroom that students are drawn to the social interaction that music affords. From that conclusion, she might then implement more activities designed to facilitate collaboration. These new activities might then compel her to find out what kinds of collaborative activities other teachers around the country are doing in their music classrooms, which then gives birth to a new study and continues the spiral. The term *teacher research* refers more generally to teacher research where the findings may or may not lead to a subsequent study, or even a change in future actions.

Designing and Implementing a Teacher Research Project

Developing a Purpose and Research Questions

The first step for teacher-researchers is to identify a problem or formulate a question regarding music teaching or learning. Since the goal of teacher research is to affect change, the most important aspect to consider is the usefulness of the inquiry in terms of one's own teaching. Teacher-researchers do not need to be concerned with generalizations to populations outside of their own context. However, in many cases, results documented in one study may be transferable to other contexts. It is important that the teacher-researcher carefully describe the setting of the research and the participants involved in the study so that other music teachers may consider how findings may relate to other contexts.

All aspects of a study—design, data collection, and analysis—are guided by the initial research questions. For example, in an interview study a researcher may ask, "How many participants need to be interviewed?" "How many interviews should I conduct with each participant?" "Are individual interviews or focus group interviews better for this study?" The only way to address these important research issues is to reflect on the research questions for the study. Worksheet #1 at the end of this chapter addresses research idea formation and development of questions.

Curriculum Research Design Options

Although teacher researchers do not need to focus a great deal on labeling a particular research design, we believe it is important to consider various ways in which curricular questions might be explored. We also think it is important for teacher researchers to let go of old notions of "research" that may be rooted in 7th grade science. Some curricular questions may be best answered by experiments, but many other questions may utilize other elements of design. In this section we provide types of curriculum questions that might be answered through qualitative, quantitative-descriptive, correlational, and experimental designs.

Qualitative. Most teacher research projects fall within the realm of qualitative research since teachers often study small groups of students through observation, interview, or review of documents. The findings in qualitative studies provide narratives and stories of participant experiences. The advantage to this type of design is that almost any teaching-practice question can be addressed by observing students, reviewing student work, or interviewing students, parents, or other teachers. The disadvantage is that qualitative research is "messy" and sometimes hard to distill down to usable suggestions and recommendations. The "hard data" that some districts require for student growth measurement or advocacy purposes may be harder to collect in a qualitative approach. However, the reader is reminded that the primary goal of teacher research is to improve teaching and learning and promote teacher reflection. It may be that a teacher researcher examines teaching to promote reflection and collects student growth data through other means.

A teacher researcher doing a qualitative study might invite students to keep journals about their responses to various classroom activities, and then analyze the student responses. Or, a music teacher might do focus group interviews with other teachers in the school building to better understand some phenomena of the school. Again, most any question that is specific to a teaching context can be addressed through observations, interviews, document analysis, or some combination of these techniques.

Quantitative-descriptive research. Different from qualitative research, quantitative-descriptive research often involves the collection of data outside of the teacher's classroom and from a much larger population. An example of quantitative-descriptive research that we can all relate to are polls where large numbers of people are surveyed regarding what they do in a given situation or what they think about a particular topic. We see research of this type every day in the media such as where professional polling organizations survey samples of the population regarding the political candidate they support, the television shows they like, and whether they think the economy is heading in the right direction, only to name a few. Political organizations, marketing firms, and economists rely heavily on quantitative-descriptive research to inform their decisions and future actions.

Quantitative-descriptive research can also be helpful to music teachers. Perhaps a teacher researcher is interested to know what method books other teachers around the country are using in their music classrooms, or what teaching techniques other teachers use in their classrooms. Or perhaps a teacher is interested in knowing more about what other teachers think about a particular topic such as the new music standards, teacher evaluation systems, or the Common Core. In such instances, the teacher researcher could develop a Likert-type survey instrument (strongly agree, agree, neither agree nor disagree, disagree, strongly disagree) and distribute the survey to a large number of respondents in a target population. The researcher could then examine the means and standard deviations among the population to provide answers about what the sampled population does in their classrooms or thinks about particular topics. Of course, the larger percentage of the target population who respond to the survey, the more reliable the data becomes.

Correlational research. Correlational research seeks to answer the question: "What is the relationship between X and Y?" Traditional correlational research looks to see if there is a relationship between two variables but does not try to answer if one variable *causes* the other. A correlation exists if, when one variable changes, the other changes in a consistent manner. To conduct correlational research, data are collected regarding two or more characteristics of the same participants. The data are then compared to see the relationship. Results from correlational research reveal if there is a relationship between two variables and to what degree they are related.

An example of correlational research in music education would be to answer the question: "Is there a relationship between grade level and sight-singing ability?" Data would be collected from multiple grades singing the same melody to see if sight-singing ability improved as students matured. There would be a correlational relationship if there were a consistent result, i.e., the 7th grade students were able to sing the melody more correctly than the 4th grade students. Correlation, however, does not indicate that one variable influenced the other. Even though the older students may be better sight-singers, age may not be the cause. They may have received private lessons, for example.

Experimental research. Perhaps the most familiar type of research is experimental. In this type of research a cause-and-effect relationship is sought—does X cause Y? The researcher must investigate how many conditions might influence one variable. There are often a control group and a treatment group. The control group receives no special treatment and is used for comparative analysis. The treatment group receives an intervention intended to create some form of change. Within the treatment group researchers are looking at two variables: the independent and dependent variables. The independent variable is the intervention that researchers are looking at to see if it will alter the group—the cause. The dependent variable is what is potentially changed—the effect.

An example of experimental research in music education would be to answer the question: "Will students perform better if I talk less and they perform more in rehearsal?" The teacher would then use two similar classes as groups. The teacher would not change instruction for one class (the control group). The teacher would make a concerted effort to talk less and have the students perform more in the other class (treatment group). The students' performance would be the dependent variable (because it *depends* on the other variable) and the amount of teacher talk would be the independent variable. There would be a causal relationship if the decreased teacher-talk resulted in a marked difference in student performance.

Collecting Data to Answer the Questions

Once research questions have been identified and a design has been considered, the teacher-researcher must begin to gather information and create documentation of the issues relating to the question. Many teachers find it valuable to keep a diary or a teaching journal so that they may keep track of daily incidents that may relate to the research. In some cases, a teacher may want to videotape his classroom and use the videotape transcript as a form of observation data. Interviews with students, parents, and colleagues may also be appropriate data, depending on the study. Existing documents such as student grade reports, student compositions, portfolios, practice records, concert programs, audiotapes of performances, etc., may also be used as data in the inquiry. In studies done in collaboration with university researchers or other teachers, classroom observations performed by the collaborative partner may provide valuable insight for the study.

Doing teacher research is not so different from teaching. Music teachers collect many artifacts of teaching (student work, videos, concert reflections) and many of these may be used as data. Some school districts may require extra permission if you are interviewing students or parents outside of regular class interaction, so these types of data collection should be cleared with an administrator. Worksheet #2 at the end of this chapter addresses data collection.

Analysis and Reporting: Who Is the Audience?

The teacher-researcher must reflect throughout the research process to determine when enough data has been collected. The data collection and analysis phases of a teacher research project meld together so that thoughts regarding the meaning of the data begin to emerge during the process of the project. The researcher must search for meaning in the data collected by coding the data and developing categories that help to describe and organize the themes presented in the observations, diary notes, interviews, etc. In collaborative research projects, teachers and university researchers may analyze the data together. This discussion adds another important dimension of reflection to the research process.

The final steps for the teacher-researcher include making decisions regarding teaching and learning based on the results of the study. In a less systematic way, good teachers make these kinds of decisions every day. What teacher research does is provide a model for teachers to use in reflecting on their work. The documentation of these decisions and reflections contribute to the knowledge base of teaching. Collaboration with university researchers may be helpful in terms of preparing this documentation for sharing with others. Worksheet #3 at the end of this chapter addresses analysis and reporting.

Conclusion

It seems self evident that intentional and systematic reflection on one's teaching followed by informed changes in action is a good thing. However, Cochran-Smith and Lytle (1999) remind us that with this level of reflection and change comes additional considerations. First, teacher researchers need to make sure that their research, if they are to claim it as research, is rooted in accepted notions about the nature of knowledge. That is, teacher research should be more systematic and rigorous than simply claiming a hunch or an experience as a research finding. This is not to discredit tacit knowledge or even experiential knowledge as legitimate ways of knowing, but that such ways of knowing do not require the same level of methodological rigor or justification of findings that is required of the systematic inquiry to be considered "research." Teacher researchers should be systematic and rigorous in their methods and justify their conclusions with evidence from their findings.

Second, teacher researchers should remember that it is difficult to remain objective and critical in events in which the researcher is also a participant. While the dual role of participant/researcher can aid in elucidating complexities of a problem, it can also make more difficult the task of seeing the larger picture; it is difficult to see the forest when you are among the trees. Working with another teacher researcher or a university researcher can help maintain a healthy balance between insider and outsider perspectives.

Lastly, although teacher research has the *potential* to fundamentally alter the nature of practice and the role of teachers, its power is severely diminished if it is used to perpetuate the status quo. Teacher research should be rooted in an understanding of social structures with the objective of changing them. Teacher researchers should conduct research as a means of critically examining their teaching and students' learning, rather than as a justification for their former practices, or as a way of maintaining traditional power structures.

RESEARCH IN YOUR CLASSROOM
FORMULATING YOUR QUESTIONS

DESCRIBE YOUR INSTRUCTIONAL SETTING (What do you teach, Who do you teach, Where do you teach, What are your resources?):

_____

_____

_____

_____

_____

_____

BASED ON THIS SETTING WHAT QUESTIONS DO YOU HAVE OR WHAT WOULD YOU LIKE TO SEE IMPROVED? (What is the problem you would like to see fixed?):

_____

_____

_____

_____

_____

_____

CONTINUE TO DESIGN AND DATA COLLECTION WORKSHEET

RESEARCH IN YOUR CLASSROOM
DESIGN AND DATA COLLECTION

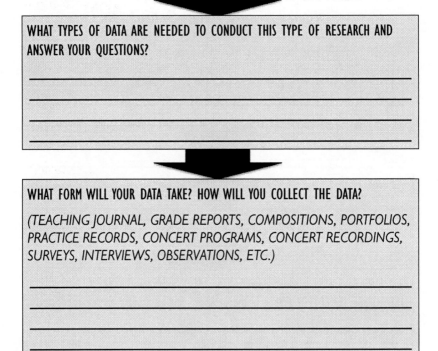

WHAT TYPE OF DESIGN WOULD YOU LIKE TO USE? (CIRCLE ONE)

QUALITATIVE

SURVEY

CORRELATIONAL

EXPERIMENTAL

WHAT TYPES OF DATA ARE NEEDED TO CONDUCT THIS TYPE OF RESEARCH AND ANSWER YOUR QUESTIONS?

WHAT FORM WILL YOUR DATA TAKE? HOW WILL YOU COLLECT THE DATA?

(TEACHING JOURNAL, GRADE REPORTS, COMPOSITIONS, PORTFOLIOS, PRACTICE RECORDS, CONCERT PROGRAMS, CONCERT RECORDINGS, SURVEYS, INTERVIEWS, OBSERVATIONS, ETC.)

CONTINUE TO ANALYSIS AND REPORTING WORKSHEET

RESEARCH IN YOUR CLASSROOM
ANALYSIS AND REPORTING

HOW WILL YOU ANALYZE/REFLECT ON YOUR DATA TO SEE IF YOU HAVE ANSWERED YOUR QUESTIONS?

WHAT DID YOUR DATA TELL YOU? WHAT DID YOU LEARN?

WHAT ARE YOU GOING TO CHANGE? WHAT ARE YOUR NEXT STEPS?

DO YOU HAVE NEW QUESTIONS? IF SO, WHAT?

DO YOU WISH TO PUBLISH/PRESENT YOUR FINDINGS IN A JOURNAL OR AT A CONFERENCE? IF SO, WHERE?

P–12 Teacher Action Research and Teacher Research Examples in Music Education

These lists of published and unpublished examples of teacher research are provided to give readers ideas regarding the possibilities of topics for teacher research.

Published Works

Bannan, N. (2004). A role for action research projects in developing new pedagogical approaches to aural and musicianship education, in J. W. Davidson (Ed.), *The Music Practitioner: Research for the Music Performer, Teacher and Listener*. Aldershot: Ashgate.

Barrett, M. (1994). Music education and the primary/early childhood teacher: a solution, *British Journal of Music Education, 11 (3)*, 197–207.

Black, C. (1998). Improving group dynamics and student motivation in a Grade 9 music class, *The Ontario Action Researcher*, 1 (1), www. nipissingu.ca/oar/archive-Vol1.htm accessed 23/01/07.

Byrne, C. & Sheridan, M. (2001). The SCARLATTI papers: development of an action research project in music, *British Journal of Music Education, 18* (2), 173–185.

Cope P. (1999). Community-based traditional fiddling as a basis for increasing participation in instrument playing, *Music Education Research, 1* (1), 61–73.

Davidson, J.W. (2004). Making a reflexive turn: practical music-making becomes conventional research, in J.W. Davidson (Ed.), *The Music Practitioner: Research for the Music Performer, Teacher and Listener*. Aldershot: Ashgate.

Edwards, R. H. (1992). Research: Going from incredible to credible. *The Quarterly Journal of Music Teaching and Learning, 3* (1), 5.

Gaunt, H. (2007). Learning and teaching breathing and oboe playing: action research in a conservatoire, *British Journal of Music Education, 24* (2), 207–231.

Hookey, M. (1994). Music education as a collaborative project: insights from teacher research, *Bulletin of the Council for Research in Music Education, 123*, 39–46.

Howard, J., & Martin, J. (1997). Developing musical creativity: the Sinapore Young Composers' Project as a case-study, *Research Studies in Music Education, 8(1)*, 71–82.

Mackworth-Youn, L. (1990). Pupil-centered learning in piano lessons: an evaluated action-research programme focusing on the psychology of the individual, *Psychology of Music*, 18, 73–86.

Major, A. E. (2007). Talking about composing in secondary school music lessons, *British Journal of Music Education, 24* (2), 165–178.

Miller, B. A. (2004). Designing compositional tasks for elementary music classrooms. *Research Studies in Music Education*, 22, 59–71. doi: 10.1177/1321103X040220010901

Miller, B. A. (2003). Integrating elementary general music instruction with a first grade whole language classroom. *Bulletin of the Council for Research in Music Education*, No. 156, 43–62.

Parker, E. (2010). Exploring student experiences of belonging within an urban high school choral ensemble: An action research study. *Music Education Research, 12*(4), 339–352. doi:10.1080/1461380 8.2010.519379.

Reynolds, A., & Nancy, B. (2007). Reflective practice in a middle-school instrumental setting. *Bulletin of the Council for Research in Music Education*, 174, 55–69.

Robbins, J., Burbank, M. K., & Dunkle, H. (2006). Teacher research: Tales from the field. *The Mountain Lake Reader, Vol. 4*. 60–68.

Strand, K.(2008). A narrative analysis of action research on teaching Composition. *Music Education Research, 11*(3), 349–363. doi:10.1080/14613800903144288.

Strand, K. (2005). Nurturing young composers: exploring the relationship between instruction and transfer in 9–12 year-old students. *Bulletin of the Council for Research in Music Education*, 165, 17–36.

Wiggins, J. (1999/2000). The nature of shared musical understanding and its role in empowering independent musical thinking. *Bulletin of the Council for Research in Music Education*, 143, 65–90.

Wiggins, J. (1995). Building structural understanding: Sam's story. *Quarterly Journal of Music Teaching and Learning, 6* (3), 57–75.

Wiggins, J. (Winter, 1994/1995), Teacher-research in a general music classroom: Effects on the teacher. *Bulletin of the Council for Research in Music Education*, 123, 31–35.

Wiggins, J. (1994). Children's strategies for solving compositional problems with peers. *Journal of Research in Music Education*, 42 (3), 232–252. doi: 10.2307/3345702.

University of Michigan Thesis Documents – Teacher Inquiry Projects

Male Peer Models in the Kindergarten Classroom (Megan Warzecha, 2014)

Composition in Third Grade General Music: The Student Perspective (Lisa Duprey, 2013)

A Description of Individual Practice Sessions of Four Ninth Grade String Students (Jill Soussek, 2013)

'I Don't Sing': Exploring Perceptions of Selected High School Students (Sarah Bowman, 2012)

Strategies for Self-Assessment in Middle School Band: Perceptions of Students, Parents and the Teacher (James Shouldice, 2012)

An Examination of 5th Grade Students' Descriptions of "Their Music" (Corynn Nordstrum, 2008)

Producing Lifelong Music Learning: Comparing Musical Motivations of Adult Community Musicians and Upper Elementary Students (Cathy Wilkinson, 2008)

Out of School Activities and Achievement in 8th Grade Band: Perceptions of Students, Parents and the Teacher (Michelle Wank, 2008)

The First Weeks of Practice: Case Studies of Beginning String Students (Daniel Mollick, 2008)

Perceptions of Fourth and Fifth Grade Students Regarding Motivation in
General Music (Lindsey Micheel-Mays, 2007)

Experiences of Middle School Band Students Regarding Gender and
Musical Instrument Selection (Bethany Maumee, 2007)

Student Perceptions of Cooperative Learning in Instrumental Music
(Sarah Djordevic, 2007)

Perceptions of Female Students in a Same Sex School: Gender and
Instrument Choice (Sommer Buttu, 2007)

Anxiety and the High School Musician (Matthew Forsleff, 2007)

References

Cochran-Smith, M., & Lytle, S. (1999). The teacher research movement:
A decade later. *Educational Researcher 28*(7), 15–25.

Conway, C. M., & Borst, J. (2001). Action research in music education.
Update: Applications of Research in Music Education, 19 (2), 3–8.

Conway, C. M., & Jeffers, T. (2004). The teacher as researcher in
beginning instrumental music. *Update: Applications of Research
in Music Education, 22* (2), 35–45.

McMahon, T. (1999). Is reflective practice synonymous with action
research? *Educational Action Research, 7*(1), 163–169.

Nieto, S. (2003). *What keeps teachers going?* New York: Teachers College
Press.

Robbins, J., Burbank, M. K., & Dunkle, H. (2006). Teacher research: Tales
from the field. *Journal of Music Teacher Education*, 17, 42–55.

Robbins, J. (2014). Practitioner inquiry. In C.M. Conway (Ed.). *The
Oxford Handbook of Qualitative Research in American Music
Education*. New York: Oxford University Press.

Walker, D. (1980). A brainstorming tour of writing on curriculum. In
A. Foshay (Ed.), *Considered action for curriculum improvement*
(pp. 71–81). Washington: Association for Supervision and
Curriculum Development.

West. C. (2012). Action research as a professional development activity.
Arts Education Policy Review, 112 (2), 89–94.

PART TWO:
FRAMEWORKS
FOR CURRICULUM
DEVELOPMENT

CHAPTER 4

THE INTERSECTION OF STUDENT UNDERSTANDING AND CURRICULUM: UNDERSTANDING BY DESIGN IN THE MUSIC CLASSROOM

Sommer H. Forrester
The University of Michigan

A primary goal of education is the development and deepening of student understanding of important ideas and processes within, and across, disciplines so that they can transfer their learning to new situations. (Wiggins & McTighe, 2012, p. 2)

Introduction

The purpose of this chapter is to introduce the rationale behind the Understanding by Design (UbD) framework, outline the salient components of UbD, and provide music teachers with the necessary tools for designing curricula, unit and/or lesson plans. In this chapter I will summarize the UbD framework and provide examples for using the design templates. This chapter is not intended to replace the work outlined by the UbD authors Grant Wiggins and Jay McTighe; rather, it is a way for music teachers to think critically about the relationship between curricular design, instruction, and student learning.

What does understanding look like?

Since the early 1960s, the developments in cognitive psychology have impacted the practice of teaching and learning (Tunks, 1992). Instructional trends have moved away from the top-down approach where the teacher is the bearer of all knowledge and passes information to the student, toward a more dynamic, dialectic, and process-orientated approach whereby teachers and students are co-creators of knowledge. This active process, known as enculturation, honors and builds on students' prior knowledge and encourages students to construct their understanding through the careful balance between skill acquisition and knowledge (Bransford, Brown, & Cocking, 2000; Brown, Collins, & Duguid, 1989; DeCorte, 2003; Wiske, 1998; Wiggins & McTighe, 2005). Learning (skill acquisition and knowledge development) and cognition are the fundamental building blocks in developing *autonomous learners* who are able to *think flexibly* and *apply their knowledge* to new and different contexts throughout their lives (Brown et al., 1989).

Music educators are charged with the task of designing and implementing curricula, units, and lesson plans that address established state-driven content standards and the national arts standards. Such standards define what students are expected to know and be able to do. Teachers must translate these standards into engaging curricula, and instruction. Most recently, the National Coalition for Core Arts Standards (NCCAS) advocated for the integration across subjects, grade levels, and long term learning goals that foster student understanding (Siebert, 2013). While the NCCAS stress the enduring principles of fostering student understanding and promote transfer of learning to other domains, music teachers are left to put the pieces of the puzzle together and find a way to design curricula and instruction to the standards (Wiggins & McTighe, 2012). In order to apply these standards to practice, we must first step back and examine the term *understanding*, and how teachers facilitate this development with students.

Education writers Grant Wiggins and Jay McTighe contend that understanding is both a verb and a noun (2005). "To *understand* [verb] a topic of subject is to be able to *use* (or *apply*) knowledge and skill wisely and effectively. An *understanding* [noun] is the successful result of trying to understand—the resultant grasp of an *unobvious* idea, an interference that makes meaning of many discrete elements of knowledge" (2005, p. 43). In order to foster student understanding and nurture autonomous thinking, teachers must "unpack" content and illuminate core concepts and essential questions for learners (Wiggins & McTighe, 2012).

"Uncovering" student thinking is vastly different than "covering" material. As a noun, the word cover refers to something on the surface. When we apply this to teaching, it suggests addressing surface details and/or stating the facts, but falls short of connecting concepts to the bigger picture. Conversely, *uncovering* suggests getting inside the process and the argument, questioning past and present understandings, and testing claims. Teachers must "uncover" student questions, assumptions, misunderstandings, and core ideas. In doing so, learners are given the space to actively and thoughtfully make meaning of facts, apply their knowledge and skills to other tasks and domains, and ultimately transfer learning to new situations. Wiggins and McTighe (2012) indicate the six facets of understanding serve as indicators of student understanding: i) the capacity to explain, ii) interpret, iii) apply, iv) shift perspective, v) empathize, and vi) self-assess. Therefore, evidence of understanding involves assessing "students' capacity to use their knowledge thoughtfully and to apply it effectively in diverse settings—that is, to *do* the subject" (p. 48, 2005). As such, learners must actively develop their understanding with the support of the teacher.

Understanding the UbD framework

Backward Design

Understanding by Design is a way of thinking purposefully about curricular planning, assessment and school reform. It builds on the premise of a goal-orientated model for learning that emphasizes ideas, processes, relationships, and promotes understanding through student inquiry. The UbD framework provides teachers with flexible tools to structure their curriculum around the development of understanding in the learning environment. The framework is not a linear approach and does not prescribe a formulaic or rigid program. Developed by Grant Wiggins and Jay McTighe in 1999, the UbD framework is grounded in the idea that "Teaching is a means to an end, and planning precedes teaching. The most successful teaching begins, therefore, with clarity about desired learning outcomes and about the evidences that will show that learning has occurred" (Wiggins & McTighe, 2010, p. 7). Thus, understanding is achieved through purposeful *design* as opposed to piecing facts and content together with the hope that learners will connect the dots.

UbD advocates using a three-stage "backward design" that emphasizes purposefully aligning curriculum with the desired learning outcomes. The three stages of the backward design include: "i) Desired results, ii) Evidence, iii) Learning plan" (p. 18). Rather than starting with content, teachers identify the learning goals and outcomes first. In doing so, teachers avoid the "twin sins" of curricular planning and unit design: covering content and activity-orientated design (Wiggins & McTighe, 2005). The "twin sins" approach to design overgeneralizes content material and provides no guiding intellectual purpose or clear priorities to frame students' learning. The priority of the backward design is to help students know and understand the *purpose* of the activity, the *goal* of the task, and how these goals lead to *understanding*. Through this design, students are encouraged to go beyond knowing facts and figures and are encouraged to develop an understanding of the conceptual underpinnings of the discipline, make connections, and ultimately transfer the application of their understanding in new problems and diverse situations (McTighe & Davis, 2012).

The authors summarize the three stages of the backward design used in the UbD framework:

Stage 1 – Desired Results
• What long-term transfer goals are targeted?
• What meanings should students make to arrive at important understandings?
• What essential questions will students keep considering?
• What knowledge and skill will students acquire?
• What established goals/standards are targeted?
Stage 2 – Evidence
• What performances and products will reveal evidence of meaning-making and transfer?
• By what criteria will performance be assessed, in light of Stage 1 desired results?
• What additional evidence will be collected for all Stage 1 desired results?
• Are the assessments aligned to all Stage 1 elements?
Stage 3 – Learning Plan
• What activities, experiences, and lessons will lead to achievement of the desired results and successes at the assessments?
• How will the learning plan help students achieve transfer, meaning, acquisition, and independence?
• How will the unit be sequenced and differentiated to optimize achievement for all learners?

Figure 1: *Graphic representation of the logic of backward design (Wiggins & McTighe, 2010, p. 8)*

Music teachers looking to use the UbD framework can start by thinking through a unit of study and answer the aforementioned questions to frame their planning. Consider a middle school instrumental chamber music unit as our first example of how to apply the logic of the backward design:

Stage 1 Desired Results	Stage 2 Evidence	Stage 3 Learning Plan
If the desired end result is for learners to understand that...	*then you need evidence of the learners' ability to (explain, interpret, apply)*	*then the learning events need to...*
Musicians make informed, independent musical decisions	Lead peer directed rehearsals and independently make musical decisions	Help students understand the rehearsal process (reading a score, breaking sections down, chunking) Help students articulate their musical goals Help students learn how to self-assess Apply previous knowledge about the rehearsal process

Figure 2: *Adapted from: Figure A.1 The logic of Backward Design (Wiggins & McTighe, 2010, p. 9)*

From this example, we can see that music teachers typically use a backward design without even realizing it! In this example, students who have worked in a large ensemble setting will likely already have the tools required to complete this task. Thus, the role of the teacher is three-fold: i) *Transfer*: Guide students to think back to their past and present understanding: What are the sequence of events that happen when a new piece is handed out in the large ensemble context? ii) *Meaning*: Guide students to reflect and analyze on their music making: How do musicians make musical decisions? How have the students approached these decisions in the past? What knowledge and skills do they need to inform their decisions? iii) *Essential Questions*: Guide students towards drawing inferences, and asking questions that push them toward connecting ideas, and applying strategies: How do conductors and musicians decide which elements of musical style to use in performance? Are there multiple ways to interpret stylistic markings in the score, and/or parts? What makes a performance musical?

Design

The nature of the backward design encourages teachers to think carefully and strategically about curriculum design and unit plans. In this section, I will describe in detail the three-stage design process outlined in UbD. Teachers who wish to learn more about specific UbD templates and modules are encouraged to visit the Association for Supervision and Curriculum Development (ASCD) website: http://www.ascd.org/research-a-topic/understanding-by-design-resources

Stage 1 – Desired Results

The three-stage design encourages teachers to align unit goals, assessments, and instructional plans. When charged with the task of designing unit plans, where does one start? Are certain questions, learning goals, and activities more suitable than others? The short answer to these questions is: yes! Instructional design is challenging and complex work. The key component of the backward design is determining the desired goal of the instructional design. Based on the goal, the architect of the design (i.e., the teacher) can determine the assessments and learning events that will help students reach the goal. Thinking about instructional design from this vantage point encourages aligning the three stages to ensure that each stage supports the next.

UbD encourages teachers to approach this work through flexible entry points that are broad-based and focused on enduring ideas: Big Ideas and Essential Questions (Wiggins & McTighe, 2005; 2010). Wiggins and McTighe offer the following definitions:

> [Big idea]: By definition, big ideas are important and enduring. Big ideas are transferable beyond the scope of a particular unit...big ideas are the material of understanding. They can be thought of as the meaningful patterns that enable one to connect the dots of otherwise fragmented knowledge. Such ideas go beyond discrete facts of skills to locus on larger concepts, principles, or processes. (2005, p. 338–339)

[Essential questions]: A question that lies at the heart of a subject or curriculum (as opposed to being either trivial or leading), and promotes inquiry and uncoverage of a subject. Essential questions thus do not yield a single straightforward answer (as a leading question does) but produce different plausible responses, about which thoughtful and knowledgeable people may disagree. (2005, p. 342)

As teachers think about the big ideas and essential questions, they must also consider how these ideas and questions align with overall expectations, i.e., state-adopted music content standards. Transfer goals require teachers to think about how students will independently use their learning and apply it to other contexts. The big ideas and essential questions anchor the instructional design and help focus the transfer goals. Figure 3 provides two music examples of how the overall expectations, transfer goals, big ideas, and essential questions are realized.

The final component in the Stage 1 design is acquisition. What will students know and recall at the end of the unit? What skills and processes will students use? Clearly outlining the knowledge and skills in relation to the long term understanding goals helps connect and focus summative and formative assessment: Stage 2 of the framework.

Stage 2 – Evidence

In order to craft evaluations that get to the heart of assessing student understanding, teachers must "think like assessors" (Wiggins & McTighe, 2010, p. 22). What evidence is needed to determine if students have achieved the desired results outlined in Stage 1? What types of assessments reveal student understanding? The structure of the backward design requires that each of the three stages are aligned and interconnected. As such, approaching assessment through questions that link to the desired results is crucial.

Assessing for understanding has many layers as it involves determining the degree to which students understand the meaning of the

Stage 1				
			Meaning	
Topic	**Overall Expectations**	**Transfer Goals**	**Big Ideas/ Understandings**	**Essential Questions**
Listening unit	State content standard	• Develop a lifelong appreciation of music as performer and listener.	• There are many different types of musical sounds, traditions, colors, and styles.	• What did I hear? • How might this experience inform your playing as a musician and a member of a musical ensemble?
Beginning band/ orchestra/ choir performance unit	State content standard	• Develop a lifelong appreciation of music as performer and listener. • Acquire a basic understanding of reading music notation while singing or playing an instrument. • Develop a basic understanding of musical elements through participation in musical experiences that involve listening, creating, and performing.	• Being a member of a musical ensemble requires collaborative, creative, and technical knowledge and skills.	• How do rhythm and melody affect my playing? • How can you interpret the expressive markings in music? • What is tempo? • What is pitch? • What is the role of dynamics in music?

Figure 3: *Example of partial Stage 1 Design in Music*

learning task and if they are able to transfer their understanding to other situations. What do we want learners to understand? What do we want learners to be able to *do*? This approach to assessment goes beyond measuring knowledge and skill through traditional evaluations that simply assess correctness (i.e., tests, recall, demonstration).

Assessing for understanding requires that teachers look beyond correct answers to how students use their knowledge flexibly, and apply it to new situations. Moreover, assessing for understanding involves examining student choices: what sources do they draw from (past and present knowledge), what informs their decisions (arguments and rationales), are they able to make connections beyond the task at hand, are they able to draw meaning and make transfers without prompting from the teacher? Thus, assessing understanding and the assessment tasks in Stage 2 need to include opportunities for students to: "(1) explain—in their own words—what inferences they have drawn and why (by providing appropriate evidence and reasons); and (2) apply their learning to new situations" (Wiggins & McTighe, 2010, p. 49). In doing so, students have the opportunity to connect and communicate their understanding.

In order to craft assessment tasks in the UbD framework we must first begin with the evaluation criteria: "What criteria will be used in each assessment to evaluate attainment of the desired results? Regardless of the format of the assessment, what qualities are most important?" (Wiggins & McTighe, 2010, p. 17). Notice that we are not starting with the types or format of the assessment (i.e., playing tests, essays, etc.). Rather, we begin with criteria that link back to the specific tasks of the desired results. Let's refer back to the evidence of understanding for the listening unit and examine how to begin crafting assessments (see Figure 4). From this point teachers would devise a list of performance task(s) that enable students to demonstrate their understanding. Continuing with the concert review assignment, performance tasks might include: having students write a comparison of two concerts, develop a journal that chronicles their listening habits throughout a semester, provide a written or oral critique of a concert from the perspective of a musician, conductor, or music critic. In addition to stating the performance tasks, students may demonstrate that they achieved Stage 1 goal through related forms of evidence. In the case of the concert review assignment this could include the students' ability to analyze and describe their interpretation of their own playing vis-à-vis responding to a concert or solo recording.

	Stage 1	Stage 1	Stage 2
	(Specific tasks) Acquisition of Knowledge - *Students will know...*	(Specific tasks) Acquisition of Skill - *Students will be skilled at...*	Evaluative Criteria
Listening unit	• That there are several different styles and genres of music • That there are several different ways to perform a piece of music (performance practices) • The elements of music • That art is informed by socio-political factors	• Interpreting and expressing an informed personal opinion about a performance • Applying the elements of music to their interpretation of a performance	• Effective use of music elements to communicate opinions • Insightful, supported analysis • Clear and appropriate reflection • *NB: Teachers would include more fine grain assessment that fit the needs of their classroom and unit.*

Figure 4: *Stage 2 Evidence*

Stage 3 – Learning Plan

By now, you can probably anticipate that the contents of the Stage 3 learning plan will connect with Stages 2 and 1. Now that we have connected the broader learning goals with the assessments we can proceed with creating a plan of action that summarizes the learning events. It is important to note that the backward design is a not a rigid template that functions in a linear manner. Rather, the design is flexible and circular. Teachers can work on any of the stages in any order although there is some logic to making sure the goal is clear before doing the rest. As teachers work on each stage, rethinking may cause them to change any of the stages they have already completed; thus the process is iterative and builds understanding as you move through it. Stage 3 may take the form of specific lesson plans, or it may not.

Teachers may use this stage to summarize the learning events and types of instruction needed to facilitate student success at meaning, transfer, acquisition, and overall understanding of the learning tasks. In addition, Stage 3 is the place where teachers can determine what pre-assessments might be needed to determine the student's prior knowledge, skill level, and possible assumptions. It is also the place where teachers can think broadly about how they will continue to monitor and support student progress and understanding at the completion of the unit.

Alignment

Aligning the three stages of the backward design is a critical component of the UbD framework. This requires teachers to reflect back on their work and assess the fluidity of the design. Do the three stages connect to the stated goals in Stage 1? Wiggins and McTighe (2010) offer the following questions as a way to self-assess the alignment in the backward design:

1. Could students do the proposed assessment(s) well but not really have mastered or understood the content in the question?
2. Could students do poorly on the specific assessment(s) but really have mastery of the content in question?
3. Could students do all the designer-proposed activities in Stage 3 but not really be ready to explain/justify/infer meaning or transfer their learning as demanded by assessments in Stage 2?
4. Could students fail to do all of the proposed activities in Stage 3 but still be ready to handle tasks in Stage 2 that require higher-order inference and other kinds of meaning-making? (2010, p. 53–54)

If the answer to any of these questions is *yes*, the activities likely do not align with the goals in Stage 1 and/or the assessments in Stage 2, and require revision.

Empowering learners to know, understand, and *do*!

Teaching and learning is a complex and dynamic endeavor. As educators we have the opportunity to work with students and provide them with powerful opportunities to develop understanding that they can use beyond the classroom walls. Facilitating this growth and participating in this process is exciting and rewarding work! In order for this process to be fully realized, teachers must think carefully and thoughtfully about how they approach curricula, course syllabi, content materials, assessments, and instruction. In doing so, they can make the purpose and goals of the classroom experience known to students from day one. Giving students the tools to see how education connects to the real world is a necessary step in promoting curiosity and life long learners.

Teaching for understanding is dependent on the conditions for learning that are established by teachers. Creating an environment where students are encouraged to think critically and reflectively requires an approach to instruction that is process-orientated and rooted in the development of understanding. This learner-centered model involves the dynamic interaction between the teacher and student. Younker (2012) indicates: "Questioning, inquiring, and being curious in communities of learning involves all participants, who are recognized as stakeholders and knowledge bearers, and who construct understanding and meaning through active participation" (p. 169). Music students in classroom settings must see this type of instruction modeled and cultivated throughout their development as musicians and learners if we hope to enculturate it as an integral part of the classroom practice and thus enable students to autonomously act as musicians. Creating dynamic curricula, instructional plans, and learning environments where learners are challenged to develop understanding and apply their knowledge to new contexts reinforces the ultimate goal of education: for learners to think critically and apply their understanding as they navigate the real world.

References

Bransford, J. D., Brown, A. L, & Cocking, R. R. (Eds.). (2000). *How people learn: Brain, mind, experience, and school.* Washington, DC: National Academy Press.

Brown, J. S., Collins, A., & Duguid, P. (1989). Situated cognition and the culture of learning. *Educational Researcher, 18*(1), 32–42.

DeCorte, E. (2003). Transfer as the productive use of acquired knowledge, skills, and motivations. *Current Directions in Psychological Science, 12*(4), 142–146.

McTighe, J., & Davis, S. (2012). Proceedings from: *Understanding by Design 2.0.* Toronto, Ontario: McTighe.

Tunks, T. W. (1992). The transfer of music learning. In R. Colwell (Ed.) *Handbook of Research on Music Teaching and Learning* (pp. 437–447). New York: Schirmer.

Wiggins, G. & McTighe, J. (2005). *Understanding by design, Expanded 2nd Edition.* New York: Prentice Hall.

Wiggins, G. & McTighe, J. (2010). *The Understanding by design guide to creating high-quality units.* New York: Prentice Hall.

Wiggins, G., & McTighe, J. (2012). From the common core to curriculum: *Five big ideas.* Retrieved from: http://nccas. wikispaces.com/file/view/From%20Common%20Core%20 Standards%20to%20Curriculum%20-%20Five%20Big%20Ideas. pdf/375975758/From%20Common%20Core%20Standards%20 to%20Curriculum%20-%20Five%20Big%20Ideas.pdf

Wiske, M. S. (1998). What is teaching for understanding? In M. S. Wiske (Ed.), *Teaching for understanding: Linking research with practice* (pp. 61–86). San Francisco: Jossey-Bass.

Younker, B. A. (2012). Focusing on critical practice and insights in the music teacher Education curriculum. In C. Beynon & K. Veblen (Eds.), *Critical perspectives in Canadian Music Education* (pp. 165–180), Wilfred Laurier Press: University of Wilfred Laurier.

CHAPTER 5

UNDERSTANDING MUSIC AND UNIVERSAL DESIGN FOR LEARNING: STRATEGIES FOR STUDENTS WITH LEARNING DIFFERENCES IN THE 21ST CENTURY

Ryan Hourigan
Ball State University

In order to examine the topic of curriculum it is important to reflect on the aim music education and how *all* students might be provided access to music within American K–12 schools. The National Association for Music Education (NAfME) provides the following mission statement:

> Music allows us to celebrate and preserve our cultural heritages, and also to explore the realms of expression, imagination, and creation resulting in new knowledge. Therefore, every individual should be guaranteed the opportunity to learn music and to share in musical experiences. (NAfME, 2014)

In looking at this mission statement, *cultural heritage, expression, imagination*, and *creation* are shared experiences for many students. Students in the United States also share a myriad of common classroom and performance experiences (within reason) due to shared cultural elements, national and state music standards, and traditional practices (i.e., band, choir, orchestra, general music) that are similar from state to state. There are also common utilitarian outcomes such as critical thinking, problem-solving, and collegiality that are also shared collective familiarities in music education classrooms.

If the outcome of an American music education aims to "guarantee the opportunity to learn and share in music experiences," then we, as a profession, sometimes fall short when serving certain populations of students such as those with learning differences. Many P–12 music education programs in the United States have one or more of the following attributes: 1) focuses solely on performance; 2) base most programmatic decisions on Euro-centric traditions within a hierarchy that assumes some music is of higher quality than other music; and 3) does not provide equal access to requisite knowledge and opportunities for engagement and expression, all of which excludes a large majority of students (e.g., students with disabilities, diverse backgrounds, and socioeconomic status) in our schools from participation and provides a "one size fits all" approach to music education. Dewey states, "The belief that all genuine education comes about through experience does not mean that all experiences are genuinely or equally educative. Experiences and education cannot be equated to each other. For some experiences are mis-educative" (Dewey, 1938). We, as music educators, should look beyond standard goals and current promising practices to include dispositions such as inclusive attitude, compassion, diversity, and acceptance as a true goal in our profession.

How is this to be done within the growing demands and pressure on music education programs? Walker and Soltis state, "...there are lots of things like good health that curriculum theorists have wished for people-such things as just society; a harmonious, progressive, democratic nation; the abilities to think critically, act morally, and live responsibly" (Walker and Soltis, 2004). The first steps in providing a more inclusive practice are to expand traditional offerings, curricula, and materials to be more student-centered in order to foster life-long learners and consumers of music. Much of what Dewey, Walker, and Soltis mention above can be taught while attaining goals of student-centered instruction and inclusive music education.

In the early 1990's, Meyer, Rose, and Gordon at the Center for Applied Special Technology (CAST) began developing a new approach to teaching and learning (Meyer, Rose, and Gordon, 2014, p. 5). In their many years of research, they found that students with and without disabilities faced similar barriers at some point along their path that kept them from being academically successful. Meyer et. al (2014) states: "The education community began to recognize that many students—not just students with disabilities—faced barriers and impediments that interfered with their ability to make optimal progress and to develop as educated and productive citizens" (p. 5). *Universal Design for Learning* (UDL) became the catalyst for rede-signing the teaching and learning process for all students regardless of learning differences and to provide equal opportunities for all students to gain access and learn. The UDL framework has been successfully developed over many years but three core principles have remained the same. In order for schools to provide equal opportunities to reach high standards in music we must provide multiple means of engage-ment, representation, and expression in order to meet the needs of 21st century classrooms.

Universal Design for Learning

| Multiple Means of Engagement | Multiple Means of Representation |

| Multiple Means of Action and Expression |

Figure 1: *The Principles of Universal Design for Learning.*

Unfortunately, for students who have learning differences, traditional teaching and learning requires the student to be flexible rather than the curriculum. Meyer et. al states (in referring to traditional education): "Classrooms became textbook-centered rather than student-centered" (p. 128). Over the years, music education followed suit with traditional education by offering "cookie cutter" textbook series, literature lists, lesson planning and curricular models rather than considering the myriad of learning differences in the music classroom. Many of our textbooks and method books still do not provide accommodation examples for students with learning differences.

Universal Design for Learning moves the emphasis away from traditional learning and on to curricular experiences that are positive, educative, and student-focused. Glass, Meyer, and Rose state:

> To be effective in a more inclusive, more demanding teaching environment, arts educators will have to be more responsive to individual differences by recognizing the variation in difficulties that their students will have and addressing them in productive ways. At its roots, UDL is a framework for understanding and responding effectively to individual differences. (p. 104)

This chapter will examine each of the principles of UDL as they relate to challenges in providing inclusive music education curriculum for all students. These ideas will be examined at the macro (building or district-level) and micro level (classroom level). Some of the examinations of music curriculum below will cross over between macro and micro levels with the overall target of providing inclusive music opportunities for *all* students.

Principle 1: Multiple Means of Engagement in Music Education

Macro-level. Multiple means of engagement as part of UDL is described as "How learners get engaged and stay motivated. How they are challenged, excited or interested" (Meyer, Rose, and Gordon,

2014, p. 90). The first large missing component within American music education is access. Students cannot engage in music without opportunity. How are we to address engagement if there is not equal access to instruction for all music students? At the fundamental macro level, the basic means of engagement in music education is participation; however, many school music programs still are not available to students in poverty and students with special needs (Hourigan, 2014). This is a shared disadvantage that is common across the United States. In addition, many school districts who carry partial or even full programming still continually break the Zero Reject/Least Restrictive Environment principles of the Individuals with Disabilities Education Act by not allowing full access to programming for students regardless of disability[1]. For example, many elementary schools do not allow an opportunity for self-contained special education classes to receive a music education or to participate in all school music programs or concerts. This may or may not be appropriate for all students; however, some students are not given the opportunity. In addition, many secondary performance classes have no entry-level for students who may have exceptionalities. Often students with disabilities are not developmentally able to join band and orchestra at the traditional entry points (e.g., 5th or 6th grade) and it would be more developmentally appropriate to give them this experience beginning later in their schooling.

The obvious solution to this larger curricular problem is to find ways at *all* levels to include *all* students regardless of ability and background and provide as many access points to music education as possible. This presents a host of challenges. The biggest obstacles for accomplishing this goal are models for inclusion and professional development for music educators (Hammel , 2007).

One of the guiding principles of UDL in the area of engagement is "Sustaining effort and persistence—providing opportunities where students naturally work with their peers, focus on the task at hand,

---

[1] The Individuals with Disabilities Education Act requires that all students, regardless of disability be "equally educated." In addition, IDEA mandates that all students receive a "Free and Appropriate" education.

and receive directive and supportive feedback from the instructor" (Nelson, 2014, p. 44). For most students, the collective ensemble experience accomplishes these goals. Students naturally work with their peers, focus on the end goal of a polished performance and receive directive and supportive feedback from the music educator. However, how can we accomplish this same task as the macro-level for students who have learning differences? Just providing music experiences for students with disabilities is not enough. Students with learning differences must have the same opportunity to thrive in music.

Inclusion Models and Examples. Inclusion models for instruction have continued to improve over the years. Because of thirty-plus years of mainstreaming and inclusion, students are more aware of the needs of their peers. Students being educated for many years in inclusive environments are more likely to assist and provide ideas for shared music education experiences. Within performance music education, partner ensembles have been popping up as a way to provide performance access at the secondary level (Hammel and Hourigan, 2013, p. 136). Partner ensembles are typically set up for students with special needs to perform with students who do not have special needs. These ensembles provide opportunities for peers with and without disabilities to be paired together in elementary and secondary performance experiences and fold right into UDL philosophy (i.e., naturally work with peers, task oriented, mentored or given feedback from peers and music educator). This highly successful strategy can provide multiple means of engagement for many students, affording not only the typical curricular offering (band, choir, orchestra, general music), but a less threatening more inclusive experience (partner ensemble) as well.

Reverse inclusion is also another macro-curricular idea for music education scheduling. This is where students who are not challenged by disabilities attend music (or any other curricular activity) with students who have special needs, often this culminating in a shared experience either in performance or the classroom. This can and should happen at both the elementary and secondary level. Students making music with peers are the biggest motivator for lifetime performance and consumption of music.

As students reach the secondary level of music education, the curriculum is often tilted towards large-group ensembles in many middle and high schools. Large ensembles often require a level of independence that many students who have learning challenges struggle with because there are so many students around them with a variety of distractions. Yes, there are classroom-based experiences that often appear in the secondary curriculum (e.g., guitar, piano, or music theory); however, these particular experiences often require fine motor development (e.g., piano, guitar) or a requisite knowledge base (music theory). One solution may be to offer small-group performance experiences to begin before engaging in the large group. Peer music lessons and chamber music can often be a good starter experience prior to joining the large group. Having the peer-helper follow the student into the large group (when ready) can also add to the experience.[2]

Striving to provide equal curricular access at the state, district, or school level can be important to students for a variety of reasons. Students with developmental disabilities become adults with developmental disabilities. Some require assisted living; however, many could be provided with skills to engage the community, socialize, and add to their quality of life. This may not be a national or state standard; however, in invoking some of the strategies mentioned above, students may gain the ability to experience community-based music experiences for a lifetime of music making which will add to their quality of life. For students who do not end up with this lifestyle, the underlying goal would be to motivate students to pursue a lifetime of music making. This will only come by cultivating a personal love of music.

Micro-level. Glass, Blair, and Ganley (2012) state:

Part of the process of UDL implementation is providing engaging and relevant content with flexible low-and high-tech

---

[2]   United Sound (July Duty) is an excellent example of reverse inclusion in instrumental music (http://www.unitedsound.org)

tools to support various pathways to learning. We also need to make a transition in our thinking as educators—from retrofitting modifications in response to particular disabilities of students or groups of students, to designing learning opportunities and spaces from the beginning that are more universal. (p. 106)

In other words, many music educators often think of adapting lessons to meet the individual need of a specific student. In many cases this is a very worthwhile and relevant planning technique; however, this often can result in a one shot, event-based system of planning and instruction. As lessons come up, we accommodate not thinking of the overall opportunity to engage the art form or long-term independence of students gaining knowledge and skills. Fortunately, music provides many access points. Glass et. al (2012) states, "The arts can provide engaging alternatives for the representation of content and for meaning expression and action" (p. 107). For example, as students with disabilities continue through middle school and high school, opportunities for music education decrease. We often move from classroom instruction in the United States to performance-based music. Ensemble conductors, if challenged to include students with disabilities, often attempt to fit the student in the mold of the ensemble. This can come from adapting parts, finding instruments that are easier to access, offering limited opportunity (less music), and other accommodations.

Re-examining the Traditional Approach to Engagement. Engagement is considered the "why" of learning within UDL. Meyer et. al state, "In the all-important affective domain, expertise involves developing interest, purpose, motivation, and most importantly, strong self regulation as a learner" (p. 90). For all students, including those who are challenged, finding the motivation to participate and set self-motivating goals can be difficult. Instead of trying to make the student fit the group, music educators should attempt to identify and remove barriers allowing the group to fit the student (Glass et. al 2012). For example, some students with disabilities often have unique interests or skills. There is an example of "Mike and the Didgeridoo" in Hammel and Hourigan (2011) where a band director was able to incorporate Mike's interest in the didgeridoo into middle school band. This not only allowed Mike to participate (who happens to have special needs) but also allowed exploration of multicultural music.[3]

The story referred to above is an example of a traditional band program that was completely evolved to accommodate an individual student. This raises the question: How can students with exceptionalities participate in secondary ensembles with the same autonomy, choice, motivation, and contribution as their peers on a long-term basis (which is a principle of UDL)? First, there must be an examination of the traditional band, choir, and orchestra in the secondary public school. Could there be alternative ensembles that are more engaging for students with disabilities?

Band and orchestra conductors should also think outside of traditional approaches to rehearsal and performance. Could we have partner bands and orchestras? This would involve peer-supported lessons at the secondary level that could encourage future teachers to learn about pedagogy with an exceptional group of students. In addition, there have been great successes using iPad ensembles with applications like garage band, soundation[4], and cosmovox[5] to allow more options for performance for students who are challenged by traditional instruments. These tools allow students the opportunity to make music with traditional instrument patches and sounds without the barrier of traditional approaches to pedagogy. All of the tools mentioned above are just the first step in reevaluating traditional practice to include a more diverse offerings and opportunity within music education, especially at the secondary level.

---

[3] A full vignette of this story can be found on page 125 of *Teaching Students with Special Needs: A Label-free Approach* (Hammel & Hourigan, 2011)

[4] http://soundation.com

[5] http://leisuresonic.com/cosmovox

An excellent example of this can be found at PS 177 in New York City.[6] The instrumental ensemble at this school uses a combination of acoustical instruments and the iPad. Students who struggle with disabilities tend to find the iPad less threatening and the technology allows a fusion with traditional acoustic instruments. The easy touch-screen allows students with fine motor challenges to participate, perform, and practice at home.

- Garage Band
- Band (MooCowMusic Ltd.)
- Barrel Tones (Barrel Squid)
- Bloom (Opal Ltd.)
- Capo (SuperMegaUltraGroovy)
- Instruments (Mobilsoft)

More apps can be explored at the Children with Exceptionalities SRIG website: https://sites.google.com/site/exceptionalitiessrig/home/resources/related-website

Figure 2: *Instrumental Music Applications for the iPad*

One goal of UDL is finding ways for students to remain motivated and to set internal goals for themselves and to remain musical over a long period of time. The key to motivating students to improve musically is to strip away as many barriers as possible (many mentioned above) and then provide them with multiple pathways to remain musical. The last component of UDL that applies to this section (multiple means of engagement) is feedback. With the right feedback, students will find a way to regulate between internal and external motivators to find success. Formative feedback should be honest, regular, and positive with concrete solutions to challenges. Peer feedback within the framework mentioned could enhance the motivation to continue with lifetime music making.

---

6   Information about PS 177 and the iPad band can be found at: http://www.npr.org/blogs/ed/2014/06/07/319223328/high-school-band-theres-an-app-for-that

How would this feedback look for students with disabilities? Nelson (2014) explains (in referring to sub-principles of UDL in regard to multiple means of engagement), "Offering options for self-regulation, students gain skills in self-monitoring to gauge their behaviors and their learning..." (p. 44). One technique would be to record rehearsals or lessons and follow up with reflective questions (see Figure 3). Smartphones have expanded these opportunities for many settings. Another technique, have a peer sit with the student and ask him or her the following questions (these could be spoken for those who have difficulty with writing): 1) How would you describe your performance in rehearsal today (see Figure 3 below)? What are your goals for improving tomorrow? How do you plan to achieve these goals?

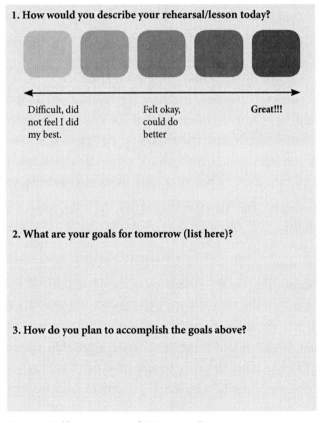

Figure 3: *Self-assessment and Motivation Discussion*

The above discussion should start the next day's lesson or rehearsal. This will remind students of their goals from the previous day. Often students with disabilities are given many things to focus on in music. This is a concrete set of goals for a student with special needs and will lead to measureable improvement.

Questions to Readers:

- Is there a pathway in your program for all students to participate in and learn music?
- How have you incorporated technology to assist with including students at various learning levels?
- Have you examined the opportunity and type of feedback that your students are receiving?
- Do your students seem self-motivated?

Principle 2: Multiple Means of Representation

Macro-Level. "Multiple Means of Representation" is the second of three guiding UDL principles. Nelson (2014) states, "The principle of representation introduces us to ways we can provide students access to ideas, concepts, and themes present within text-based information" (p. 63). Within music education, this could also include notational-based and aural-based information. Representation is seen in UDL circles at the "what" of what we are learning. Again, there are implications at the macro (building or district) and micro (classroom) level for music education.

Unfortunately, at the macro level, opportunities are not always represented in a way that is meaningful for all students. Many students come with a variety of contexts and worldviews. English may not be their first language and traditional music education may not be as familiar. Music educators may have a mixture of students at various socioeconomic levels or who are in poverty or have exceptionalities. This requires the music teacher to adapt to an ever-changing set of values and requisite experiences in the music classroom.

Again, music programs traditionally become driven by large ensembles at the secondary level. These large ensembles are primarily Euro-centric in instrumentation and repertoire and require requisite skills and knowledge that are not always available to students with diverse backgrounds and exceptionalities. This provides an insufficient context for understanding and progression in music education at the secondary level. This institutional foundation is unfortunately counter to the goals of UDL.

When setting the stage for "Multiple Means of Representation," Meyer et. al (2014) states, "Learners may also struggle due to lack of needed background knowledge or contextual understanding." For example, Fort Wayne, Indiana is home to a large population of Burmese families that were provided assistance by the United States State Department.[7] Many of these students arrived in Fort Wayne speaking their native language with no contextual or background understanding of traditional school music in the United States. However many of these students were interested in making music. Many of the Fort Wayne choral music programs used this opportunity to not only teach students choral music traditions, but also to aid with English skills, and provide a creative outlet for students to come to terms with their past life in refugee camps. This also allowed students to move faster in acclimating to their new home and socializing with their peers in their communities. Most important, this example provided students with contextual understanding of American life while also providing background knowledge of American music making and how it may relate to their own culture. The added benefit to the students from Indiana was their ability to learn about Burmese culture.

This example is unique and may or may not translate to many traditional music programs. However, establishing a set of requisite understandings and pathways to music making at all levels is imperative. Many students with disabilities have parallel experiences to the

---

[7]   Information on this population can be found at:
http://www.journalgazette.net/article/20110804/LOCAL/308049978

Burmese refugees. By the time they develop language skills, fine motor skills, classroom self-help skills, and social skills, it is too late for them to join our traditional secondary music ensembles (band, orchestra, and choir). They may be three, four, or five years behind their peers in all areas. Does this mean that students do not deserve a music education?

They key is providing pathways for all students to gain knowledge. This should include both small group and large group experiences, traditional and non-traditional literature, and contextual understanding. The most important aspect, at the macro-level, is to "activate or supply background knowledge" and "maximize transfer and generalization" (Meyer et. al, 2014. p. 99). In other words, there should be a process at all levels for students to participate and gain the same skills and knowledge either by remediation (traditional experiences) or providing alternative experiences for students (e.g., song-writing, small-group vernacular ensembles, secondary general music, etc). At the macro-level, traditional music programs should provide representation through multiple means, not just large-group traditional experiences.

Micro-level. In order to discuss this area of UDL at the micro-level, we must first examine some of the umbrella challenges of many students with learning differences. First, Theory of Mind affects many students, especially students with autism and students who do not speak English as their first language. Theory of Mind (ToM) is defined as "the awareness of how mental states such as memories, beliefs, desires, and how intentions govern the behavior of self and others" (Baron-Cohen, 2000, p. 3). Students with a variety of disabilities have difficult predicting the intentions of others based on body language, facial expression, and other non-verbal communication.

In discussing context or background knowledge in music, emotional and non-verbal context must be part of the conversation. Much of what we teach relies on the ability of a person to understand the nuances of emotional and non-verbal communication. For students with learning difficulties, music may be difficult for this reason. Imagine sitting in a traditional band, orchestra, or choir rehearsal. A traditional conductor often uses facial expressions, conducting gestures, analogies, and references all within a shared context. This shared experience is not the same experience for most students with disabilities. Many of them are still working on age-appropriate interests, language contexts, and socially appropriate interaction. These gestures and nuances need to be clearly defined with a combination of pictures and text. For example, taking photos of conducting gestures used along with text explaining what each gesture signifies would be helpful, especially for those students who come to the rehearsal with a variety of backgrounds (see Figure 3). These can be posted in a very visual place in the room. The key is to look into your planning through the eyes of *all* of your students. Figure 4 provides a framework for planning within the representation area of UDL through student-centered instruction.

Figure 4: *Visualization and Explanation of Conducting Gesture*

Options for Comprehension (Educator's Perspective)

- Activate or supply background knowledge
  - Provide avenues to gain requisite skills at all levels (do not leave children behind)

- Highlight patterns, critical features, big ideas, relationships/maximize generalization
  - Relate musical patterns and features to student experience

Options for Language and Symbol Systems in Music (Educator's Perspective)

- Always clarify vocabulary and symbol systems in music (Do not assume students have requisite knowledge)

- Illustrate using multiple media (e.g., screen as well as model)

Options for Perception in Music (Educator's Perspective)

- Offer ways to customize music
  - Reduce, change, adapt written music.
  - Aural-based approach
  - Read music on multiple forms of media (ipad).

- Offer a variety of aural and visual references (electronic or paper).

Options for Comprehension (Student Opportunity)

- Students supply information on their experiences (teacher then relates to subject matter).

- Students create concept maps based on their context and ideas (teacher guides based on subject matter).

Figure 5: *Multiple Means of Representation in the Music Classroom (for students with learning differences)*

Question to Readers:

- How can music educators clearly articulate background information such as vernacular, slang, non-verbal gestures, emotional content, and requisite skill sets?

Principle 3: Multiple Means of Action and Expression

Macro-level. The third fundamental guiding principle of UDL is "Multiple Means of Action and Expression." The foci of this principle are three fold: 1) "guide appropriate goal-setting"; 2) "support planning and strategy development"; and 3) "enhance capacity for monitoring progress all with the final goal of developing expertise in executive functions" (Meyer et. al, p. 102). Within music education this requires a break from traditionally held values and a movement toward student-centered options for "expression and communication including multiple media, multiple tools for construction and composition, and support for development of fluency through graduated support in practice and performance" (p. 103).

How does this look at the building or district macro-level? How are teachers being encouraged to set appropriate, individualized goals for students? Are students being allowed multiple ways to solve musical problems? For example, in a performance classroom, are students being permitted to contribute to musical decisions of the group? Are most of these decisions coming from the conductor? Of those students, are all students regardless of their talent or skill levels being allowed to contribute? When students set goals for a classroom or ensemble, are we guiding them to completion? These are all reflective questions at the programmatic level that should be addressed. Again, the fundamental idea here is that the curriculum must be flexible in order to assist students in solving. At the macro-level, there should be a shift to learner-centered goal setting rather than curriculum- or conductor-centered goals. These goals should be long-term and monitored with student input along the way. Figure 6 on the following page offers some ideas and guidelines for performance-based classrooms in regard to multiple means of action and expression:

1. **Guiding appropriate goal-setting (reflective questions from the conductor):**
   - Require the individual player/singer to provide a goal-setting essay for the semester or year detailing their individual goals for executive function (e.g., tuning, balance, tone quality).
   - Require written statements from the ensemble about overall group goals (musical) for the year. Provide opportunity for tracking of individual goals.

2. **Support planning and strategy development.**
   - Offer multiple opportunities to address group goals and plan for accomplishing these goals.
     - Make these discussions a part of regular rehearsal.
     - Ask reflective questions during process referring back to goals and recent progress.
     - Monitor individual progress through journaling, portfolios, or Wiki spaces.

3. **Enhance capacity for monitoring progress with the final goal of developing expertise in executive functions.**
   - Record individual or group at the beginning of a segment (e.g., semester) and then at the end.
     - Lead discussion of original goals for the group and whether or not these goals were met. Start process again for next segment.

Figure 6: *Multiple Means of Action and Expression in Music Performance*

It is important to point out that in Figure 6, there are many ways to adjust this process for students who have learning differences. For example, a peer could transcribe goals from a student. These goals could be very simple; for example under number 1, the goal could be as simple as learning a B-flat scale. A group goal could be to learn one of the three pieces on an adapted part. Providing multiple means of action and expression should be a building- or district-wide philosophy for learning.

Concerts or Public Performances (as a means of Action and Expression)

Concerts or public performances and programs in some instances can be seen as "informances" allowing for another means of "Action and

Expression" as opposed to the traditional concert. This works well for self-contained classes of students with special needs—beginning band and orchestra and other process-based demonstrations. Audience members can sit side-by-side with students and join into the music that is experienced in the classroom. The music educator walks through a "day in the life" of a student in music showing the process not the product. This allows parents, teachers, students, and administrators a shared look into the process of music education. A tertiary benefit of such events is the shared understanding of progress that can sometimes lead the way for advocacy for music education. The idea is that students are given another opportunity to express their understanding as opposed to the traditional concert or program.

Micro-level. Students come to our music classrooms with a variety of skills, experiences, and understandings. The challenge with this principle of UDL is the idea of setting learning goals, monitoring progress, and providing multiple ways to demonstrate understanding. Specifically, when music educators see in average more students than a typical teacher and for less time, this may require our profession to begin looking away from traditional methods of teaching during the time we see our students and focusing more time on when we don't.

For example, Thompson Junior High School in Oswego, Illinois (Dan Harrison, Director) has moved to a "flipped classroom" concept for beginning and intermediate band.[7] In order to accomplish this goal, he posts on his website a series of youtube videos with either he or model students demonstrate the executive function skills (e.g., fingerings, hand position) that are required for class. When class begins he is able to focus more time on individual learning goals of each student. If a student is unable to accomplish these learning goals within the time frame allowed, he offers alternative strategies for use during the next practice segment and also has an "ask the teacher" blog in place so students can contact him outside of class. Students can scan

---

[7]   Thompson Junior High School is located in Oswego, Illinois, Dan Harrison is Director of Bands. The website example URL is thompsontigerband.weebly.com

the blog to see if anyone has asked the question in mind and allows for a non-threatening environment for questions instead of in front of peers. This type of learning environment serves students with exceptionalities in a variety of ways. Videos can be played over and over for better understanding. Having peers demonstrate to peers via video can be very powerful and less threatening to a student who is challenged.

In all of the examples above the music educator is afforded more opportunities to "guide appropriate goal-setting", "support planning and strategy development", and "enhance capacity for monitoring progress all with the final goal of developing expertise in executive functions." The key is thinking of ways to reach the individual learner and also addressing group goals. This is all done to allow students to eventually self-regulate their own goals as a group and as individuals within a program that provides equal opportunity.

Questions for Readers:

- How are students in your program allowed to set their own goals for achievement?
- How do you share the monitoring of these goals? Do you provide constant feedback?
- In what format are these goals assessed?

Assessment

Assessment and evaluation has long been a subject of discussion in music education. Where UDL, students with learning difference, and music education meet is in providing many pathways for demonstrating understanding. In many music education settings there are only a few of these pathways (e.g., playing test, written test, worksheet, etc.). Recently, there has been much discussion regarding student portfolios as a means of summative assessment in music education (Hammel & Hourigan, 2011; Goolsby, 1995). However, within UDL, the added component for assessment thought is the idea of a "feedback loop."

Nelson (2014) states, "Most commonly viewed as a part of communication, a feedback loop confirms what information has been shared and that everyone involved has interpreted the information similarly" (p. 80). In other words, do the students (on an individual level), teachers, and sometimes parents see information similarly? How do we involve the rest of the learning community in regards to feedback?

This requires feedback to be often from both the teacher and the student perspectives. The teacher is assessing not only understanding of content, but also the quality of transfer of information and concepts to the student. In addition, can the student generalize the concept to another context? In other words, did the student play in tune? Can the student recognize when she is out of tune? Can she adjust her instrument or voice to be in tune at the next rehearsal? Is this a shared understanding (what it means to be in tune)?

One curricular component of UDL is to "provide options for expression and communication" using multiple media for communication (Meyer, et. al, p. 103). One option to provide positive feedback within an online space for students is using a Wiki (Burnard, p. 119, 2007). Wiki spaces are online portfolios that allow students or groups of students to add content in a web-based, multimedia format. Videos, music files, graphics, pictures, and links are all components that can be added to Wiki spaces. Again, this just provides one more tool for students to demonstrated their understanding of music. Many students with special needs find computer-based projects as less threatening than traditional projects. They feel as though they have more control and may be fascinated with the computer (and the web).

The next step would be to find concrete ways to monitor progress that is understandable to the student. The music student should also participate in "Using their background knowledge to identify and use patterns, critical features, big ideas, and relationships they recognize" to collaborate in assessing their work (Nelson, 2014, p. 82). With the Wiki and the portfolio mentioned above, this would require the student not only to create the work, but also create the evaluation at whatever level she understands. The instructor should collaborate in this feedback.

In all aspects of teaching music to students with exceptionalities, appropriate feedback to the student in an understandable format is often left out of the discussion; however, if a student does not feel as though he is making progress, he may not engage the music in the same way. These strategies can also provide information to music educators about the accommodations they are providing and any adjustments that need to be made. Like all students, students who have learning challenges want to know if there are succeeding. Therefore, it is imperative that we give them appropriate feedback on their progress.

Conclusion

The UDL framework examined above is an important consideration for music educators who are seeking to reach all students regardless of "talent," ability, disability, or background. With Universal Design for Learning, the student becomes the focus rather than the curriculum. Goals are set and students are taught to be internally motivated due to constant, honest, positive, and appropriate feedback. Most important, there are different pathways to gaining understanding and context in music education. It is hoped that through UDL we can begin to examine the experiences of all children and focus the pursuit of a broad understanding of personhood and context from all perspectives in designing music education curricula.

References

Baron-Cohen, S. (2000). Theory of mind and autism. In S. Baron-Cohen, H. Tager- Flusberg, & D. Cohen (Eds.), *Understanding other minds: Perspectives from developmental cognitive neuroscience* (2nd ed., pp. 3–20). Oxford, England: Oxford University Press.

Burnard, P. (2007). Reframing creativity and technology: Promoting pedagogic change in music education. *Journal of Music, Technology and Education 1*(1), 16, 37–55

Dewey, J. (1938/1997). *Experience and Education*. New York: Touchtone (originally copyrighted by Kappa Delta Pi).

Glass, D., Blair, K., and Ganley, P. (2012). *Universal design for learning and the arts Option*. In (T. Hall, A. Meyer, & D. Rose, Eds.), Universal design for learning in the classroom. New York: The Guilford Press.

Glass, D., Meyer, A., & Rose, D. H. (2013). Universal Design for Learning in the Arts. *Harvard Educational Review, 83I* (1), 98–119.

Goolsby, T. W. (1995). Portfolio assessment for better evaluation. *Music Educators Journal, 82*(3), 39–44.

Hammel, A. M., & Hourigan, R. M. (2013). *Teaching Music to Students with Autism*. New York: Oxford University Press.

Hammel, A. M., Hourigan, R. M. (2011). *Teaching music to students with special needs: A label-free approach*. New York: Oxford University Press.

Hammel, A. M. (2007). Professional development research in general education. *Journal of Music Teacher Education, 17*(1), 22–32.

Hourigan, R. H. (2014). *Intersections between school reform, the arts, and special education: The children left behind*. Arts Education Policy Review, 115 (2), 35–38.

Meyer, A., Rose, D. H., and Gordon, D. (2014). *Universal Design for Learning: Theory and Practice*. Wakefield, MA: CAST Professional Publishing. The National Association for Music Education (nafme.org).

Nelson, L. L. (2014). Design and deliver: Planning and teaching using universal design for learning. Baltimore, MD: Paul H. Brooks Publishing.

Walker, D. F., & Soltis, J. F. (2004). *Curriculum and Aims*. New York: Teachers College Press.

CHAPTER 6

21ST CENTURY SKILLS AND THE COMMON CORE

Johanna J. Siebert

Webster Central School District, Webster, NY

Movements in educational thought and practice have always been grounded in contemporary and political relevance. Whether devised to assist immigrant education in the early 1900s or to promote and develop tolerance in the late 20th century, such priorities had major influences on the cyclical design of general education, and certainly on the inclusion of music education within the school community. Current reform movements demonstrate no exception. In this chapter I will discuss two major and related educational themes, 21st Century Skills and the Common Core State Standards (CCSS) movement, and their effect on school music programs.

21st Century Skills

In 2005, Thomas Friedman's *The World is Flat: A Brief History of the 21st Century* alerted readers to increased globalization in the world marketplace. Likening the environment to a continually "leveled playing field" unbounded by geographical limitations, the author shared his concern that America was growing less competitive due to its ignorance of international themes, diminishing prowess in math and science fields, and lack of adaptability. Friedman argued for the accelerated updating of requisite knowledge, and his clarion call reinforced the growing need for "21st century skills" that would help America regain its position as a global leader. Multiple organizations emerged and expanded to build partnerships and develop resources that could define and provide for such skills that would help prepare students (and the workforce) for their future. Educators have come to understand these as essential skills that children will need to succeed as citizens and workers in the 21st century.

However, even before publication of *The World is Flat*, coalitions existed that united the business community, education leaders, and policymakers in designing resources to position graduates for 21st century global success. Among these groups, the Metiri Group and its EnGauge Framework, the Center for 21st Century Skills, North Central Regional Education Laboratory (NCREL), and the Partnership for 21st Century Skills, perhaps the most well-known is Partnership for 21st Century Skills, or P21 (2012). Currently P21's organization combines partner states and well-known organizations and companies (e.g., College Board, Council of Chief State School Officers, National Education Association, The Walt Disney Company, Lego Education, Ford Motor Company, Pearson Foundation, National Board for Professional Teaching Standards, and Public Broadcasting System). Strong interest among states prompted legislators John Rockefeller (West Virginia), Olympia Snowe (Maine), and John Kerry (Massachusetts) to propose the bipartisan 21st Century Skill Incentive Fund Act in 2009. This act was to provide matching funds to states pairing core courses with 21st century skills, and create additional partnerships among federal government, states, private businesses, and schools. While the bill did not progress beyond the Senate, P21 has continued to grow in size to include nineteen states and twenty-six organizations and businesses.

The Four Cs

Supported by the interdependence of appropriate learning environments, professional development, curriculum and instruction, and standards and assessments, P21 detailed seventeen individual skills within those designated areas of core subjects based upon 2002 No Child Left Behind mandates; life and career; learning and innovation; and information and technology (figure 1). Over time, these skills (as well as those named by other organizations) have been categorized under the more common "Four Cs"—critical thinking, collaboration, creativity, and communication. While collaboration, for example, has always been valued across centuries as a desirable trait in the workplace, the need for a collaborative and communicative *capacity* has grown in order to facilitate work that is accomplished by teams of people (as opposed to individuals doing isolated work in an industrial setting). Furthermore, such interactions often take place simultaneously across multiple settings, via varying mediums, and require interpretation skills in order to communicate effectively in "real time."

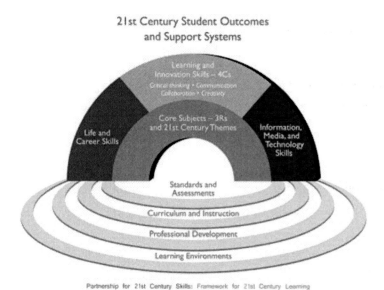

Figure 1. *Partnership for 21st Century Skills: Framework for 21st Century Learning, 2010.*

Education advocates of 21st century skills favor student-centered methods—such as project-based learning and problem-solving—that allow students to collaborate as they work on authentic tasks. While music classrooms and ensembles make regular use of these activities, traditional general education classrooms are often restrained in providing such opportunities due to time constraints, large class size, required assessments, and overall lack of student independence. Conspicuously absent in these skills and accompanying documents is mention of their application to the arts, even though their actualization in music classes is particularly evident to music teachers.

21st Century Skills for the Arts

To alleviate this absence of the arts, the Partnership for 21st Century Skills solicited and gained input from arts educators in 2009 for its "21st Century Skills Map for the Arts." Designed in collaboration with national arts education organizations and their members, this resource was published in 2012 to provide arts-based outcomes in line with P21's original skills. Multiple examples from dance, music, theater, and visual arts were detailed for grades four, eight, and twelve to align with areas of critical thinking, collaboration, creativity, and communication (among others). Among the many resulting outcomes of the P21 Arts map is a subsequent study by the College Board that compares P21 skills with the 1994 National Arts Education Standards (2013). This College Board study was used to inform the development of the new national voluntary arts standards.

It was within this setting that the field of education started identifying greater opportunities for more open-ended and performance-based learning activities and assessments to provide students with more authentic ways of achieving and demonstrating mastery of disciplinary and interdisciplinary knowledge. While all of these options were part of the push toward 21st century skill application, more needed to be done to ensure their implementation and set America's future work force on par with that of other industrialized nations.

Common Core State Standards Initiative

In 2008, the National Governors' Association (NGA), the Council of Chief State School Officers (CCSSO), and Achieve, Inc. convened an advisory group consisting of governors, state commissioners of education, business leaders, researchers, former federal officials, and state and local officials. Their task was to investigate what states would need to do to have educational standards that would rival those of top-performing countries. Led by former Arizona governor Janet Napolitano, the task force acted upon its concerns of current American teaching standards. They published the report "Benchmarking for Success: Ensuring U.S. Students Receive a World-Class Education," and called upon states to upgrade their learning standards by adopting a common core of internationally benchmarked standards in math and language arts for grades Kindergarten through twelve. It was believed that state-developed standards were at times weak and undemanding, and that they covered too many topics that were often repeated across various grades (ultimately leaving American students lagging years behind their counterparts in other countries, especially in science and mathematics). The wide variety of individual states' content standards was also problematic as they contributed to students' contradictory performances on international assessments, and it was felt that common outcomes would help to ensure consistency among the nation's teacher preparation programs in the training of teachers and implementation. In 2009 the task force launched an initiative to write Common Core State Standards (CCSS) in English Language Arts (ELA) and Mathematics.

While the effort was led by NGA, CCSSO, and Achieve, other national organizations were also asked for input. Both the American Federation of Teachers and the National Education Association—the two largest teacher unions in the country—contributed, as well as members of the International Reading Association and the National Council of Teachers of Mathematics. The CCSS were written by examining high-performing states' education standards (e.g., Massachusetts, Minnesota), international standards, and current research that detailed what students needed to know and be able to do to be successful in college and careers. Evidence cited was gleaned from the National Assessment of Educational Progress (NAEP) assessment data in English Language Arts, college surveys and student success rates, and findings from the Trends in International Mathematics and Science Study (TIMSS) and other international studies.

Various individuals have been credited with the creation and development of these standards. The mathematics standards team was headed by Jason Zimba (co-founder of Student Achievement Partners, or SAP, from Achieve the Core), and David Coleman (often cited as the "architect of the Common Core") began his work on the ELA standards as a writing team member in 2009, under the direction of Sue Pimentel (the other co-founder of Student Achievement Partners). During the standards-writing process, Coleman became a co-director at SAP. In 2012, he was named President and Chief Executive Officer of the College Board, thus ensuring greater promotional value for the philosophies and mission of the CCSS.

What ARE Common Core State Standards?

The Common Core State Standards spell out ELA, literacy, and mathematical skills that students should gain as they progress from kindergarten through high school. Its comprehensive website states its mission to:

> ... provide a consistent, clear understanding of what students are expected to learn, so teachers and parents know what they need to do to help them. The standards are designed to be robust and relevant to the real world, reflecting the knowledge and skills that our young people need for success in college and careers. With American students fully prepared for the future, our communities will be best positioned to compete successfully in the global economy (2014).

Adopted by forty-five states, the District of Columbia, and the Department of Defense, CCSS stress in-depth learning of subject matter over breadth of coverage. The standards are not a curriculum, with daily lessons and a scope and sequence guide; rather, they emphasize attention to "college and career readiness" for high school graduates. They are considered more rigorous than previous standards because they require more reasoning, student independence and self-knowledge, and multiple ways to demonstrate knowledge.

Unlike mathematics, the ELA standards cross multiple content areas. The ELA Standards comprise six "shifts" in practice: balancing informational and literary texts; knowledge in the disciplines; staircase of complexity; text-based answers; writing from sources; and academic vocabulary. (The shifts signify a change to stronger reliance on non-fiction texts to build deeper knowledge of subject matter.) Depending on state and local policies, teachers in non-mathematics core content areas may be expected to incorporate these standards into their discipline's content and to follow and teach the implied grade level competencies. However, the introduction to the ELA Standards states:

> Literacy standards for grade 6 and above are predicated on teachers of ELA, history/social studies, science, and technical subjects using their content area expertise to help students meet the particular challenges of reading, writing, speaking, listening, and language in their respective fields. It is important to note that the 6–12 literacy standards in history/social studies, science, and technical subjects are not meant to replace content standards in those areas but rather to supplement them (2014).

While the arts are not included in Common Core grade level standards, specific mention is made of using arts materials for teaching and learning. Interpreting visual and performing works of art is mentioned frequently in the ELA Standards as a means of using academic vocabulary to analyze and make comparisons, and some exemplar lessons are available. Another resource is the paper "Guiding Principles for the Arts, Grades K–12," authored by David Coleman (2012). In it are seven principles that define the arts' connections to linguistic literacy and knowledge, and promote intersections of study among the arts that strengthen and complement Common Core tenets. Most of these principles encourage the study of art works and their creators; the works' role in various social, political, cultural, and economic contexts; and associated careers in the arts. There is no mention of developing individual musicianship and/or musical behaviors. Behaviors that are described, however, are the "capacities of the literate individual" and include such attributes as demonstrating independence, valuing evidence, responding to varying needs of audience, having strong content knowledge, using technology strategically and capably, and understanding various perspectives and cultures.

College and Career Readiness Anchor Standards

Included in the ELA standards are the College and Career Readiness (CCR) Anchor Standards. The College and Career Readiness Standards address what students are expected to know and understand by the time they graduate from high school. These broader standards were developed first to improve literacy in all content areas through reading, writing, speaking, listening, and language; they were then incorporated into the K–12 standards in the final version of the Common Core. These literacy standards apply to all content in the lower grades (Kindergarten–grade five), and to core content and career and technical education (CTE – the arts, woodworking, and business courses, among others) in grades six through twelve. The CTE content areas have been termed "technical subjects," and their teachers are to be held accountable for the teaching of the CCR Standards.

Music Education and the College and Career Readiness Standards

In considering music as a technical subject and discipline with its own literacy component, music teachers have had success in aligning the artistic processes of creating, performing, responding, and connecting to the CCR Standards of writing, reading, speaking, listening, and language. A side-by-side comparison of the artistic processes to the CCR Standards provides obvious parallels between the two forms of literacy. Well-informed state education departments and school district administrators recognize the strong connections artistic literacy goals share with linguistic literacy, and encourage the development of these connections through attention to the content in arts disciplines.

Unfortunately, not all state and school officials are so informed. Because the CCSS continue to be "unpacked" and built into existing or revised curriculum, some districts are enforcing a "one size fits all" approach to implementation. Music teachers often relate how they are required to be formally observed teaching a reading or vocabulary lesson, and are expected to include written performance evaluations as a regular component of their ensemble rehearsals. Multiple teaching websites suggest CCSS resources to arts teachers that offer little connection to making music, but rather to the discussion, identification, and documentation of knowledge about music. These practices are problematic for music education, as they ignore the development of artistic literacy essential to college and career ready students.

The growing lack of bona fide music supervisors further compounds these concerns. It is uncommon to find a school district that can provide its music teachers with a knowledgeable music administrator. Too often the voice of the arts is absent from district conversations, interpretations, and shared decision-making, as well as at the state level within larger school-reform initiatives. Appropriate professional development for music faculty is also inconsistent. Without knowledgeable arts leadership a common district default is to implement a "one size fits all" approach to mandates. Such adherence to misguided interpretations and inappropriate alignment of the CCSS to arts content has led to growing dissatisfaction with the CCSS among arts educators.

Assessment of Student Learning in the Common Core

Part of the design for evaluating the national success of the CCSS is based on common measures, yet the implementation and support of these standards has been uneven at best, even within individual states. Teachers note that the lack of a curriculum, scope and sequence, and specific content and skills has created a difficult and challenging teaching and learning environment for the delivery of the new standards. Of great worry are the consequences of student test results based on common, state-driven assessment that does not consider uncommon implementation practices and instruction, as well as previous years of non-common core learning standards.

The use of common assessments for measuring the impact of uncommonly implemented standards has caused myriad concerns to arise in various states and districts, and from multiple stakeholders (Bidwell, 2013; 2014). Questions of reliability and validity arose when first year assessments (often non-piloted) were used in high stakes environments. The increased battery of tests frequently extended the actual assessment period by hours and days, and the adequate preparation of students for new assessment formats and knowledge required additional and multiple practice tests. It was not uncommon to see schools stop other classes and activities for such practice, as well as for the actual days of assessment. Schools and parents worried that students were being over-tested, and some families decided to "opt out" of the assessments and practices. Students' results caused comparisons of teachers' practice, as well as those of school districts. Some states tied funding formulas to the students' achievement rate, a cause for further concern for both schools and their communities.

In addition to these issues, teachers and principals began facing a new use for students' achievement results. Over 40 states had applied and received grant money from President Obama's Race to the Top Fund (RTTT), a $4.35 billion competitive grant funded through the American Recovery and Reinvestment Act of 2009. This grant was designed

> ... to encourage and reward states that are creating the conditions for education innovation and reform; achieving significant improvement in student outcomes, including making substantial gains in student achievement, closing achievement gaps, improving high school graduation rates, and ensuring student preparation for success in college and careers... (2009).

One important stipulation for the award (28 percent of the application's total points) was to provide evidence of a rated teacher evaluation system that included the use of common standards and assessments for measuring student achievement, and for that achievement rate to be used in computing the overall individual teacher evaluation score. Depending on the individual state's proposal to the US Department of Education and state legislative action, a teacher's composite evaluation score may be used for district staffing decisions and potentially for salary incentives and/or adjustments. In turn, teachers' and students' scores are used in determining principals' scores, with similar accountability. RTTT states could choose to use Common Core, Smarter-Balanced Assessment Consortium, Partnership for Assessment of Readiness for College and Careers (PARCC, 2014), or other state standards assessments (until the mandated use of CCSS assessments in school year 2014–2015). To date, forty-six states and the District of Columbia have submitted comprehensive reform plans in hopes of gaining this grant; nineteen states have already received funding, and thirty-four have amended their plans and are waiting on notification of their success.

While separate from the Common Core itself, the federally mandated accountability plan in many districts and states, requires that a percentage of the school-wide student results of ELA and mathematics common assessments be applied to *all* teachers as part of their evaluation, even if they didn't teach in those subjects. This has caused an uproar among music teachers (and in other elective areas), who were being a) evaluated against the results of students they didn't teach, and b) held accountable for content for which they were not responsible. Such districts argued that everyone should be held responsible for student literacy, that tested students had been taught in previous years by other district staff, and that the nature of interdisciplinary teaching espoused by the tenets of the CCSS was such that all educators could share in student outcomes; with this explanation the application of ELA and math assessment results to all faculty were judged to be appropriate. In this way, the high stakes assessments of CCSS came to impact all populations in many school communities in Common Core states.

Common Core Assessment Design

There has been variety in the creation of Common Core assessments. Some have opted to revise or design their own statewide assessments, while others plan to use standardized (purchased) assessments. At this time, national testing companies and state education departments are designing assessments for all grade levels of the CCSS. There is no doubt that the high stakes nature of the standards has been a boon to the testing industry. Pearson, Smarter Balanced, and PARCC are creating assessments that measure deeper learning, critical-thinking and problem-solving skills. Many designs require student use of computers in their administration—even more evidence of technology's connection to college and career readiness. (ICT—Information and Communication Technology—is yet another tenet of the standards movement.) The 2013–2014 school year found testing companies collaborating with districts and teachers to create, field test, and review the assessments before their widespread use in 2014–2015.

As of this writing, all states identified as PARCC or Smarter-Balanced have participated in piloting items from their respective tests. Kentucky was the first to fully implement and assess the CCSS in 2012, and—as expected in its first year of implementation—students experienced a significant drop in student proficiency in both ELA and Mathematics. Minnesota and New York students also scored significantly lower on their states' newly aligned ELA and mathematics assessments (2013); state education officials decreed it was more a reflection of students' lack of familiarity with the higher standards than of declining achievement. Despite these drops in test scores, it is predicted that student scores will consistently improve as teachers gain more experience with teaching the standards, state-designed learning modules that accompany the grade-by-grade standards are implemented, and students receive standards-based instruction in subsequent grade levels.

Growing Issues with Implementation

Feelings regarding the acceptance and future success of the CCSS are mixed. It is too soon to determine student success as relevant assessments have yet to be designed and administered. In general, educators in classrooms feel that the CCSS have been implemented all too quickly and in a top-down manner. Teachers are accustomed to developing lessons based upon teacher-written curriculum, with teacher-selected resources according to a well-planned timeline that includes familiar knowledge, skills, and assessments. With no choice or voice in adopting CCSS, many teachers have become frustrated in their attempts to plan for high quality instruction.

Politically, CCSS may be seen as an attack on states' constitutional rights of educational governance. Prior to the CCSS, states varied widely in the rigor of their own standards. According to our federal constitution, education is a state's right. This establishes a strong argument that such decisions should be made at the state or local level. Many also believe that the federal government was involved in the development of the standards, due to the Obama administration's support for the Common Core and the use of RTTT funds that persuaded almost every state to improve its standards. Partisan politics are adding to the tension in the implementation of the standards and accompanying assessments, as Republican positions continue to threaten derailment of the Democratic administration's support for reform.

To this point, multiple states have made alterations to their planned implementation of CCSS testing. Responding to popular opinion from teachers, administrators, and parents, New York State Education Department is still administering CCSS assessments (2014), but has delayed the impact of low students' scores in teacher evaluation scores until school year 2015–2016. State lawmakers in Georgia are working on Senate Bill 167 to stop Washington's interference in state curriculum and assessments, and other states are questioning the rights of the federal government to drive education. California most recently applied and received a one-year waiver from federal testing requirements while the state field tests its computer-based Smarter Balanced assessments. These early scenarios prompt the question of how to accomplish compliance with the RTTT requirements: in the absence of state test scores, what will states use to determine student achievement results to be used in teacher evaluation?

Effects of the Common Core Assessments on School Music Programs

These changes have had an overall negative effect on the status of music programs in many school districts. Numerous music resources—financial, staffing, scheduling, sequenced programs, access to students—have been reduced to support the expanding needs of the CCSS. Expectations for compliance in teaching literacy lessons have increased as well, and music teachers in schools and districts around the nation are frequently tasked to align their content with standards in ELA and mathematics. This is a remarkably challenging and difficult time for arts programs, especially in districts with low student achievement and inadequate arts advocacy.

Despite these tough times, there continues to be a high value for the role of the arts in developing and enhancing student skills in the Four Cs: collaboration, communication, creativity, and critical thinking. In 2012 the College Board surveyed district leaders on behalf of the National Coalition for Core Arts Standards (NCCAS) to identify the primary benefits of an arts-rich education. District and building leaders responded (n=980) and identified many elements of the CCSS that reference the same broad goals and behaviors of strong school arts programs. These values for the creative aspects of music and the arts are addressed in the philosophical foundations and lifelong goals of the new National Core Arts Standards, as well as through the interdependence of the four artistic and complementary processes of creating, performing, responding, and connecting.

While a deep commitment to the teaching and assessment of the CCSS has been demonstrated by most states' education departments, negative reactions from concerned stakeholders abound. It is still too early to predict if this educational reform model will in fact improve college and career readiness for America's students. These issues (and others) have caused much debate regarding the future of the reform effort. It behooves music educators, however, to have a working knowledge of CCSS; in this way teachers whose evaluations include any responsibility for the standards' implementation can choose to highlight positive areas of intersection through music instruction as well as recognize the Common Core's limitations regarding active music making. If music educators strive to produce *artistically literate* students using rigorous standards as a means to accomplish this, then they will truly prepare their students for the 21st Century.

References

Allie Bidwell. (2013). "Minnesota Reading Scores Plummet in Common Core Assessments." *USNews and World Report*, August 2. Retrieved from http://www.usnews.com/news/articles/2013/08/27/minnesota-reading-scores-plummet-in-common-core-assessments

Allie Bidwell (2014). "New York Voters Undecided on Common Core." *USNews and World Report*, February 26. Retrieved from http://www.usnews.com/news/articles/2014/02/26/new-york-voters-undecided-on-common-core

Charleroy, A., Gentry, C., Greco, A., Rubino, N., & Schatz, M. (2011). Arts education standards and 21st century skills: an analysis of the national standards for arts education (1994) as compared to the 21st century skills map for the arts. New York; The College Board.

Coleman, D. (2012). "Guiding Principles for the Arts." New York State Education Department. Retrieved from http://usny.nysed.gov/rttt/docs/guidingprinciples-arts.pdf.

College Board. (2012). Education Leaders and the Arts: A National Survey of Superintendents and Principals. Retrieved from http://media.collegeboard.com/digitalServices/pdf/advocacy/policycenter/education-leaders-arts-presentation.pdf

Common Core State Standards Initiative. (2014). English Language Arts Standards. Retrieved from http://www.corestandards.org/ELA-Literacy/

Friedman, T. L. (2005). *The world is flat: A brief history of the twenty-first century.* New York: Farrar, Straus, and Giroux.

Govtrack.us. (2009). S.1029 (111th): 21st Century Skills Incentive Fund Act. Retrieved from https://www.govtrack.us/congress/bills/111/s1029

International Benchmarking Advisory Group. (2008). "Benchmarking for Success: Ensuring U.S. Students Receive a World-class Education." Achieve. Retrieved from http://www.achieve.org/

National Coalition for Core Arts Standards. (2014). Retrieved from http://nccas.wikispaces.com/

New York State Education Department. (2014). "Regents Adjust Common Core Implementation." Retrieved from http://www.oms.nysed.gov/press/regents-adjust-common-core-implementation.html

Olsen, C. A. (2014). Music education and 21st century skills. Teaching Music, 21 (5), 24.

PARCC. (2014). Partnership for Assessment for Readiness for College and Careers. Retrieved from www.parcconline.org

Partnership for 21st Century Skills. (2012). 21st Century Skills Map for the Arts. P21.org. Retrieved from http://www.p21.org/storage/documents/P21_arts_map_final.pdf

Partnership for 21st Century Skills. (2010). P21 and the Council of Chief State School Officers Form Strategic Management Relationship. Retrieved from http://www.p21.org/news-events/press-releases/968-p21-and-the-council-of-chief-state-school-officers-form-strategic-management-relationship

Student Achievement Partners. (2014). Achieve the Core. Retrieved from http://achievethecore.org

The White House. (2009). "Race to the Top." Knowledge and Skills for the Jobs of the Future. Retrieved from http://www.whitehouse.gov/issues/education/k-12/race-to-the-top

Uijfusa, A. (2014). Common-Core Delay Approved by N.Y. Assembly, Challenging Gov. Cuomo. Ed Week. Retrieved from http://blogs.edweek.org/edweek/state_edwatch/2014/03/common-core_delay_approved_by_ny_assembly_challenging_gov_cuomo.html

U.S. Department of Education. (2014). No Child Left Behind; Elementary and Secondary Education Act. Retrieved from http://www2.ed.gov/nclb/landing.jhtml

PART THREE:
MUSICAL DEVELOPMENT

CHAPTER 7

MOVEMENT FOR MUSICAL DEVELOPMENT: CURRICULUM AND ASSESSMENT

Heather A. Russell
Cleveland State University

Jill Reese
The State University of New York at Fredonia

"Musical consciousness is the result of physical experience."
(Jacques-Dalcroze, 1921, p. 8)

Educators value movement as a way of knowing (Eisner, 1998; Gardner, 2011) and a mode for learning (Swassing, Barbe, & Milone, 1979; Wiggins, 2009). Movement and music are natural partners, and because of this, movement has long been an important component of music education methodologies and approaches in the United States (Ferguson, 2005). With their students' development in mind, music educators often use movement as a tool to make concrete the abstract concepts inherent in music (Haraksin-Probst, Hutson-Brandhagen, & Weikart, 2008; Jacques-Dalcroze, 1921; Wiggins, 2009). Though music teachers commonly use movement as a tool in general music classes, especially at the elementary level, students in performing ensembles benefit from movement instruction as well (Jordan, 1989). In the context of a comprehensive music curriculum, sequential movement instruction has the potential to affect all students' abilities to create musical sounds and to express musical meaning.

When creating successful music curriculum, teachers must consider developmentally appropriate practice. For example, they consider the range of songs when choosing appropriate literature in general music classes; and they consider key when choosing appropriate literature for beginning band students. These choices affect student success. So, too, must teachers consider developmentally appropriate movement practices and the ways in which movement affects students' successes or failures in the context of music activities. Similarly, teachers' knowledge of developmentally appropriate movement will affect what they plan, how they teach, and the ways they assess and interpret students' achievement. In this chapter, we will synthesize literature regarding movement development, describe a sequential approach to engage students in movement to develop beat competency and musical expression, and describe ways in which teachers can assess students' movement development and interpret the assessment data to inform future instructional choices.

Movement and Music Development

Movement is considered the first way in which children respond to music (Reynolds, 2005) and is a common medium through which young children demonstrate musical ability and expression (e.g., Moog, 1976). For elementary age students, movement and music are seamlessly intertwined (Gromko & Poorman, 1998). Movement instruction contributes positively to rhythmic development, singing and pitch development, improvisation, and listening and discrimination abilities. Though sequential movement instruction seems to contribute to the musical development of young students, it might be an especially useful tool for students with little to no formal music training (Sadek, 1987).

Teachers use various approaches to structure movement instruction and to enrich music experiences in general music settings. Common techniques include eurhythmics-based movement instruction, Laban-based movement instruction, and Curwen-Glover hand signs. In general, students benefit from learning environments in which teachers and students interact via modeling, describing, and suggesting movement, and these experiences become richer when extended beyond imitation through creativity and discussion (Weikart, 2000).

In addition to being a tool for scaffolding musical development, movement activities are also highly motivational. When teachers include movement during music instruction, students demonstrate increased on-task behaviors and more favorable attitudes toward music (Moore, 2002). For these reasons, authors of elementary music textbooks and other materials for music teachers often include movement as a vehicle for experiencing music concepts and for musical expression.

Though it is common for music teachers to include movement in elementary general music settings, the lack of literature regarding movement in secondary music settings may indicate a paucity of movement instruction in secondary music curricula (Ferguson, 2005). Some music teachers at the secondary level assume adequate movement instruction occurred at previous levels and that the students will not need further instruction. This assumption may be incorrect, and may run counter to the physical and developmental needs of adolescents.

Students at the secondary level require movement to scaffold their understanding and engage their interest (Saylers & McKee, 2002). A lack of movement during music classes may contribute to a lack of interest in the curriculum at the secondary level. "Part of the reason for the alienation of some older pupils is that the needs of the body are severed from the mind" (Philpott, 2001, p. 89). Despite the need for movement, some students will seem more self-conscious and less willing to move in the context of class. Often, their self-consciousness is compounded by a growing lack of coordination caused by rapid physical growth (Ruffin, 2009). Regardless of adolescents' more adult-like fine-motor skills ability to synchronize their bodies to music in spite of tempo fluctuation and syncopation (Reifinger, 2006), coordination cannot be taken for granted and can be a challenge. Even with these social and physical challenges, music teachers should include a variety of movement activities through which secondary students can experience musical concepts, express themselves musically, and demonstrate their understanding of music. Resources that support the use of movement in ensemble settings are increasingly available for secondary music teachers (Conway, Marshall, & Hartz, 2014; Dilworth, 2006; Feldman & Contzius, 2011; Weikart, Boardman, & Bryant, 2003). These resources emphasize using movement to enhance pitch accuracy, rhythmic development, literacy, and expression in the context of choral and instrumental rehearsals.

Suggestions for Sequencing Movement Instruction for Music Development

When movement instruction is developmentally appropriate and carefully sequenced from simpler to more complex, students can successfully focus on the music concept and use movement as a tool to demonstrate their understanding and skill. When movement instruction is not developmentally appropriate or not carefully sequenced, students' learning might be impeded, and their ability to demonstrate their understanding and skill deterred. When teachers are aware of how to successfully sequence movement instruction, they teach more clearly and efficiently, assess more accurately, and adapt instruction more successfully. In the following sections, we provide movement-development information, illustrative examples, and suggestions for sequencing movement instruction, assessing movement, and using assessment data to inform future instruction. The information and suggestions we offer are based on the work of Phyllis Weikart (2006) and Rudolph Laban (1974), and can be used by teachers regardless of teaching context (elementary or secondary; general, instrumental, or vocal), philosophy, or methodological approach. Table 1 contains definitions of terms we will use throughout the rest of the chapter.

Movement Core: Simpler to More Complex

At its most basic level, the Movement Core is the "what" of movement instruction. With the Movement Core, Weikart (2006) provides a summary of locomotor and nonlocomotor movement development

Movement Development Terms

- *Coordination* refers to general body coordination, and eye-hand and eye-foot coordination.
- *Movement awareness* refers to a metacognitive understanding of how, when, and where one's body is moving (or parts of one's body). It includes body awareness, language awareness, and space and time awareness.
  - *Body awareness* is knowing how each part of one's body can move.
  - *Language awareness* is being able to label and describe what and how one is moving (Weikart, 2006, pp. 36–37).
  - *Space and time awareness* is understanding one's body in relation to time (e.g., quickness, duration) and personal and general space (e.g., where and how one is moving).
- *Locomotor* movement requires a complete transfer of weight between one body part and another (e.g., from one foot to the other, as when walking). Locomotor movement can be done in place (i.e., stepping in place) or traveling about a space. Sometimes music teachers use the words "personal space" and "general space."
- *Nonlocomotor* movement requires that some body part is anchored, or remains touching a secure surface (e.g., when standing and one or both feet do not leave the floor, or when lying on one's back). No weight is transferred between body parts.
- *Integrated* movement is locomotor and nonlocomotor movement at the same time, or upper and lower body movement at the same time.
- *Individually Preferred Tempo* refers to the speed at which each person prefers to move steady beat. Moving steady beat in one's preferred tempo is easier than moving steady beat in a faster or slower tempo (Walters, 1983). The ability to move steady beat in one's preferred tempo precedes the ability to move steady beat in a tempo set by someone else (e.g., a teacher, recorded music), also known as steady beat competence.
- *Steady Beat Competence* is the ability to feel, express, and keep steady beat independently (Weikart, 2006, p. 35).

Table 1

from simpler to more complex for students of all ages. Other factors also contribute to movement complexity when combined with the basic ways to move outlined in the Movement Core. These factors include single and sequenced movements, movement in place (stationary) and movement through space (traveling), gross and fine motor movement, movement with a tactile endpoint and no tactile endpoint, movement with or without objects, and integrated locomotor and nonlocomotor movement. With the Movement Core and these other factors in mind, teachers can begin to accurately assess musical and movement abilities, diagnose barriers to achievement and understanding, and use that data to plan movement instruction that contributes to music development.

Reading the Movement Core figures. The locomotor and nonlocomotor figures (Figure 1) contain a set of three terms inside the circles (*alternating, one side...other side,* and *two-sides*) and two pairs of terms outside the circles (*single & sequence,* and *static & dynamic*). The terms at the top and left represent simpler movement; the terms at the bottom and right represent more complex movement. Notice the

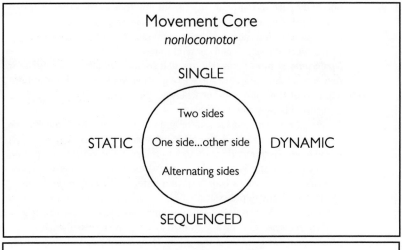

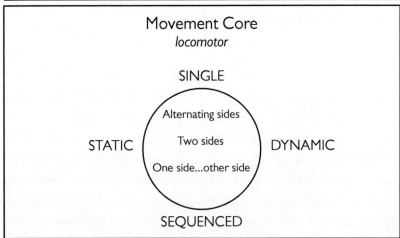

Figure 1: *Movement Core Figure*

terms inside each circle are in different orders. They are in different orders because locomotor and nonlocomotor have different sequences of simpler-to-more-complex movement. For example, when moving in locomotor ways, alternating sides is simplest, however, when moving in nonlocomotor ways, two-sides together is simplest. See Table 2 for descriptions of the movement demands of some common music class activities using Movement Core terms.

Movement Demands of Common Activities (Elementary through Secondary)

Percussion Instruments (Non-locomotor, moving with objects)
- Hand-Held percussion (e.g., triangle, tambourine, wood block, finger cymbals, hand drum, boomwhackers, rhythm sticks, shakers)
  - One side (shakers can be two-sides symmetrical if held with both hands or one in each hand), fine and gross motor
- Pitched percussion, (e.g., xylophone, metallophone, glockenspiel, tone bars)
  - Often two-sides symmetrical (simple bordun), sometimes alternating (broken or crossover bordun, or when playing rhythmic patterns)
- Free standing drums (e.g., conga, djembe, bongos, tubano)
  - Usually alternating (note: When drums are not on a stand but held between the legs, could be considered integrated movement)

Stringed Instruments (e.g., dulcimer, ukulele, guitar, zither, autoharp, fiddle, orchestral strings)
- Non-locomotor, moving with objects, two sides asymmetrical, fine motor (fingering, using noter, pushing buttons, holding a pick, fingerpicking) and gross motor (strumming)

Wind Instruments
- Non-locomotor, moving with objects, hands = two sides (may be symmetrical or asymmetrical), fine motor (fingering, embouchure), integrated

Keyboard/Piano
- Non-locomotor, moving with objects, two sides, gross motor (mostly symmetrical), fine motor, integrated (hands doing different movements and feet operating pedals)

Folk Dancing, Play Parties, Singing Games, Marching (marching band)
- Locomotor, mostly alternating, single or sequenced, integrated, complex use of space (all but finger plays), marking time while keeping toes on the ground is non-locomotor, gross and fine motor, some singing games may be non-locomotor (e.g., cups song), marching band and some singing games require moving with objects

Finger Plays
- Non-locomotor, can be two sides or alternating (often asymmetrical), and sequenced

Table 2

Single movements and sequenced movements. One movement repeated over and over again (single movement) is simpler than a pattern of two or more movements repeated (sequenced movement). For example, a single movement like walking (step-step-step-step) is simpler than a sequenced movement like step-kick-step-kick. A single movement like repeatedly tapping on the head is simpler than a sequenced movement like tapping back and forth between the head and shoulders (head-shoulders, head-shoulders, etc.). If teachers ask students to move in a sequence and the movements are inaccurate, they can have the students do a single movement instead.

Locomotor movement: Stationary and traveling. Locomotor movement (e.g., marching, hopping, jumping) is simpler in place (stationary) than moving from place to place (traveling). Traveling is more complex than stationary movement because it requires paying attention to objects (chairs, desks, instruments, etc.) and other people in the room to maneuver around them. If more than one student is traveling at once, each must coordinate his or her movements (direction, speed, length of stride) with everyone else to avoid collision. If teachers ask students to travel and the movement is inaccurate or the students seem distracted by running into or avoiding each other, they can instruct students to do the movement in place instead.

Gross motor and fine motor movement. Movement ability development follows human neurological development, which proceeds from the head to the feet (cephalocaudally), and from the central part of the body outward (proximodistally). Thus, gross-motor abilities are simpler and precede fine-motor abilities (Nucci, 2009). Playing musical instruments usually requires refined and coordinated fine motor movement (e.g., holding a mallet or bow, holding and playing small percussion, fingering notes on an instrument, forming the embouchure). If students experience difficulty with fine motor movements, they may not have had enough foundational experiences with gross motor movement. When a student is struggling with fine motor movement, teachers might consider representing the fine motor movement with gross motor movement to help the student experience more success with the fine motor movement. For example, students might struggle with the fingering pattern of *Hot Cross Buns* on the recorder (perhaps they mistakenly begin the third phrase on *mi*). The teacher can have students put down their recorders and move their arms up and down to show the melodic contour (perhaps tapping hands on shoulders for *mi*, waist for *re*, and knees for *do*), calling attention to the beginning of the third phrase. After students move the pattern correctly, they can return to playing the song on the recorder.

Tactile endpoint and no tactile endpoint. Movement with a tactile endpoint on the body (e.g., patting hands on the legs) is simpler than movement with a tactile endpoint on an object (e.g., tapping a hand drum). Movement with no tactile endpoint is the most complex (e.g., playing an imaginary xylophone in the air). A tactile endpoint on the body aids precision because it provides a target (the legs) and kinesthetic sensory information from two sources (the hands and the legs). A tactile endpoint on an object aids precision because it provides a concrete stopping point or target, but it provides kinesthetic sensory information from only one source (the hand). A movement that ends on an object also involves varying degrees of eye-hand coordination, depending on the size of the object (e.g., a hand drum versus a glockenspiel bar). A movement that has no tactile endpoint is more abstract and complex because it provides no concrete stopping point or target, and provides kinesthetic sensory information from only one source (the moving body part). If teachers ask students to do movement with a tactile endpoint on an object (e.g., using mallets on a xylophone) and the movement is inaccurate, they can have students play with the mallets on the legs. Then when students can play accurately on their legs, they can return to playing on the xylophone.

Moving without objects and moving with objects. Moving with an object is more complex than moving without an object because the object is an extension of the body. For example, we know how far our hand is away from our body because we can feel it. Adding an object extends the length of our reach, and requires a more refined eye-hand coordination and understanding of space. Objects include equipment such as scarves, bean bags, playground balls, and hula hoops, and musical instruments such as sticks, mallets, recorders, and trombones. If teachers ask students to move with an object and the movement is inaccurate, they can remove the object and have students move without it until they can move accurately, then return to moving with the object. For example, if students are performing a bordun inaccurately, the teacher can remove the mallets and have students practice playing the part using their fingers on the xylophone. When the students play accurately with fingers, they can return to using the mallets.

Integrated movement. Integrated movement is simultaneous locomotor and nonlocomotor movement, and it is more complex than locomotor movement alone or nonlocomotor movement alone. Examples of integrated movements are walking while clapping or playing an instrument, doing jumping jacks, jumping rope, and dancing. If students are not ready for integrated movement, their musical accuracy will suffer. If teachers ask students to perform integrated movement and the movements are inaccurate, they can have students practice each mode of moving (locomotor and nonlocomotor) separately. When students can accurately demonstrate each part of the movement separately, they can again combine the two parts.

Using the Movement Core. As shown in the descriptions of the Movement Core and other factors contributing to movement complexity, teachers can use the Movement Core to analyze the difficulty of various movement activities included in their lesson plans. For example, plain walking is simpler than walking with a kick between each step. Both types of walking are *locomotor* (transferring weight between feet), *alternating* (first one side one time, then the other side one time, back-and-forth), and *dynamic* (continuous). Plain walking, however, is a single movement, while walking with a kick between each step is a sequenced movement. One can see that single movements are simpler than *sequenced* movements because the word single is at the top of the locomotor Movement Core figure and the word sequence is at the bottom.

Analyzing movement in this way can help teachers understand how to increase or decrease complexity to support student success and engagement in movement activities or tasks. For example, if teachers ask students to perform a step-kick movement and the movements are inaccurate (i.e., off the beat, too slow or fast), they can change the movement to plain walking. Making the movement simpler supports students' musical development because they are more likely to successfully coordinate their movement to music. Likewise, if teachers ask students to walk to music (single) and the movements are consistently accurate (i.e., on the beat, in the correct tempo), they have the option to add more complexity to the movement, possibly by having students step-kick (sequence). Another factor in movement is moving steady beat or moving rhythm.

Steady Beat Competence and Moving Rhythm

Performing music with others (in general music classes and performing ensembles) is a common expectation in most music programs. To do so, students must be able to move rhythmically and maintain steady beat within a context of group timing. The ability to express accurate rhythms with the voice, body, or an instrument depends on a foundation of experiences moving steady beat and developing basic timing, or steady beat competence (Weikart, 2006). To plan instruction and assess student achievement, teachers need to understand how steady beat movement develops beat competence, which supports rhythmic movement.

Steady beat competence. Moving steady beat is the foundation of moving to music and moving to make music. Beat competence is proficiency expressing and keeping steady beat while moving, singing, or playing instruments (Weikart, 2006). It is the most basic level of achievement in moving to music. There are two stages in developing beat competence: moving steady beat at one's individually preferred tempo, and matching an external tempo—one set by recorded music or another person (Weikart, 2006).

Students of all ages who are beginners (inexperienced at moving) need to spend a lot of time moving steady beat in both locomotor and nonlocomotor ways. Many students begin school having already reached this milestone, but some will not have had enough experience to reach even this most basic level of musical achievement. All students in the earliest years of elementary school, and even upper elementary, middle school, and high school students who are inexperienced movers, will need many opportunities to move steady beat in their own tempo and matching an external tempo to develop and strengthen beat competence—the foundation for rhythmic movement.

Moving rhythm. Students with beat competence can transition to moving rhythm. An appropriate transition to moving rhythm begins with pairing chanted rhythm with steady beat movement. Teachers should chant simple rhythm patterns while moving steady beat; students imitate the teacher's steady beat movement and echo the chanted patterns. Teachers should then have students try out their own patterns while continuing to move steady beat (all students chanting and moving simultaneously). During these activities (echoing rhythm patterns and exploring their own patterns), teachers should call attention to how the long and short durations of the chanted rhythms fit in and around the steady beat.

After students have had opportunities to try chanting their own rhythm patterns while moving steady beat, they can begin moving the same rhythm patterns they are chanting. For example, students could chant a rhythm pattern while tapping the same rhythm with their hands on their laps (alternating hands) or step the rhythm with their feet (in place first, then traveling). When walking rhythms while traveling, it is important to keep walking forward during faster notes instead of shuffling so students can feel the quickness of shorter durations and keep the movement flowing through the pattern. Once students are successful chanting while moving, they could then play or finger the rhythms on an instrument.

Imprecise tempo or inaccurate rhythmic movement is sometimes a symptom of a lack of steady beat competence. Ensembles that struggle to stay together (by rushing or slowing the tempo, e.g.) likely have members who have not yet achieved steady beat competence. For example, some elementary students are capable of performing parts of an Orff arrangement on their own, but struggle to keep up or stay together with group members when the class plays as a whole. Some instrumentalists and vocalists are capable of performing passages from literature accurately, unless they are required to perform with an accompaniment or with others. These are all examples of how a lack of steady beat competency manifests itself as inaccurate rhythm or imprecise tempo during a performance task.

Expressive Movement

When students have experiences moving expressively to music, they are more likely to transfer that expression to the music they perform and create with their voices or instruments. Laban's movement theory (Laban & Lawrence, 1974) provides guidance for teachers and students exploring musical expression through movement (Jordan, 1989; Newlove & Dalby, 2004). Laban believed movement consists of an interaction of four *effort factors*: flow, weight, space, and time. Each effort factor exists on its own continuum that spans from one extreme of that element to another; these extremes are called *effort elements*. For example, the continuum for the effort factor, flow, spans from the effort element *free* to the effort element *bound*. Similarly, the weight continuum spans from *light* (or gentle) to *heavy* (or strong), the space continuum spans from indirect to direct, and the time continuum spans from *sudden* (or quick) to *sustained* (or slow).

Every movement of the body and every expressive musical gesture consists of a combination of all four effort factors. Gliding is a movement that combines sustained, light, and direct movement with bound flow (Newlove & Dalby, 2004) and could be a movement we associate with conducting or moving to *Skater's Waltz Op. 183* by Waldteufel. Imagine the quality of flow, weight, space, and time required to perform *Suite No. 2* from *O Fortuna* from *Carmina Burana* by Orff. Imagine the quality of flow, weight, space, and time required to perform Satie's *Trois*

Gymnopedie (No. 1) arranged by Debussy for orchestra. Both musical works require musicians to engage in and employ combinations of the effort elements. *O Fortuna* demands bound, strong, direct, and sudden movement; *Trois Gymnopedie (No. 1)* yearns for free, gentle, indirect, and sustained movement.

Though no effort element exists in complete isolation from any other effort element, students benefit from activities in which teachers focus the students' attention and movement on a single effort element. After students experience each side of a continuum separately, they are ready to combine the two. For example, during one class, teachers might have students explore bound movement by having them suggest ingredients that might be sticky and stir them in an imaginary pot. During the next class, the teacher might have students explore free movement by having them suggest ingredients that might be slippery, and stir them in an imaginary pot. Then, during the next class, the teacher might have students choose secret ingredients to add to an imaginary pot, demonstrate stirring, and have other students describe the movement and identify whether they thought the ingredients in the pot were sticky (bound) or slippery (free).

Students with less experience moving benefit from having concrete experiences with the effort element before we ask them to imagine moving using a particular effort element. While some students might accurately embody bound flow when asked to move as if they are swimming through molasses, others will struggle. For the students that struggle, concrete experiences will inform their imagination. Students could experience bound flow concretely by pressing palms against the teachers' hands and stirring the imaginary sticky ingredients as partners. See Table 3 for examples of concrete and imaginary experiences with the effort elements.

As we noted earlier in the chapter, some students may feel self-conscious about moving, especially moving expressively. One way to ease self-consciousness is to move with an object, which shifts the focus from the student's movement to the object's movement. Though moving with objects is, in a pure sense, more complex than moving

Effort Element	Concrete Experiences	Imagined Experiences (Appropriateness may depend on your students' age and life experiences.)	Repertoire Selection
Flow - Bound	Place your palms against your student's palms; both people press simultaneously to experience the resistence of bound flow.	Imagine you are stirring a bowl full of molasses.	O Fortuna - Orff
Flow - Free	Move with a scarf through space to feel free flow.	Imagine you are seaweed flowing in the current underwater.	Hedwig's Theme - Williams
Weight - Heavy/Strong	Lifting a medicine ball or push it on the ground away from your body	Imagine you are a giant walking across the countryside shaking the ground with each step.	Romeo and Juliet - Prokofiev
Weight - Light/ Gentle	Students carry a feather, or catch a bubble	Imagine you are walking across the surface of the moon, totally weightless.	Trois Gymnopedie (No. 1) - Satie
Space - Direct	Teacher uses string to create a straight line. Students walk that straight line.	Imagine you are walking in a parade, or walking a tightrope.	Washington Post March - Sousa
Space - Indirect	Teacher uses string to create a curvy pathway. Students follow the string.	Imagine you are a bee returning to the hive, but you must stop at each flower along the way.	Flight of the Bumblebee - Rimsky-Korsakov
Time - Sudden	Snap into a new statue shape each time the teacher plays a single note on the bass xylophone. Teacher varies the space between sound events providing some spaces with lengthy silences in which students are frozen.	Imagine you are a corn kernel (crouch down as small as possible) and burst suddenly into a fluffy piece of popcorn of varying shapes and sizes.	Waltz in D-flat, Op. 64, No. 1 (Minute Waltz) - Chopin
Time - Sustained	Students move fluidly in their space and do not stop moving while the teacher rolls on a single note on the bass xylophone. Each student freezes into a statue when the teacher stops rolling. Teacher varies the length of the rolled notes and the lengths of the silences providing varied lengths of sustained movement and frozen statues.	Imagine you are a snowman melting slowly in the sunshine.	Kinderszenen, Op. 15, No. 7 (Traumerei) - Schumann

Table 3: *Examples of Concrete and Imagined Experiences, and Repertoire for Effort Elements*

without an object, movement with an object for expressive movement can ease social anxiety for older students.

Similar to steady beat, effort elements are best introduced without related musical accompaniment before asking students to coordinate their movement with music. Once students have experienced moving an effort element without musical accompaniment, however, consider connecting the movement to a piece of music in which that movement element contributes to musical expression. See Table 3 for examples of repertoire selections for each effort element.

Though it is imperative for students to be exposed to and explore Laban's effort elements in the context of general music classes, students benefit from exploring the effort elements in the context of elementary and secondary performing ensembles as well. Teachers can provide expressive movement experiences with the effort elements as a part of warm-ups, or as a way of focusing energy during transitions between pieces, especially between pieces that vary in expressive quality. Prior to rehearsing *Siyahamba*, a choir director might have the ensemble move to a recording of the piece by dabbing the steady beat (direct, sudden, light, and free flow) to prepare the students for the buoyant style of performance required for the piece. Prior to rehearsing *Suite No. 2* from *Romeo and Juliet, Op. 64* by Prokofiev, an orchestra director might have the ensemble move to a recording of the piece by pushing the steady beat against the wall (direct, sustained, strong, and bound flow) to prepare the students for the pesante style of performance required for the piece. After asking their students to move expressively by focusing on the effort elements, teachers should help students connect the movement to the act of performing on their instruments or with their voice by asking them to reflect on what the musicians might have done to play their instruments with the certain effort element. Teachers might also consider assigning students the task of finding recordings of music they believe correspond to certain effort elements: one group of students brings in recordings of music that represents bound flow, another indirect space, and another sudden time. Then each group can exchange recordings and move expressively to each other's music. After experiencing the effort elements through movement, encourage the students to connect that movement with their performances. A band director might choose an excerpt from the current repertoire, assign small groups of students to different effort elements, and ask each to perform that excerpt using their assigned effort element. Students could then evaluate the performances based on the success of the small group to express their assigned effort element.

These Laban-based experiences help students manifest the effort elements through musical expression while performing. When students have the ability to control and manipulate the flow, weight, space, and time of their bodies, they are able to transfer that ability to their musical expression through their instruments.

Additional Considerations for Movement Instruction

Exploring movement. Students need time to explore move-ment, meaning a few seconds to a few minutes to experiment with a movement "idea" within parameters set by the teacher. Exploration before sharing ideas with the class or teacher activates students' prior knowledge and bolsters their confidence. One way teachers can have students explore is to give them time to work out movements (e.g., dance sequence, fingering pattern, mallet pattern) in their own timing (i.e., faster or slower than the teacher's tempo) before asking them to move at a certain tempo all together (group timing or with music). After having time to work out the movements in their own timing, students will be better able to do the movements in group timing.

Another way teachers can have students explore is to have them move to represent a music concept, which gives them a concrete expe-rience of the concept and prepares them to build on that experience to deepen their understanding. Before asking students to move their bodies to show the contour of a specific melody, for example, teachers could give students the opportunity to explore high and low move-ments and sounds. Teachers could do this by asking students to find ways to move their bodies at high and low levels, then add vocal sounds to match the movements, and then share their movements and sounds with each other and copy each other. After this exploration activity, the teacher could have students sing a familiar song and find ways to show the melodic contour with their bodies matching their voices. Exploring high and low movements in general and coordinating voices to match those high and low movements activates students' prior knowledge and prepares them to experience and understand the melodic contour of a specific song.

Modeling movement. One of the keys to successful exploration experiences is whether or not teachers model movements or ideas for students to copy before or during the exploration time. Though modeling is often thought to support student success, teachers should consider two factors before choosing to model: the experience level of students, and the objective or goal of the activity or lesson.

If students are inexperienced movers, teachers will need to build their movement "vocabulary," or repertoire, by modeling many ways to move and having students copy, label, and describe that movement. As students gain experience and expand their movement vocabulary, teachers should model less, and instead have students explore. During initial exploration time, teachers should describe and label the ways they see students moving to call students' attention to their own movements, build body awareness, and support their understanding of the concept they are exploring through movement. Teachers should also have students model movements for each other while the other students and the teacher copy them. Inexperienced movers of any age will need teachers to model movements for them to copy so they can build a vocabulary of movements and language to describe movement. If students are more experienced movers, teachers will need to model less because they will likely possess a large movement vocabulary and the language to describe it.

A second consideration when deciding whether to model movement for students is the objective or goal of the activity or lesson. When teachers model, students perceive the demonstrated movements as the "correct" way to move, and tend to limit themselves to those movements. Therefore, if there *is* only one correct way to move, or immediate correctness is the goal, teachers should model the movement for students to copy. However, if there are many possible correct ways to move, teachers should refrain from modeling. Any activity in which creativity, independence, or critical thinking is the goal should have many possible correct ways to move, and teachers should not model. For example, teachers should not model movements when students are exploring a music concept through movement (as described in the Time to explore movement section). Additionally, if teachers intend to assess or evaluate students' movements or understanding, they should refrain from modeling. Just as it is important to stop singing with children and to provide them opportunities to sing alone, it is important to stop moving with and for students and let them move alone. Refraining from modeling in this instance frees teachers to assess and record their assessments while students move.

Purposeful movement. To develop body awareness and metacognition, students must move purposely, that is, they must move with specific intent (a plan) and attend to the movement while moving. Students who move without purpose cannot replicate their movements and may seem to move in ways that are awkward, wild, or disconnected from the task or activity at hand. These students may lack body awareness or vocabulary (a repertoire of movements and labels for those movements). Teachers support purposeful movement by setting parameters for exploration (e.g., find ways to move to show high and low, choose "sticky" ingredients to stir in your imaginary pot), by asking students questions about their movement and how they are representing ideas through movement, and by labeling and describing students' movement.

Differentiating instruction. Teachers must consider, as always, the range of skill and experience among a group of students, whether in an elementary class, ensemble, or lesson group. If teachers demand that all the students in a class move in the same way at the same time, some students will be unsuccessful and some students will be unchallenged (both of which can cause disengagement and misbehavior). Teachers can differentiate instruction and meet the needs of all students at the same time by building students choice into lessons.

Teachers could build choice into lessons by offering two or three specific ways to participate (i.e., "correct" ways to move), either from the start of an activity or after seeing that individual students are struggling or seem ready for increased challenge. (Refer to the section on the Movement Core for ways to move from simpler to more complex.)

Another way teachers can offer choice is to have students "make a plan" for how to participate, sometimes giving examples of how students might leave out or add something. For example, if, while teaching a new song on the guitar, the teacher notices that some students are ready to perform all four chords using a challenging strum pattern, some students are struggling to accurately perform the strum pattern, and others are struggling to form the chords in time, the teacher can have students make a plan to participate at a level they can achieve. In this instance, students who can successfully form the chords in time, but struggle to perform the strum pattern, can play the chords using a simple downward strum on each beat. Students who are struggling to form all the chords in time can choose two of the four chords to perform with a downward strum on each beat, or they can choose one chord and perform that one chord in time using the challenging strum pattern.

Choice can also take the form of exploring within parameters set by the teacher: students who are more adept or experienced will be able to choose more difficult or complex movements, and students who are less adept or experienced will be able to choose easier or simpler movements. In this way, all students can participate and experience success at the same time. In any of the examples in this section, while students are making choices and participating in the activity at a level at which they can be successful, the teacher is free to observe and assess, noting the choices students are making and evaluating their achievement.

Assessing Movement and Using Data to Inform Instruction

Assessing, at the core, is observing and recording what is observed. Evaluating is making judgments about cause and achievement based on what is observed. A teacher may observe, for example, that students are playing incorrect notes on their instruments. They may also move awkwardly, use incorrect technique, or play mechanically (note-by-note rather than expressive phrasing). These observations make up the assessment of the students' playing. The teacher then makes evaluations based on what may be the cause of what he or she observed. In this example, the teacher might think students did not practice enough, that they do not know the piece well enough to play it, or that they do not recognize the musical phrases. When teachers know how the Movement Core and expressive movement influence musical performance, they can consider other possible causes of the incorrect playing, too: perhaps the movement required to play is beyond students' current capability, or that the combination of several factors was too complex.

Teachers then use their assessments and evaluation to plan the next steps of instruction. Traditionally, music teachers might break down the piece and have students work on component parts (e.g., practice individual phrases, chant the rhythm, play the rhythm on a single pitch, play the pitches out of rhythm, sing the tune while fingering the notes). Armed with understanding of the Movement Core and expressive movement, teachers could also have students move steady beat while chanting the rhythm, walk the rhythm (gross motor), move arms in an arc while singing the tune to show the phrasing, represent the fingering in gross motor movement (see the recorder example in the Gross and Fine Motor section of this chapter), represent the pitches with hand, arm, or whole body movement, or practice one of Laban's effort elements that matches the expressive qualities of the piece (see examples in the Expressive Movement section of this chapter).

Music teachers commonly assess student achievement in informal, formative ways, such as those described in this section. With the increasing emphasis in education on formal assessment, teachers must also consider ways to codify and record student assessment and evaluation. In the following section, we offer some ideas and tools for formal assessment.

Tools For Assessing Movement

Beat competence assessment. Phyllis Weikart (2006) has developed two assessments of beat competence that teachers can use with students of any age. In these assessments, teachers use recorded music and model movements that progress from simpler to more complex. As students copy the teacher's movements, the teacher watches to see at what level the movement becomes too complex for students (i.e., when students are unable to copy the movements accurately in tempo). The assessments can be administered to individual students or groups (though video-recording the group assessment would help the teacher assess accurately in the group setting). The assessments are described in detail in Weikart's book, *Teaching Movement and Dance* (2006, pp. 449–456). Teachers can use the results of the beat competence assessment to tailor instruction to individuals and groups.

Using the Movement Core for assessment. When assessing students' achievement in moving to music, teachers can use Movement Core terms, Laban effort elements, and other terms in this chapter. For example, an elementary general music teacher could keep a checklist of movement skills for each student that contains columns for moving steady beat in varied ways (see Table 4), or one for rhythmic movement. A band teacher could use a rating scale for marching using Movement Core terms (see Table 5). Since marching with an instrument is integrated movement, the checklist separates each movement skill into *with instrument* and *without instrument*; since it also includes traveling as a group, the checklist is also separated into *alone* and in *formation* (i.e., with the group). One more layer of complexity is included in the checklist of marching band movement skills: *facing judges*, which allows teachers to assess students' skills while they are facing straight ahead for the other columns. Teachers could use these checklists to record informal assessments (e.g., after each class period

Checklist of Steady Beat Movement Skills

Student Name	Locomotor							Non-Locomotor				
	In Place				One side...Other side		Two-sides	Two-sides		One side...Other side		Alternating
	Alternating		Traveling		Left Foot (Hop)	Right Foot (Hop)	(Jump)	Upper Body	Lower Body	Upper Body	Lower Body	Upper Body
	Single	Sequence	Single	Sequence								
Student 1												
Student 2												
Student 3												
Student 4												

Table 4

Checklist of Marching Band Movement Skills

Student Name	In Place (Locomotor)	Forward (Traveling)								Backward (Traveling)							
		(Locomotor)			(Integrated)					(Locomotor)			(Integrated)				
	Marching in Place (Stat.)	Alone	Facing Judges	In Formation	Alone	Facing Judges	In Formation	Forward at Angle	Macrobeat/Slow March	Alone	Facing Judges	In Formation	Alone	Facing Judges	In Formation	Backward at Angle	Macrobeat/Slow March
Student 1																	
Student 2																	
Student 3																	
Student 4																	

Table 5

or rehearsal) or as formal checkpoints at the beginning, middle, or end of a semester or school year.

Conclusion

Comprehensive music curricula include a wide variety of ways for students to experience music and express themselves musically. Movement is an important tool for scaffolding the music development of students in general music classes and performance ensembles, elementary through secondary and beyond. With the proper knowledge about developmentally appropriate sequencing and with tools to assess movement behaviors, teachers should be able to successfully plan, teach, and assess their students' music and movement abilities. By capitalizing on the partnership between movement and music, teachers skillfully weave in movement from elementary music classes through secondary music classes to create a curriculum that is engaging and enriching for all students.

References

Dilworth, R. (2006). *Choir builders: Fundamental vocal techniques for classroom and general use.* New York: Hal Leonard Corporation.

Eisner, E. W. (1998) *The kind of schools we need: Personal essays.* Portsmouth, NH: Heinemann.

Feldman, E., & Contzius, A. (2011). *Instrumental music education: Teaching with the musical and practical in harmony.* New York: Routledge.

Ferguson, L. (2005). The role of movement in elementary music education: A literature review. *Update: Applications of Research in Music Education, 23*(2), 23–33. doi:10.1177/87551233050230020104.

Gardner, H. (2011). *Frames of mind* (3rd ed.). New York: Basic Books.

Gromko, J. E., & Poorman, A. S. (1998). The effect of music training on preschoolers' spatial-temporal task performance. *Journal of Research in Music Education, 46*(2), 171–181. doi:10.2307/3345621

Haraksin-Probst, L., Hutson-Brandhagen, J., & Weikart, P. S. (2008). Making connections: *Movement, music, & literacy.* Ypsilanti, MI: High Scope.

Jaques-Dalcroze, E. (1921). *Rhythm, music and education.* (H. F. Rubinstein, Trans.). New York, NY: G. P. Putnam's Sons. (Original work published in 1920). Retrieved from https://play. google.com/books/reader?id=WhMWAAAAYAAJ&printsec=fr ontcover&output=reader&authuser=0&hl=en&pg=GBS.PP1

Jordan, J. M. (1989). Laban movement theory and how it can be used with music learning theory. In D. L. Walters & C. C. Taggart (Eds.), *Readings in music learning theory* (pp. 316–332). Chicago, IL: GIA Publications.

Laban, R., & Lawrence, F. C. (1974). *Effort: Economy of human movement* (2nd ed.). London: MacDonald & Evans.

Moog, H. (1976). The development of musical experience in children of pre-school age. *Psychology of Music, 4*(2), 38–45. doi:10.1177/030573567642005

Moore, R. S. (2002). Influence of mulitcultural singing games on primary school children's attentiveness and song preferences in music classes. *International Journal of Music Education, 39*, 31–39. doi:10.1177/025576140203900104

Newlove, J., & Dalby, J. (2004). *Laban for all.* New York: Routledge.

Nucci, L. (2009). *Nice is not enough: Facilitating moral development.* Upper Saddle River, NJ: Pearson.

Philpott, C. (2001). The body and musical literacy. In C. Philpott & C. Plummeridge (Eds.), *Issues in music teaching* (pp. 79–92), London: Routledge Falmer.

Reifinger, J. L. (2006). Skill development in rhythm perception and performance: A review of literature. *Update: Applications of Research in Music Education, 25*(1), 15–27. doi:10.1177/8755123 3060250010103

Reynolds, A. M. (2005). Guiding preparatory audiation: A moving experience. In M. Runfola & C. C. Taggart (Eds.), *The development and practical application of music learning theory* (pp. 87–113). Chicago, IL: GIA Publications.

Ruffin, N. (2009). *Adolescent growth and development* (Publication 350–850). Blacksburg, VA: Virginia Polytechnic Institute and State University, Virginia Cooperative Extension.

Sadek, A. A. M. (1987). Visualization of musical concepts. *Bulletin of the Council for Research in Music Education, 91,* 149–154.

Saylers, F., & McKee, C. (2009). *The young adolescent learner.* Retrieved from http://www.learner.org/workshops/middlewriting/images/pdf/W1ReadAdLearn.pdf

Swassing, R. H., Barbe, W. B., & Milone, M. N. (1979). *The Swassing-Barbe modality index: Zaner-Bloser modality kit.* Columbus, OH: Zaner-Bloser.

Weikart, P. S. (2000). *Round the circle: Key experiences in movement for young children.* Ypsilanti, MI: High Scope.

Weikart, P. S. (2006). *Teaching movement & dance: A sequential approach to rhythmic movement.* Ypsilanti, MI: High Scope.

Weikart, P. S., Boardman, B., & Bryant, E. (2003). *75 ensemble warm-ups: Activities for bands, choirs, and orchestras.* Ypsilanti, MI: High Scope.

Wiggins, J. (2009). *Teaching for musical understanding.* Oakland, MI: Center for Applied Research in Musical Understanding.

Chapter 8

Rhythm

Amy West
Johnson City Central School District, New York

When you think of a musician, or group of musicians, who have "good rhythm," what comes to mind? A soloist who skillfully performs complex rhythms in the context of steady time and can make deliberate changes to that time? Ensembles in which individual members perform their part with rhythmic accuracy, even while other members of the group are performing different rhythms? Someone who can create rhythms that make sense within a given context, as a jazz drummer might improvise a solo? All of these are skills that music educators can develop in their students through a sequential and skill-based rhythm curriculum. It is important to note that all of the musicians described above could be performing "good rhythm" with or without traditional music notation. To fully develop our students' rhythmic abilities, we must address rhythmic skills beyond interpreting notation and mastering theoretical knowledge of rhythms. A rhythm curriculum should include, and in fact begin with, experiences that help children develop an internal sense of steady beat, the ability to divide that beat into twos and threes, a feeling of the meters that result from the juxtaposition of the beat and its divisions, the ability to perform rhythms in various meters with their voices, bodies, and instruments, and the ability to create rhythms that make sense within a given musical context. If students first develop these skills, they can then bring more meaning to the study of rhythmic notation, as they will have thoroughly experienced and internalized the sounds that those symbols represent.

This chapter addresses ways in which teachers can structure a rhythm curriculum with these goals in mind. Broad, overarching principals are discussed first, followed by more specific descriptions of rhythmic skill sequences, as well as activities and assessments that could be used to teach those skills.

Overarching Principals

The approach outlined in this chapter is based upon several overarching principals. First are the notions that rhythm should be taught as a separate element of music and that a rhythm curriculum should include work in various meters. Teachers are also urged to consider the value of experiencing musical sounds before visually interpreting notation, working in a whole-part-whole format, and spiraling the curriculum with regard to musical content as well as musical skills. Finally, teachers are asked to explore the importance of individualizing instruction through knowledge of students' rhythm aptitudes, eliciting individual responses from students, and regular assessment of musical skills.

Rhythm and Meter

This chapter addresses the teaching of rhythm apart from the other elements of music, which allows children to focus their cognitive energy on one thing at a time. This chapter will continuously refer to three aspects of rhythm: beat, division of the beat, and meter. Beat refers to the pulse that you feel when listening to a piece of music. Division of the beat refers to the underlying division of beats into twos or threes. Meter is then defined through these divisions. For the purposes of this chapter, music in which the beats are of equal length and are divided in twos will be referred to as duple meter. Music in which the beats are of equal length and are divided in threes will be labeled as triple meter. Music can also have beats that are of unequal length, as is the case in 5/8 and 7/8. In these meters, the beats divide into both twos and threes. These will be referred to as unusual meters. This is quite an overly simplified explanation of meter and readers who are interested in a more thorough discussion of rhythm and meter are encouraged to explore the resources listed at the end of this chapter. The rhythm curriculum and skill sequences discussed in this chapter emphasize the value of working in a variety of meters. Not only does this more accurately represent the wide variety of music in the world, but also provides students the chance to learn what something is by understanding what it is not. Bluestine (2000) explains:

> Imagine a whole world in which everything were purple: purple sky, purple water, purple grass and trees, purple food, everything. Would we call anything purple? Would we even coin the word "purple?" No, we wouldn't need to. But imagine, in all that purple, you came across a single yellow flower. One yellow flower; that's all it would take. All of a sudden, yellow and purple have meaning. What is purple? Everything that isn't yellow. And now imagine a multicolored world in which our understanding of purple is dramatically more precise because we now have so much to compare it with. (p. 69)

We can lead our students to a deeper and more complete understanding of rhythm by exposing them to a variety of meters and asking them to master musical content in those meters.

Sound Before Sight

The rhythm skill sequences discussed in this chapter proceed in a manner that addresses musical sounds, processed aurally and orally, before musical notation, which is processed visually. As Bluestine (2000) points out, this is an old idea rooted in the work of Johann Heinrich Pestalozzi and, later, in the work of music educators such as Lowell Mason who:

> ...wrote music guidelines for Boston schools based on the following Pestalozzian ideas: 1. Teach sound before sign; 2. Lead the student to observe by hearing and imitating instead of explaining; 3. Teach but one thing at a time—rhythm,

melody, and expression—before the child is called to attend
to all of them at once; 4. Require mastery of one step before
progressing to the next; 5. Give principles and theory after
practice. (p. 35)

Asking students to first deal with and master musical sounds makes
sense because music is an aural art and, when students learn to think
in musical sound first, they can bring that understanding to later experiences with music notation.

Spiral Curriculum

Jerome Bruner's curriculum work included the idea of a spiral
curriculum; one in which students revisit the basic ideas repeatedly, building on them each time until they have mastered the full
concept. This chapter will discuss an approach to teaching rhythm
that spirals with regard to both musical content and musical skills. In
other words, students will repeatedly engage with the same musical
content, but at increasingly complex skill levels. They will also engage
in the same musical skills over and over again, but with increasingly
complex musical content each time. Organizing a rhythm curriculum
in this way helps teachers deliberately sequence activities to maximize
student learning. It also provides teachers a framework for discussing
curriculum with colleagues as they seek to describe and determine
what things should be learned at what time.

Whole-Part-Whole

This chapter will also make reference to whole-part-whole
sequencing. This refers to a teaching process in which students first
experience a whole, such as listening to a piece of music or learning
a tune by rote. Then, the teacher engages students in learning about
a part of that whole; rhythm patterns, for example. Finally, students
take that knowledge of the part and bring it back to the whole again.
After studying the part, they are able to perform the whole with greater
understanding.

Rhythm Aptitude and Individualized Instruction

Chapter 1 introduced Gordon's (2003) definition of music aptitude, "a measure of a student's potential to learn music" (p. 41), as well
as tests available for measuring music aptitude (Gordon, 1979, 1986,
1989). Each of these includes a rhythm aptitude test, which provides
teachers with a rhythm aptitude score for each child in their classroom.
Teachers can then use this information to tailor their instruction to
students' individual needs. It is important to note that this does not
mean limiting skills or content for students with lower aptitude. Rather,
as Bluestine (2000) explains, "...*all students, including those with low
aptitude, should learn the same musical skills and content* [italics orig-
inal]. No student should be deprived of anything" (p. 30). Applying
this to a rhythm curriculum means that all students should engage in
the same musical skills such as chanting, moving, creating, performing
on instruments, reading, and writing. It also means that all students
should work with the same musical content; for example duple, triple,
and unusual meters. However, the difficulty level within that content
can be matched to students' aptitude levels. For example, a student
with high rhythm aptitude might be asked to chant or play duple meter
rhythm patterns of greater complexity while a student with a lower
aptitude would be given simpler duple meter rhythm patterns. For
more information on the relative difficulty of various rhythm patterns,
readers are encouraged to consult the rhythm register books listed in
the resources section at the end of this chapter.

In order for individualized instruction to occur, teachers must
include regular opportunities for individual response in the music
classroom. Specific examples of this will be described later in the
section on formal learning. In addition, individual response provides
an opportunity to foster musical independence in our students. When
students must respond alone, they cannot imitate their peers. They
must master the skill and musical material themselves. Additionally,
individual response allows both the teacher and the student a precious
opportunity for assessment.

Informal Instruction

Chapter 14, Early Childhood Curriculum, addresses the importance of early music instruction and describes the kinds of activities that are the most beneficial for young children. This early instruction can be thought of as informal learning because students are not expected to give "correct" musical responses on cue. Rather, the focus is on providing a rich musical environment in which students can absorb and interact with a wide variety of musical content. Activities should provide children with opportunities to move their bodies in response to music and encourage them to engage in music babble, which is equivalent to the language babble children engage in before they start to speak recognizable words. With regard to rhythmic development, these early childhood experiences should expose children to music in many different meters and tempos. The tempo should remain steady throughout any given piece of music, however, as young children can have difficulty with gradual tempo changes. Children should be encouraged to move their bodies in many ways in response to the music, including the Laban effort factors of flow, weight, space and time, which were discussed in detail in Chapter 7, Movement. Learning to move in a continuous, fluid manner is an important aspect of rhythmic development because it helps students to feel the time and space which the music occupies. If students do not learn to feel the space in between each beat of the music, they may rush or drag instead of maintaining a steady tempo when performing music.

Informal learning experiences should also include opportunities for children to babble rhythmically by echoing short (two beat) rhythms. At this stage, a correct, in-time response is not expected as children are still learning to coordinate their responses with a feeling of steady pulse. Chapter 14 provides an in-depth discussion of early musical development as well as sample activities and lesson plans to use in informal learning. School music teachers should observe students in their classes in order to determine if they are ready to begin formal rhythm instruction or if they might benefit from informal instruction first. Once a teacher determines that the students are ready to move on to formal instruction, they can begin to work on the skill sequences described in the next section.

Formal Instruction

In formal instruction, accurate musical responses are desired and students develop their rhythmic skills in a sequential manner. The following approach to teaching rhythm is a skill-based curriculum which, as was discussed in Chapter 1, focuses on skills such as moving, chanting, playing instruments, and creating through improvising and composing. The ability to aurally recognize musical concepts such as a steady beat, divisions of the beat, and the resulting meter are also emphasized. These skill sequences are aimed at developing students' inner sense of rhythm and meter, which they can later apply to their study of traditional music notation. Music reading skills will not be discussed in this chapter as they are addressed at length in Chapter 12, Music Literacy.

When developing a curriculum for formal rhythm learning, it may be helpful to consider two related skill sequences. One sequence deals with developing students' sense of steady pulse, sometimes referred to as beat competency, while the other focuses on learning and interacting with rhythm patterns of ever-increasing complexity.

Beat Competency Skill Sequence

As was discussed in Chapter 7, beat competency is proficiency expressing and keeping a steady beat while moving, singing, or playing instruments (Weikart, 2006). A helpful first step in developing this skill is to have students listen to music, in various meters and tempos, and move their bodies in a continuous, fluid manner, as was discussed in the previous section on informal instruction. Once students are able to do this, they can then be asked to superimpose the steady beat of the music onto that flow. For example, students might flick their hands to the steady beat as they move the rest of their arms and body in a flowing manner. This movement will help them to feel the space between the beats and develop a kinesthetic understanding of steady beats. Since the flicking motion is silent, students must feel the beat internally. They cannot simply imitate their classmates a split-second after they hear them perform the beat. Of course, they can watch their classmates' movements and imitate that a split-second later, so it is sometimes helpful to have students do this with their eyes closed. Activities such as this provide teachers an opportunity to individually assess their students, even while the whole class is engaged and participating in the activity. A teacher could use the following rating scale to track which of their students have mastered this skill:

1. Student is learning to move with flow.
2. Student moves with flow and attempts to superimpose beat movement.
3. Student moves with flow and superimposes steady beats for some of the song.
4. Student moves with flow and superimposes steady beats for all of the song.

Students need many opportunities to move to the steady beat and teachers should plan activities that incorporate a variety of movements. Chapter 7, Movement, provides extensive information about factors that make movements simpler or more challenging. Teachers should be aware of these factors and take them into account when planning steady beat movement activities and assessments. For example, bilateral movements, in which the two sides of the body are moving at the same time, are easier than movements in which the two sides of the body alternate. Also, movements with a tactile endpoint on the body are easier than movements with a tactile endpoint on an object, such as an instrument. When teachers are aware of the difficulty of the movement task, they can make intentional choices about the difficulty level of steady beat assessments. An example of assessing steady beat with a simpler movement would be to have students listen to a song and pat the beat on their lap with both hands at the same time.

If students do this with only their fingertips instead of their whole hand, the activity would be quiet, which would allow the teacher an opportunity to assess beat competency using the following rating scale (Taggart, 2001, p.221):

1. The student is unable to maintain a steady beat.
2. The student maintains a steady beat that does not correspond with the beat of the music.
3. The student maintains a steady beat for some but not all of the song.
4. The student maintains a steady beat for most but not all of the song.
5. The student maintains a steady beat for the whole song.

Sometimes a student will play the steady *division* of the beat for the whole song. If this happens, the teacher could circle level 1. Or, she could circle level 5 but make a note that the student played divisions of the beat instead of the steady beat. This provides important information about the student and indicates that, perhaps, he perceived the beats of the song differently than the teacher or that maybe he does not understand the difference between the steady beat and divisions of that beat. Further assessments would help to clarify this issue. Once students are able to demonstrate the steady beat with a simple movement, teachers can increase the difficulty of the movement by asking students to perform the steady beat on an instrument, for example. Or, students could pat the beat on their knees in an alternating motion. The above rating scale can still be used as an assessment tool, even as the difficulty of the movement increases. Table 4 in Chapter 7 provides a sample document for teachers to track multiple steady beat assessments, utilizing different movements, over time.

It is recommended that teachers engage students in beat movements that go beyond patting their laps. One reason for this is because movements that involve the weight of the whole body can help students to feel the weight of and space between the beats. For example, asking students to bounce their heels to the beat or swaying side-to-side while standing are two beat movements that involve the weight of the entire body. Teachers can further expand these activities by asking students to keep the beat with various body parts (e.g., head, shoulders, hips) and by having students perform locomotor beat movements such as walking, marching, and hopping. Again, Chapter 7 addresses the relative difficulty of these types of movements.

Teachers may also have students perform movements together. This can provide support for students who have lower rhythm aptitudes or who are struggling for another reason. For example, teachers may pair a strong student with a weaker one and ask them to tap the beat on each other's knees. In this way, the weaker student can learn by comparing their movement to that of the stronger student. Or, the two students could stand with their hands on each other's shoulders and sway to the beat. When teachers have aptitude data and current assessments for all of their students, they are able to make deliberate pairings that will allow these peer teaching moments to occur.

In addition to moving to the steady beat of the music, students should also learn to move their body to the divisions of that beat. Once students are comfortable moving to both beats and beat divisions, they can be asked to switch between them. For example, the teacher could sing a song for the students and ask them to begin by moving to the beat. When the teacher sings "switch" at some point during the song, the students switch their movement to divisions of the beat.

It is important to note that all of the beat competency activities described thus far should be done in both duple and triple meters. Therefore, when students are comfortable with both beats and divisions of the beats, they can begin to juxtapose them together and discover the meter that is created by doing so. For example, half the class could move to or chant—with or without rhythm syllables—the beats while the other half of the class moves to or chants the divisions of the beats. Students should also learn to combine these two beats together in their bodies. For example, they could bounce their heels to the beat and tap their fingertips to the divisions of the beat. In these ways, students can begin to experience and internalize the meter of the music. They can then learn to label duple and triple meter and identify the meter of a piece of music based on the beat divisions they hear and feel.

Table 1 summarizes the skills discussed in this section and provides teachers a way to track their students' progress in terms of both musical skill and content. This chart also shows how the curriculum can be spiraled according to both skill and content. For example, at a given point in the school year, a class may have reached the point of moving to simultaneous beats and beat divisions in duple meter, moving with flow and superimposed beats in triple meter, and moving with flow

Skills	Content		
	Duple Meter	Triple Meter	Unusual Meters
Move with flow			
Move with flow and superimpose beats			
Move to the beat ___bilateral ___alternating			
Move to the beat ___stationary ___locomotor			
Perform the beat on instruments			
Move to divisions of the beat ___stationary ___locomotor			
Perform divisions of the beat on instruments			
Simultaneously perform the beat and divisions of the beat			
Label meter			
Identify meter			

Table 1: *Steady Pulse/Beat Competency Skill Sequence*

only to a song in unusual meter. This chart also helps to define the readiness activities which students may need in order to perform more advanced skills or content. For example, if a teacher wants his ensemble to perform a piece in 5/8, he may benefit from first engaging students in some of the beat competency skills on this chart.

Rhythm Pattern Skill Sequence

Along with developing students' beat competency and sense of meter, it is recommended that a rhythm curriculum include instruction on rhythm patterns. Rhythm patterns are short rhythms; perhaps the length of four underlying beats. Figure 1 provides two examples of rhythm patterns, one in duple meter and one in triple meter.

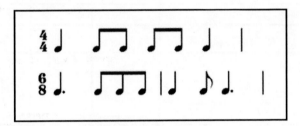

Figure 1: *Rhythm Patterns*

Rhythm pattern instruction should include work in duple, triple, and unusual meters. Additionally, teachers should be aware of the opportunity to individualize instruction by aligning the complexity of the rhythm patterns with students' rhythm aptitude levels. Students with higher aptitude should be given more challenging patterns. Students with lower aptitudes can be given simpler patterns to work with. However, this is not to say that students with low aptitude should never be given more challenging patterns.

When students begin formal rhythm instruction, they first echo rhythm patterns on a neutral syllable such as bah. This should be done by the whole class as a group as well as by individual students. Again, individual response requires students to internalize and master the material for themselves and provides teachers an opportunity for assessment. At this skill level, teachers should record whether or not the student performed the rhythm pattern correctly and in steady time. If students are hesitant to perform individually in front of the class, the use of a toy or prop may help them feel more comfortable. For example, the teacher might perform a chant or song about snowmen and, in between repetitions of the chant, pass a stuffed snowman to individual students and ask them to echo a rhythm pattern. Establishing the practice of individual response early on will help students to understand that it is an expected part of the classroom culture.

After students are successful at performing rhythm patterns on a neutral syllable, they should then perform, as a group and individually, the same rhythm patterns with rhythm syllables. Introduced in this way, students are simply adding labels (rhythm syllables) to sounds that they have already performed and internalized. Echoing rhythm patterns with syllables does not happen in the same class period as the echoing on neutral syllable. Rather, it would occur in a later class period as the curriculum spirals. A detailed discussion of two rhythm syllable systems appears at the end of this chapter.

In the two skills described above, the teacher performs musical material and the student gives the same material back. This kind of rote learning is important for building students' rhythm vocabularies. To help students become independent musicians, though, we must engage students in skills beyond rote learning. We must ask them to draw on what they have learned and use their rhythm vocabularies in creative thinking and musical problem solving. For example, the teacher could chant a rhythm pattern on a neutral syllable and ask the student to chant the rhythm pattern back using the correct rhythm syllables. This requires the students to master which syllable goes with which musical sound and represents a deeper level of understanding than simply echoing the teacher's rhythm pattern. Again, this can be done as a group and individually with a prop, toy, or game to help elicit responses from students. For example, students could pass a glow-in-the-dark ball from one to another while performing a song or chant. The student holding the ball when the music stops would be the individual to chant the rhythm pattern back using syllables. Teachers can assess students' individual responses based on whether or not they chant the same rhythm back with correct or incorrect syllables. This type of assessment does take time so, to avoid boredom and behavior problems, it is recommended assessing only part of the class on any given day. Teachers may have to devote a few minutes of several class periods to such activities in order to assess each student. It is, however, time well spent because of the information it provides about the students, their learning, and where to go next.

Another way to move beyond echoing and rote learning is to have students create their own rhythm patterns. Again, this requires students to be independent musicians and utilize the rhythm vocabulary they developed through rote learning. The teacher might first begin by asking students to listen to two rhythm patterns and indicate whether they think the patterns were the same or different. Students can use hand signs to silently indicate their choice. Both hands open could indicate the same, while different could be one hand open and one hand closed in a fist. After this, the teacher could ask students to create rhythm patterns that are different from the ones she chants. This can be done on a neutral syllable or with rhythm syllables, depending on where students are in their skill development. Teachers can place parameters on students' responses such as the kinds of notes they can use (e.g., use beats and divisions of the beat only) or the length of their response (e.g., your rhythm must be four beats long). Or, teachers can let their students answer freely. Asking students to create their own music provides teachers important insights into what students have truly learned and internalized.

Table 2 summarizes the skills discussed in this section and, as before, illustrates that each skill should be performed with musical content from duple, triple, and unusual meters. Due to the spiral nature of the curriculum, teachers would guide their students through these skills multiple times, using different sets of rhythm patterns each time. This is why each meter column has been divided into further columns by the dashed lines. For example, a teacher

Skills	Content		
	Duple Meter	Triple Meter	Unusual Meters
Echo rhythm patterns on neutral syllable ____Group ____Individual			
Echo rhythm patterns with rhythm syllables ____Group ____Individual			
Listen to a rhythm pattern performed on a neutral syllable and chant it with correct rhythm syllables			
Identify whether two rhythm patterns are the same or different			
Create rhythm patterns (without or with rhythm syllables)			

Table 2: *Steady Pulse/Beat Competency Skill Sequence*

may begin by introducing duple rhythm patterns comprised of beats and divisions of the beat (e.g., quarter notes and eighth notes). Once students have mastered some of the skills with that set of patterns, the teacher might introduce duple meter rhythm patterns that are more complicated. For example, they might include further subdivisions of the beat (e.g., sixteenth notes) or rests. Later patterns might include elongations—notes with durations longer than one beat—or syncopations. Each time a new set of patterns is introduced, the teacher would begin at the beginning of this skill sequence, echoing on a neutral syllable. In this way, the curriculum spirals around through skills and content of increasing complexity. Readers who are interested in more information about a possible sequence of patterns to use are encouraged to consult the materials listed in the resource section at the end of this chapter.

Back to the Whole: Music Making

The beat competency and rhythm pattern skill sequences discussed above represent two of the "parts" of a whole-part-whole curriculum. The first "whole" is the experience of a new piece of music. Then, instruction focuses on one of the "parts" using the sequences above. Finally, students return to the "whole" again, performing the music with greater understanding. Teachers can think of the "wholes" as the making of real music in the classroom. This is again skill-based and includes skills such as, but not limited to: performing beats and/or beat divisions on an instrument to accompany a song; performing a rhythmic ostinato, with voice, body percussion, or instrument, to accompany a song; performing multiple rhythm ostinati simultaneously; aurally identifying where certain rhythm patterns occur within a song; performing rhythm patterns found in a song; aurally identifying the meter of a song; and creating rhythm patterns that could be used as introductions, ostinati, or codas for a song. Though the repertoire and instruments may change, these same skills could be part of music classrooms K–12.

Curriculum Alignment

The skill and content sequences above represent just one of many ways to organize a rhythm curriculum, yet they highlight some important ideas that teachers should consider when creating a rhythm curriculum. One such idea is the concept of readiness for each next level of learning. As Bluestine (2000) states, "*Before* is a crucial word in curriculum planning!" (p. 7). Another consideration is that assessment should be an integral and planned part of the curriculum so that the curriculum proceeds in a sequential manner where students master one skill or set of content before moving on to another, more challenging one. A curriculum that includes specific skills and assessments is likely to be more helpful to teachers than a document that simply lists rhythm values by grade level. For example, in some school curricula the rhythm column simply states Kindergarten: quarter note, pair of eighth notes; 1st grade: quarter note, pair of eighth notes, quarter rest;

2nd grade: quarter note, pair of eighth notes, quarter rest, half note; and so on. What does this actually mean, though? What musical skills are students demonstrating and mastering in relation to these notes values? Teachers are encouraged to develop curriculum documents that include specific skill development goals as well as content goals.

In doing so, teachers can address some of the challenges that are often encountered in music teaching. As was discussed in Chapter 1, one such challenge is that students in the same class are not necessarily all at the same level of learning. For example, students may go from two different elementary programs into one middle school program. Or, students may be in a music class that includes multiple grade levels. In these situations, it is important to remember that "musical age," the skill and content levels which students have achieved, is more important than chronological age.

Another related challenge is that music teachers often work with the same students for multiple years (e.g., grades K–5 or 9–12). Again it is important to focus on students' musical ages. As teachers begin to implement a sequential curriculum with the same group of students over several years, they may find the need to continually revise the curriculum and move skills and/or content between grade levels. For example, if an elementary music teacher implemented the skill sequences discussed earlier in this chapter, students in most grade levels would probably need to start with the simplest skills and content, depending on their previous music experiences. However, after a year or two, that teacher may find that their second graders are ready for more advanced skills and content than were second graders in previous years. This is because their musical age will have increased due to the sequential instruction they received in Kindergarten and 1st grade.

Another challenge music teachers face is vertical alignment within their departments and what happens to students when they go from one music teacher to another. A spiral rhythm curriculum that focuses on both skill and content offers an opportunity for music departments to be consistent in what they are teaching across classes and grade levels. Additionally, it provides a common framework or vocabulary for students as they travel between or among teachers. It also provides teachers a common vocabulary in order to discuss how far a certain group of students has advanced. One area that music departments should be sure to discuss is the use of a rhythm syllable system. As was mentioned in Chapter 1, lack of consistency in this area can inhibit the transfer of learning for students between years of instruction whereas consistency can enhance transfer and deepen learning.

Rhythm Syllable Systems

A rhythm syllable system is to rhythms what "do, re, and mi" are to pitches. Syllable systems provide a tool for labeling sounds so that they can be conceptually understood and discussed. Rhythm syllable systems can also aid students in remembering rhythms. As Taggart (1989) points out:

> Without providing labels for rhythm patterns by associating them with rhythm syllables, most students would be able to retain only a small number of patterns in their audiation. In the same way that words serve as labels that help one to classify and remember things in the environment, rhythm syllables serve as labels that help one to classify and remember rhythm patterns in his audiation. (p. 55)

Additionally, a rhythm syllable system can help students learn to read and write music notation. "They are designed to help students learn, remember, and quickly identify recurrent patterns, and they provide a link—a translator—between aural and visual domains" (Hoffman, Pelto, & White, 1996, p. 8).

The skill sequences outlined in this chapter are based upon a "sound before sight" philosophy. Therefore, the skill sequences are most likely to be successful when used in conjunction with a rhythm syllable system based on beat function. A system based on beat function applies syllables to rhythms based on how they sound and function in the context of meter (i.e., what we hear and feel) as opposed to how they are notated (i.e., what we see). Such a system allows students to associate labels (rhythm syllables) with given sounds without yet having to understand how those sounds could be notated. Two such syllable systems are the Froseth/Gordon system (Gordon, 2003) and the Takadimi system (Hoffman, Pelto, & White, 1996). Table 3 summarizes the basic syllables used in each of these systems.

Froseth/Gordon System			
	Duple Meter	**Triple Meter**	**Unusual Meter**
Beat	Du	Du	Du
Division of the beat	Du De	Du Da Di	Du Be and Du Ba Bi
Subdivision of the beat	Du Ta De Ta	Du Ta Da Ta Di Ta	Du Ta Be Ta and Du Ta Ba Ta Bi Ta
Takadimi System			
	Duple Meter	**Triple Meter**	**Unusual Meter**
Beat	Ta	Ta	Ta
Division of the beat	Ta di	Ta ki da	Ta di and Ta ki da
Subdivision of the beat	Ta ka di mi	Ta va ki di da ma	Ta ka di mi and Ta va ki di da ma

Table 3: *Basic syllables of the Froseth/Gordon and Takadimi rhythm syllable systems.*

The lack of musical notation in this table is meant to emphasize the fact that these systems are based upon how rhythms sound, feel, and function rather than on how they are notated. For example, the steady beat receives the same syllable (*Du* in the Froseth/Gordon system and *Ta* in the Takadimi system) regardless of how it is notated or where it falls in the measure. This is reflective of the fact that the steady beat has the same function regardless of its notation. Bluestine (2000) explains:

The fact is that macrobeats are not necessarily quarter notes or half notes. They can be notated as a series of quarter notes, half notes, eighth notes, whole notes, double-whole notes, dotted-half notes, and so on. Their specific time value is irrelevant; all that's relevant is their temporal consistency. (p. 121)

Figure 2 demonstrates how these rhythm syllable systems can be applied to common rhythms. Additionally, it shows how rhythms that sound and feel the same can be notated in different ways, yet would still receive the same rhythm syllables.

Figure 2: *Froseth/Gordon and Takadimi Syllables Applied to Common Rhythms*

The ability to develop aural skills before notational skills is one strength of the rhythm syllable systems outlined above. Another strength is the presence of distinct syllables for each meter. Duple divisions of the beat are labeled with different syllables than triple divisions of the beat. Using distinct syllables for different meters helps ensure that students make a one-to-one correlation between the sound and the syllable. The syllables can, therefore, be used as a tool to identify and understand different meters. Finally, the systems described above provide students with a labeling tool that is internally consistent and, therefore, works even with complex musical material. Readers interested in further examination and comparison of rhythm syllable systems are encouraged to consult the resources suggested below. It is important that music departments take time to discover the strengths and weaknesses of various systems in order to make an informed choice regarding which system to use in their curriculum. In addition, the more consistency there is among teachers, the more students will be able to transfer their learning between music classes.

Suggested Resources

The following resources are recommended to readers who are interested in further exploration of the ideas presented in this chapter:

Teaching Movement and Dance: A Sequential Approach to Rhythmic Movement (Weikart, 2006) - This book offers a detailed discussion of teaching movement, including information about developing beat competency and body coordination. Movement activities and folk dance instructions are included. The CDs that go with this book are an excellent resource for movement activities.

The Complete Conductor's Guide to Laban Movement Theory (Billingham, 2009) - This book provides an introduction to Laban's life and theories. While this book is geared towards conductors and the application of Laban's movement theories to conducting gestures, music educators at all levels may find it helpful for understanding Laban's ideas. Practical movement exercises are included.

Music Play (Valerio, Reynolds, Bolton, Taggart, & Gordon, 1998) - This book provides information about a music curriculum for early childhood, which can be used to guide children through informal music learning experiences. Information on various stages of informal learning is presented along with songs, chants, and sample activities.

Jump Right In: The Music Curriculum (Taggart, Bolton, Reynolds, Valerio, & Gordon, 2000) - This series of books presents a skill-based music curriculum intended for use in elementary general music classes. Currently, there are five books available—K, 1, 2, 3, and 4—though it is important to note that teachers may need to use activities from various books depending on their students' prior musical experiences and current level of skill development. In other words, the book number does not necessarily correlate directly to the grade level of that same number. This curriculum spirals both musical content and skill and these books include a wealth of songs, chants, and teaching plans that address the skills discussed in this chapter.

The Ways Children Learn Music (Bluestine, 2000) - This book offers a more in-depth explanation of the ideas presented in this chapter and is an accessible resource for teachers looking for information on this type of curriculum.

Learning Sequences in Music (Gordon, 2003) - This book provides a much more in-depth discussion of the ideas presented in this chapter. It includes extensive, detailed discussions of the Froseth/Gordon rhythm syllable system, music aptitude, and other topics.

Rhythm Register Book 1 (Gordon, 1990a), *Rhythm Register Book 2* (Gordon, 1990b), and *Reference Handbook for Using Learning Sequence Activities* (Gordon, 2001) - Together, these three books provide a comprehensive explanation of one approach to rhythm pattern instruction. Rhythm patterns are identified by level of difficulty, which can be used to individualize instruction based on aptitude level. These books also illustrate the spiral nature of the curriculum, with the same rhythm patterns revisited at higher skill levels in later units of study.

www.takadimi.net - This website provides links to information about the takadimi rhythm syllable system including a short guide that summarizes the syllables, audio examples, and information on *The Rhythm Book*, published by Richard Hoffman, which includes materials for rhythm instruction at the high school and college levels.

Conclusion

A comprehensive rhythm curriculum includes rhythmic skill development beyond counting note values and reading notation. A skill-based curriculum helps students develop a kinesthetic understanding of rhythm and meter by moving to beats, divisions of the beats, and rhythms. Students also develop a rich vocabulary of rhythm patterns in various meters and are able to call upon those vocabularies for use in unfamiliar music and in creative endeavors such as improvising and composing. In mastering these skills, students develop an internal sense of rhythm that will inform their music reading and writing abilities later on. As the curriculum spirals both musical content and skill, students develop to their fullest potential and foundations are laid for playing and singing with "good rhythm" for the rest of their lives.

References

Bluestine, E. (2000). *The ways children learn music: An introduction and practical guide to music learning theory*. Chicago: GIA Publications.

Billingham, L. (2009). *The complete conductor's guide to Laban movement theory*. Chicago: GIA Publications.

Gordon, E. E. (1979). *Primary measures of music audiation*. Chicago: GIA Publications.

Gordon, E. E. (1986). *Intermediate measures of music audiation*. Chicago: GIA Publications.

Gordon, E. E. (1989). *Advanced measures of music audiation*. Chicago: GIA Publications.

Gordon, E. E. (1990). *Jump right in: Rhythm register book one*. Chicago: GIA Publications.

Gordon, E. E. (1990). *Jump right in: Rhythm register book two*. Chicago: GIA Publications.

Gordon, E. E. (2001). *Reference handbook for using learning sequence activities*. Chicago: GIA Publications.

Gordon, E. E. (2003). *Learning sequences in music: Skill, content, and patterns: A music learning theory*. Chicago: GIA Publications.

Hoffman, R., Pelto, W., & White, J. W. (1996). Takadimi: A beat-oriented system of rhythm pedagogy. *Journal of Music Theory Pedagogy, 10*, 7–30.

Taggart, C. (1989). Rhythm syllables: A comparison of systems. In D. Walters & C. Taggart (Eds.), *Readings in music learning theory* (pp. 55–65). Chicago: GIA Publications.

Taggart, C. (2001) *Examples of assessing in a classroom setting*. [Coursepack for mus 467: Teaching general music in elementary school]. East Lansing, MI.

Taggart, C., Bolton, B., Reynolds, A., Valerio, W., & Gordon, E. (2000) *Jump right in: The music curriculum Book 1*. Chicago: GIA Publications.

Valerio, W., Reynolds, A., Bolton, B., Taggart, C., & Gordon, E. (1998). *Music play: The early childhood music curriculum, guide for parents, teachers, and caregivers*. Chicago: GIA Publications.

Weikart, P. S. (2006). *Teaching movement & dance: A sequential approach to rhythmic movement*. Ypsilanti, MI: High Scope

CHAPTER 9

SINGING AND TONAL AUDIATION FROM EARLY CHILDHOOD TO SECONDARY

Christina Hornbach

Hope College

"Intelligence is musical when its background is a storehouse of musical knowledge, a dynamo of musical interests, an outlet in musical tasks, and a warmth of musical experiences and responses." (Seashore, 1967, p. 8)

Singing is one of the most common public school music experiences and is a basic construct of musicianship. Singing, much like speaking one's native language, is a common and instinctive childhood experience. The earliest roots of American music singing education can be traced back to the eighteenth-century singing schools. Young children with singing experience will begin to sing accurately. However, if the skill of singing (how to use your singing voice) and with what timbre, as well as the skill of tonal audiation (what you comprehend/think) are not modeled and developed through social interaction and musical experience, these skills will most likely not develop. Most parents/ adults easily speak to children, connect, and respond with language. Children develop their listening vocabulary for language based on these interactions. It is from this listening vocabulary that children start to respond or speak language; intermixed in the process is the development of thinking and comprehension. Then, armed largely with their listening, speaking, and thinking (audiating) vocabularies, children may begin to read and finally write. Audiation is to music what thinking and understanding are to language (Gordon, 2007). The following will be an introduction to Music Learning Theory and how teachers can learn these ideas to develop audiation and singing skills for newborns through students in high school.

How Children Learn Music

Children learn music in markedly the same way that they learn a language. In order to form a listening vocabulary in music, children must first be exposed to sounds and the musical syntax of the culture. This is a similar process to how the listening vocabulary develops in children's native language. Eventually, children experiment with producing musical sounds (musical babble) and hopefully progress to singing and chanting in context (the speaking vocabulary of music). In order to learn to speak, children informally listen to people talk all day long; this language learning even begins in the womb. Similarly, children acquire musical knowledge and a means of sharing it (singing or chanting), through human, and in this case, specifically human musical interaction. During the first year of life, infants' brain growth is rapid. Early childhood is a critical time for brain development as a large percentage of the neurological synapses are formed (Gordon, 2007). With a stimulating musical environment, children lay brain pathways that enhance the potential (aptitude) for future musical understanding and growth.

Unfortunately, most children do not come to school with the same depth and level of experience (listening and speaking vocabulary) for music as their native language. In Pre-K, kindergarten, and first grade especially, the music teacher must initially provide informal music guidance to fill this need for a listening vocabulary in music (Valerio, Reynolds, Bolton, Taggart, & Gordon, 1998). Most preschool and kindergarten music classes will consist of primarily informal music guidance. If first grade students have had appropriate informal music guidance in kindergarten, they may only need informal instruction the first month or so of first grade. If second grade students have already started formal instruction in first grade, they may only need a few weeks of informal music guidance at the beginning of the year and have formal instruction the rest of the year.

Informal music guidance in general music classes, taught by a professional musician and teacher, gives children the opportunity for exposure to an extensive music vocabulary and to play and experiment with music. Then, as students develop the readiness, music teachers may progress to formal, sequential instruction and assessment. Children must develop both a large listening vocabulary, which provides the basis for their "thinking" or audiation vocabulary (tonal audiation), and the skill of using their singing voice (an executive or physical skill). Elementary general music classes should provide developmentally appropriate, quality one-to-one and group interactions with music that lay the foundation for a lifetime of musical growth, understanding, and expression. By participating in regular music making time, children cultivate a working music vocabulary (listening/ tonal audiation) and the skill to share it (singing).

The philosophical underpinning of elementary general music education should be to provide young children with a rich, developmentally appropriate musical environment in which they have an opportunity to grow musically and become fluent in "music." So, how do teachers pass on musical skills? How specifically do music teachers develop the skill of singing? How do they teach young children to sing and respond to music? "Learning how to sing, like learning language, is a long process that begins at birth" (Greenberg, 1979, p. 173). The development of a tonal language expressed with the singing voice is a primary facet of the sequential instruction of Edwin Gordon's Music Learning Theory. Music Learning Theory is not a methodology or curriculum, but rather it describes how we learn music and the guidelines for learning. The Gordon sound-to-symbol concept, though not focused on specifically developing physiological singing skills, has the "potential to accomplish musicianship and literacy" (Jordan-Decarbo, 1986, p. 41).

Children's music learning and development is a complicated and often misunderstood system. So, how do we navigate singing in the elementary general music classroom? Do we teach music in a way where we expect children to have certain skills and content knowledge before we have shared that skill and content with them? In order to avoid this mistake, music teachers need to practice sequential instruction that is aligned with the assessment of tonal skills and classroom content. If children are taught singing and tonal audiation skills in this manner, they become actively involved in their learning, and this, in turn, may help foster an already innate love of singing. Essentially, we have two "instruments" or "skills" to develop in order to create students who are independent singer musicians: the singing voice and the internal instrument (the comprehension or tonal audiation). Practice and research have shown the importance of singing in the elementary students' musical development. Despite this fact, it is unclear as to what extent singing-related activities are a part of the general music classroom and what skills and vocal techniques are used. Hence, we, as a profession, need to plan instruction with a list of developmental skills or benchmarks for each grade level; yet, always provide a spiral-based curriculum that continues to provide the foundational musical skills in a developmentally-appropriate manner at all levels and also adapt instruction to meet individual needs.

Informal Instruction

Informal music instruction lays the aural and oral foundation for all sequential tonal learning in music. Informal teaching is guided or facilitated; formal teaching is direct instruction. Singing is a learned behavior, and there is a significant amount of evidence that validates vocal coordination instruction, a psychomotor skill (Cooper, 1995; Green, 1989; and Jersild & Bienstock, 1934). Levinowitz, Barnes, Guerrini, Clement, D'April, and Morey noted that children "vacillate between the speaking voice and the singing voice" and that this does not appear to be a product of maturation, as is range, but that the use of the singing voice is a "learned" skill (1998, p. 41). Despite the fact that numerous experts agree that singing is a teachable skill (Atterbury, 1984; Gordon, 1971), there exists no structured approach on how to teach children to sing (Atterbury, 1984). Students need to find and develop their singing voice and their "thinking" voice (audiation) simultaneously. The singing voice is the primary instrument through which students can predominantly become involved in their musical learning; but, if they do not also in turn develop their tonal audiation, they will never be able to create or improvise in music, merely imitate (e.g., echo patterns). Audiation is the ability to comprehend, not just echo tonal patterns.

First and foremost, we must purposefully provide time in instruction where we sing for children. The teacher sings for the students and in doing so provides both musical listening vocabulary and also models an appropriate singing voice (light, energetic, free). Informal guidance requires the teacher to 1) sing for students, 2) sing in a variety of tonalities, 3) be mindful of pitch range, and 4) encourage developmental and age appropriate activities (we learn through play). We teach children how to sing through modeling, what songs we chose to sing provides students with a rich and varied tonality and meter "diet." Teachers should set a goal for two to three minutes of instructional time every class period where they are singing for students; students may be engaged by doing another musical activity while listening. For instance, sing a song for children and have them give beanbags a "ride" on different body parts. The listening to and singing of songs in a variety of tonalities provides students with a large listening vocabulary. This informal music "bath" supplies the readiness and context for future tonal learning. Ideally, this would have happened before children enter formal schooling. Since, for the majority of children, this type of music instruction is not happening, music teachers must provide this informal learning in the early years of elementary school before continuing on to formal music instruction.

Music teachers must sing for children in a variety of tonalities; music teachers should develop a curriculum (and a working song repertoire for themselves) with songs predominantly in the following tonalities: major, harmonic minor, Aeolian, Dorian, Phrygian, Lydian, and Mixolydian. *The Early Childhood Music Curriculum: Experimental Songs and Chants* (Gordon, Bolton, Valerio, & Taggart, 1993), *Music Play* (Valerio, Reynolds, Bolton, Taggart, & Gordon, 1998), and *Jump Right In: General Music Series* (Taggart, Bolton, Reynolds, Valerio, & Gordon, 1999) are three rich resources for teaching materials and songs in a variety of tonalities, as well as selected folk songs and hymn tunes. A varied song repertoire in turn provides students with listening vocabulary that serves as a foundation for all future music learning. Singing should be done in an age appropriate range to encourage the use of the head voice versus chest voice in young children. This range should be limited further when the teacher expects a singing response from the children (resting tone and tonal patterns); student singing should be done within a limited range to set them up for success. In the beginning, the majority of class time should be spent singing and chanting in a variety of tonalities and meters. For tonal development, teachers should limit song range, sing for children, and develop and use playful singing activities that provide students initially with a singing model of resting tone and then eventually an opportunity to sing the resting tone and tonal patterns as a group and individually. Informal music guidance must start with context first (singing songs for children in a variety of tonalities). Teachers should not teach content (e.g., tonal patterns), until they have provided students with context (the song in major, the song in minor, etc.). The music is in the tonal audiation; the notation is on the page. The more music students have heard a variety of tonal contexts (e.g., Major, Aeolian, Dorian, etc.), the more comparisons they can make and the more music they can comprehend and make on their own.

As music teachers, our goal for our students should be that they can function as independent musicians; students who can comprehend and perform music without us. The new National Core Arts

Standards are designed to coordinate a core curriculum for all and ensure that students are equipped for either a career or college. The National Coalition for Core Arts Standards (NCCAS) had developed a web-based music curriculum that coordinates anchor standards and performance standards by artistic processes (creating, performing, responding, and connecting). Please note the correlation of the National Core Arts Standards with Tonal Skill Learning suggested below for tonal activities. The National Core Arts Standards are voluntary, but quite easy to align with a developmentally appropriate music curriculum, though in and of themselves are not substantive enough, especially for a novice teacher, to use as a guide for content and skill sequences of learning in the music classroom. The following are some examples of informal singing activities.

Informal Singing Activities

Goal: Development of Tonal Audiation Skills

Example Informal Tonal Audiation Activity

"Alex's Song" (Lydian)

Objective: Students are exposed to songs in a variety of tonalities.
Objective: Teacher sings for children (providing singing model).

NCCAS Pre-K Performance Standard for the Artistic Process of Creating

"Students will, with guidance, explore music ideas (i.e., sing) to use for specific musical purpose (e.g., activity)."

Teacher sings song; students listen and flow with scarves. Teacher sings songs several times and asks students to flow with scarves as "high as they can flow" one time and as "low as they can flow" another time.

Alex's Song

Allegro

Christina M. Hornnbach

Goal: Development of Singing Skill

Providing vocal exploration activities is not a new activity for elementary general music teachers. However, teachers can maximize instructional time by providing vocal exploration within the tonal context of a song.

Example Informal Singing Activity

"Ding Dong" (major)

Objective: Student explores vocal exploration as a group and individually.

NCCAS K Performance Standard for the Artistic Process of Performing

"With support, students will perform with expressive qualities (i.e., dynamics, tempo) in a manner appropriate to context."

Teacher has the "cats" (the children) sit down and rest on their imaginary blankets or carpet squares if available. Teacher sings the song on a neutral syllable. Teacher makes meowing vocalizations (e.g., "Me-ee-ee-ow" on a sustained downward sigh; "Me-ow" from low to high; etc.) and has children echo in between repetitions of the song. Teacher models cat sounds in a variety of ranges and also encourages group response (by gesturing to class with both hands) and also offers the opportunity for individual response (by gesturing to one student at a time).

Ding, Dong, Di-Gi-Di-Gi Dong

Traditional

By offering and expecting students to respond to teacher gesture as a group and individually, teachers are building a social construct of interaction of the expectation of group and individual response in every music class. Initially, this is just developing a class culture of interaction. Eventually, teachers will capitalize on this by assessing students' response to adapt instruction. This develops a culture for group and individual response as a norm in music class and should be included at least once in every music class.

Goal: Development of Tonal Audiation and Singing Skills - Resting Tone

The resting tone is the "home note" of whatever tonality you are singing. So, if your song is in major tonality, the resting tone or tonic note is *Do*. In informal guidance, the resting tone should be sung frequently and on a neutral syllable, such as bum.

Goal: Development of Tonal Audiation and Singing Skills - Resting Tone

Example Informal Resting Tone Activity

"Band of Angels" (major)
Objective: Students sing resting tone as a group and individually with the teacher.

NCCAS K Performance Standard for the Artistic Process of Creating

"Students will, with guidance, develop and refine musical ideas (i.e., rhythm, tonal, or melodic)."

Teacher sings the song on a neutral syllable and has students "paint" with body parts in a continuous, fluid style. Teacher sings the following on dominant: "What color do you want to paint with?" The teacher picks a student response, and sings the answer on tonic, "Ok, let's paint with red today!" Teacher sings the resting tone on bum or a neutral syllable and pretends to dip the "paint brush" in a new paint color. Teacher sings the resting tone and encourages students to imitate singing the resting tone echoing him/her or by singing the dominant note on a neutral syllable (here d) and then responding with the resting tone (here g) in between song repetitions.

Band of Angels

Traditional

There was one, there were two. There were three lit-tle an-gels. There were four, there were five. There were six lit-tle an-gels. There were sev-en, there were eight. There were nine lit-tle an-gels. Ten lit-tle an-gels in the band.

Giving students opportunities to sing individual and group patterns is important. The more that they have a chance to sing individually, the more comfortable students will become with the process. It also offers them an opportunity to hear themselves, so they can adjust if need be. Initially, what students think they are singing and what they actually are singing might not match. When students are given the opportunity to hear this difference, it in turn gives them a chance to correct/adjust their singing.

Goal: Development of Tonal Audiation and Singing Skills - Resting Tone

Example Informal Resting Tone Activity

"Two Little Birds" (Major)
Objective: Students sing resting tone as a group and individually. Students sing tonal patterns on neutral syllables.

NCCAS First Grade Performance Standard for the Artistic Process of Performing

"Students will identify how a musical element is used in the music and demonstrate their analysis." [Here, the demonstration is singing the resting tone and their analysis is actually singing it in the correct tonal context.]

Have children sit down and rest in their nests. Teacher sings the song for them. Teacher sings the resting tone or tonic note on *bum* or *peep*. Teacher gestures to the whole group (two hands with a breath gesture first) or individual birds (one hand) to sing the resting tone on *bum*. Teacher sings the answer (*do* on a neutral syllable of *bum* or *peep*) at the same time as student sings the answer. This is teaching mode or discrimination learning.

Extras: Sing tonal patterns in Major for them in between repetitions of the songs. Give children the opportunity to echo your patterns.

Two Little Birds

Iowa

Two lit-tle birds sat on a hill. One named Jack and the oth-er named Jill.

Fly a-way Jack,   Fly a-way, Jill.   Come back Jack.   Come back Jill.

As previously mentioned, in kindergarten, most of the year may be informal tonal music guidance. As an established music teacher begins to implement these objectives in his/her program, the switch to formal music instruction will begin sooner as the teacher becomes more skilled in his/her instruction and also builds up a group of students who have the foundational tonal audiation and singing skills. A teacher starting in a new skill will also need to incorporate informal music instruction at all levels initially. This informal environment has a mix of the teacher singing for the children, but the teacher also remembers to stop singing and let the children sing alone as a group and individually. The goals of informal tonal music instruction are to develop both the singing voice and the "thinking" voice (tonal audiation skills). Teachers do this by providing singing activities where students sing; explore their own voices (students should be encouraged to experiment with and use head voice from a young age); correctly use singing voice; sing the resting tone as a group; sing the resting tone individually; sing tonal patterns as a group; and sing tonal patterns individually. When students are able to correctly sing the resting tone in major, they are ready for more formal instruction. The teacher must continue a mix of informal instruction in other tonalities (Aeolian, Dorian, etc.) to continue to build students' listening vocabulary (this is a life-long endeavor). For tonal instruction, a music teacher should be asking: Have my students figured out how to use their singing voices and do they audiate tonal syntax (do they hear home, resting tone or tonic)?

When teachers have provided students with the appropriate tonal vocabulary via playful and interactive music activities and the students can sing the resting tone in major on a neutral syllable, they are ready to move on to formal instruction. When students have found and are using head voice while singing, formal instruction may begin.

Formal Instruction for Singing in Elementary School

There are two basic means of learning in the music classroom: discrimination and inference (Gordon, 2007). Imitating tonal patterns and singing a song by rote are examples of discrimination learning (recalling familiar songs); the teacher has taught the student "the answer" and the student has memorized it (though he/she might not know why, they just know the answer). Discrimination learning is readiness for inference learning. Discrimination is rote; inference is conceptual (Gordon, 2007). For instance, a student must have listened to and sung a large number of familiar songs in major tonality (discrimination learning), before he/she can hear an unfamiliar song and decide that it is in major (inference learning). The levels of Discrimination Learning are Aural/Oral, Verbal Association, Partial Synthesis, Symbolic Association, and Composite Synthesis (Gordon, 2007). For the purposes of this chapter, the teaching examples are designed for discrimination learning Aural/Oral and Verbal Association Levels. The Aural/Oral Tonal Levels primarily consists of activities (on neutral syllables) where students sing the resting tone (usually performed on the neutral syllable *bum*); sing tonic and dominant; sing the first and last pitches of songs; echo tonal patterns; find tonal patterns in songs; and sing chord root melodies. The Verbal Association Tonal Levels includes activities (performed with solfege syllables) where students sing the resting tone; sing the first and last pitch of songs; echo tonal patterns; find tonal patterns in songs; label tonalities of songs sung in class; sing tonic ostinati; and sing simple melodic ostinati. For the purposes of this chapter, examples of solfege will use moveable *do* with a *la*-based minor.

Goal: Development of Tonal Audiation and Singing Skills through the Aural/Oral Skill Level of Learning

Example Tonal Activities for Aural/Oral Learning

1. "Ships" (Dorian)
Objective: Students sing resting tone as a group and individually (without syllables).

NCCAS First Grade Performance Standard for the Artistic Process of Responding

"Students will identify how a musical concept is used in musical selections and demonstrate the analysis." [Here, the musical concept is comprehending the resting tone in context (audiating) and the response is singing the resting tone (singing skill or demonstrating their analysis).]

Teacher sings song - students listen and do gentle neck or other appropriate stretch. Teacher singing resting tone on a neutral syllable. Teacher gestures to the group and individuals to sing the tonic or resting tone on bum in between repetitions of the song.

Ships

Christina M. Hornbach

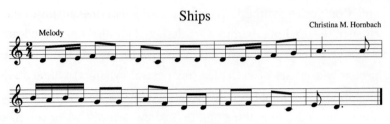

2. "Froggie Went A-Courtin'" (major)
Objective: Students sing on tonic and dominant in harmonic context.

NCCAS Second Grade Performance Standard for the Artistic Process of Performing

"Students will identify and demonstrate how musical elements (e.g., form) are used in the music."

Teacher sings song. Have children be frogs and hop around the room. Teacher models singing and hopping. Teacher sings the dominant on the preparation to jump [either low 5 (*so*) or high 5 (*so*)] and the tonic [1 (*do*)] on a neutral syllable in between repetitions of the song.

Froggie Went A-Courtin'

Traditional Folk Song

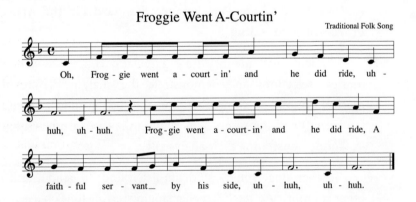

3. "Let's Go to the Sea" (major)
Objective: Sing first and last pitches of songs without syllables.

NCCAS First Grade Performance Standard for the Artistic Process of Performing

"Students will identify how a musical element is used in the music and demonstrate their analysis."

Teacher sings the song and students pretend to swim around the room as dolphins. Students freeze at end of the song. Teacher sings the first pitch of the song (here a c) on a neutral syllable and gestures to students to sing first pitch (sing high c on *bum*). Teacher then sings the last pitch of the song on a neutral syllable (f on *bum*) and gestures to students to sing last pitch (f on *bum*). Teacher sings first pitch (c on *bum*) and then questions, "Is that the first pitch of this song?" Teacher then sings first pitch of song (c on *bum*) and answers his/her own question by singing, "Yes!" on the first pitch of the song. Teacher does the same for the last pitch of the song.

Let's Go to the Sea

Guatemalan Folk Song
Adapted by C. Hornbach

Let's go to the sea, sea, sea, to en - joy the best fish, fish,

Let's go to the sea, sea, sea, to en - joy the best fish, fish.

Adaptation © 2011

4. "Six Little Ducks" (major)
Objective: Students echo sing tonal patterns without syllables.

NCCAS K Performance Standard for the Artistic Process of Creating

"With guidance, explore tonal and rhythmic patterns…"

Teacher sings song and models swimming in the water. Children join in swimming. Teacher stops swimming at end of song and sings tonal patterns in major on a neutral syllable or quack.

Teacher sings song and continues swimming around the room. Teacher provides opportunity for group and individual responses by gesturing to the group as well as individuals for tonal responses. The expectation is that the students will echo the tonal patterns.

Six Little Ducks

5. "Wind the Bobbin" (Major)
Objective: Students find tonal patterns in songs.

NCCAS K Performance Standard for the Artistic Process of Creating

"With guidance, explore tonal and rhythmic patterns…"

Teacher sings song for students. Teacher sings the tonal patter *mi-do* on a neutral syllable (bum) and gestures for students to echo. Teacher sings song again and has students wind their arms (one arm over the other in a circle). Teacher sings the *mi-do* tonal pattern again on a neutral syllable. Teacher sings song again on a neutral syllable and asks students to raise their hand when they hear the *mi-do* pattern. Teacher does not identify the *mi-do* pattern with solfege; teacher sings it for students on a neutral syllable.

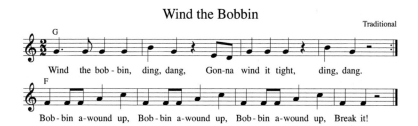

Wind the Bobbin

Traditional

Wind   the bob - bin,   ding, dang,   Gon-na wind it tight,   ding, dang.

Bob - bin a-wound up, Bob - bin a-wound up, Bob - bin a-wound up, Break it!

6. "Bow Belinda" (Major)
Objective: Students sing chord root melodies.

NCCAS Second Grade Performance Standard for the Artistic Process of Performing

"Students will perform with expressive and technical qualities, appropriate interpretation and appropriate performance expectations in a manner appropriate to the context."

Teacher sings song and walks in a circle on microbeat (small beat) with children. Teacher sings song and walks in a circle on macrobeat (big beat) with children. Teacher sings song and pulses microbeat with knees. Teacher sings chord root melody as if it were a separate song. Teacher asks student to sing his new song and helps him by gesturing with the pointer finger for tonic and five fingers for dominant while singing the chord root melody.

Bow, Belinda

American Singing Game

Melody

Chord Root Melody

Goal: Development of Tonal Audiation and Singing Skills through the Verbal Association Skill Level of Learning

Example Tonal Activities for Verbal Association Learning

1. "Early One Morning" (Major)
Objective: Students sing resting tone with syllables.

NCCAS K and First Grade Performance Standard for the Artistic Process of Creating

"Students will with guidance, develop and refine musical ideas."

Teacher sings the song on a neutral syllable. Teacher models singing the resting tone (for this song, sing *do* on e-flat). Have students sing the resting tone on *do* whenever you stop and gesture to them as a group and as individuals. This can be between song repetitions or at other places in the song (musical phrases).

Early One Morning

England

2. "Yonder Stands A Handsome Lady" (Dorian)
Objective: Students sing first and last pitch of songs with syllables.

NCCAS First Grade Performance Standard for the Artistic Process of Performing

"Students will identify how a musical element is used in the music and demonstrates their analysis."

Teacher sings song on a neutral syllable and pretends to stir soup. Teacher sings, "What shall we put in our" (on dominant) and "soup today?" (on tonic). Teacher takes students' feedback on what to put in soup as an opportunity to sing the song again and stir the soup. Teacher sings first pitch of song on *re* and gestures to students to echo. Teacher then sings on the tonic (here it is d), "When our song is in Dorian, our resting tone is *re*." Teacher sings on dominant (here a) "Interestingly enough (pause)" and then sings on tonic "our resting tone *re* and our starting pitch of this song, *re*, are the same."

3. "Bridge at Avignon" (Major)
Objective: Students echo tonal patterns with syllables (solfege).

NCCAS K Performance Standard for the Artistic Process of Creating

"With guidance, explore tonal and rhythmic patterns…"

Have students drive their cars around the room or on the "bridge" as you sing the song. Have students freeze when you stop singing. Sing tonal patterns using tonal syllables (e.g., *do-mi-so*, *so-mi-so*, *so-fa-re-ti*, *do-mi-do*) in Major for them. Give students the opportunity to echo your patterns as a group and as individuals.

4. "Oh, Where Has My Little Dog Gone?" (Major)
Objective: Using syllables, students find tonal patterns in songs.

NCCAS K Performance Standard for the Artistic Process of Creating

"With guidance, explore tonal and rhythmic patterns..."

Teacher sings song and flows with little butterfuly nets. Teacher sings the tonal pattern *mi-so-mi* and has the students echo. Teacher sings the song again. Teacher again sings the tonal pattern *mi-so-mi* and has the students echo. Teacher provides opportunities for the group and individuals to imitate. Teacher asks students to raise their nets in the air when they hear the pattern *mi-so-mi* as teacher sings the song on a neutral syllable. (Teacher sings pattern on solfege.)

Oh, Where Has My Little Dog Gone?

Traditional

5. "I'm Gonna Sing" (Major)
Objective: Teachers label tonalities of songs. Teacher sings first and students imitate answers through rote learning. (Move to Verbal Association, first major and then minor, teachers should remain at the Aural/Oral level with other tonalities).

NCCAS Third Grade Performance Standard for the Artistic Process of Responding

"Students will select music from varied familiar sources to experience, and demonstrate and explain connections to a specific purpose." [For the purposes of this activity, the purpose is musical—the learning and labeling of musical tonalities.]

Teacher sings the song. Teacher then establishes the major tonality by singing "*so-la-so-fa-mi-re-ti-do*." Teacher explains that the song is in a major tonality because the Major tonal sequence works with what we are audiating during this song. Teacher talk is "*Do* is the resting tone and when *do* is the resting tone we know we are in Major tonality."

6. **"Old Joe Clark" (Mixolydian)**
Objective: Teacher labels tonalities of songs, he/she singing first and students imitate answers through rote learning. (Move to Verbal Association, first major and then minor, teachers should remain at the Aural/Oral level with other tonalities).

NCCAS Third Grade Performance Standard for the Artistic Process of Responding

"Students will select music from varied familiar sources to experience, and demonstrate and explain connections to a specific purpose." [For the purposes of this activity, the purpose is musical— the learning and labeling of musical tonalities.]

Teacher sings the song. Teacher then establishes the Mixolydian tonality by singing "*re, mi, re, do, ti, la, fa, so*." Teacher explains that the song is in a Mixolydian tonality because the Mixolydian tonal sequence works with what we are audiating during this song. Teacher talk is "So is the resting tone and when So is the resting tone we know we are in Mixolydian tonality."

Old Joe Clark

American Folk Song

7. "Canoe Song" (Minor)
Objective: Students sing tonic ostinato.

NCCAS Second Grade Performance Standard for the Artistic Process of Responding

"Students will identify and demonstrate how musical elements are used in the music..." [For the purposes of this activity, the musical element is harmony, and the students demonstrate the ability to sing a harmonic accompaniment.]

Students learn song by rote.
Students learn melodic ostinato by rote.

Canoe Song

Camping Song

8. "Hush, Little Baby" (Major)
Objective: Students sing simple melodic ostinato.

NCCAS Second Grade Performance Standard for the Artistic Process of Responding

"Students will identify and demonstrate how musical elements are used in the music..." [For the purposes of this activity, the musical element is harmony, and the students demonstrate the ability to sing a harmonic accompaniment.]

Students learn song by rote.
Students learn melodic ostinato by rote.

Hush, Little Baby

The above teaching examples are designed for discrimination learning Aural/Oral and Verbal Association Levels in elementary. These same activities may be adapted to the choral classroom, elementary or secondary.

Formal Instruction in the Choral Context

Whether teaching young children, or singers in the upper elementary, middle/junior high, or high school, teachers must help students develop their listening and thinking vocabulary (audiational skills), as well as the executive skills. Executive skills are the physical and technical skills that are necessary to perform. One artistic process for music is performing (e.g., singing or playing an instrument). Examples of executive skills for instrumental performance are fingerings and embouchure. For singing or vocal performance, examples of executive skills are posture, breathing (breath awareness and energy), vocal production and resonance (tone quality).

Singing is a skill. It is through this skill that students may express their audiation of music. In order to be able to express their musical ideas, students must possess the executive skills. The choral warm-up is the traditional place for singers to engage in developing executive skills. If choral teachers also include the teaching of audiational skills in both warm-ups and rehearsal, overall performance practice will increase. Excellence in choral singing requires mastery of both audiational and executive skills.

In order to develop audiational skills in the choral setting, students should experience the same tonal activities as outlined above for the elementary setting (Aural/Oral and Verbal Association Tonal Activities), but in a developmentally and discipline appropriate context.

Goal: Development of Tonal Audiation and Singing Skills through the Aural/Oral Skill Level of Learning in the Choral Context

Example Tonal Activities for Choral Aural/Oral Learning

1. "If Ye Love Me" by Thomas Tallis (edited by Shenenberger, 2006) (Major)

Objective: Students sing resting tone as a group and individually (without syllables).

Teacher rehearses the octavo. Singers sing octavo. Teacher singing resting tone on a neutral syllable *bum*. Teacher gestures to the group and individuals to sing the tonic or resting tone on *bum* in between repetitions of the song or rehearsing sections.

Objective: Sing first and last pitches of songs without syllables.

Teacher rehearses the octavo. Singers sing octavo. Teacher sings the first pitch of the song for each section on a neutral syllable and gestures to just that section to sing the first pitch on a neutral syllable. For instance, the teacher sings an F on *bum* and gestures to the sopranos to imitate. He/she repeats with each section.

Objective: Students echo-sing tonal patterns without syllables.

Teacher rehearses the octavo. Singers sing octavo. To set the context for rehearsal, teacher sings tonal patterns without syllables in F major and gestures to the group or individuals to echo. For example, the teacher may sing *do, mi, so* on *bum, bum, bum* and gesture to the group to imitate.

2. "Il est bel et bon" by Pierre Passereau (edited by Shenenberger, 2007) (Dorian)

Objective: Students find tonal patterns in songs.

Teacher sings tonal patterns from the song. Students echo. Students locate and identify pattern in the song. For example, the teacher sings "*re, mi, fa, so, la*" and the students imitate and locate in their own parts and other parts.

Example Tonal Activities for Choral Verbal Association Learning

1. "If Ye Love Me" by Thomas Tallis (edited by Shenenberger, 2006) (Major)

Objective: Students sing resting tone as a group and individually with syllables.

Teacher rehearses the octavo. Singers sings octavo. Teacher singing resting tone *do*. Teacher gestures to the group and individuals to sing the tonic or resting tone, *do*, in between repetitions of the song or rehearsing sections.

2. "Il est bel et bon" by Pierre Passereau (edited by Shenenberger, 2007) (Dorian)

Objective: Students sing resting tone as a group and individually with syllables.

Teacher rehearses the octavo. Singers sings octavo. Teacher sings resting tone, *re*. Teacher gestures to the group and individuals to sing the tonic or resting tone, *re*, in between repetitions of the song or rehearsing sections.

Teachers must think strategically and continually evaluate and adapt the classroom to maximize instruction. The ideal classroom environment for music making enables students to focus on music making by providing a physical environment that provides open space for movement, free from distractions. Teachers should consider setting up their elementary classroom with no chairs and ask students to sit in a circle. Setting up the teaching space in this manner offers direct visual and physical proximity to all students. Teachers may sit on the floor in the circle with students (or on a low stool or milk crate). In the secondary setting, chairs should be used as a rehearsal organizational tool in a traditional tiered, sectional seating arrangement; however, teachers should remember to vary seated singing with standing singing and provide ample opportunity for singing in a circle or in varied seating arrangements. The music teacher's energy level, excitement, preparation, and delivery of song material will determine or set the baseline for students' attitude, energy, and involvement.

Singing instruction is progressive, all students/classes are the continuum of instruction. After you teach something, repeat it. Find a way to do it again, and again. If you ever want your students to take risks in your classroom environment, you have to take risks yourself and model that it is fine to make a mistake—continually foster a healthy learning environment.

In informal instruction (primarily kindergarten and first grade for most teaching environments) and formal instruction, music teachers are charged with immersing students in a rich tonal environment; they acculturate students to different tonalities by singing whole songs, singing parts of songs (resting tones and tonal patterns), and fitting those parts back into the harmonic context of the whole song (providing an opportunity to sing the whole song again). Teachers should strive to provide an interactive and playful environment where they are not directly teaching, but modeling musical behaviors (singing, singing resting tone, singing tonal patterns, etc.). This is best done in an open space, with space for movement that is free from distractions. Initially, the songs should be sung mostly without text. Providing students with opportunities to "play" with musical vocabulary during informal music making will simultaneously help develop students' listening vocabulary and the speaking vocabulary (singing) will follow.

Strategies for the Successful Incorporation of Singing and Tonal Audiation in the Informal and Formal Music Environment

The following are a few suggestions for ways in which to incorporate more singing and tonal audiation skills in the elementary general and secondary vocal music classroom.

1. **Teachers must have a clear idea of an age-appropriate singing tone and educate students by their vocal model, teacher talk, and by posting expectations in the classroom.** Decide on an appropriate and healthy goal for vocal quality. Encourage an appropriate singing vocal quality through teacher vocal modeling and specific descriptions of the singing voice through "teacher talk." Students will gravitate towards a chest voice singing production—this requires training/coaching to find head voice (have an idea of what it sounds like) and use verbal reminders and post singing voice goals in the music. Children should learn from an early age to use their head voice. Habits are formed early. Research suggests that singing should be done in the head voice to improve tonal accuracy (Gordon, 1971). What vocal tone should music educators associate with the healthy use of the singing voice? While the quality of the singing voice may be arguably subjective, the one objective mandate is a model that encourages no vocal or physical stress/strain.

2. **Sing on a neutral syllable (*bum* or *loo*).** Removing text allows students to target just the "skill of singing" and takes

away the crutch of language. Sing without text. Text may be distracting or confounding factor in finding and focusing on the singing voice.

3. **Teacher must have knowledge of and incorporate a rich song repertoire in a developmentally appropriate range.** Initially, songs should have a range of approximately d (one step above middle c) to an octave above. The tessitura (or notes where students should initially be expected to produce accurate responses) should be approximately a fifth (the d right above middle c to a fifth above is a good guide). These ranges are a guide; teachers should use their discretion when using repertoire or patterns that fall out of this initial range. If initial singing responses are presented and asked for in a developmentally appropriate range, students will have more success. Singing instruction should be rounded out with vocal exploration that gently explores/stretches the singing voice range. Pick repertoire and actually sing it in appropriate range to develop head voice. Ideally, teachers should not sing for children in their speaking voice range (it encourages use of the speaking voice).

4. **Provide an interactive teaching environment** (Hornbach, 2005). The ideal music environment is most effective when it is an interactive environment, not unlike improvisatory theatre.

5. **Provide a playful and improvisatory environment. Provide a playful model for students.** In a teaching environment, you get what you give. Teachers should be playful and uninhibited in their movement and music making. The children will only be as playful and adventurous in their music making as the teacher is in his/her modeling.

6. **Seek individual responses from children (Hornbach, 2005).** Teachers must continue to find ways to elicit individual responses from students as it provides information

on the students' musical learning and development. Eliciting responses is important in order to meet instructional needs. Through listening to children's responses, teachers are able to gain insights into developmental levels. Based on this, they can adapt instruction to better serve the individuals in their classroom. If the children do not respond individually, teachers are unsure of the children's developmental levels and are unable to adapt instruction to best meet students' needs. Also, children need to hear their own voices. Goetze & Horii (1989) found that singing accuracy was greater when children sang individually versus in a group. Rutkowski (1996) recommends the use of individual and small group singing activities.

7. **Provide opportunities for practice and repetition.**

8. **Provide opportunities for silence in instruction (Hornbach, 2005).** Silence (wait time) is an important instructional tool in the music classroom. It helps teachers elicit student responses. "Teachers who consciously managed the duration of pauses after their questioning and provided regular intervals of silence during explanation created an environment where thinking was expected and practiced" (Tama, 1989, p. 3).

9. **Spend more instructional time singing.** Track and manage your instructional time. Teachers should periodically track how many minutes of a class period are spent actually singing (teaching singing or student singing). Basically, students need to sing. Teachers first model singing and then label or describe (e.g., teacher sings directions for students; teacher labels own "singing voice"; or teacher manages classroom behavior and labels musical behaviors at the same time by singing on the dominant of the key of the current song "My job is singing right now" and then on the tonic "Your job is listening right now"). Next, students should have a lot of time to sing individually and as a group. Sing directions for students. Sing songs

for students. Build a song repertoire for each grade level where students own and can reproduce entire melodies.

10. **Sing without accompaniment or recordings.** The playing of chords may inhibit accuracy. Stauffer (1985) established that students sang more accurately with no harmonic accompaniments. Warning, proceed with caution! This does not mean to stop playing harmonic accompaniments in your classroom. Rather, it means that teachers should strive to provide a balance of singing experiences with and without accompaniment; and, early on, the majority of song experiences should be without accompaniment. Also, when teachers are specifically measuring the singing voice, the song should have no accompaniment.

11. **Teachers need to establish a systematic and regular way to establish tonal context before starting a song.** For instance, before singing a song in Major tonality, the music teacher should sing the tonality sequence in major (*so-la-so-fa-mi-re-ti-do*). Then, the teacher should set the students up for success by communicating the tonal context, rhythm context, and the students' job before a song begins.

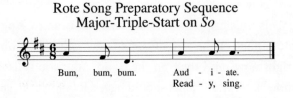

Conclusions

The majority of the listening vocabulary for singing and future music making is heavily reliant on the attention and skill of the elementary general music teacher; however, the secondary choral teacher should include audiation skill instruction alongside executive skill instruction in the choral setting as well. There are many different ways of approaching singing instruction; teachers are charged with finding options that work the best that day, for that song, and to differentiate instruction for the individuals in each class. This can be a daunting task, yet is an area where music educators must examine and change instruction, or society will continue to face the slow decline of singing as skill. Music educators need to reclaim our focus on the singing voice as the primary means of instruction in the general music classroom. Do you know what to teach and when to teach it? The training and experience you provide will change your students' musical brain. In music, there is no "you have it" or "you don't." Music aptitude (potential to achieve in music) is developmental until approximately age nine. Singing is a psychomotor skill that improves with instruction. While music educators seem to agree on the significance of singing and musicianship skills to overall musicianship, the music education community varies greatly on the actual practice in the elementary general music classroom.

Singing and tonal audiation are an essential part of music instruction at both the elementary and secondary level; despite this fact, there does not seem to be agreement among music educators on the most effective way to teach the skill of singing or the recognition of the development of tonal audiation as an indispensable part of the process of developing tonal musicianship. The early and middle childhood years are the most crucial for the development of the singing voice. Singing is paradoxically often relegated to one of those things that "everyone can do," so students are not specifically taught how to do it. Music teachers have the responsibility of developing a classroom environment with specific goals and objectives for musical behaviors.

There must be a sense of community and a developed culture of inter-action and response. Of particular note is the use of play and teacher improvisation as teaching tools in the strategies suggested to enhance singing and tonal audiation in this chapter. A critical change in singing instruction in the classroom must occur if we are to develop and improve the level of use of singing voice and music making (tonal music audiation) skills for children.

The above chapter is based in part on the dissertation, *Ah-eee-ah-eee-yah-eee, Bum, and Pop, Pop, Pop: Teacher Initiatives, Teacher Silence, And Children's Vocal Responses In Early Childhood Music Classes*, granted in 2005 by Michigan State University.

References

Atterbury, B. W. (1984). Are you really teaching children "how" to sing? *Music Educators Journal, 70*(8), 43–45.

Bruckner, A. (2004). *Pange lingua* (edited by James Jordan). Chicago: GIA (G-6481).

Cooper, N. A. (1995). Children's singing accuracy as a function of grade level, gender, and individual versus unison singing. *Journal of Research in Music Education, 43*(3), 222–231.

Goetze, M., & Horii, Y. (1989). A comparison of the pitch accuracy of group and individual singing in young children. *Bulletin for the Council for Research in Music Education, 99*, 57–73.

Gordon, E. E. (1971). *The psychology of music teaching*. Englewood Cliffs, NJ: Prentice-Hall.

Gordon, E. E. (2007). *Learning sequences in music: Skill, content, and patterns*. Chicago: GIA Publications.

Gordon, E. E., Bolton, B. M., Valerio, W. H., & Taggart, C. C. (1993). *The early childhood music curriculum: Experimental songs and chants*. Chicago: GIA.

Green, G. A. (1989). The effect of vocal modeling on pitch-matching accuracy of elementary schoolchildren. *Journal of Research in Music Education, 38*(3), 225–231.

Greenberg, M. (1979). *Your children need music.* Englewood Cliffs, N. J.: Prentice-Hall.

Hornbach, C. M. (2005). Ah-eee-ah-eee-yah-eee, bum, and pop, pop, pop: Teacher initiatives, teacher silence, and children's vocal responses in early childhood music classes (Doctoral dissertation, Michigan State University, 2005).

Jersild, A. T., & Bienstock, S. F. (1934). A study of the development of children's ability to sing. *The Journal of Educational Psychology 25*(7), 481–503.

Jordan-DeCarbo, J. (1986). A sound-to-symbol approach to learning music. *Music Educators Journal, 75*(6), 38–41.

Levinowitz, L. M., Barnes, P., Guerrini, S., Clement, M., D'April, P., & Morey, M. J. (1998). Measuring singing voice development in the general music classroom. *Journal of Research in Music Education, 46*(1), 35–47.

Music Learning Theory Elementary General Music Level One Materials. Gordon Institute for Music Learning.

National Core Arts Standards: Music (Draft, June 2013 – Final, Jun 2014). State Education Agency Directors of Arts Education (SEADAE) on behalf of National Coalition for Core Arts Standards (NCCAS).

Passereau, P. (2007). *Il est bel et bon* (edited by M. Shenenberger). Chicago, GIA (G-6504).

Rutkowski, J. (1996). The effectiveness of individual/small-group singing activities on kindergartner's use of singing voice and developmental music aptitude. *Journal of Research in Music Education, 44*, 353–368.

Seashore, C. E. (1967). *Psychology of music.* New York: Dover Publications.

Stauffer, S. L. (1985). An investigation of the effects of melodic and harmonic context on the development of singing ability in primary grade children. *Dissertation Abstracts International, 46*(07), 1862A.

Taggart, C., Bolton, B., Reynold, A., Valerio, W., & Gordon, E. (1999). *Jump right in: General music series*. Chicago, GIA.

Tallis, T. (2006). *If ye love me* (edited by Marilyn Shenenberger). Chicago: GIA (G-6519).

Tama, M. C. (1989). *Critical thinking: Promoting it in the classroom*. Bloomington, IN: ERIC Clearinghouse on Reading and Communication Skills. (ERIC Document Reproduction Service No. ED306554).

Valerio, W. H., Reynolds, A. M., Bolton, B. M., Taggart, C. C., & Gordon, E. E. (1998). *Music play*. Chicago: GIA Publications.

Christina M. Hornbach is associate professor of music and coordinator of music education at Hope College, Holland, Michigan. She received a Bachelor of Music and a Master of Music from the University of Michigan (Ann Arbor), and a Doctor of Philosophy from Michigan State University (East Lansing). She has taught general music in the public schools in Michigan and Minnesota as well as early childhood music at Michigan State University's Community Music School and Eastern Michigan University's Community Music Academy. Hornbach founded an early childhood music program, Early Bird Music, for the west Michigan community. Hornbach has presented workshops at the state, regional, and national NAfME In-Service Conferences, as well as local and international venues. She has published her research in the *Journal of Research in Music Education, Listen to Their Voices: Research and Practice in Early Childhood Music,* and *Learning from Young Children: Research in Early Childhood Music*. She is currently serving as Past-President for the Michigan Music Educators Association.

CHAPTER 10

CREATIVE MUSIC MAKING

C. Michael Palmer
Ball State University

Shannan L. Hibbard
University of Michigan

If "Musical creativity and musicianship are mutually interdependent and interactive" as David Elliott (1995, p. 227) asserts, then a curriculum fundamentally focused on musicianship alone is insufficient to cultivate all facets of music interaction and production. Equal attention must be given to musical creativity. The United States has a strong tradition of music education in performance, but less attention has been focused on other creative music making practices, namely composition and improvisation (Sarath, 2002), engaged listening, and interpretive performance. This chapter will outline the importance of creativity in music education and provide ideas on how to cultivate creative dispositions through composition, improvisation, performance, and listening.

Creativity

Creativity is commonly understood as the use of imagination for the production of original work. It is the making of something new, unique, or original, while demonstrating its relationship to a formerly established tradition or cultural domain. A creative disposition or habit of mind is adaptable and flexible through the interaction and response to new situations and contexts. In music, creativity is the process often associated with composition and improvisation. In this chapter, composition is defined as the process of creating music and its resultant product over an extended period of time, while improvisation is the simultaneous creation and performance of a musical work within a specific moment in time. The key differences between the two practices are the amount of time spent creating original musical ideas and the ability to edit those ideas. Composition can take place over an extended period of time and include editing and revision, while improvisation is bound to the present moment and cannot be edited once it is performed. These two differences produce unique challenges for music educators in teaching these practices, suggesting the need for a variety of strategies and approaches when including it in a comprehensive curriculum.

Although improvisation and composition are commonly viewed as the two creative musical behaviors, other elements of a music curriculum such as interpretive performance and listening can require creativity. All curricular aims in music are strengthened when teachers encourage students to create. Whether reading a score, deciding how to perform a song, or listening to a new piece of music, students may be involved in a myriad of creative problem solving. In this chapter, creative approaches to interpretive performance and music listening will be discussed, with suggestions for ways to involve students in creative activities across the music curriculum. Interpretive performance is defined as the execution of previously determined musical content, whether notated or taught by rote.

What is the value of including creative approaches in the curriculum in the first place? They explore divergent and convergent thinking practices. Music learning in the area of traditional band, choral, and orchestral music performance is focused predominantly on convergent thinking: Learning the correct way to sing and to play an instrument and to be able to perform music in its requisite authentic style. Yet, composition, improvisation, and creative approaches to interpretive performance and listening promote divergent thinking practice, which is the ability to come up with a wide variety of ideas to test, play with, and consider before settling on an idea as a part of convergent thinking. As Webster (2002) notes, "The interplay between divergent and convergent thinking is almost magical in scope and is at the centre of creative thinking" (p. 28–29). (For a visual representation of this process, see Webster's (2002) Model for Creative Thinking in Music.)

Another benefit of exploring these practices is that they provide spaces for students to develop their own ideas and interpretations of sounds in time. "Through the process of making music up, people learn whatever can be learned of self and others and of the world beyond music" (Campbell, 2009, p. 120). Creative music making involves figural or intuitive thinking. Keith Swanwick (1994) describes intuition as an exercise of imagination and the impetus for all other ways of knowing. In order to bridge the divide between sensation and cognition, we rely upon our imagination. "Intuitive knowledge is…the medial exchange between sense and significance" (p. 31). Providing opportunities for students to draw upon their own intuitive impulses leads to a sense of ownership, empowerment in the learning process, and ultimately, to a deeper realization and understanding of musicianship. In essence, composition, improvisation, and creative interpretive performance and listening are inherently constructivist practices because the learner is creating the music based on his/her musical understanding and experience.

Composition

Learning to manipulate sounds and silences in novel ways using pitch, rhythm, articulation, and dynamics provides students opportunities to demonstrate and cultivate their musical creative capacity. Such experiences provide a different perspective from the traditional role as interpreter/performer, thereby enriching students' understanding of music. Music composition gives students a voice for expressing their own thoughts and feelings through sound. For those who choose not to enroll in a music performance class, composing can be the activity that draws out their musical potential.

Composing music in a school setting often demands carefully structured activities over an extended period of time; structure can be loosely defined or strictly defined, based on the teacher's goals for the composition task and the students' developmental level. The important idea is for teachers to set their students up for success. By carefully planning out the sequence of events (e.g., starting, developing, and finishing a composition) and providing parameters (i.e., guidelines on what to include/exclude in the composition), students will have greater opportunity to learn about the compositional process and much about themselves.

Thanks to technology, anyone is capable of composing with or without formal musical knowledge. The idea that a composer is a solitary figure who spends time sitting at a desk notating his musical thoughts is passé. Most of us see young people creating songs individually and together using their tablets, computers, or other forms of technology. We have seen singer/songwriters perform songs they have composed and committed to memory. The idea that a piece of music must be written down is only one way of preserving that music for a future performance. Other forms of preservation include memorization, recordings, and computer software programs.

Including composition in the music curriculum requires forethought, particularly if the music class is a performance ensemble with a demanding concert schedule. The extent to which each class explores this creative practice will depend on its purpose and objectives and the teacher's experience and comfort level in teaching composition. For directors of ensembles, relinquishing control of the ensemble for student-directed work and learning activities is a major shift in the classroom dynamic. However, it is an opportunity to observe what students know and understand about music as they use their imaginations and intuition to create new music.

Scope and Sequence

In planning composition activities for students in any grade level, it may be helpful to center instruction on students' compositional capacities: intention, expressivity, and artistic craftsmanship (Kaschub & Smith, 2009). Intention is the impetus for composing, the desire to compose, often based on a feeling, memory, experience or extra-musical object, such as a poem. Expressivity is an individual's recognition of a connection between sound and feeling. Artistic crafts-manship is the technical skill that composers utilize in expressing their musical intentions. Each of these capacities is important for young composers to develop.

Intention. Another way to understand intention is to examine the generative processes of composing. How does one begin composing? How do musical ideas emerge from one's imagination? This can be one of the most exhilarating or frustrating stages of the composition process for many students, so it is particularly important for teachers to be aware of a variety of strategies for prompting musical thought. As Wilkins (2006) suggests in her book *Creative Music Composition: The Young Composer's Voice*, the use of programmatic (i.e., extra-musical) or abstract (i.e., specific musical elements) sources are common prompts for starting a composition.

Programmatic prompts exist in a variety of forms. For example, in an elementary classroom, children may be given storybooks and asked to compose pieces to accompany them. Similarly, a group of middle school choir students may find inspiration in a poem from their English class and want to create a melody with which to sing it. Or consider a high school orchestra class studying Mussorgsky's *Pictures at an Exhibition*. As part of this unit of study, students visit a local museum to find paintings that could serve as the prompt for their own compositions.

Alternatively, abstract musical ideas may serve as important starting points for composing. Students with some formal understanding of the elements of music may choose to begin their composition with a pre-set structure/form, a specific rhythm, melodic idea, etc. Consider a request from a flutist for a short composition that features fast rhythms, high trills, while featuring the full range of her instrument. Or a teacher providing strict parameters for a composition: Compose an eight-bar melody that utilizes the Dorian mode in triple time.

Improvisation can also serve as an important tool for gener-ating musical ideas. Instrumentalists, vocalists, and students using computers and other electronic equipment often find ideas through the act of performance. It is common knowledge that many popular musicians create songs by improvising with their band mates. They select the most salient musical ideas that emerge from this process and build upon them to create their songs. As part of the generative process, a representation of divergent thinking, teachers should provide time and space for improvisatory activity to occur.

Expressivity. A fundamental characteristic of musicianship is expressivity, one's recognition of the connection between sound and feeling. In music composition, this is experienced through the unique combination of musical elements (e.g., pitch and rhythm) with musical principles (e.g., sound versus silence) employed by the composer. Cultivating expressivity in music composition can be achieved by focusing students' attention on the interaction of these two categories.

Among the musical elements (i.e., pitch, rhythm, dynamics, form), timbre is one of the most important qualities for composers to consider. Students should have time to explore timbre and to think about the quality of sound(s) they wish to have in their compositions. Although all music classrooms have different inventories, having access to a wide variety of instruments, whether acoustic or electronic, provides a rich and varied tonal palette with which young composers can work. Learning about timbre can occur through listening to other composers' works and through play. Teachers should make a point to discuss timbre as an important component of a composition.

Musical principles are the ways in which composers manipulate the elements for expressive purposes. The ideas of motion/stasis, unity/variety, sound/silence, tension/release, stability/instability (MUSTS) are all identifiable musical principles (Kaschub & Smith, 2009). Focusing on one or more of these in a composition activity helps students to develop expressive musical products. For example, elementary students could be asked to create short compositions demonstrating dynamics through sound and silence. Similarly, high school band students could create small group compositions focusing on timbre, rhythm, consonance, and dissonance. As students become aware of their expressive capacities through manipulation of sound, they begin to discover their own compositional voice.

Artistic craftsmanship. Musicians steeped in the Western classical tradition can readily identify a work by Mozart, Hindemith, or Ravel because of the characteristic sound of the music. In these compositions, the composer's voice is clearly heard due to his artistic craftsmanship of organizing the musical elements and principles in unique ways. Novice composers have the least amount of experience with artistic craftsmanship, creating musical ideas and putting them together in an experimental fashion until it "sounds right." When they begin using conventional musical formulas (e.g., a particular harmonic progression or musical form) and stylistic characteristics in their compositions, these composers demonstrate a developing sense of craftsmanship. Through continued study and practice, advanced composers are capable of innovating beyond conventional forms to create musical works that are unique. They understand how to manipulate the elements of music in ways that reflect awareness of established musical norms and styles while creating new ones (Kaschub & Smith, 2009).

Helping students to develop their artistic craftsmanship through composing leads to greater clarity of their musical ideas and their overall understanding of music. Learning how the elements of music can work with one another, how to orchestrate various timbres, how to create musical phrases ending in cadences, how to compose an accompanying harmony to a melody, are all examples of developing artistic craftsmanship. This dynamic interaction of divergent and convergent thinking helps students in cultivating and focusing their creativity, lending a different experiential perspective to developing musicianship than solely performing music.

There are many ways in which to cultivate students' artistic craftsmanship. Listening to recordings and discussing composers' approaches to working with the musical elements and principles is often the easiest way. Teachers can point out or have students select musical characteristics heard on recordings and have them experiment with those in their own works. If students are proficient readers of notation, they can analyze music scores for techniques to use in their works. Providing access to these resources and/or allowing students to access resources using their own technology (i.e., computers, smart phones, and tablets) promotes broader interaction and learning in a music culture and community.

Performance and Assessment

For composers of all ages and abilities, it is vitally important to hear their works performed. Performances of compositions will vary, based on curricular goals and the student's willingness to share his/her creation. They might include listening to a MIDI file version of their piece performed by a computer, a live performance by classmates during class, or formal performances at a school concert. Establishing performance dates provides the necessary endpoint in the composition process, resulting in a product to be shared and evaluated by others. In many cases, performances validate a composer's efforts and even in circumstances in which a composer is not satisfied, s/he learns about the evolution from process to product and what others think of the work.

Assessment of music composition should be both formative and summative. Teachers should provide feedback and assistance as students compose. Caution is important, however, because music teachers listen with adult ears that are well developed through years of musical training and study. Because students have not had the same amount of musical experience, their compositions may sound overly simple or lacking important musical elements. It is important for teachers to understand that composing is a developmental process and too much guidance and instruction can hinder or stifle the voice of the young composer (Kaschub & Smith, 2009). Another consideration to be made is if a composition should be assessed based on its performance, which may or may not be successful in realizing the composer's intentions. A poor performance may be reflective of factors such as limited rehearsal time and difficulty level, while the composition, preserved on paper, is sophisticated and well-written. Teachers and students should discuss how and to what extent the performance should factor in to the overall assessment.

Summative assessment takes place once a composition is finished. It can be conducted in a variety of ways, including asking students for self-assessment of their work, peer-assessment, teacher assessment, community assessment, and/or assessment by a professional composer. It is recommended that for summative assessments, a rubric be designed that takes into account the goals of the composition unit. One popular approach is to ask students for assistance in designing the rubric. Such an arrangement empowers them to set goals for their compositional outcomes and provides opportunities for self-learning and self-assessment. (Table 1 provides an example of what such a rubric might look like and what could be assessed. Each category can be further defined by the teacher and/or students, based on grade level and curricular goals.)

Criteria	3	2	1
Musical Elements	Composition contains all necessary musical elements	Composition contains many of the necessary musical elements	Composition lacks necessary music elements
Use of Musical Instruments	Composition demonstrates knowledge and appropriate use of musical elements	Composition demonstrates knowledge and appropriate use of musical elements, with a few exceptions	Composition demonstrates a lack of knowledge and appropriate use of musical elements
Use of Musical Principles	Composition demonstrates knowledge and appropriate use of musical principles	Composition demonstrates knowledge and appropriate use of musical elements, with a few exceptions	Composition demonstrates a lack of knowledge and appropriate use of musical principles
Mode of Preservation	Composition is preserved in an appropriate manner (i.e., aurally recorded, memorized, or written) for performance	Composition is preserved in an appropriate manner (i.e., aurally recorded, memorized, or written) for performance, but there are some challenges in remembering or reading what was created	Composition lacks a form of preservation for future performance
Performance	Composition is performed successfully, realizing the composer's or composers' intentions	Composition is performed successfully, but with some exceptions in realizing the composer's or composers' intentions	Composition is not performed successfully, lacking the several details in realizing the composer's or composers' intentions

Table 1: *Music Composition Grading Rubric*

Fitting Composition into the Curriculum

For many music teachers, music composition is an add-on to an already packed performance curriculum. Finding the time to implement a unit on composition and to achieve successful outcomes can be challenging. However, it is our belief that any amount of composition experience is preferable to none. Create a plan that works best for your program and keeps the enrichment and development of student musicianship as its focal point. Consider the following as you develop a unit:

1. Will the composition unit be a short-term or long-term project?
2. What are the intended outcomes for the project?
3. Will the students perform their compositions or have them performed?
4. What type of performance setting will it be?
5. When and where will students compose?
6. Will students work alone or with others?
7. Will the teacher provide specific parameters (e.g., what rhythms or pitches to use) based on developmental level?
8. How will students preserve their works? (e.g., recordings, notation, memorization, computer?)
9. How will the teacher encourage development of students' compositional capacities (i.e., intention, expression, and artistic craftsmanship)?
10. What type of assessments will the teacher use for each project?

Improvisation

Although often associated with the jazz idiom, improvisation is at the heart of many musical styles and traditions. It is a highly complex, multi-dimensional process of music creation involving a knowledge base, technical fluency, memory, and expertise. As a creative practice, it represents the highest level of human cognition in Benjamin Bloom's Revised Taxonomy (Anderson & Krathwohl,

2001). Composers such as Bach and Beethoven were known to be skilled improvisers. Yet, both the rise of the formal concert hall and the industrial era in the nineteenth century gradually put an end to concert improvisation (Nachmanovitch, 1990; Sarath, 2013). The division of labor fragmented musicians' roles in interpretive performance from the creative practices of composition and improvisation. Today, the structure of music schools further encourages the fragmentation of musicians' roles and music teachers often report feeling unprepared or lacking confidence in teaching improvisation after their undergraduate education.

Reflective of life, the act of improvisation is process-based and responsive in nature. Such a view of improvisation places it at the core of life rather than in the margins (Paton, p. 115). In this way, the act of improvisation should be a vital component of any music education. Consider the value of improvisation when it is viewed more broadly than an element of jazz, and more deeply than a component of curriculum standards. Improvising vocally and on instruments allows students the opportunity to be creative and expressive in a spontaneous manner unattainable through interpretive performance alone. The process of improvisation can be a fertile endeavor where students' inner voices and expressivity may be turned outward and musical development can thrive. The act of improvising music, framed by the teacher or student, and further stimulated by the musical ideas of others, can also be an important reflection of musical knowledge (Della Pietra & Campbell, p. 125).

Getting Started in Improvisation

Providing improvisational experiences involves frequent, well-planned activities that include a balance of freedom of choice and useful constraints. As with compositional experiences, the goal is to set up students for success using activities that are simple and include attainable goals. Volz (2005) describes how teachers must be careful not to overwhelm students:

As music teachers, we may inadvertently place our students who are learning to improvise on the equivalent of the Daytona 500. The musical variables are much too complex for success and often result in a number of audio accidents. Chord symbols, scales, patterns, licks, and style are all integral to advanced improvisation but too difficult for beginners who are trying to improvise for the first time. (p. 50)

The manner in which students are introduced to improvisation is critical. Musical improvisation requires a level of comfortability and safety on the part of the performer. Students in improvising roles must feel safe with the level of vulnerability necessary for their musical voice to be heard amongst the potential scrutiny of their peers and instructors. Music teachers should carefully consider how they may establish a trusting, safe classroom for any type of improvisation. This starts with the instructor modeling a willingness to improvise openly, effectively on several occasions before students are asked to participate themselves. Strengths and challenges presented by students' developmental stages and school culture should also be taken into account. Instructors may ask students to focus less on technique and more on where to put their thoughts. Specific considerations may include "intuition, listening, suspending judgment (of self and others), exploration, ensemble interaction (group awareness and equality) and the difference between process and product" (Goldstaub, 1996, p. 46). Teachers will also want to consider how the physical space, such as lighting and furniture may contribute to students overall comfortability in improvising.

Designing Improvisational Experiences

When designing improvisational experiences for students, it is helpful to break down the various roles improvisation can play in the music curriculum. What types of improvisation are most appropriate for certain students, learning spaces, educational outcomes, and programs? Campbell (2009) provides insight into these questions when describing three ways of viewing the role of improvisation:

"improvising to learn music," "learning to improvise music," and "improvising music to learn."

Improvising to learn music. "Improvising to learn music" is to incorporate improvisation within musical training. In the system of western European art music, this approach is a means to an end, the result of which is a developed musician with a more comprehensive sense of music. It is what teachers do when they design lessons and activities in improvisation as a part of the larger music curriculum. When improvising to learn music, activities can be integrated into any music curriculum at any skill level, and are best for students' musical development when presented regularly and with consistency. Improvisation activities can be structured around dimensions of music such as rhythm, texture, timbre, harmony, expression, and form as they are being explored in class or through repertoire. Activities can also be organized around technique, musical style, or mood. Improvisatory experiences may be used as an alternative to a warm-up, or as a way to encourage class or ensemble unity.

Agrell (2008) provides over 500 musical games that teachers may use to structure "improvising to learn music." Two of such games titled "Duet-eventually" and *"Entrainment"* borrow a term used in drum circles, meaning the tendency of players to fall into a synchronized beat. Students are instructed to begin playing percussion instruments at the same time—independently, with no set beat or pulse. The group or duo is asked to unite on a common beat. Agrell suggests musicians could begin this activity by facing away from each other, then gradually turning toward one another as entrainment sets in. An additional game titled "So What?" (Agrell, 2008) calls for players of any age or instrument to play a short musical passage, then a responding player improvises music that is as contrasting as possible. For instance, if the first passage is slow, soft, and mournful, the second player may respond with music that is frantic, loud, and wildly exuberant. For students with little improvisational experience, teachers may choose to give students prompt cards with musical or non-musical words to stimulate imagination.

These experiences allow students the chance to "play" with concepts that not only reinforce their learning, but provide fertile ground for musical flexibility, dexterity, and possibility. Music teachers are encouraged to use their contextual knowledge about students' developmental levels, strengths, and challenges to design meaningful and engaging improvisational experiences. Teachers should consider creating time for students to present their own games and activities to each other, as their musical imagination and curiosity are stimulated. To allow students a chance for musical expression within concepts that are often taught and tested by rote is to provide a window of opportunity for comprehension at a deep and personal level.

Learning to improvise music. *Learning to improvise music* is to learn within genres that are purposefully embedded in rich improvisatory material, such as jazz, solo interpolations in gospel choirs, various drumming traditions and bluegrass music on fiddle and banjo. Experiences in these types of traditions have an important place in the music education curriculum, both as a part of specialized ensembles based around such traditions and traditional ensembles such as band, choir, or orchestra.

Jazz improvisation. For many music educators, learning how to improvise is typically explored in a jazz setting, due to its cultural context as improvised music, popularity in many schools, as well as the amount of aural and notated materials available. The variety of styles (e.g., blues, Latin, swing) included in the jazz idiom provides a rich tapestry of cultural experiences for students with opportunities to add their personal voices through improvisation. Yet, it seems that far too often, music teachers allow only their best and most confident improvisers the opportunity to solo in performances. How will others learn to improvise and how does this improve the musicianship of the other members in the ensemble?

All students participating in a jazz ensemble should be encouraged to improvise in each rehearsal. I (Palmer) typically begin rehearsal with an open jam session featuring the solo section of one of the jazz charts we are rehearsing. Whether playing a backing track (recorded rhythm section) or having the rhythm section play, I ask all musicians to improvise in one of a variety of ways (i.e., collectively, trading fours, solo). This type of activity is preceded by an explanation of how to approach improvising over the particular chord progression, emphasizing chord tones and scales. I encourage my students to experiment with these "tonal tools" to find what mode of expression and sound reflects their personal voices. By making improvisation a regular activity for all musicians in the ensemble, each person learns to view it as a fundamental aspect of jazz where each person's voice is validated and heard.

For those who try, jazz improvisation is one of the most challenging forms of artistic creativity they will undertake as musicians. They will feel most comfortable approaching improvisation in an atmosphere that feels safe for taking risks and being vulnerable. Providing proper structural support to improvisation activities is important to building students' confidence in this practice. For example, having students improvise collectively using a particular scale provides the opportunity to experiment without the pressure of having to "sound good" in front of others. When all students are comfortable improvising collectively, the teacher can ask for small groups to improvise. This can then be pared down to a call and response or trading fours exercise between two players. As the musicians become accustomed to improvising regularly, their confidence and willingness to take risks will grow.

Finally, learning how to improvise in the jazz idiom demands the development of aural imitation ability, technical facility, and frequent practice. Regular listening to and playing along with jazz recordings is one of the best ways to develop these skills. In addition, improvising with others, particularly those with more advanced improvisation skills will heighten awareness and sensitivity to nuances of the practice. Over time, a knowledge base develops that serves as a fertile source for musical ideas and the technical prowess to realize them.

Improvising music to learn. *Improvising music to learn* is to create music, to learn more about oneself, others, and the world outside of music. Improvising in this context occurs when students spontaneously express themselves through rhythmic sounds and movements. Most often, young children express themselves in this way, and therefore opportunities for pre-primary and early elementary-age students to improvise openly in the music classroom are extremely valuable. An example of this is "Arioso" (Feierabend, 2006) where students are given the space and time to create songs on the spot using their voices. Such experiences in improvisation reinforce the importance of children's musical ideas and encourage them to use their voices to express themselves and learn about their environment.

> In the process, children improvise music to learn who they are, what their relationship may be with others, and how they may go about doing whatever it is they are doing—eating, bathing, dressing, playing with Legos and Lincoln Logs, skipping, swinging, and riding in cars. More than most people, it is children who quite regularly learn their world through the music they make. (Campbell, 2009, p. 121)

Performance and Assessment

While not all types of improvisation practiced in the music classroom are desirable for a stage performance with a formal audience, it is important for students of all ability levels to understand and experience the importance of the improvisation in live musical performance. Students should be formally prepared for such performances so they are confident in the form and structure of the experience. Just as teachers should set up their students for success in classroom improvisation activities, the detail and preparation of formal performances should be carefully considered as well. However, the considerations for improvisational performance are different than in the context of the classroom. Some questions that music teachers should consider are: How comfortable are students with this particular improvisational challenge? Have students practiced enough to be comfortable, yet still retain the flexibility to allow for spontaneity in the moment? How might the performance space contribute to/distract from performance? Do students understand the structure of the performance and what that means for beginning, ending, and taking turns? Are students prepared to adjust within the structure if "mistakes" are made? Are all students invited to improvise, not only those performing at a high level?

The assessment of creative activities is a difficult task. Various psychometric tests of creativity are available to measure students' divergent thinking abilities, but are not ideal when assessing curricular classroom activities designed by teachers and students. Improvisation can be assessed based on perceived effort, but this approach is problematic due to its inability to measure concrete objectives or musical development over time.

Ideally, improvisational assessment will happen in formative and summative manners, as with composition. In both forms of assessment, involving students in the process can be enriching. Discussions based on the assessment of improvisational performances help students develop musically by reflecting upon how they and others responded in the moment. When talking about improvisation, it is important to encourage students to understand the difference between descriptive and evaluative comments (Goldstaub, 1996). Students should be encouraged to first discuss descriptive elements such as pitch, rhythm, dynamics, texture and color.

Evaluative likes, dislikes, and personal preferences should be discussed separately, as students reflect on what descriptive elements lead them to their conclusions. A discussion session that separates these two types of comments encourages musical analysis, concentration and memory. When students are actively involved in formative assessment, they may develop rubrics for summative assessment in an informed manner.

Creativity throughout the Music Curriculum

Although creativity is most often associated with composition and improvisation, it may also be encouraged in activities throughout the music curriculum. With the understanding that creativity is the use of imagination for the production of original work, we propose components of every music curriculum include space for students to think and perform creatively. With this approach, the goal is to give students agency and power through the ability to guide musical decisions and express musical ideas. This section of the chapter will focus on creative approaches to interpretive performance and music listening.

How can music teachers encourage such an approach? To believe that interpretive performance and music listening may be creative endeavors is to adopt the assumption that the voices of all students are important. The ideas, visions, and imaginations of all students must be valued and accessed for the group to reach its creative potential. The often meritocratic structure of music classrooms and ensembles makes this type of equality potentially challenging. Musicians often vest power and attach worth to individuals according to playing or singing ability. Therefore, music educators must be aware of how they may work to value the musical and intellectual voices of all students, despite notions of perceived "talent." Instructors' attitudes and assumptions regarding student voice are critical, as ways in which they value or dismiss students' voices will be emulated throughout the group. As teachers who wish to honor all students, assumptions and beliefs about students should be examined often. To reflect the creative capacity of the entire ensemble, every student should have the ability to be heard, both musically and verbally.

Interpretive Performance

Creativity in interpretive performance is evident when one compares the performances of the same work by two different artists. For example, the performance of a Bach fugue by Glenn Gould has a different sound (i.e., interpretive approach) than when it is played by Andras Schiff. Each performance includes an authentic realization of the rhythms and pitches of the original score, but will have different non-syntactic nuances (e.g., dynamics, tempo and articulation). As such, each performance takes on a life of its own, sounding "original," representing the "voice" of each artist.

Interpretive performance in P–12 school contexts traditionally involve students performing previously composed works as a part of general music classes or traditional ensembles such as band, orchestra, and choir. A limited amount of student creativity and decision-making is often associated with participation in such groups. A portrait of typical interpretive performance involves a teacher-conductor figure leading students to gain the skills and knowledge required to play a piece "correctly" in terms of rhythms, pitches and stylistic idioms. Yet, interpretive performance experiences can involve students' creative decision-making abilities as well as serve as prompts for creative play with improvisation and composition.

Decision-making. Performing previously composed works involves limitations framed by musical notation. Within these parameters, however, there are a myriad of decisions that must guide performance. For example, just how loud is forte in this context? Who will sing the solo? What should members of the trumpet section envision in order to create a unified sound? How will the ensemble be situated on the stage? How long should the fermata last? Music teachers can allow for creativity in performance by giving students the chance to make these types of decisions in interpretive performance. Music teachers can encourage student creativity by thoughtfully considering the balance of decision-making. Which elements must be determined by the notation or teacher, and which are malleable, to be open for student imagination and creativity? Consider how different it feels as a student to perform in a group where you are allowed to actively contribute to decision-making rather than acting as a channel through which a predetermined notion of a musical product is passed. Through this manner of creative approach to interpretive performance, students can be empowered to develop and contribute their unique ideas to the good of the larger group. Though a concern could be that this type of creative approach might compromise the integrity of the musical "product", we believe it only strengthens it. Allowing students to make creative decisions in interpretive performance promotes their musical development and motivation, suggesting positive outcomes for both individuals and performing groups alike.

Creative prompts. Within the context of rehearsal or preparation for performance, creative prompts may be used as a way to promote musical development and understanding. These activities can be short, yet used to provide richness and depth to the understanding of the unique elements of a musical work by stimulating students' imaginations. Examples of such creative strategies are: students creating short compositions or improvisations in the style of a piece being studied and students composing or improvising alternative endings to musical sections or phrases. Students can play a composed musical passage in a different meter, style, or tonality. A band director could ask students to warm up for a piece in concert b-flat by asking them to improvise on the scale. A choir director could ask students to remove a section of a song and create a passage with an "opposite" feel. There are many ways in which students can be asked to tap into their creative possibilities while learning composed musical pieces.

Listening

Music listening is the foundation of all other musical activities and behaviors and is a personal, individually constructed process. Teachers often construct classroom music listening experiences, however, around the identification of "correct answers" such as dynamics or form, ignoring the fact that we all listen differently and uniquely (Kratus, 2014). Traditionally, listening experiences in classrooms are guided by an instructor asking students to hear elements of a piece in a very specific, pointed manner. In real life settings, however, listeners create their own uniquely personal experiences, situated within their own cultural and cognitive milieus (Kerchner, 2014). Kerchner challenges music teachers to consider that the cognitive processes involved in music listening lead to creative products. Because there is no direct access into listeners' minds, music teachers are forced to rely on external modes to gain access to the mental processes and creative products that come from listening experiences. She suggests exploring students' multisensory responses through talk-alouds, musical maps, and movement as behaviors that embody or "mirror" musical thinking.

When designing music listening experiences in the classroom, teachers should consider how they may allow students to create an external representation of their unique multisensory responses. Verbal prompts should allow for a multitude of correct answers, such as "when the music changes, name the first three dimensions you noticed" or "what do you hear as the most important instrument in this passage?" Music mapping, using iconic and contour representation, can guide students of all ages and abilities to express their creative listening in a way that is not limited by language or musical notation. Additionally, movement activities using props such as scarves or ribbons to respond to musical passages can provide students with a means of embodied expression. Careful consideration should be given to the introduction and organization of such activities, as props and materials can be a potential distraction and a hindrance to expression rather than an aid.

Kratus (2014) suggests listening experiences in the classroom should be designed as divergent activities, encouraging a range of responses based on students' creative listening experiences. Kratus suggests four concepts from the psychology of creativity fluency to guide musical listening: fluency (the ability to generate many responses), flexibility (the ability to generate a variety of responses), elaboration (the ability to enhance ideas through change), and originality (the ability to generate unique responses) may be helpful in crafting creative listening experiences. The directions below are examples of how these concepts can encourage listeners to develop divergent listening practices (Kratus, 2014):

- Fluency: As you listen to the music, make a list of at least five things that you hear, think of, or feel.
- Flexibility: As you listen to the music, write at least one thing you notice about the rhythm, one thing you notice about the timbre, and at least one image or story you imagine.
- Elaboration: When the music changes, write down at least two changes that you hear.

- Originality: As you listen to the music, write down at least one thing that you hear, think of, or feel that you think no one in the class will think of.

Assessment across the curriculum

The four concepts of fluency, flexibility, elaboration, and originality can be used to frame assessment in creativity across the curriculum. Summative and formative assessments framed around these concepts can give students and teachers a picture of creative development over time. Kratus (2014) suggests sequencing listening across multiple musical examples can allow students practice in divergent thinking and provide a way to measure creative listening. Kerchner (2014) provides music teachers with a variety of ways to assess responses to student listening, establishing the importance of goal-setting in teacher-student learning partnerships. She gives practical examples of how to set up and assess musical listening portfolios for students of all developmental stages. Based on her research, she gives detailed suggestions of how teachers may assess verbal, visual, or kinesthetic responses to music listening. Informal teacher observation checklists, rubrics, and student self-assessment forms are all encouraged in assessing students' responses to music (Kerchner, 2014).

Conclusion

Students' creative development hinges upon the guidance of music teachers who believe that all students can be creative. Instructors have the powerful ability to discourage or encourage creativity simply through their underlying attitudes and beliefs. "We block creativity by labeling it as unusual, extraordinary...we segregate it by establishing systems of star performers" (Nachmanovitch, 1990, p. 121). Rather, if the music curriculum is to value creativity as an integral part of musicianship, it will be viewed as something important for each student to cultivate, practice, and express. Creative activities within the broader music curriculum allow students the chance for a musical grounding not otherwise gained only through convergent forms of thinking and performing. "The ultimate aim of a musical education may be to give balance to 'our music' and 'their music,' to the old and the new in music, to what's notated and what's not, to traditions and their potential for change" (Campbell, 2009, p. 140). Reflecting this balance, when a part of a comprehensive music education, creativity can allow students to express the musical voice inside and reach a deeper realization of their musical potential.

References

Agrell, J. (2008). *Improvisation for classical musicians.* Chicago, IL: GIA Publications.

Campbell, P. S. (2009). Learning to improvise music, improvising to learn music. In G. Solis & B. Netti (Eds.), *Musical improvisation: Art, education and society* (pp. 119–142). Urbana: University of Illinois Press.

Anderson, L. W., & Krathwohl, D. R. (Eds.). (2001). A taxonomy for learning, teaching and assessing: A revision of Bloom's Taxonomy of educational objectives: Complete edition, New York : Longman.

Elliott, D. J. (1995). Music matters: *A new philosophy of music education* (Vol. 14). New York: Oxford university press.

Feierabend, J. M. (2000). *First steps in music for preschool and beyond.* Chicago, IL: GIA Publications.

Goldstaub, P. (1996). Opening the door to classroom improvisation. *Music Educators Journal, 82*(5), 45–51.

Kaschub, M., & Smith, J. (2009). *Minds on music: Composition for creative and critical thinking.* Lanham, Maryland: Rowman & Littlefield Education.

Kerchner, J. L. (2014). *Music across the senses: Listening, learning, and making meaning.* New York: Oxford University Press.

Kratus, J. (2014, April 11). *Music listening as "in the moment" creativity.*
    Presentation at National Association for Music Education
    Biennial Conference, St. Louis, Missouri.

Nachmanovitch, S. (1991). *Free play.* New York, NY: Tarcher.

Paton, R. (2011). *Lifemusic: Connecting people to time.* Wimborne, UK:
    Archive Publishing.

Sarath, E. W. (2002). Improvisation and curriculum reform. In R. Colwell
    & C. Richardson (Eds.), The new handbook of research on
    music teaching and learning (pp. 188–198). New York: Oxford.

Sarath, E. W. (2013). *Improvisation, Creativity, and Consciousness: Jazz as
    Integral Template for Music, Education, and Society.* SUNY Press.

Swanwick, K. (1994). *Musical knowledge: Intuition, analysis and music.*
    London: Routledge.

Volz, M. D. (2005). Improvisation begins with exploration. *Music
    Educators Journal, 92*(1), 50–53.

Webster, P. (2002). Creative thinking in music: Advancing a model. In T.
    Sullivan & L. Willingham (Eds.), *Creativity and music education*
    (pp. 16–34). Edmonton, Canada: Canadian Music Educators'
    Association.

Wilkins, M. L. (2006). *Creative music composition: the young composer's
    voice.* New York: Routledge.

CHAPTER 11

TEACHING MUSICAL EXPRESSION AND SENSITIVITY

Ryan Shaw

Michigan State University

Ah, expression! It's what the majority of musicians believe music to be. Yet, for some unknown reason, it's rarely talked about. (Vosskuhler, 2005, p.1).

Musical expression and sensitivity can be elusive and difficult to approach. Many music teachers seem at home determining the scope and sequence of rhythmic concepts or of the overall difficulty of repertoire. Many educators also seem to feel comfortable sequencing physical skills such as the development of two-hand independence in piano playing or the learning of new instrument fingerings. But the teaching of musical expression and sensitivity can sometimes be veiled in ambiguity. Few teaching methods explicitly address their development, and the popularly held notion of expressivity as a mysterious or intuitive "gift" can hinder the music teacher interested in thinking purposefully about these topics. How can music teachers think about and approach a topic that is so vital to musical communication yet so nebulous and vague?

In this chapter, I offer ideas for how to think about the teaching of musical expression and sensitivity. To be clear, *there is no single way to approach these musical constructs*. Teaching expression is a little bit like teaching love or friendship—everyone's conception of what it is and how it develops differs. But it is also hazardous to dismiss the idea that such subjective aspects of music can be taught, as this invites hit-or-miss instruction on these topics (or none at all). I first define what I mean by expression and sensitivity. I then offer lesson planning concepts, teaching strategies, and principles for assessing students.

Defining *Expression* and *Sensitivity*

Think about the words one sees used interchangeably with "musical expression." These include *musicality, artistry, feeling, aesthetic,* and *mood.* While it can be difficult to agree on a singular definition when the usage is so varied, many people would probably agree that musical expression *describes the way in which musical sound conveys meaning to a listener.* It is an active process of "doing" something, and for the purposes of this chapter, I will limit this "doing" to performing. Beyond this baseline definition, there is quite a bit of disagreement about the concept of expression. Is it the actual combination of sounds that is expressive on its own, or is the music expressive because of how it is performed and received? Put another way, does meaning reside in the harmonies and melodies or in how music conjures up experiences, memories, and other extra-musical associations? Is the expression *in the music, in the performance, or in the listener's perception*? Is it some combination of all three?

If this discussion seems like a trivial philosophical game, consider how one's views might shape music teaching. If you believe that musical expression is only in the sound, you may choose a very "technical" approach, encouraging students to manipulate their dynamics and tempo to achieve more expressivity. On the other hand, if you believe that musical expression is a function of the listener's experiences, you may take a more "holistic" approach, encouraging students to think of metaphor when shaping a musical phrase. If you acknowledge that expression is in both places—the piece of music and the person—you may borrow from several approaches.

If music expression involves conveying meaning through sound, then musical sensitivity can be thought of as *how someone receives the musical communication*. The more sensitive you are to different kinds of music, the more you may notice and be able to understand in the sound. A sensitive listener begins to hear musical characteristics much the same way as someone learning a language. What previously was nondescript or non-relatable comes into sharper focus through *heightened aesthetic awareness*. Though perhaps less controversial than musical expression, some have argued about sensitivity. Is musical sensitivity about perception of things like variations in pitch and volume? Does it depend on hearing musical characteristics like tension/release, or pattern grouping? Is sensitivity dependent on being acculturated to certain kinds of music?

As one thinks about the definitions of these words, it becomes clear they are really two parts of a single process. Expression is the extent to which one *conveys* musical meaning, and sensitivity is the extent to which one *receives* musical meaning. Some have even suggested that the most direct way to build someone's musical sensitivity is to him/her to be an expressive musician (Elliott, 1995). Of course the reverse may also be true: the more distinctly one perceives and understands musical elements, the more likely he/she may be able to express musical meaning through performance. Returning to the language learning analogy, this two-sided process is not unlike what happens in a language immersion context. As a visitor to a Spanish-speaking country hears more Spanish words and phrases (sensitivity), they become acutely attuned to the conventions of the language and are more likely to speak meaningfully (expression). At the same time, the more they speak Spanish (expression), the more they will develop an "ear" for the idiosyncrasies of the language (sensitivity).

If expression and sensitivity are two parts of a related process, it stands to reason that what a performer intends to express should be at least close to what is received by the listener. Researchers have used this approach widely by asking performers to express specific emotions, and then asking listeners to indicate what emotions they perceived. Not only has this extensive body of research shown that it is indeed possible for specific emotions to be communicated and received, researchers have also been able to tie certain expressive choices—referred to as "cues"—to specific emotions (Juslin, 2002). For example, "sadness" is often expressed through slow tempo, quiet volume, legato articulation, soft timbre, and other choices related to attack/decay and amount of variation in tempo (Juslin, 2002). When the intended cues overlap with the perception of the cues, there is a high degree of "matching." Over and over, research has suggested there are clear matches for many expressive cues and the emotions they indicate.

Planning for Expression/Sensitivity Instruction

Teachers who value expression and sensitivity must be purposeful about prioritizing and selecting goals and must then plan instruction to achieve these ends. Of course, this can be quite difficult in practice. Constraints include large class sizes, wide varieties of student ability, and uneven student-teacher contact time, all of which can mediate the way that these objectives are pursued. Planning for expressiveness/sensitivity also is complicated by the particularities of most music classrooms. By this, I mean that it is not logical (and probably not desirable) to teach expressive fundamentals as a separate month-long unit. As Conway mentions in Chapter 1, curricular approaches in music often necessitate the "spiraling" of concepts. In this sense, expressive concepts must be introduced and then approached on a recurring basis with the overarching goal of deepening understanding and application on each successive "trip around the spiral."

So what are some expressive goals and objectives? Parsing these out can feel somewhat artificial, since research has suggested that performers manipulate almost all available musical parameters to communicate intended ideas and emotions (Juslin, 2002). As a result, what teachers and students often desire is the cumulative effect of several (or all) of these at the same time. For example, an expressive performance of a melody may start with a purposefully meek, almost

inaudible sound that then warms through the use of vibrato, acceler-
ates and loudens to a high note, before slowing down and becoming
purposefully shrill and metallic. Expressivity is often complex, which
necessitates a variety of discrete and holistic teaching strategies. Some
specific objectives may include (but are not limited to) the ability to:

- Perform with desired dynamic (volume) contour
- Perform with desired tempo manipulation (e.g., accelerating,
  slowing, rubato)
- Manipulate articulations/accents to create desired perfor-
  mance "style"
- Perform with a desired tone/sound concept (e.g., beautiful,
  raspy, piercing)
- Vary the color/timbre of one's sound during performance
- Manipulate vibrato/straight tone during performance
- Manipulate physical presentation (e.g., use of facial expressions,
  body movements)

Obviously missing here are goals such as performing correct
pitches and rhythms, performing pitches and intervals in tune, and
maintaining a steady pulse. While these are absolutely essential to
enabling expressive performances, I omit them for the sake of clarity.
On the flip side of expression, one can brainstorm possible objectives
for musical sensitivity. These might include being receptive to all of the
above-mentioned expressive objectives and, as is the case with expressive performance goals, these are likely to be combined and spiraled.

Context is paramount in selecting expression/sensitivity goals.
Not all genres share the same conventions for expressivity. What may
be expressive in *bel canto* singing style may be almost the opposite of
what is emphasized in certain popular/folk genres. On the other hand,
there are "rules" that govern whether something is perceived as expressive within a given musical context. For example, in Classical era art
music (e.g., Mozart, Haydn), certain ways of grouping and accenting
notes will lead to an audience perceiving expression. At the same time,
slight differences in grouping or accenting will lead to an audience

perceiving something as nonsensical. In sum, there is (within genres and contexts) a fine line between expressive conventions and a performance that is perceived as full of errors or mistakes.

Because expression and sensitivity are somewhat context-specific and personal, teachers should develop goals *in conjunction with students*. Teachers rarely ask students what they want to learn, which can lead to teachers imposing goals that students do not share or understand. Inviting students to be part of the goal-setting process fosters ownership, empowers students to think for themselves, and encourages ambition, metacognition, and motivation. In terms of expression and sensitivity, teachers should solicit ideas about both the content and the approach of instruction. What do students want to know and be able to do? How do they want to develop this knowledge and skill set?

Teaching Strategies—Expression

Music researchers who have investigated the teaching of expression have discovered both a wide range of strategies and some commonalities across teachers. One of the interesting findings is that often the specific teaching strategy is not "effective" or "ineffective" in and of itself. In the hands of a convincing and passionate teacher, students tend to rate whatever strategy the teacher uses as influential and enjoyable (Woody, 2006). And while teachers may use certain strategies more or less than others, it is likely that a given educator will sample numerous strategies, even mixing the mode of instruction within a single lesson. Indeed, experienced music teachers often draw on a "bag of tricks," modifying and differentiating their instruction to meet the needs of their students.

General Aural Modeling

In this largely non-verbal strategy, a music teacher demonstrates an expressive concept through singing or playing. Verbal descriptions are not part of this strategy, though they may work well in tandem with modeling. In a sense, modeling can be viewed as a strategy to encourage expressivity *through* sensitivity. For this approach to be effective on its own, the student must aurally take in the teacher's performance, recognize the expressive parameters emphasized in the performance, and make a translation to his or her own performance. Because of the translation process, this can be thought of as a high-inference strategy in which the student must independently interpret the teacher's modeling.

Examples of this strategy may include performance without comment, or with a simple suggestion to listen. The teacher may also frame it explicitly as a model to discuss: "I'll perform that section now—listen for how I approach the phrasing." Finally, teachers could set up the model as a basis for a verbal answer from the student(s): "I'll perform the piece. Listen and tell me what you hear."

Teachers who prefer modeling expressive performance must be careful to remember the limitations of the strategy. As Woody (2006) noted: "Students cannot simply tape-record the model into their memories and then play it back. Preexisting musical knowledge, expectations, and preferences always influence—and sometimes interfere with—hearing and encoding a model" (p. 22). In other words, teachers who use modeling may need to combine it with other strategies or be conscious of meeting a student in "the middle," between the character of the teacher-modeled performance and the version they hear back from the student.

Modeling "Deadpan" vs. Expressive Exemplars

Under the umbrella of modeling, there are a number of potential choices. A teacher may choose purposefully to model "right" and "wrong" exemplars in close proximity. The "wrong" exemplar can either be "deadpan" (purposefully boring, drab, and unaffected) or what I call "counterintuitive" (gestures chosen at random or that go against written or unwritten conventions). Teachers who use this strategy often preface it with a verbal set-up, such as "I'll play this two ways—tell me which you prefer," or "I'll sing this two ways—one with very little expression, and one with more expression."

This strategy has an obvious basis in how humans learn. Human brains make sense of new stimuli and new information by categorization. Early on, these categorical schemas are unsophisticated. For example, a toddler who has a dog at home may learn to say "dog" whenever the canine passes by. But what does "dog" signify to that toddler? He or she may know that humans are not dogs, but beyond this distinction, the toddler can only learn "dog-ness" by introducing something that is similar to a dog, but not a dog. When the toddler first sees a cat, he/she will likely still say, "Dog." More "same/different" experiences must occur for this child to become attuned to identifying the distinct categories of "dogs" and "cats." The same is true of identifying and then producing expressive performances. Students can benefit from closely situated exemplars that differ in some important respect.

Physical Gesturing

Teachers frequently attempt to show or embody the music through physical gesturing. While common in ensembles, this strategy is not confined to a podium and need not require a baton. A crescendo may be shown through expanding or rising arm motions. Accents may be shown through jumping, leaning, or pushing. Harmonic tension and release (or cadential closure) can be shown in a number of ways through physical tension and release. A potential advantage of this strategy is that it can easily occur simultaneously with a student's performance. Because it is not based in sound, it stands a better chance of its impact not being obscured by the performance itself—that is, students can respond to the strategy while still performing. Furthermore, this strategy is also a potential "time saver," especially if a teacher wants to keep students engaged in uninterrupted music making as much as possible during a lesson period. In certain contexts, this can also easily be combined with aural modeling.

If this strategy sounds an awful lot like conducting, it's no accident. A conductor who speaks very little and still encourages expressive results is relying on gesturing to both "show" expressivity and to enable musicians to perform together. But even for elementary general music teachers, the upside to this strategy is its emphasis on active musicianship. A wise professor of mine once told me that the more a music teacher kept the flow of a lesson going without verbal interruption, the better the experience for students. To this professor, making this flow continuous meant using verbal gestures and aural modeling whenever possible, and only stopping to discuss the music as a last resort.

Verbal Instruction about Musical Parameters

When using this strategy, the teacher engages in discussion of specific, discrete musical parameters to influence the expressivity of the students' performance. This is a low-inference strategy, meaning the student does not have to infer or interpret much as he/she makes sense of the instruction. Examples abound: "I think that part is getting too loud too soon. Let's wait longer to start that crescendo." "I hear you really accentuating that syllable—is that what you want?" Whether taking the form of a question, a statement, or a direction, the common aspect is the direct, clear emphasis on a *specific musical parameter* (such as volume, accent, intonation).

Is this strategy only for beginning musicians or is it equally appropriate for experts? It certainly makes sense for beginners, who may need to think discretely before attending to a number of parameters at the same time (a more holistic experience). During my student-teaching semester, my co-operating teacher impressed upon me the necessity of being clear and specific with beginners. He told me that a beginning clarinet player needs to hear where to put his/her fingers and tongue and how to create an appropriate tone. This beginner should not be told that he/she should "make a note more of a light blue." In saying this, my co-operating teacher was arguing against inappropriate use of metaphors/imagery in favor of simplicity and clarity. In this spirit, I would urge the reader to consider this strategy—and all others discussed—as tools upon which to draw, and to be responsive to student needs and the demands of the context, regardless of the experience level of the student. After all, there is research that suggests specific verbal feedback can improve the expressiveness of even experienced performers (Juslin & Laukka, 2000).

Verbal Instruction Using Imagery and Metaphor

This strategy involves the teacher using vivid metaphors or images as a means of enabling the students' expressive performance. As is the case with aural modeling, this strategy requires a level of inference/interpretation—perhaps the most inference among all of the strategies discussed. Because of the high level of inference required, there is a much greater chance that the metaphor or image used will be subject to mediating factors involved with past experience. In other words, there is a greater chance of the instructional strategy getting "lost in translation." That being said, there is also a potentially high reward if the metaphor or imagery used connects in a rich, deep way with the student, enabling personal attachment and ownership to an expressive concept. Therefore, this strategy is "high risk, high reward."

There are subtle differences between metaphor and imagery in this context. For my purposes, metaphors are used holistically, and imagery is used more discretely. Examples of metaphors are as follows:

> I like to think of that crescendo as a vacation car trip. When you begin, you are filled with anticipation—I can't wait to get to Florida! But you're still so far away. As you get further south, you start to sense the changing weather. The air smells different. You shed your long-sleeved shirt and turn off the heat in the car. As you cross into Florida, you start to see palm trees—your anticipation is building and your heart is pounding until ... finally! You see the ocean. Can you treat the crescendo just like that?

That example is holistic in the sense that it uses an extended metaphor—a "road trip"—to stand in for all the discrete aspects that make a crescendo expressive (potentially including volume, air speed, tone, timbre). Here's another holistic metaphor example:

We have to treat this slow movement like we're putting a little baby down to sleep at night. Any quick motions, surprising noises, or disruptions to the quiet, peaceful mood we're creating—we'll wake the baby. At the end of the piece, as the last note fades *al niente*—down to nothing—it's just like you're creeping out of the room once the baby is asleep.

Clearly, this metaphor is subject to interpretation and requires inference. After all, what if students have never been on such a road trip? What if putting a baby to sleep means nothing to them? Therefore, thoughtful choices about the chosen metaphors are crucial. And as Woody (2006) reminded us about modeling, teachers may need to "unpack" these holistic metaphors into more discrete parts. If a metaphor does not seem to connect with a student, it may be time to turn to the previous strategy—clearly addressing musical parameters. It may also be true that metaphors "prime" students to be more receptive to other strategies. Some writers have suggested that this is the key to their effectiveness—that they put the student into an affective state that makes him/her more sensitive to aural modeling (Davidson, 1989).

For the purposes of this discussion, using imagery means comparing expressive concepts to sensory experiences. For example, a teacher may say, "Can you make those staccato notes more like a rooster pecking (or ping pong balls bouncing, or popcorn popping, or grains of rice)?" A teacher might also say, "Can your airstream be steady like the water coming out of a fire hose?" The possibilities are endless, but the common feature here is that these examples are more discrete than the metaphors above. They reference a single expressive concept. As with metaphor, there is still translation required on the part of the student. After all, "popcorn popping" may mean different things to different students. If one needs proof of these differing interpretations, simply ask a group of students for an image to describe staccato—the range of responses will be enlightening.

Verbal Instruction Using Emotions/Moods

Another possibility that is closely related to using extended metaphors is to suggest emotions or moods. These can range from simple descriptors of a section of music ("Can you make that more sad?") to more extended descriptions ("Play with the thoughtfulness and patience of an old man looking back on his life."). These moods may be directly related to the piece's background. As an example, a teacher whose students are studying Wagner's *Trauersinfonie* might be asked to think about losing a loved one. Obviously, these extended mood descriptions resemble aspects of the metaphors discussed above. One key difference, however, is that the emotion/mood strategy addresses how to feel (or how to make the audience feel) when performing. The metaphors, by contrast, address how to treat certain aspects of the music. It's a small but important distinction to make as one thinks through a desired strategy.

Asking students to "feel" an emotion brings up an interesting question: can the performer's emotional state help them to be more expressive? People disagree on this, with some acknowledging the benefits of purposefully getting into an emotional state, and some suggesting that this is at best a recipe for distraction. Ultimately, it may depend on the situation and the student. If a performer needs to execute a passage of music that is fast and frantic, requiring extensive technique and control, it probably does not help (and may hurt) to "feel" frenzied. In other situations, the failure to put oneself in a certain frame of mind may cause a performance to feel mechanical or unaffected.

General Teaching Strategies—Sensitivity

Increasing musical sensitivity has been a goal of music education for many years. In fact, one could say it was the primary goal of music teaching, especially at the elementary level, from around 1970 to the mid-1990s. Influential texts such as Bennett Reimer's *A Philosophy of Music Education* (1970) argued for the value of *aesthetic education*. In aesthetic education, students become attuned to the beauty of music (or any art form) through exposure to great works. They develop sensitivity and become sophisticated judges of quality through expert guidance from a teacher. While this aim of music education has gone somewhat out of style in favor of more active music making, the contributions of the movement remain very influential.

Teaching strategies aimed at developing sensitivity to musical expression are numerous. In general, they are based on the assumption that music listening—separate from other activities—is the primary mode of encouraging sensitivity. As mentioned above, it is possible to include instruction aimed at sensitivity simultaneous with instruction aimed at expression. Because expression and sensitivity are two sides of the same process, teaching for expression can develop sensitivity (and vice versa). But in this section, I focus specifically on *music listening strategies* separate from performance. For the purposes of this discussion, I follow Kratus's (2014) lead, breaking these listening strategies into two categories of listening: *convergent* listening and *divergent* listening.

Convergent Listening

In a convergent task, there is one right answer. Therefore, in a convergent listening strategy, teachers draw students' attention to specific musical concepts such as tempo, texture, form, range, cadences, dynamics, and timbre to name a few. Students are asked to listen for specific things, and the convergent nature of the task intentionally limits the focus of the listening and the range of acceptable responses: "What instrument is playing at the beginning of the piece?" "How many times does the rhythmic motive repeat?"

This strategy can be used both with beginners and with students who are more familiar with a variety of musics. For beginners, this strategy may help to "cut through the noise" of a multi-faceted musical example. Just as with a room full of multiple conversations, a musical example may seem too "busy" or incomprehensible to a novice listener. Focusing convergently on single aspects can direct the ear toward a characteristic with the goal that musical aspects begin to stand out more and more distinctly upon repeated listenings. For more experienced students, convergent listening still can be used to focus on specific musical characteristics. For example, advanced students in a jazz choir can benefit from focusing on a famous artist's timing, treatment of a motive, or practice of "quoting" from another tune.

While the root of convergent listening is perception, perception alone does not translate into sensitivity. Perception involves merely recognizing characteristics of sound like duration and volume, and while perceiving these sound qualities is an important precursor to musical sensitivity, it does not guarantee that one can understand the factors that make sound distinguishable as music. As an example, a morse code operator can be (and must be) highly perceptive of duration of sounds. But musical sensitivity means going beyond perception of those durations to understanding the duration in a musical context (e.g., meter, metric modulation, melodic augmentation). Therefore, in convergent listening strategies, teachers must be careful to choose questions/prompts that attend to musical details in musical contexts.

Divergent Listening

While there is always a place for convergent listening strategies and activities, Kratus (2014) urges teachers to take students beyond "single right answer" listening. In divergent listening activities, there are multiple ways to respond and multiple acceptable responses. Students are asked to take ownership for their listening and must also infer more, since there is less scaffolding provided (i.e., what to listen for). Examples of divergent questions/prompts include "Identify and discuss the three most interesting features of this singer's tone," "In what ways does the composer's choice of rondo form affect the way you experience this piece of music?" "Discuss three ways this musician changes the articulation of the main melody."

Divergent listening can be thought of as working in tandem with convergent listening, as well as a strategy to encourage different kinds of listening from convergent strategies. If the two strategies are thought of as working in tandem, one can sequence early lessons to focus on predominantly convergent listening tasks, and then design divergent listening tasks that cover the same content. In this way, the students are given structure and scaffolding (convergent) and must then demonstrate a "working knowledge" and ownership of musical characteristics (divergent).

Divergent listening is about more than just providing open-ended ways to demonstrate technical sensitivity. As Kratus (2014) points out, most people do not listen to music for pleasure with the goal of identifying the meter, key, and form. Instead, many people listen to music because of how it makes them feel. From the casual radio listener to the serious connoisseur, this brand of musical sensitivity includes the ability to relate to and make personal sense of the feel of the music. Encouraging this kind of sensitivity is less straightforward than encouraging sensitivity through focus on hearing discrete musical characteristics and changes, but is no less worthy of a goal. Divergent listening strategies, therefore, should focus on holistic listening as well as technical listening. Questions of this sort might read: "How does this piece of music make you feel?" "What do you picture when you hear this piece—why?" "Describe how the music changes character at measure 25."

No matter the selected sensitivity strategy, it is important to remember that students are already making sophisticated musical judgments at a young age. Students as young as 6 years old are consistent in classifying music as "happy or sad" or "excited or calm" (Kratus, 1993), and children can differentiate between musical styles at the age of 3 or 4 (Marshall & Shibazaki, 2011). In other words, certain activities and strategies aimed at developing sensitivity may be a waste of time for students. It therefore becomes crucial for teachers to assess students' developmental capabilities and keep them in mind as they design instruction.

Assessment of Musical Expression and Sensitivity

As mentioned, a dominant feature of elementary general music in the second half of the 20th century was a focus on developing aesthetic sensitivity. As a result, a significant amount of intellectual energy went into designing tests to assess students' abilities. Most of these tests, such as Herbert Wing's *Tests of Musical Ability and Appreciation*, the *Gaston Test of Musicality*, and the *California Tests of Aesthetic Judgments in Music* are no longer in use. However, Edwin Gordon's *Music Aptitude Profile* (1965, updated 1995) is still a popular means of providing researched, standardized measures of sensitivity. The test is intended for students in grades 5–12 (ages 9–17) and includes sections on phrasing, balance, and style. In the phrasing section, students listen to two versions of the same string instrument melody performed with different dynamic contrasts, rubato, tone quality, and/or intonation choices. Students are asked to choose which of the two they prefer. In the balance section, students select which of two phrase endings better complements the beginning of the phrase. Finally, in the style section, students hear the same melody played at two different tempi and select the one they prefer.

Because the *Music Aptitude Profile* is meant to be a test of innate potential and not achievement, its uses in a classroom context are limited. It can and ideally should provide information that a teacher can use to differentiate instruction based on students' strengths and weaknesses. It should not, however, be used to assess achievement levels in a particular course. The administration time for this test is also an issue: the full battery of subtests takes approximately 3.5 hours, making it all but prohibitive in most classrooms.

Most assessments of expression and sensitivity are designed by music teachers in the contexts of their instructional settings. The form and specifics of assessments will obviously vary widely based on student ability, curricula, and a host of other factors. While a complete discussion of how to create "good" assessments is beyond the scope of this chapter, there are several guiding principles that may be helpful to consider when designing such assessments:

1. *Assessments should be based on the desired long-term "take away."* What do you hope students can express in their

performance as a result of your teaching? What do you hope students perceive and understand in the expressive performances of others? Basing assessments on these long-term considerations may seem obvious, but often other factors such as tradition or logistics end up unduly governing the choice of assessments. Teachers should also pay constant attention to how instruction in specific and discrete aspects of expression results in an overall "ownership" of expression.

2. *Assessments should provide descriptive feedback on skill and knowledge to both the teacher and the student.* Assessments in which the results are only reduced to a number in the teacher's grade book are of little use to students' learning. When appropriate, students deserve helpful information that allows them to make sense of their growth (this may not always be necessary in early elementary experiences). This is especially true in terms of assessing expression because of the large amount of possible musical parameters. Rating scales and rubrics provide a good format for recording specific feedback.

3. *Assessments should occur in authentic contexts of performing, creating, or responding—not done via a proxy.* Students should demonstrate their expressiveness by playing or singing, not by answering questions about expressiveness. Similarly, students should demonstrate their ability to hear and understand expressive features of music in the context of actual music listening, rather than writing abstractly about sensitivity.

4. *Assessments should provide multiple ways to demonstrate one's abilities.* Whenever possible, students should be provided with multiple ways to demonstrate what they know and can do. Differentiating an assessment can allow students to demonstrate achievement *where they are*, and the choice of a single assessment, while easier to administer than multiple forms, can unnecessarily privilege certain students over others. For example, it may be more inclusive to allow students to choose individually a portion of a piece of music to perform

expressively, rather than to dictate the same portion for all students. Similarly, some students may be able to demonstrate listening skills via discussion (or voice recording) in a more sophisticated way than in a short-answer writing sample.

5. *Assessments of sensitivity should include convergent questions and divergent questions.* Assessing the convergent (single correct answer) aspects of sensitivity is fairly straightforward and can be approached in a number of ways. But how do you assess when every answer could be (and should be) different? In these cases, a teacher must find a way to assess on criteria related to the students' thoughtfulness rather than content.

Rating Scales (Expression)

Figures 1 and 2 below give examples of rating scales that can be used to assess expressivity. In both figures, the rating scale is *continuous,*

5	Dynamic contrasts are used effectively in accordance with the natural rise and fall of the melodic line.
4	All dynamic markings are observed.
3	Student observes most of the dynamic markings and creates some contrast.
2	Few dynamic markings are attempted and little contrast is created.
1	All pitches are played at the same volume.

Figure 1: *Sample analytical rating scale for dynamic contrast*

5	Performance uses dynamic contrast to accentuate melodic line, and creates interest through articulation style and purposeful use of vibrato.
4	Student observes dynamic markings, articulation markings, and uses some vibrato to create interest.
3	Performance engages the listener through its uses of articulation variety and dynamic contrasts.
2	Correctly performed articulations add some variety to performance.
1	Performance is monotone and creates little or no interest.

Figure 2: *Sample holistic rating scale for expression*

meaning that to achieve a higher rating, the student must first achieve at the lower levels of the scale. In other words, a "1" describes the lowest level of achievement and each higher level assumes that the student has achieved at the lower levels in addition to the highest level achieved. This is contrast to *additive* rating scales, in which single points are awarded for achievement (e.g., "uses dynamic contrasts," "varies tempo appropriately") and totaled up to provide a score. In general, continuous rating scales tend to provide more useful information and do a more statistically sound job of measuring achievement.

There are clear differences in the amount of information covered in figures 1 and 2. Figure 1 presents an *analytical* rating scale, meaning that it is focused on a single dimension of expressivity. Figure 2, by contrast, presents a sample *holistic* rating scale: it includes several dimensions of expressive performance. Both types of rubrics are useful. Analytical rubrics can provide more specific information, while holistic rubrics can help students see the bigger picture of how different dimensions influence an overall performance. In deciding which to use, logistics also may be a determining factor to some extent: designing four or five analytical rating scales may be unrealistic or too cumbersome, making a single holistic rating scale the preferred choice. But since every assessment need not cover all skills, an educator could teach toward holistic performance but assess narrowly using different analytical rating scales (focused on use of vibrato, manipulation of timbre, etc.) at different points in the semester or year.

In certain contexts such as private or small group instruction, teachers' verbal comments can serve the same function as rating scales, at least in terms of providing feedback. Rating scales, however, have multiple benefits. These scales allow teachers to make their assessments more valid across a large group of students. They also form a tangible record of the assessment, which can be helpful in a number of ways. This potentially gives students something to reference, allows students to self-assess in an organized manner, and helps with assigning grades and discussing progress with parents.

Selected Response, Constructed Response, and Performance Items (Sensitivity)

There are a number of written options to assess students' sensitivity to musical expression. Multiple-choice questions, also known as selected response, have the benefit of easy scoring and quick feedback. But good questions are difficult to construct and the questions do not easily assess complex knowledge. Short answer/short essay, also known as constructed response, can assess higher-order thinking skills but have tradeoffs with the amount of time it takes for students to write their answers and for teachers to score responses. Performance tasks in this context refer to *extended written responses* that include a broad range of content (across multiple content standards) and are designed to assess what selected response and constructed response items cannot. This terminology is borrowed from the most recent Common Core consortium tests, but can be confusing, since music educators often use the same words to refer to actual musical performance.

A full guide to writing effective items in each of these categories is beyond the scope of this chapter. In general, choice of assessment should be guided by the nature of the skill or knowledge to be demonstrated. As mentioned above, this means that authentic contexts should rule the day: musical expression cannot be authentically assessed by any means other than direct performance. Therefore, students should demonstrate their expressive abilities by performing and receiving verbal or written feedback. In the same way, assessment of students' sensitivity should be situated authentically around *actual music listening*. In other words, there is more validity in students listening to their own performance or the performance of others and using any number of response formats (selected response, constructed response, performance task) than there is in asking context-less questions about crescendos.

As mentioned above, students also should have options when presenting their knowledge and skills. Students should be encouraged, when appropriate, to select music individually from among several options to perform for an assessment. Similarly, there often is value in having students select both the questions they wish to answer and the manner in which they want to discuss their knowledge/opinions. Creating a spoken word piece, a blog, a podcast, a video—these options are no less valid than writing a traditional paragraph. These are all meaningful ways of assessing the content of the work.

Sample Lesson Plan Activities

Thus far, I have tried to define some important terms, explore some important debates around expression and sensitivity, and discuss some teaching and assessment strategies. On pages 260 and 261, I put a variety of these ideas into sample lesson plan activities. These lesson plans are not in any way meant to act as "ready-made" templates or scripts for music teaching, but should be considered samples of how these elements might co-exist in a sample class period.

For each activity, several strategies are listed alongside a few other notes on anticipating interactions that occur during teaching. A growing body of research suggests experienced teachers value a lesson plan as a *mental organizer* rather than as an actual step-by-step plan. Experienced teachers also value flexibly-designed instruction, and the flexibility to respond to student needs is enabled by having multiple activities to achieve goals, and by having multiple strategies within selected activities. Just as an improviser uses a musical theme as a jumping off point for experimentation, veteran educators make "in-flight decisions" to guide lessons. This approach to lesson planning values the professionalism of teachers as responsive, reflective practitioners. Lesson plan 1 offers activities for an elementary general music class, and lesson plan 2 is based on a high school orchestra class.

Conclusion

Having recently attended three live performances, I have been reminded of the power of musical communication. Concert one featured a guitar-playing folk singer/songwriter in a historic theatre. Concert two highlighted a jazz saxophonist leading a quintet in a basement of a New York City club. And concert three featured a collegiate wind ensemble at a conference for music educators. In all three

Sample Lesson Plan Activities: Elementary General Music Class

Lesson objectives:
- Students will listen to and identify (through movement) tension and release in a crescendo.
- Students will perform a chant with a crescendo.

Activity: *As students walk in to the room, "Also Sprach Zarathustra" (by Richard Strauss) is playing. Students sit in a circle and listen to piece. Students are given scarves, using them to show the growing volume and throwing them at the climactic moment.*	**Notes:** *Students' prior experience? Students may have heard this piece before in popular media (commercials). As far as skill/knowledge, students have experienced volume changes, but have not labeled it as a crescendo.* **Anticipated issues (difficulty, "emergent moments")?** *Because the crescendo in this piece lasts a long time, and occurs without an obvious underlying pulse, students may lose track of the climactic moment. Also, students may want to discuss when they've heard this music before (TV, movies, etc.).*
Multiple strategies: • Add movement (stand up and show crescendo in body). • Teacher is aural model, students imitate with voice. • Teacher verbally describes the growing tension. • Imagery: teacher asks students to picture sun rising and bursting through.	**Assessment:** *Observation of students' responses (checking whether students demonstrate gradual crescendo in their movement, whether they can demonstrate the climax).*
Activity: *Students sing a chant called "Rocketship"[1] and do body percussion. They experience the crescendo, tension, and release. Students add rocketship motions.*	**Notes:** *Students' prior experience? Most students are probably familiar with a rocketship taking off, but not necessarily everyone will have the same level of confidence with interpreting this.* **Anticipated issues (difficulty, "emergent moments")?** *The compound meter may present problems (when adding body percussion) with respect to the performance of the crescendo. Also, depending on comfort with the chant, students may be ready to conceptualize the decrescendo that occurs after the climax.*
Multiple strategies: • Modify movement: take a prop for a rocketship ride around the room (locomotor). • Modeling: teacher models both with and without a crescendo. • Metaphor: teachers asks students to imagine being in a rocketship about to take off.	**Assessment:** *Use analytical rating scale to assess students' ability to demonstrate gradual crescendo with their voice. Also, informally assess through observation their ability to demonstrate crescendo through movement, and their ability to perform body percussion beats.*

---

[1] Piece by Rebecca Frezza; available at www.bigtruckmusic.com/rrrlyrics6.html

Sample Lesson Plan Activities: High School Orchestra

Lesson objectives:
- Students will identify features of a performance that affect expression.
- Students will evaluate the effectiveness of a performance, defending choices with details.
- Students will incorporate expressive elements into a group performance.

Activity: *Students listen to three different recordings of Rachmaninoff's "Vocalise"[2] and compare expressive features through group discussion. Students also pick the version that they consider most effective and say why*	**Notes:** *Students' prior experience? Students have likely not heard this piece, but will be somewhat familiar with the style through previous listening/performance in orchestra class.* **Anticipated issues (difficulty, "emergent moments")?** *Pulse/rubato may be difficult to discern; students may have difficulty raising hands to indicate when they hear certain aspects of the piece. Also, students may not be skilled at using specific vocabulary in group discussion (this may require scaffolding or clarifying).*
Multiple strategies: • Ask students to tap along with pulse (to experience rubato). • Convergent questions: ask them to close their eyes and raise hands when they hear certain features (vibrato, crescendo, rallentando). • Divergent questions: ask them what emotions are expressed in various performances. • Pair-share: with a partner, students select the most effective example, then "share out" with the full orchestra.	**Assessment:** *Monitor students' responses to the full group discussion; monitor pair/share activity for participation. Also, observation of hand-raising to assess whether predominance of class is hearing expressive features.*
Activity: *Orchestra performs Rachmaninoff's "Vocalise," and alters performance based on expressive features discussed in aforementioned activity.*	**Notes:** *Students' prior experience? Students are growing more familiar with the piece's expressive possibilities based on the activity above, but may not be used to drastically altering a group performance.* **Anticipated issues (difficulty, "emergent moments")?** *There is bound to be difficulty associated with execution of expressive concepts, as well as difficulty agreeing as a class on the "best" interpretation.*
Multiple strategies: • Group exploration: perform with and without a given expressive feature (vibrato, rubato). • Recording: record ensemble and listen back to see progress. • Singing: demonstrate intentions with singing before playing.	**Assessment:** *Self-assessment of group performance through holistic rating scale (each student uses rating scale to give the orchestra a score on their effective use of expressive features in performance).*

---

[2] See album titled "Rachmaninoff – Vocalise," RCA Records (2000) for multiple versions.

settings, the performers did something that made my jaw drop; did something that made me want to leap out of my seat and move with the music; did something that put a lump in my throat and almost brought tears to my eyes. I saw some of the same reactions in the people sitting around me, too. It was difficult in the moment to put my finger on what exactly was expressive, but the lack of clarity did not diminish the power of the experience.

Though isolating what is expressive can be harder than identifying a problem with rhythm or pitch, this difficulty should not be an excuse for avoiding instruction in expression and sensitivity. Researchers and music teachers have made important strides in clarifying how expression/sensitivity may work. By devoting time and energy to choosing specific goals, fulfilling instructional strategies, and thoughtful assessments, teachers can help students to embrace their musicianship more fully.

References

Davidson, L. (1989) Observing a yang ch'in lesson: Learning by modeling and metaphor. *Journal of Aesthetic Education, 23*, 85–99.

Elliott, D. (1995). Music matters: *A new philosophy of music education.* New York: Oxford University Press.

Juslin, P. N. (2002). Emotional communication. In R. Parncutt & G. McPherson (Eds.), *Science and psychology of music performance: Creative strategies for teaching and learning* (pp. 219–236). Cary, NC: Oxford University Press.

Juslin, P. N., & Laukka, P. (2000). Improving emotional communication in music performance through cognitive feedback. *Musicae Scientiae*, 4, 151–183.

Kratus, J. (1993). A developmental study of children's interpretation of emotion in music. *Psychology of Music, 21*, 3–19.

Kratus, J. (2014, January 17). *Teaching music listening as a creative activity.* Presentation at the Michigan Music Conference, Grand Rapids, Michigan.

Labuta, J. A., & Smith, D. A. (1997). *Music education: Historical contexts and perspectives.* Upper Saddle River, NJ: Prentice Hall.

Marshall, N. A., & Shibazaki, K. (2011). Two studies of musical style sensitivity with children in early years. *Music Education Research, 13*(2), 227–240.

Reimer, B. (1970). *A philosophy of music education.* Englewood Cliffs, N.J.: Prentice-Hall.

Vosskuhler, B. (2005). Musical expression and ways to teach it. *Music Staff: Teacher Lounge, 24,* 1–4.

Woody, R. H. (2006). The effect of various instructional conditions on expressive music performance. *Journal of Research in Music Education, 54*(1), 21–36. doi:10.1177/002242940605400103

CHAPTER 12

HELPING STUDENTS DEVELOP MUSIC LITERACY

Heather Nelson Shouldice
Eastern Michigan University

Most music educators would agree that helping students develop music literacy should be a primary outcome of music education in schools. This is evidenced by the fact that most K–12 music curricula include a music literacy component. But what exactly do we mean when we say "music literacy?" For many, music literacy likely implies the ability to read music notation. However, we might broaden our concept of music literacy by considering the idea of literacy in terms of language. Rather than focusing on a narrow view of language literacy as simply the ability to read and write, the United Nations Educational, Scientific, and Cultural Organization (2004) advocates a broader view:

> Literacy is the ability to identify, understand, interpret, create, communicate and compute, using printed and written materials associated with varying contexts. Literacy involves a continuum of learning in enabling individuals to achieve their goals, to develop their knowledge and potential, and to participate fully in their community and wider society. (p. 13)

This definition of literacy focuses not on the mere decoding of printed material into language sounds but the larger goal of understanding by bringing meaning to printed materials and using them as a tool for communication, both sending and receiving. We might apply this definition to music literacy as follows:

> [Music] literacy is the ability to identify, understand, inter-
> pret, create, communicate and compute [musically], using
> printed and written [music notation] materials associated
> with varying [musical] contexts. [Music] literacy involves a
> continuum of learning in enabling individuals to achieve their
> [musical] goals, to develop their [musical] knowledge and
> potential, and to participate fully in their [musical] commu-
> nity and wider society.

This broader conception of music literacy implies that, although the ability to read and write music notation is indeed a component of being musically literate, it is not an end in and of itself. Developing the ability to read and write music notation should serve as a tool for students to achieve the larger goal of participating independently and meaningfully in musical activities in real-life contexts. When an individual is able to use music notation to interact with music in this way, we can say that he or she is musically literate.

Another misunderstanding about music literacy is that of what constitutes the ability to "read" music notation. We would not say that a child could read written language just because he has the ability to name the letters he sees on the page, and yet reading music notation is often misunderstood in this way. Some music educators confuse music reading with the mere ability to name rhythmic time values or pitch letters on the staff and to push the appropriate keys on an instrument. However, as Feierabend (1997) argues, "the ability to identify 'letter names' (i.e., F, A, C, E, D-sharp, B-flat, etc.) when looking at notes on a staff and to press the corresponding keys on an instrument should not be confused with true music literacy" (p. 34). Similarly, according to Mills and McPherson (2006), "the functional literacy of knowing where to put your fingers [on an instrument] after having seen a visual cue on a score, represents a very limited form of comprehending staff notation" (p. 158).

In order for students to use music notation in a meaningful way, they should be able to read and write notation in a meaningful way—with comprehension of the musical sounds that the notation represents. Gordon (2004) refers to this as notational audiation. According to Gordon, notational audiation is the ability "to hear the musical sound and give contextual meaning to what you see in music notation before you perform it, before someone else performs it, or as you write it" (p. 5). Although Gordon coined the term *notational audiation*, the concept existed long before he did so. Kodály referred to music literacy as "being able to look at a musical score and think sound" (Choksy, 1981, p. 15). In addition to Kodály and Gordon, others who have advocated a similar approach include Guido d'Arezzo, Lowell Mason, Sarah Glover, and John Curwen (Feierabend, 1997).

Although many would agree that developing the ability to look at music notation and know how it sounds without needing to consult an instrument is ideal, some might consider it a lofty or even unattainable goal for students in school music programs. After all, many music teachers may not have developed this skill until college-level sight-singing and aural skills classes (if at all)! However, the key to understanding the ways in which we might help our students to read and write music notation with comprehension of musical sound lies in the idea of sequential music learning.

Sequential Music Learning: Music/Language Parallels

In order to understand the idea of sequential music learning, it is helpful to consider the sequence through which we learn our native language, as it has been theorized that music and language are learned through similar processes (Bluestine, 2000; Burton, 2011; Feierabend, 1997, 2001; Gordon, 1999, 2004). After we are born, we begin learning our native language through listening. We are immersed in the language environment around us and gradually become acculturated to the sounds of our native language. During this time, we develop our "listening vocabulary" for language (Gordon, 1999). Once we have heard a sufficient amount of language and are developmentally ready, we begin to imitate the language sounds we hear. This imitation begins through babble—experimenting and playing with language sounds—and eventually progresses to the ability to imitate whole words with accuracy. At this point, we are developing our "speaking vocabulary" (Gordon, 1999). As we develop our listening and speaking vocabularies, we begin to think in language and develop the ability to interact with others through conversation, during which we are able to understand the words and thoughts of others and spontaneously respond with thoughts and words of our own. These "conversational interactions" help us develop a larger, richer vocabulary and further develop our readiness for learning to read and write language with comprehension (Burton, 2011). Only after years of developing our listening, speaking, and conversing vocabularies do we begin developing our reading and writing vocabularies, and when we do, we learn to read and write in tandem rather than learning one before progressing to the other. Finally, after we have developed a sufficient reading and writing vocabulary, we begin to learn the theoretical explanations for our language system, such as the parts of speech or the etymology of words.

Now imagine if we were expected to learn our native language by being taught how to read, write, and understand the theory of how language is constructed before we could even speak the language. Few would fail to see the absurdity in this, and yet it is often the very way we expect students to learn music! According to Mills and McPherson (2006),

> Many children exposed to a traditional approach to music instruction begin learning notation from the very first lessons. Without being taught to link the sound of musical patterns with notated patterns these children will probably learn to rely on sight vocabulary, going directly from the visual image to the fingering required to execute this on their instrument. This is what Schleuter (1997) refers to as "button pushers" to whom notation indicates only what fingers to push down. (p. 160)

If we compare this process to the one through which we learn language, we can see that the traditional way in which many *teach* music—by expecting students to begin learning to sing or play an instrument via music notation and theory—does not fit the sequence through which we learn music—by first developing our musical listening, speaking (i.e., singing, chanting, moving, playing), and conversing (i.e., improvising) vocabularies. By providing our students with extensive experiences and opportunities to develop these first three vocabularies—listening, making music by ear, and improvising—*before* expecting them to read and write music notation, we will better prepare them to read and write music notation with comprehension of the musical sounds the notation represents rather than training them to be musical "button pushers." As Bartholomew (1995) emphasizes, before we teach our students music notation, we must help them develop the ability to think in and be responsive to musical sounds and to "develop an inner sensing of the musical relationships present in sequences and combinations of sounds" (p. 7).

Readiness for Music Notation

Before a student is ready to read and write music notation with understanding, she must first develop what Campbell (1989) refers to as musical "orality," the transmission of music through the aural/oral mode. This ability to understand and make music through listening and doing provides readiness for learning to understand and make music through notation. The ability to sing in tune and the ability to move rhythmically are fundamental aspects of this readiness (Feierabend, 1997; Gordon, 2004).

Children first begin developing musical orality through immersion in a rich musical environment (Burton, 2011). Music teachers should provide students with extensive opportunities to be immersed in music and should model singing, chanting, and moving for their students. Teachers should also encourage students to begin imitating the musical sounds that they hear and acknowledge students' attempts at music making regardless of their accuracy. (See Chapter Fourteen on preschool curriculum for further details on guiding children's early musical development.)

Once students are beginning to use their singing voices and move to a steady beat with some degree of accuracy, teachers should encourage further development of their tonal and rhythmic skills. Encouraging students to audiate and sing the tonal "home" of music (i.e., resting tone, tonic, first scale degree) and audiate and move to layers of beat (i.e., macrobeat/microbeat, beat/subdivisions) will help them develop a sense musical context, which will not only improve tonal and rhythmic accuracy but will aid in students' ability to make sense of notation in the future (Henry, 2008; Hodges & Nolker, 2011; Killian & Henry, 2005; McCabe, 2006). Just as children develop a vocabulary of words, teachers should also guide students in developing a vocabulary of tonal patterns and rhythm patterns that they can sing and chant (or play by ear). Once students have developed these basic tonal and rhythm skills, tonal and rhythm solfege/syllable systems can be added, which will help students better understand and retain musical sounds as well as serve as a tool for notation reading and writing in the future (Azzara, 1993; Cassidy, 1993; Colley, 1987; Hodges & Nolker, 2011; Jacobi, 2012; Shehan, 1987). In addition to singing and chanting patterns with these syllables, students might learn to use the syllables as a tool for labeling aspects of music such as meter, tonality, and function. It is also helpful to guide students in developing the ability to apply those syllables to patterns given on a neutral syllable or played on an instrument as further readiness for applying the syllables to music notation. (See Chapter Seven on movement, Chapter Eight on rhythm, and Chapter Nine on singing and tonal audiation for more information on developing children's skills in these areas.)

Finally, it is important that students develop their ability to create and improvise music by ear before learning music notation. "With the achievement of improvisational dexterity, children are ready to *bring* meaning to music notation" (Gordon, 2011, p. 6). The opportunity to tap into their listening and "speaking" vocabularies and spontaneously create their own music will help students take ownership of their music making and their ability to express their own musical thoughts rather than relying on music notation as the sole determining factor of how music should go. Additionally, evidence suggests that experiences with improvisation may actually improve music reading skills (Azzara, 1993; Bradley, 1974; McPherson, 1995). (For more on creative music making, see Chapter Ten.)

Developing Emergent Music Literacy: Informal Experiences with Notation

As students develop their skills in listening, singing, chanting, moving, and improvising, another way in which we can help prepare them for formal music reading/writing instruction is by providing informal experiences with music notation. The purpose of these informal notation experiences is to expose children to music notation before expecting them to read and write it with understanding and correctness. During these informal notation experiences, students can begin to explore notation and develop awareness of important aspects of notation that will better prepare them for formal instruction in notation reading and writing later.

The rationale for providing students with these early informal notation experiences is rooted in a language concept known as emergent literacy. According to Whitehurst and Lonigan (1998), "emergent literacy consists of the skills, knowledge, and attitudes that are presumed to be developmental precursors to conventional forms of reading and writing" (p. 849). Existing research suggests that "children who arrive to beginning reading instruction with well-developed emergent literacy skills progress more rapidly and readily than those who do not have these skills" (Justice, Bowles, & Skibbe, 2006, p. 224). Just as we can better prepare children to learn to read and write by developing their emergent literacy skills, we can better prepare children to read and write music notation by developing their emergent *music* literacy skills through informal experiences with music notation.

Awareness that music notation has meaning. One of the most basic components of emergent literacy is developing the awareness that print carries meaning and is used to communicate (Tompkins, 1997). Parents encourage this awareness when they read to their children, and literacy teachers help students develop this awareness by modeling the reading and writing of print through activities such as read-alouds. By hearing written words spoken aloud (and even seeing the parent or teacher point to each word as it is read), children begin to understand that the visual symbols they see are connected to the sounds that they hear. Additionally, literacy teachers model the conversion of spoken words to written language; for example, the teacher might lead the students in creating a simple story, which he/she writes on the board as they do so (Pinnell & Fountas, 2011).

Similarly, one of the most basic understandings about music notation that a child can develop is the fact that notation represents musical sounds. As music teachers we can help students begin to develop this awareness simply by modeling the reading and writing of music notation for students. Similar to a read-aloud, you might do a "sing-aloud," during which you show the notation for a song and perform it for the students (or invite them to sing if it is a familiar song) and point along in the notation. You might also lead the students in creating a song and notating it on the board for them as you do so.

In a study of music acquisition in an early childhood music class, Burton (2011) incorporated "rhythm and melody books" she had created. Each displayed the notation for a short melody or rhythmic chant, which she would perform for the class while they looked at the page. Burton also modeled writing familiar rhythm patterns that the children had heard, echoed, and improvised with in class and would even invite the students to dictate patterns for her to write. Burton referred to these as "musical messages," reinforcing the idea that the notated symbols the children saw were intended to communicate musical meaning.

General concepts about music notation. A second aspect of emergent literacy involves developing a sense of general concepts about prints, also referred to as "print knowledge" (Justice et al., 2006; Pinnell & Fountas, 2011; Tompkins, 1997). This includes three main types of concepts about print: 1) book-orientation concepts, 2) directional concepts, and 3) letter and word concepts (Tompkins, 1997). Book-orientation concepts encompass such understandings as how to hold a book, how to turn the pages, and the difference between print and pictures. Directional concepts include left-right directionality—the awareness that we read from left to right—as well as top-bottom directionality. Letter and word concepts involve basic understandings about words and letters, such as the awareness that words are made up of letters, sentences are made up of words, and one printed word matches up with one spoken word.

In modeling the reading and writing of music notation for our students, we can call attention to similar basic concepts about music notation. Students can start to develop a sense of left-right and top-bottom directionality by watching the teacher point along in the notation for a familiar song while they sing it. Students can also exercise their understanding of these directional concepts by being invited to point along in the notation (albeit without an expectation of correctness). For example, Figure 12.1 shows an image that could be used as a handout to accompany the singing of the traditional song "Sally Go 'Round the Sun." The teacher might pass out a copy to each student (as well as displaying it on the board) and lead the students in informally pointing along to each line of the song while singing. (The pictures provide visual cues to aid the students in pointing to the appropriate line.) The teacher could extend this by pointing out (or leading students to discovering) that each line of the song sounds different, therefore each line of the song notation looks different.

Figure 12.1: *Song notation for "Sally Go 'Round the Sun."*

Similar activities can help students also develop their awareness of note and pattern concepts in music notation. While students are developing their vocabulary of tonal and rhythm patterns that they can sing and chant, the teacher can informally show students the notation for these patterns to develop their awareness that one pattern that they sing or chant is represented by one notated pattern. Similarly, by seeing the teacher point to each note of the pattern while singing or chanting it, students begin to develop a sense that each sound being sung or chanted corresponds with one note in the printed notation. For example, after learning to sing the traditional folk song "Love Somebody" and identifying the pattern *Do-Mi-So* (which is heard/sung three times in the song), you might show students the notation for that pattern through a visual aid like the one in Figure 12.2. After modeling singing and pointing to each pitch in the pattern, the teacher could model singing the song and pointing to the pattern each time it is sung/heard. Additionally, copies could be made for each student to point along. Another example would be to teach the students to sing a rhythmic ostinato (notated in Figure 12.3) as accompaniment for the traditional song "Donkeys Love Carrots" and then show the visual displayed in the figure while singing and pointing along.

Figure 12.2: *Pattern notation for "Love Somebody"*

Figure 12.3: *Ostinato notation for "Donkeys Love Carrots"*

Experimental reading and writing. As students develop their awareness of print concepts, they also begin to experiment with reading and writing. This can include pretending to read and write (Whitehurst & Lonigan, 1998), in which "the child knows that marks on paper represent meaningful language, and he wants to try it for himself" (Pinnell & Fountas, 2011, p. 148). During this time, children "play at" reading and writing and typically make "gross approxima-tions" of letters and words (Pinnell & Fountas, 2011). Activities for guiding and encouraging students' experimental reading and writing include "shared reading" or "interactive writing" (during which the teacher reads or writes most of the text but invites children to join in on familiar words) as well as creating "literacy play centers" that provide opportunities for students to experiment with reading and writing (Pinnell & Fountas, 2011; Tompkins, 1997).

Similarly, music teachers can encourage students to engage in experimental reading and writing with music notation. This can be as simple as providing opportunities for students to pretend to read and write notation or informally try to copy symbols they see in nota-tion. These "gross approximations" of music reading and writing are valuable opportunities for children to "play at" music notation. In her study of early childhood music acquisition, Burton (2011) encouraged her students to try reading and writing "musical messages" similar to the ones she had modeled. She found that, although the children may not have used "traditional conventions of musical print," at least one student often was able to "read" his messages with fluency, demonstrating that "he had conceptualized what he had put into print" (p. 25). Music literacy play centers could provide students with further opportunities to experiment with reading and writing music notation.

It is important to remember that there should be no expectation of correctness or immediate understanding when students are engaging in these informal music notation experiences, just as students are not expected to read and write language correctly while developing emergent literacy skills. The purpose of these informal music notation experiences is simply to expose students to notation and help them begin exploring notation so that their emergent music literacy skills can develop. These informal music notation experiences and resultant emergent music literacy skills form a necessary readiness for formal instruction in music notation.

Transitioning to Formal Music Notation Instruction

Once students can aurally sense and perform tonal and rhythmic context ("home" tone and layers of beat), are able to sing and chant tonal and rhythm patterns with accuracy, have some level of comfort with tonal and rhythm solfege/syllable systems, have had opportunities to create and improvise music, and have begun to develop emergent music literacy skills, they are ready to begin formal instruction in music notation. (See Jacobi, 2012 and Junda, 1994 for more on specific readinesses for preparing students to formally learn music notation.) Teachers can help their students learn music notation more effectively by considering three general guidelines: 1) sounds before theory, 2) familiar before unfamiliar, and 3) rote learning before inference learning.

When students begin formally learning to read and write music notation, they should initially do so by associating musical sounds to the notated symbols rather than learning theoretical knowledge about notation. Music theory concepts, such as letter-names of pitches on the staff or time-value names of notes, are important things for students to know eventually but are not necessary when students are initially learning to read and write notation. In fact, focusing on theoretical concepts can even hinder students' progress, as they easily can become "bogged down" and overwhelmed in trying to understand this superfluous information. Explaining or "talking about" notation should be preceded by focusing on the sounds that the symbols are intended to represent.

It is also important that students begin learning notation by associating it to musical content that is familiar to them, just as children begin reading and writing language through familiar words (Feierabend, 1997; Gordon, 2012; Jacobi, 2012; Mills & McPherson, 2006). According to Mills and McPherson (2006), this provides students "the opportunity to cross-check material they are reading [or writing] with material that they know, and to relate it within an aural system that they already understand" (p. 159). Learning the notation for musical sounds that students have already heard and performed allows them to focus solely on their newly developing reading and writing skills without being forced to learn new content as well (McPherson & Gabrielsson, 2002). Once students have developed sufficient skill in reading and writing familiar material, they will be better able to apply their notation reading and writing skills to unfamiliar material. Initially learning to associate notation to familiar musical examples also enables students to give meaning to the notation because they already have a sense of the sounds the notation represents, rather than trying to use the notation to decipher what the music should sound like. In this way, beginning to read and write notation through focusing on familiar sounds lays the foundation for the development of notational audiation—the ability to mentally hear the musical sounds represented in notation without having to consult an instrument.

Finally, we can encourage students' overall success with notation reading and writing by providing them with ample experiences to learn notation by rote before expecting them to make inferences. Many teachers present students with a few basic note values (such as quarter notes and eighth notes) and then expect students to be able to read ALL rhythms that use these note values. This scenario forces students to quickly assimilate these note values and immediately make inferences by applying their understanding to new combinations of rhythms. While some students are able to make this leap right away, many are left feeling overwhelmed and frustrated. Initially providing students with numerous opportunities to learn through rote imitation—a process Gordon (2012) calls "discrimination learning"—helps them develop the readiness to figure out new material independently—which Gordon refers to as "inference learning." When we initially present notation to students, we should model for them *how* to read and/or write familiar musical examples and have students repeat, recognize, and discriminate between them before we ask students to make inferences by reading and writing what they have not previously seen read/written and have not read/written yet themselves. Once students have had sufficient experiences in which the teacher shows them how to read and write by rote, they will be better equipped to apply their knowledge and skills in figuring out how to read and write new and/or unfamiliar musical examples.

Formal Music Notation Skills

When children begin learning to make sense of printed language material, they learn to read and write in tandem. According to Freire and Macedo (1987), "to read and write are inseparable phases of the same process" (p. 47). Similarly, students should not learn music notation through reading alone but in conjunction with writing because these are mutually reinforcing skills (Burton, 2011). Additionally, learning to write along with learning to read music notation helps students realize that notation not only represents sounds but that they have the power to use that notation to represent those sounds within any context and know how it will sound. Waller (2010) explains,

A beginning student who is given the opportunity to write out the very simple melody of "Hot Cross Buns" (or any other manageable melody she knows intimately from her childhood or other experience) learns not merely how to reproduce "Hot Cross Buns" but also that she has the power to visually represent the sound of the musical figure E-D-C (or mi-re-do), for whatever purpose she likes. Whether she then desires to write out (among other endless possibilities) a series of triplets like so: E-D-C E-D-C E-D-C E-D-C, or like so: E-E-E D-D-D C-C-C C-C-C, she knows exactly how those triplets will sound. She is already writing out original music without having to consult an instrument—a hallmark of full music literacy, yet one that is needlessly put off until advanced studies in theory or composition. (pp. 35–36)

Not only does writing reinforce reading (and vice versa) but it also enables students to create and notate new music using the material they have learned to read and write and to do so with notational audiation.

The next question to address is that of what students should begin to read and write. Many traditional approaches to music reading have students begin with learning individual pitches or durations, which they label with a letter or time-value name and practice reading (or writing) in an isolated fashion. However, this may lead students to read in a note-by-note manner, which research suggests is an inefficient means of music reading. Goolsby (1994) studied eye movement during music reading and found that the eyes of a less successful sight-reader tended to fixate on virtually every note while the eye movement of a more successful sight-reader suggested that he/she tended to process the notation in larger chunks. Similarly, Gromko (2004) found that students whose eyes tended to focus on larger structures or patterns were better sight-readers than those who tended to focus on individual figures. These findings suggest that, rather than teaching students to read in a note-by-note fashion, it may be more effective to help them learn to process music and music notation in "chunks" or patterns.

Experiencing instruction in reading and performing patterns seems to have a positive effect on students' music reading ability. Several researchers have found that students who had tonal pattern instruction were better sight-readers than students who had not had tonal pattern instruction (Grutzmacher, 1987; MacKnight, 1975; Reifinger, 2012). Similarly, Azzara (1993) found that students who learned tunes by ear, developed a vocabulary of solfege/syllables, and improvised tonal and rhythm patterns performed significantly better when performing prepared and sight-read etudes than students who did not have these experiences. As Hodges and Nolker (2011) point out, "Both basic and applied research support the important role that pattern recognition plays in successful music reading. Teachers should stress knowledge of musical patterns as opposed to note-by-note recognition" (p. 82). Thus, music teachers might prepare students to read more effectively by focusing on rhythm patterns and tonal patterns when beginning formal notation instruction.

Reading/writing rhythm patterns. Students can begin formally learning to read and write by associating notated symbols with the sounds of familiar rhythm patterns. In doing so, the teacher should not attempt to explain theoretical information about rhythm (such as note values, time-signatures, etc.) but should simply show the notation for a rhythmic pattern and perform it for the students, inviting them to read and perform it back. Once students have read several rhythms in this manner, the teacher can begin to mix them up, having the students recognize and read these familiar rhythms in new/unfamiliar orders. Students should also practice writing the notation for these familiar rhythms, first by copying and then by notating from memory. Teachers can challenge students to engage in a rudimentary form of rhythmic dictation by chanting or playing familiar rhythms for students to write without having the notation in front of them.

The use of a rhythm syllable system can assist students in learning to read and write rhythmic notation. Whereas researchers have found mixed results as to which particular syllable system may be most effective, the findings of numerous studies suggest that the use of *some* form of rhythm syllables can help students learn to read more effectively (Azzara, 1993; Colley, 1987; Hodges & Nolker, 2011; Shehan, 1987). In order to preserve sequential music learning by initially avoiding theoretical explanations of notation, some advocate the use of a system based on beat-function, such as the Froseth/Gordon or Takadimi system, rather than one based on time-values because beat-function systems are based on how we feel rhythm in the body whereas time-value systems relate to note durations and how they are symbolized. By using rhythm syllable systems such as these, the music teacher is able to introduce rhythmic notation in a way that focuses on the sounds of the notation rather than explaining theoretical information such as mathematical relationships of note values, thus facilitating the development notational audiation—the ability to convert symbols to sounds and vice versa. (For more on rhythm syllables, see Chapter Eight on rhythm.)

After students have had experiences reading and writing familiar rhythm patterns by rote (discrimination learning), they can begin to figure out how to read and write unfamiliar rhythm patterns (inference learning). This might involve familiar rhythmic figures/note-values being used in unfamiliar combinations or unfamiliar rhythmic figures/note-values that are incorporated with those that are familiar. In either case, the student uses what he or she learned at discrimination learning to make inferences about the unfamiliar. For this reason, providing students with many initial opportunities to read and write rhythms by rote will better enable them to figure out unfamiliar rhythmic material later.

In order to effectively scaffold the development of students' rhythm reading/writing skills, teachers should consider the content and difficulty level of the rhythm patterns and the order in which this notation is introduced to students. Table 12.1 outlines one possible sequence for introducing rhythm pattern content to students. In this sequence students would first learn to read and write rhythm patterns in both duple and triple meters that are comprised of only macrobeats and microbeats. Once students demonstrate a basic mastery of reading and writing patterns containing only macrobeats and microbeats, they could begin learning to read and write rhythm patterns that also include divisions, later adding in macrobeat rests, followed by elongations, and so on. Regardless of the exact sequence used, the teacher can help students continually build rhythm reading/writing skills over time by first introducing simpler rhythms and gradually adding in more complex rhythmic figures.

Rhythm Pattern Content	Examples in Duple Meter	Examples in Triple Meter
1. Macrobeats/ microbeats		
2. + Divisions		
3. + Macrobeat Rests		
4. + Elongations		

Table 12.1: *Sample Rhythm Pattern Content Sequence*

It is important that students learn to read in various meters and time signatures as soon as possible. Many teachers stay in one meter and time signature (e.g., duple meter written in 2/4 or 4/4) for weeks, months, or even years before switching to a new meter and/or time signature (e.g.,

3/4, 6/8, or 2/2), which makes transitioning to these new meters and time signatures all the more difficult because students may get "stuck" in that first meter/time signature. For example, many students begin rhythm notation by learning that a quarter note (in 2/4 or 4/4) always gets one beat, which often causes confusion and frustration when later learning time signatures in which this is not the case (2/2, 6/8, etc.). Instead, teachers might avoid the use of time-value names and early on begin introducing the concept of "enrhythmic" notation: that rhythm patterns can look different when noted in different measure signatures/ time signatures yet can still sound the same (Gordon, 2004). Table 12.2 provides examples of enrhythmic patterns in various meters and measure signatures/time signatures.

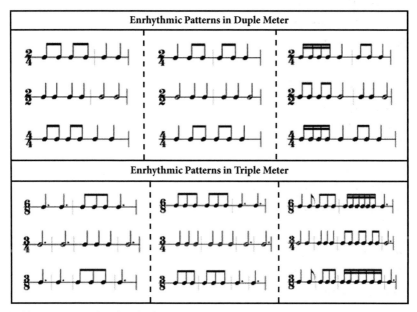

Table 12.2: *Examples of Enrhythmic Notation*

When introducing the concept of enrhythmic notation to students, you might show them that, just as the word "music" can be written with different symbols that mean the same thing, rhythms can be notated in different ways but still sound the same (see Figure 12.3). It should be noted that the use of a rhythm syllable system, rather than explaining the mathematical counting of note values, will more readily facilitate students' understanding of enrhythmic notation because it allows students to focus on sound rather than become confused by mathematical counting of note values. Introducing these various meters and time signatures early, as well as initially avoiding theoretical explanations and instead focusing on sound and movement, will help students become more flexible and fluent readers in the long run.

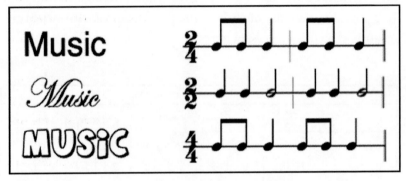

Figure 12.3: *Parallels between different print styles and enrhythmic notation.*

Reading/writing tonal patterns. Just as the use of a rhythm syllable system can aid students in learning to read rhythm notation, the use of a tonal solfege system can help students learn to read pitch notation more effectively (Azzara, 1993; Cassidy, 1993; Hodges & Nolker, 2011; Jacobi, 2012). In order to preserve sequential music learning by initially avoiding theoretical explanations of notation, some advocate the use of the movable-DO system with a LA-based minor because it is based on pitch relationships rather than on absolute pitch (as fixed-DO is) and does not require discussion of theory/scales (as DO-based minor does). (For more on tonal solfege, see Chapter Nine on singing and tonal audiation.)

If students have had the opportunity to build a vocabulary of tonal patterns that they can sing and improvise with and have developed some skill in using tonal solfege, they are ready to begin formally learning to read and write tonal patterns. One effective strategy to introduce tonal reading to students is the Kodály technique of the "hand staff" (Jacobi, 2012): turning the hand so that the palm faces you and the thumb points up, which makes the hand resemble the five lines of the staff. Choose a finger (or space between two fingers) to be *Do*, and model singing various tonal patterns while pointing to the appropriate fingers or spaces between, inviting students to echo. After singing several patterns, choose a different finger (or space between fingers) to call *Do* and repeat the activity. This helps students immediately understand that do can move, and they begin to sense pitch relationships around it. Once students understand the concept of the "hand staff," you can transition to the traditional staff by laying your hand across it so that they can see how the five lines are similar to your five fingers. After singing and pointing to several patterns in this manner, students likely will be ready to read using traditional pitch notation with note heads.

Students can then begin formally learning to read and write by associating notated symbols with the sounds of familiar tonal patterns. In doing so, the teacher should not attempt to explain theoretical information about pitch (such as half-steps/whole-steps, key signatures, etc.). Some refer to the key signature as a *DO-signature*, explaining that it indicates where *Do* is on the staff, and simply show the students where *Do* is on the staff for each particular DO-signature (without explaining what a sharp or flat does, etc.). After identifying where *Do* is on the staff, show the notation for a tonal pattern and perform it for the students, inviting them to read and perform it back. Once students have read several tonal patterns in this manner, the teacher can begin to mix them up, having the students recognize and read these familiar tonal patterns in new/unfamiliar orders. Students should also practice writing the notation for these familiar tonal patterns, first by copying and then by notating from memory. Teachers can challenge students to engage in a rudimentary form of pitch dictation by singing or playing familiar tonal patterns for students to write without having the notation in front of them.

After students have had experiences reading and writing familiar tonal patterns by rote (discrimination learning), they can begin to figure out how to read and write unfamiliar tonal patterns (inference learning). This might involve familiar pitches being used in unfamiliar combinations or unfamiliar pitches incorporated with those that are familiar. In either case, the student uses what he or she learned at discrimination learning to make inferences about the unfamiliar. For this reason, providing students with many initial opportunities to read and write tonal patterns by rote will better enable them to figure out unfamiliar tonal material later.

Just as teachers must be conscious of how they sequence rhythmic content when teaching rhythm pattern notation, teachers must also decide how they will scaffold the introduction of tonal content when teaching tonal pattern notation. The traditional approaches of Orff and Kodály structure students' tonal content learning around the pentatonic scale; in these approaches students first learn to read and write the interval *So-Mi*, and then other pitches are gradually added, beginning with *La*, then *Do*, and so on. More recently, Feierabend (2001) has advocated a different sequence through which pitches of the pentatonic scale are introduced in tonal patterns based on those he has found to regularly occur in traditional children's folksongs. In Feierabend's approach, students first learn tonal patterns comprised of the pitches *Do*, *Re*, and *Mi*, later adding in *So*, *La*, and other pitches one-by-one. Rather than focusing on individual pitches of the pentatonic scale, Gordon (2012) believes students should learn tonal patterns that are arpeggiations of harmonic functions, beginning with tonic and dominant patterns in major and minor and later adding in subdominant and other functions/patterns. Regardless of the sequence used to introduce tonal pattern content, it is important that students learn to read and write those patterns with a focus on how the patterns *sound* (rather than by talking *about* the notation, as in labeling letter names of pitches), which can be facilitated through the use of a solfege system.

It is also important that students learn to read in various tonalities and DO-signatures as soon as possible. Many teachers stay in one tonality and key signature (e.g., major tonality written in the key of C) for weeks, months, or even years before switching to a new tonality (minor, etc.) and/or key signature, which makes transitioning to these new tonalities and key signatures all the more difficult because students may get "stuck" in that first tonality/key signature. By introducing early on the idea that *Do* can be anywhere on the staff, as well as initially avoiding theoretical explanations and instead focusing on sound and pitch relationships, students will not assume that one particular line or space is always *Do*, helping them to become more flexible and fluent readers later.

Melodic reading/writing. When students have developed some basic skills in reading and writing tonal patterns and rhythm patterns, they will be ready to begin combining the two aspects in melodic notation. One basic way this can be done is to have students recognize familiar tonal or rhythm patterns within the context of song notation. For example, if students have aurally identified where the pattern *Do-Mi-So* occurs in the song "Love Somebody" and have learned to read the familiar pattern *Do-Mi-So* (in the appropriate DO-signature), they can identify where the notated pattern occurs in the song notation (e.g., by circling, as shown in Figure 12.4) and/or point to that pattern in the notation as they sing the song. This could also be turned into a writing activity by removing that pattern from the song notation and having students write the pattern in the spaces where it happens in the song.

Figure 12.4: *Identifying the pattern Do-Mi-So in song notation.*

After students are able to recognize, read, and write tonal and rhythm patterns within the context of song notation, they will be ready to begin combining tonal and rhythmic aspects into melodic reading. This can be done in three steps. First, have students read/chant the rhythm for the entire song with rhythm syllables. Then have them read/sing through the tonal patterns of the song on tonal solfege. Finally, take away solfege/syllables and have students read and perform the entire song (on a neutral syllable, such as *loo*). Once students have had practice reading familiar songs in this manner, they will be ready to try reading unfamiliar songs using the same process.

Students can practice and apply their melodic reading and writing skills through a variety of activities and exercises. In addition to ideas for pattern reading and writing games, Feierabend's (2001) *Conversational Solfege* series includes melodic pattern notation that the teacher can use to facilitate melodic reading and writing as well as a variety of worksheets in which students can practice notation writing, dictation, and even composing their own music. Jacobi (2012) gives an overview of notation activities for younger children, while Oare and Bernstorf (2010) provide a variety of strategies for notation practice that can be used with both younger and older students.

Music notation and older students. The strategies outlined in this chapter up to this point have assumed that students come to formal music notation instruction with considerable readiness experiences (including sense of tonal/rhythmic context, ability to sing/chant tonal/rhythm patterns, comfort with solfege/syllable systems, opportunities to create/improvise, and beginning emergent music literacy skills) that have enabled them to learn to read and write music notation with an awareness of the sounds that the notation represents. It is also assumed that these readiness experiences have been developed over multiple years. However, it is common for many older students, particularly those beginning in an ensemble, to lack this readiness yet still be expected to read and write notation, presenting a dilemma for the ensemble teacher.

One key factor in resolving this dilemma is communication between the ensemble teacher and the elementary general music teacher. By sharing with one another the content and skills covered in the curriculum in each setting as well as the manner in which those skills are developed, the elementary general music teacher and the ensemble teacher can gain an understanding of not only how the elementary teacher could most effectively prepare the student for learning in the ensemble setting but also how the ensemble teacher might best tap into and build on what has been learned at earlier grade levels. By communicating with one another their curricular goals and the ways in which these goals are reached, teachers can increase the likelihood that students will transition to the ensemble with the appropriate readiness.

If this solution does not prove to be an effective option, it becomes the responsibility of the ensemble teacher to provide students with remedial experiences that will help them gain the readiness for reading and writing music notation with notational audiation. First, the ensemble teacher can help students develop their musical "speaking" vocabularies by giving them opportunities to sing, chant, and move to music before introducing notation, which can include playing instruments by rote and/or by ear. While helping students develop a repertoire of songs and chants, the ensemble teacher can also help students develop a sense of tonal and rhythmic context and provide tonal and rhythm pattern instruction—first without and then with solfege/syllables—that will further develop students' musical "speaking" vocabularies. It is important that students be provided opportunities to utilize this vocabulary in musical *conversing*, i.e., creating/improvising. Once students have had these readiness experiences, the ensemble teacher can then proceed to the notation reading/writing activities described previously in this chapter. For more on providing these notation readiness experiences in an ensemble setting, see Weary (2012), Oare and Bernstorf (2010), Azzara (2005), Conway (2003), Martin (2005), Norman (2005), and Conway, Marshall, and Hartz (2014).

It is left to the discretion of the teacher to decide how much time to spend on these readiness activities before beginning formal notation instruction. It might be several weeks, several months, or even a large portion of an entire school year. For example, I know some band teachers who do not incorporate music notation until the second half of the school year, even performing the winter concert entirely without notation. Although this might seem time-consuming, it is time well-spent because students will be gaining the musical understanding and vocabulary that will enable them to read and write music notation with an understanding of musical sound and an awareness of the degree to which the sounds they produce match those indicated in the notation, thus helping them to reach true music literacy rather than becoming "'button pushers' to whom notation indicates only what fingers to push down" (Mills & McPherson, 2006, p. 160).

Assessment of Music Literacy Skills

In order to ensure that students are developing independent notation reading and writing skills, we must individually assess our students' mastery of these skills. However, this assessment should not happen in the form of worksheets, quizzes, or tests that simply ask students to identify the time-values of rhythms or pitch-letter names on the staff because this only assesses students' theoretical knowledge about notation. Figure 12.5 shows an example of such an assessment, which can be found on the website of the Conejo Valley Unified School District (n.d.). Because true music literacy involves the ability to read and write

Figure 12.5: *Example of notation assessment that is not skills-based.*

notation with a sense of how it sounds, we should assess students' notation *skills* in a way that gauges their ability to understand the relationship between sounds and symbols—by asking them to convert symbols into sounds (reading) or sounds into symbols (writing/dictation).

One basic way in which we might assess students' ability to convert symbols into sound would be to prompt individual students to read and perform tonal or rhythm patterns. For example, the teacher might display a collection of 8–10 patterns on the board and call out numbers of patterns for individual students to sing, chant, or play. Because patterns are short, all students can be assessed in a fairly quick and efficient manner. If the teacher felt it would take too long to get to all individuals in a single class period, this assessment could be broken up over several days. Additionally, alternating between having individuals or the whole class read the patterns can help keep all students engaged.

The teacher also needs to decide how he or she will measure student achievement on this type of task. One option would be a simple checklist in which the teacher indicates a yes/no judgment of whether the student correctly read the assigned pattern. A more informative option would be to develop a rating scale that could be used to measure each student's progress. For example, a rating scale for use in measuring students' ability to read and sing a tonal pattern might look like this:

> *4 = Student accurately reads the pattern, singing with correct pitches and solfege.*
>
> *3 = Student reads and sings the pattern with correct pitches but incorrect solfege.*
>
> *2 = Student reads and sings the pattern with correct solfege but incorrect pitches.*
>
> *1 = Student does not read or sing the pattern with accurate pitches or solfege.*

Using a rating scale such as this, the teacher can quickly measure and record the progress of each individual student and use this assessment data to inform future instruction.

Teachers can also assess students' ability to convert sounds into symbols through a task such as dictation. A simple way of doing this might be to sing or chant short patterns for students to notate; the teacher could perform these patterns with solfege/syllables or could make the task more challenging by performing on a neutral syllable (so that students must also apply the correct solfege/syllables in figuring out how to notate the pattern). It would not take long to have the class notate several patterns from dictation and turn in their notation for you to assess outside of class. Once students have had experiences writing tonal and/or rhythm patterns from dictation, you can challenge them with melodic dictation, requiring students to figure out both the rhythmic and tonal aspects of the example(s) as they notate the melody. In addition to helping ensure that students are understanding notation independently (as opposed to simply imitating others), assessing these snapshots of students' developing music reading or writing skills can provide the teacher with valuable guidance in planning future instruction.

Music Literacy: The Big Picture

In describing language literacy, Tompkins (1997) states, "literacy is a tool, a way to come to learn about the world and a means to participate more fully in society" (p. 6). Similarly, music literacy enables students to learn about the musical world and participate more fully in musical society. Helping students develop their music literacy skills, specifically the ability to read and write notation with an understanding of the sounds represented by the symbols, is not an easy task. However, it is a task of critical importance if we wish for our students to become independent music makers. Once students can read and write music notation with notational audiation, they have the power to represent music through notation, understand the sounds of music notated by others, and use notation to capture their own musical thoughts as well as communicate them to others. Only when students reach this point can we say that they are truly and fully musically literate, the result of which is that they are enabled and empowered to participate more fully in their musical community and wider musical society.

References

Azzara, C. D. (1993). Audiation-based improvisation techniques and elementary instrumental students' music achievement. *Journal of Research in Music Education, 41*(4), 328–342.

Azzara, C. D. (2005). Understanding music through improvisation. In M. Runfola & C. C. Taggart (Eds.), *The development and practical application of Music Learning Theory* (pp. 399–424). Chicago: GIA Publications, Inc.

Bartholomew, D. (1995). Sounds before symbols: What does phenomenology have to say? *Philosophy of Music Education Review, 3*(1), 3–9.

Bluestine, E. (2000). *The ways children learn music.* Chicago: GIA Publications, Inc.

Bradley, I. (1974). Development of aural and visual perception through creative processes. *Journal of Research in Music Education, 22*(3), 234–240.

Burton, S. L. (2011). Language acquisition: A lens on music learning. In S. L. Burton & C. C. Taggart (Eds.), *Learning from young children: Research in early childhood music* (pp. 23–38). Lanham, MD: Rowman & Littlefield Education.

Campbell, P. S. (1989). Orality, literacy and music's creative potential: A comparative approach. *Bulletin of the Council for Research in Music Education, 101,* 30–40.

Cassidy, J. W. (1993). Effects of various sightsinging strategies on nonmusic majors' pitch accuracy. *Journal of Research in Music Education, 41*(4), 293–302.

Choksy, L. (1981). *The Kodály context.* Englewood Cliffs, NJ: Prentice-Hall.

Colley, B. (1987). A comparison of syllabic methods for improving rhythm literacy. *Journal of Research in Music Education, 35*(4), 221–235.

Conejo Valley Unified School District (n.d.). *Treble clef note reading packet*. Retrieved from http://www.conejousd.org/Portals/36/TEACHERS/apayne/Treble%20Clef%20Note%20Reading%20Packet.pdf

Conway, C. (2003). Good rhythm and intonation from day one in beginning instrumental music. *Music Educators Journal, 89*(5), 2–31.

Conway, C., Marshall, H., & Hartz, B. (2014). Movement Instruction to Facilitate Beat Competency in Instrumental Music. *Music Educators Journal, 100*(3), 61–66. doi:10.1177/0027432113515929

Feierabend, J. (1997). Developing music literacy: An aural approach for an aural art. *Early Childhood Connections, 3*(4), 33–38.

Feierabend, J. M. (2001). *Conversational Solfege*. Chicago: GIA Publications, Inc.

Freire, P., & Macedo, D. (1987). *Literacy: Reading the word and the world*. Routledge.

Goolsby, T. W. (1994). Profiles of processing: Eye movements during sightreading. *Music Perception, 12*(1), 97–123.

Gordon, E. E. (1999). All about audiation and music aptitudes. *Music Educators Journal, 86*(2), 41–44.

Gordon, E. E. (2004). *The aural/visual experience of music literacy: Reading and writing music notation*. Chicago: GIA Publications, Inc.

Gordon, E. E. (2011). Early childhood music abuse: Misdeeds and neglect. *Visions of Research in Music Education, 17*. Retrieved from Retrieved from http://www--usr.rider.edu/vrme~/

Gordon, E. E. (2012). *Learning sequences in music: A contemporary music learning theory*. Chicago: GIA Publications, Inc.

Gromko, J. E. (2004). Predictors of music sight-reading ability in high school wind players. *Journal of Research in Music Education, 52*(1), 6–15.

Grutzmacher, P. A. (1987). The effect of tonal pattern training on the aural perception, reading recognition, and melodic sight-reading achievement of first-year instrumental music students. *Journal of Research in Music Education, 35*(3), 171–181.

Henry, M. L. (2008). The use of specific practice and performance strategies in sight-singing instruction. *Update: Applications of Research in Music Education, 26,* 11–16.

Hodges, D. A., & Nolker, D. B. (2011). The acquisition of music reading skills. In R. Colwell & P. R. Webster (Eds.), *MENC Handbook of Research on Music Learning: Volume 2: Applications* (pp. 61–91). New York, NY: Oxford University Press.

Jacobi, B. S. (2012). Kodály, literacy, and the brain: Preparing young music students to read pitch on the staff. *General Music Today, 25*(2), 11–18.

Junda, M. E. (1994). Developing readiness for music reading. *Music Educators Journal, 81*(2), 37–41.

Justice, L. M., Bowles, R. P., & Skibbe, L. E. (2006). Measuring preschool attainment of print-concept knowledge: A study of typical and at-risk 3- to 5-year-old children using item response theory. *Language, Speech, and Hearing Services in Schools, 37,* 224–235.

Killian, J. N., & Henry, M. L. (2005). A comparison of successful and unsuccessful strategies in individual sight-singing preparation and performance. *Journal of Research in Music Education, 53*(1), 51–65.

Landis, B., & Carder, P. (1990a). The Kodály approach. In P. Carder (Ed.), *The eclectic curriculum in American music education: Contributions of Dalcroze, Kodály, and Orff* (2nd ed., pp. 55–64). Reston, VA: Music Educators National Conference.

Landis, B., & Carder, P. (1990b). The Orff approach. In P. Carder (Ed.), *The eclectic curriculum in American music education: Contributions of Dalcroze, Kodály, and Orff* (2nd ed., pp. 109–136). Reston, VA: Music Educators National Conference.

MacKnight, C. B. (1975). Music reading ability of beginning wind instrumentalists after melodic instruction. *Journal of Research in Music Education, 23*(1), 23–34.

Martin, M. F. (2005). Music Learning Theory and beginning string instruction. In M. Runfola & C. C. Taggart (Eds.), *The development and practical application of Music Learning Theory* (pp. 225–250). Chicago: GIA Publications, Inc.

McCabe, M. C. (2006). The effect of movement-based instruction on the beginning instrumentalist's ability to sight-read rhythm patterns. *Missouri Journal of Research in Music Education, 43,* 24–38.

McPherson, G. E. (1995). The assessment of musical performance: Development and validation of five new measures. *Psychology of Music, 23,* 142–161.

McPherson, G. E., & Gabrielsson, A. (2002). From sound to sign. In R. Parncutt & G. E. McPherson (Eds.), *The science and psychology of music performance* (pp. 99–115). Oxford: Oxford University Press.

Mills, J., & McPherson, G. E. (2006). Musical literacy. In G. E. McPherson (Ed.), Child as musician: *A handbook of musical development* (pp. 155–172). New York, NY: Oxford University Press.

Norman, M. (2005). Developing thinking musicians in instrumental music. In M. Runfola & C. C. Taggart (Eds.), *The development and practical application of Music Learning Theory* (pp. 201–214). Chicago: GIA Publications, Inc.

Oare, S., & Bernstorf, E. (2010). Literacy in the instrumental classroom. *The Kodály Envoy, 37*(1), 17–20.

Pinnell, G. S., & Fountas, I. C. (2011). *Literacy beginnings: A prekindergarten handbook.* Portsmouth, NH: Heinemann.

Reifinger, J. L. (2012). The acquisition of sight-singing skills in second-grade general music: Effects of using solfège and of relating tonal patterns to songs. *Journal of Research in Music Education, 60*(1), 26–42.

Shehan, P. K. (1987). Effects of rote versus note presentations on rhythm learning and retention. *Journal of Research in Music Education, 35*(2), 117–126.

Tompkins, G. E. (1997). *Literacy for the twenty-first century*. Upper
     Saddle River, NJ: Merrill.
United Nations Educational, Scientific and Cultural Organization. (2004).
     *The plurality of literacy and its implications for policies and
     programmes: Position paper*. Paris: UNESCO. Retrieved from
     http://unesdoc.unesco.org/images/0013/001362/136246e.pdf
Waller, D. (2010). Language literacy and music literacy: A pedagogical
     asymmetry. *Philosophy of Music Education Review, 18*(1), 26–44.
Weary, K. J. (2012). Teaching musical literacy: Developing the
     independent choral singer. *Choral Director*, 12–15.
Whitehurst, G. J., & Lonigan, C. J. (1998). Child development and
     emergent literacy. *Child Development, 69*(3), 848–872.

CHAPTER 13

ENGAGING STUDENTS THROUGH MUSIC LISTENING

Cynthia Crump Taggart
Michigan State University

Introduction

Music listening is the most common form of musical engagement outside of the music classroom. Therefore, listening should have an important place in music education because of its relevance to every day life. Nearly everyone listens to music on a regular basis, either actively or passively. In fact, North, Hargreaves, and O'Neill (2000) found that 13- and 14-year-old children listened to music approximately 2.5 hours per day.

Additionally, listening is important and should be included in music classrooms because it provides access to musics that students cannot perform or experience in any other way. For example, although students may not have the resources to learn to play traditional Indian music on a sitar, technology makes it possible for them to listen to sitar music at home or in a school setting. Incorporating listening into instruction, either using live musicians or recorded music, may be the most viable option for teachers who want to give their students experiences with a variety of musical traditions.

Many more people listen to music than perform or create it. However, listening is integrally intertwined with all other forms of musical engagement. In some musical cultures and genres, persons learn to perform entirely informally through listening and doing. Yet, regardless of culture or genre, in order to be a strong performer, one must listen to what he or she is performing and adjust it on the basis of what is heard. As a member of a performing ensemble, a performer must listen to the other members of the ensemble in order to blend and contribute to the overall ensemble performance. Additionally, many performers deepen their understanding of the works that they are performing by listening to professional recordings of the same work, other works by the same composer, or other works from the same period to provide a stylistic context for their performance.

Engaging in the creation of music also involves listening. When improvising, musicians listen carefully to others in the ensemble. Strong improvisers pick up tonal, rhythmic, harmonic, and expressive cues from the other musicians and include them in their improvisations. Their improvisations are musical conversations with the other musicians. Also, when learning to improvise, jazz musicians listen to and transcribe the solos of their jazz idols as a way to become more familiar with their musical vocabulary...to learn their "licks." As they compose, most composers listen to their works realized through technology or by playing them on the piano keyboard. Then, they refine their ideas and make compositional decisions based upon what they heard. Although these are just a few examples, listening is inseparable from all other musical endeavors, and skills as a listener manifest themselves in all other realms of musical engagement.

Listening plays an essential role in the music learning process. Gordon (2013) identifies listening as the critical component of understanding music. He draws the parallel between music learning and language learning and, like Blacking (1973), believes that listening is as essential in music learning as it is in language learning. With language, the speaking vocabulary and eventually the reading and writing vocabularies are direct outgrowths of the listening vocabulary. From birth or even before, children are hearing and listening to words. They listen to the language that is all around them, play with the sounds of that language in their own babble, and eventually give meaning to the sounds that they hear. They learn their language through listening to others and to themselves. Eventually, they learn to converse (improvise in language) and learn to read and write the words that they already understand and can speak as a result of their listening experiences. Perhaps even more important, language syntax is learned through listening. No one teaches persons the order in which they put their words. Instead, syntax is learned informally through immersion in and listening to a language-rich environment. In fact, nearly all of language learning is built upon a strong foundation of listening. The richer the listening environment, the stronger the foundation will be upon which to build future language learning.

Music is learned in many of the same ways that a language is learned (Gordon, 2012). Children who are immersed in a rich listening environment musically will babble musically and eventually give meaning to the music that they hear. They will learn informally to organize the music that they hear into the syntactical systems that underpin the music in which they are immersed. For example, in the Western musical tradition, they will organize it cognitively in terms of tonality and meter. The richer one's listening vocabulary and the more styles and types of music that one has heard and to which one can bring meaning, the stronger the foundation upon which to base all other music learning.

In its National Coalition for Core Arts Standards (NAfME, 2014), listening plays a role in each of the artistic processes. For example, in Creating, students might listen to prepare for their creative process, using the works to which they listened as models for their own creations. They also might listen to their own compositions in the process of refining them. For Performing, students might listen to recordings of works as a reference when they are selecting works to perform. They also listen to their own performances as they rehearse, evaluate, and refine them. Listening has the largest function and plays the most obvious role in Responding, as it could be involved in each of the standards for that creative process, which include perceiving and analyzing an artistic work, interpreting the intent and meaning of that work, and evaluating the work itself as well as a performance of the work. It also could play a role in the process of Connecting, if the teaching/learning activity were structured in such a way.

Although listening is a part of nearly every musical activity and nearly everyone listens to music, even if they do not engage in music performance or creating music, surprisingly little emphasis is given to listening in music classrooms. Cusano (2005) found that only 1 percent to 14 percent of instructional time in elementary general music classrooms was spent on listening. Equally surprising, there seems to be little research to inform how music listening should be incorporated into music classrooms. Dunn (2011) states, "There appears to be an absence of studies directly addressing how to 'improve' listening or investigating how to help listeners reach specific goals. There do not appear to be systematic efforts to research how to move students toward becoming expert listeners" (p. 53). The purpose of this chapter is to consider what is known about music listening and to explore how this information can improve music listening practices in music classrooms.

What is Music Listening?

The music listening that I will be addressing in this chapter is an active process that requires focus and engagement; I will not be addressing music listening in which music is serving as a background to other activities (passive listening). When one actively listens to music, one is engaged in constructing meaning or "thinking" musically. Gordon (2012) would call this audiating. Peterson (2006) believes that music listening is a creative activity. She states, "During music listening, the listener constructs mental objects that not only correspond to auditory events presented by a performance, but also legitimately differ from the mental representations of other listeners" (p. 17). Even Elliott (1995), who does not include listening as one of his types of musicing, acknowledges that, "musical events are not simply received or even processed by listeners. The combined powers of human consciousness actively *construct* the complex physical events we experience as musical sound patterns" (p. 83). Morrison (2009) agrees. The cognition involved in active music listening is what differentiates listening from hearing or engaged listening from passive listening. As one listens to music, one creates a mental structure of that music, and this mental structure allows one to compare what one is hearing to what one has experienced musically in the past, to predict what comes next, and to identify what is musically important. As a result of exposure to and engagement in a musically rich environment, musicians are able to construct more sophisticated mental models and make more accurate musical predictions, and it is the responsibility of music teachers to provide these types of environments for their students.

Madsen and Geringer (2008) constructed a model of music listening that attributes the meaning-making during focused music listening to one's ability to make musical discriminations as one listens, which relates to the music cognition processes discussed above, as well as to one's ability to respond emotionally to the music, all of which occurs within the cultural context of the learner. In their model, emotional response is as important as the ability to make musical discriminations. However, the extent to which the emotional responses to music can or should be taught is a matter of debate.

Boal-Palheiros and Hargreaves (2001) state, "Enjoyment and emotion are neglected in school music listening, yet they are among the most important functions of music for children and therefore deserve more attention at school" (p. 216). Likewise, Kirnarskaya & Winner (1997) stress the need to develop both an expressive and an analytical ear. However, they found that the expressive ear or the ability to respond emotionally to music does not seem to change as a result of formal music education. At first glance, this finding is surprising. However, it could be a result of the way in which formal music education currently is constructed. Alternatively or in addition, it could be that emotional response of this type is learned better informally because of the contextual nature of emotional response and because the same context will have different meanings for different individuals. Davidson (1995) found that listeners take many of the emotional cues in music from the extramusical stimuli in the context surrounding the music rather than from the music itself. In other words, the context in which a work is experienced will to a large extent determine the emotional responses that one has to that work. In this light, perhaps the world outside of the classroom is a more authentic place than the classroom in which to learn those cues. Yet, music classrooms are a part of a student's world and are emotionally laden. Unfortunately, Sloboda (1990) posits that formal educational settings in music may foster negative attitudes about music as a result of the instructional practices in music classrooms. Woody (2004) makes the point that listening in school is different from authentic music listening, and, as a result, may help to create a disconnect between school music, which tends to be more analytical, and music as experienced outside of school, which is focused more on the emotional content of music. Likewise, Boal-Palheiros and Hargreaves (2001) found that home listening was associated with enjoyment, emotional mood, and social relationships, whereas school listening was associated with difficulty and passive listening.

Although some argue that the emotions experienced in music are as a result of extramusical factors, others argue that the emotional content in music is at least partially embedded in the music itself (Meyer, 1956; Narmour, 1990). They argue that, when musical expectations are realized or thwarted, listeners experience different emotions as a result of the fulfillment or avoidances of those expectations. However, expectations themselves are learned both informally and formally as a result of past musical experiences and exposure, so different individuals will experience different emotions to the same music, depending upon their past experiences. Researchers have found that children's cultural backgrounds and musical preferences can affect their emotional responses to music (Gregory & Varney, 1996).

Zangwill (2012) argues against collective music listening because of what he believes to be "the impossibility of perceiving the aesthetic properties of music" (p. 379) and the individualistic nature of the musical experience that makes joint listening a violation of privacy.

Yet, because of the important role of emotions in music listening, they cannot be ignored in the music classroom, but perhaps they should be explored and acknowledged rather than taught, as a way of bridging the gap between school music and music experiences out of school. And, fortunately, music classrooms can provide shared, positive experiences with music that later will result in positive associations and therefore positive emotional responses when listening to that music and perhaps even music that is similar.

Guidelines and suggestions for music listening activities

Researchers have identified some specific practices that can make listening activities more successful and meaningful for students. Some of these apply across all music settings and others are more applicable depending upon the age of the student and the type of music setting.

When choosing listening examples for students, students benefit most when listening to an entire work or a complete movement of a work. Because they are creating mental representations as a result of their listening experience, presenting them with whole works will result in more meaningful, accurate representations than using only a portion of a work. However, Sims (2004) found that, although listening time varied greatly, when given the opportunity to listen freely, most four- and five-year-old children chose to listen for between 30 seconds and three minutes. As children get older, their ability to engage in focused listening increases. Teachers need to keep these limitations in mind when choosing listening repertoire, selecting entire works but choosing works that are short enough to attend to the attention span of the listener. Suites like Saint Saen's *Carnival of the Animals*, Tchaikovsky's *Nutcracker Suite*, and Mussorgsky's *Pictures at an Exhibition* all are examples of works that have short movements that are compelling to younger children.

In addition, teachers should take students' music preferences into account when choosing the repertoire for use in music listening activities in the classroom. Young students have an "open-earedness" that decreases during K–8 schooling and then begins to rebound again during young adulthood (LeBlanc, Sims, Siivola and Obert, 1996). Young children's stylistic preferences are determined less by social pressures and expectations than those of older children, and they are more open to listening to all types of music than older students. Peery & Peery (1986) found that children with exposure to classical music in preschool continued to accept and like classical music, but those without that exposure in their curriculum showed a decline in liking classical music as they got older. In this light, it behooves music teachers to introduce their young students to as broad and rich a diversity of musical styles as possible so that children's preference for and willingness to listen to and engage with those styles continue as they mature.

Providing students a rich music listening environment in terms of styles, tonal systems, and rhythmic systems also will facilitate music learning. This is particularly is true for very young children, but it continues to be true even as children grow older. Developmental psychologists have found that children who have richer language environments develop better language skills than those from less rich environments (Moerk, 2000). Specifically, children whose parents speak with larger vocabularies have been found to develop larger vocabularies and to learn to read and write earlier and with greater comprehension than children from less rich language environments. Similarly, children who have had an opportunity to listen to a rich, diverse musical vocabulary will develop richer musical skills (Valerio, et al, 1998). Gordon (2001) calls the brain a "pattern-making system" (p. 23) that is always looking for similarities and differences between what it is processing and what it has processed in the past. Although much of the music that children hear on a daily basis is in major tonality and duple meter, they need to experience music in a wide variety of tonalities and meters. They also need to hear a wide variety of musical styles. Listening to a wide variety of music allows students to put the music that they hear in a richer context; they learn what it is by having something different to which to compare it. In this way, they can develop a deeper understanding of major and duple by learning what makes them different from other tonalities and meters (Valerio, et. al, 1998), and they can develop a deeper, more contextual, stylistic understand of the music to which they choose to listen.

As children get older, they feel the need to exert more agency and have more choice in their music learning (Kastner, 2012; Koops, 2012). As a result, beginning as early as mid-elementary school, teachers should consider including students in the decision-making processes about the pieces around which they will base listening activities. Silverman (2013) found that "students are most apt to learn music listening effectively and enjoyably when afforded democratic and creative opportunities to express their beliefs about the natures and values of the musics they decide to select, experience and discuss critically" (p. 7). Woody (2004) posits that teachers do not sufficiently value students' subjective responses to music in their preferred styles. He states, "During their schooling, students may develop the belief that certain styles of music are different from their 'regular' music and therefore are to be listened to differently" (p. 34). Perhaps music teachers should not only give students voice in selecting listening reper- toire, but they also should give them the opportunity to express what they value about their musical choices. Many adolescents have a strong liking of popular music; yet this repertoire often is not the choice of teachers for use in the classroom. Creating a place in the classroom for the music to which students would choose to listen on their own and for students to express what they value about "their own" music could help bridge the gap between music in the schools and music in the lives of students outside of the classroom, making music education in the schools more relevant.

Researchers have found that children prefer and learn more from music listening when it is active. Woody (2004) describes the traditional classroom approach to music listening as involving playing record- ings, studying history and culture, and studying the musical elements of the work, all of which he contends may be boring to students. Temmerman (2000) found that young children wanted to move and engage in other ways musically as they listened to music. One child expressed, "We always have to listen every day and be quiet and sit, but I want to do something and dance and play the tambourine" (p. 57). Fung and Gromko (2001) found that moving while listening helped children make sense of music rhythmically and that moving helped them attend to the activity. Older children may be more reluctant to move, but they can be engaged in other ways, such as being asked to map what they are hearing or asking them to make notes about and prepare to describe specific events in the music after they listen. Fung and Gromko (2001) recommended giving students problem solving tasks when they listen. Further, Dunn (2008) investigated which types of listening activities students prefer after they experienced listening with visual reinforcement, listening with moving, and listening alone. Listening alone was the least favorite presentation mode for most of the children. However, he also found that some children learned more through listening only and hypothesized that some children may be over-stimulated by attending to multiple response modes simultaneously. In other words, teachers should structure active listening activities that allow children to move, draw, solve a problem, or follow along with a visual representation of the work, while being sensitive to the needs of those students who are overwhelmed by being asked to do too many things at once.

Providing students opportunities to respond to listening in many different ways also is useful, as different response modes result in different type of thinking. Kerchner (2000) found that responding to listening through movement elicited linear thinking. Asking students to respond verbally elicited more detailed linear thinking, whereas visually mapping as they listened elicited both linear and non-linear thinking. Kerchner recommended that music educators ask children to incorporate all of these types of response modes over multiple listening activities, as developing all of these ways of thinking musically results in more flexible and deeper listeners. Flowers (2002) found that engaging children in verbal descriptions of music in response to listening activities helps them bring deeper meaning to their music listening experiences. In post-listening discussions, she encourages the use of extramusical analogies and musical vocabulary, while making encouraging comments and asking questions to help children go deeper. Like Kerchner, Johnson (2006) investigated response modes, this time with older students. He found that, when asked to respond verbally, students used more musical terms, and their responding in written result form resulted in more affective/associative responses. Both of these types of responses are valuable, depending upon instructional goals, so teachers should consider structuring listening activities so that students respond to listening in a variety of ways over time, as this will elicit deeper and different types of thinking from students.

Performing is an essential counterpart to listening and helps students develop listening skills. In reviewing the research literature, Kjelland, Kerchner and Dura (1998) found that performing helped students form better mental representations of musical works and had an overall positive effect on listening skills. Elliott (1995) argues that performance informs listening and that they are inseparable. He states, "Past music education philosophy severely underestimates what it takes to listen to and to make music well because it fails to examine the intricate relationships among listening, performing, and the performative nature of music" (p. 32).

Performing also may enhance the emotional response of students to music listening. Teachers who help to create meaningful, emotionally satisfying moments for students through performance will give students positive emotional associations to draw upon when they listen to the music that they have performed or perhaps even to similar music in the future. However, performance environments must be positive and must not induce fear in students. Sloboda (1990) found that students do not respond emotionally to music in a threatening environment. Providing students positive, nonthreatening performance experiences may be a way of encouraging emotional responses and connections to music as a result of music instruction. As a result, music teachers should try to balance listening and performance in helping students develop strong listening skills.

Finally, listening activities should be structured with children's cognitive, developmental needs in mind. Sims (1991) found that four- and five-year-old children tend to focus on one element of music at a time and have difficulty when they are asked to attend to multiple musical elements as they listen. As a result, listening activities with young children should be structured in such a way that the children are not required to concentrate on multiple musical elements at once. Hufstader (1977) found that understanding of specific musical elements emerge at different times in children, although some individual children's developmental pathways varied from this sequence and sometimes occurred at different times. For most children, understanding timbre in the context of listening activities developed first in early elementary, with melodic and rhythmic understanding developing by mid to late elementary, and harmonic understanding developing last, by seventh grade. When designing listening activities, teachers should keep in mind where their students are developmentally in light of this sequence. As children get older, they can attend to multiple musical dimensions. Woody (2004) recommends that students, especially older students, be given the opportunity to listen holistically to music, rather than for single musical elements. Holistic listening more clearly mirrors listening as it occurs outside of the classroom, therefore making classroom activities more authentic.

In summary, music teachers need to consider both the repertoire and the structure of their music listening activities. In choosing repertoire, they should use entire works of a developmentally appropriate length in a large variety of musical styles, tonalities, and meters when designing listening activities for their students. Particularly as students get older, teachers should give students input into choosing the music that is used in the music classroom and should be willing to incorporate popular music into their teaching as a way of bridging the gap between music in school and music in everyday life. In structuring their activities, teachers should make listening activities active and give students the opportunity to respond in different modes as a way of developing different ways of thinking. Also, balancing performing activities with listening activities results in better listening skills. Finally, when structuring listening lessons, teachers should keep in mind how students develop musically as well as the individual developmental pathways of students who differ developmentally from their peers.

Types of music listening activities

Dunn (2011) identified two kinds of listening activities that should be a part of every music classroom: those activities in which learning is more formal, specific, and teacher-directed, and those in which learning takes place intuitively. He expressed concern that music educators focus so much on teacher-directed learning in K–12 education that children lose touch with their intuitive sense of "what is" and what matters musically. Kratus (2014) discusses similar ideas, labeling the two types of activities as convergent listening activities and divergent listening activities. In convergent listening activities, there is a right answer ("What instruments do you hear?" or "What is the meter of this piece?"), and in divergent listening activities, there are multiple possible correct answers and ways of approaching the listening task ("How does this music make you feel and why?" or "Draw a visual map of this piece so that you and others could follow along on the map as you listen to the music."). Kratus encourages teachers to include both types of activities in their instruction (see the chapter by Shaw in this volume). Convergent tasks often tend to focus more on the elements of music and tend to be more teacher-directed, whereas divergent tasks can focus on the affective and associative elements of music as well as the more traditional elemental components. In divergent activities, students tend to construct the knowledge, whereas, in convergent activities, the teacher directs the learning. Activities can be developed that incorporate both types of learning or that are specific to one type of learning.

Convergent Listening Activities

Convergent activities tend to be used more in music classrooms than divergent activities, as they allow the teacher to make sure that students learn and understand specific features of music. This learning then can be transferred or generalized to the understanding other musical works with the same features. These types of activities can take many forms. Students can be given specific questions to answer, either in verbal or written form, before listening and then asked to answer those questions, again either in verbal or written form, as or after they listen.

Convergent activities can take the form of moving to music. When students move to the beat of the music to which they are listening, they are moving to music in a convergent way. There is a single correct answer; they are to tap their laps or take a step specifically on the beat. If they are not moving to the beat, they are not correct. Students also can move to the form of a piece in a convergent way by performing one type of movement during the A section and contrasting movements for sections other than A, moving to dynamics by making their movements larger when the music gets loud and smaller when the music gets quiet, or by moving to melodic direction by making their movements high when the melody is high and low when the melody is low. All of these are examples in which students are demonstrating or extending their understanding of the music by attaching movement to specific elements of the music.

Call charts, which were initially developed by Reimer (Dunn, 2011), often are used as a tool in directed, convergent listening. Reimer (1967) found that they were good for promoting active listening and extending listening time in junior and senior high school students, because they gave students something visual to which attend while they listen. Call charts can be developed by a teacher to represent visually exactly what he or she wants the students to notice as they listen to the music. Sections of the music can be numbered on the chart so that the teacher can "call out" the numbers as students listen, helping them to identify where they are visually on the chart. An example of a call chart for use with the "Ballet of the Chickens in Their Shells" from *Pictures at an Exhibition* can be seen in Figure 1. This particular chart focuses on form.

Ballet of the Unhatched Chicks

Figure 1

The teacher would play the recording and show or call out the A and B sections and the boxes as the students listen to the recording. This chart might be used in first grade with the teacher projecting an image of the chart and pointing to the appropriate points on the chart as the recording progresses or in second or third grade with the students having their own copies of the chart and following along with teacher guidance. After listening and asking the students questions to make sure that they understand that the A sections were similar and the B section was different (this may require playing the recording several more times), the teacher could play the recording again and see if the students can to follow along independently on the chart as they listen.

This chart, however, is not typical of most call charts in that it leaves things for the listener to do and interpret. After the students are able to follow along on their own and have internalized the larger form, the teacher could ask them if there are things that are not represented well on the chart. One example is that the second and fourth boxes of the A sections look exactly the same, but the music in them is different. The students could give ideas for how those boxes could be changed to represent the piece more accurately visually in each of the A sections. Also the students could be given the opportunity to fill in the B section of the chart, which is blank, dividing it into sections and determining what type of picture should be in each section. Students could share their ideas with one another and with the rest of the class. These extensions of the activity would require divergent thinking, as these types of questions could be answered well in many different ways, whereas the first parts of the activity would require convergent thinking and would provide the readiness for the divergent portion of the activity.

Listening maps are similar to call charts in that they are a visual representation of a work, usually with one or several specific instructional goals in mind. With a listening map, the teacher leads the children through it until they can follow it themselves. There are many choices for how music can be represented visually (pictoral representations, graphic notation, icons, etc.), and, as in the call chart above, several different levels can be represented at once; for the call chart above, the larger form was represented as well as the small sections within each larger section.

Woody (2004) expressed concern that call charts and listening maps are inauthentic, as they do not mirror "real world" listening. This certainly is true. However, the purpose for using the maps in the music classroom is so that students learn, whereas the purpose of listening to music outside of the classroom is decidedly different and usually focuses on enjoyment. In the same article, Woody (2004) questions the focus on specific elements of music in listening maps as well as in presenting historical and cultural information surrounding a piece, as persons need to take in the musical whole rather than specific parts of a work so that it can affect us emotionally. However, historical information, the stories of programmatic works, and other types of knowledge that can be depicted in listening maps can enhance the emotional effect of listening, because they enable listeners to bring greater meaning to their listening. Listening to Penderecki's *Threnody for the Victims of Hiroshima* without an understanding of the work's context might result in a different emotional experience than knowing that the work was dedicated to the victims of the bombing in Hiroshima and the details surrounding the tragedy and loss that was endured by the people of Japan as a result of the bombing. Again, however, the activity does not need to require entirely convergent thinking. Students could be asked to think about and discuss how the sounds of the piece express that tragedy as a way to encourage divergent thinking.

Giving students a convergent problem to solve in small groups can allow for students to learn from one another and work together. For example, after students have had many opportunities to learn the sounds of the band instruments, in mid-to-late elementary school they could be given the task of identifying and making a map of which instruments have the melody in an unfamiliar work. Or, after being given a recording to use as a listening reference during their problem solving process, small groups of students could be given a call chart or listening map that has been cut apart into sections and asked to re-assemble the chart in the correct order. These students then could have the opportunity to describe the rationale behind their choices. Both of these would require that students have had previous, teacher-guided experience, and the second would require that students have had experience with call charts or listening maps. However, in these activities, students would be applying what they had learned to new repertoire and would be generalizing and making inferences, albeit convergent in nature.

For older students who are studying form, Indiana University has created a tool that allows students to map form visually, called *Variations Audio Timeliner*. This program is free on line (http://variations.sourceforge.net/vat/). What is unusual is that the listening maps are attached to recordings rather than scores, so analysis is aural rather than visual. By clicking on the visual map of the work, it takes the listeners to that place in the recording, so, for example, students can hear that the second theme of the recapitulation is exactly the same as that of the exposition, only in the tonic rather than the dominant key center. Teachers could use their own graphs to help students understand the form of a piece that the ensemble is learning, and they could play a recording and help the students "unpack" the visual representation of the form. Eventually, they could ask students to listen to pieces and graph them visually as a way of applying their knowledge to different repertoire. Figure 2 is an example of visual representation of form using Variations Audio Timeliner as well as the window that students would see as they work within the program.

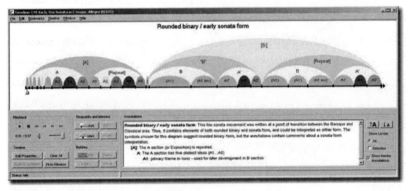

Figure 2

Convergent activities are easy to assess because there is a single right answer. Typically, if students can do the assigned task correctly, they would receive credit for learning the content. With convergent activities, students usually learn first by rote and then should be asked to apply what they have learned to new musical examples. If they are not able to generalize and apply their knowledge to unfamiliar musical works, they need more practice and guidance with the concept. Students should be able to apply their knowledge independent of the teacher or their learning will not have a life outside of the music classroom.

Divergent Listening Activities

Blacking (1973) believed that listening is a creative act, and with creative acts there is no single right answer. Peterson (2006) states,

"Although mental models of musical works are, indeed, important products of creative listening, an even more fertile (and immeasurably more complex) area for investigation into creative listening is the idea of world making and self making. The experience of living in musical time and space, however briefly, has the potential to stimulate feelings as deep and as subtle as the experiences of life itself" (p. 20). Dunn (1997) agrees, stating, "Creative listening appears to be an active process involving unique, individual cognitive and affective response to listening to music that extends beyond listeners' technical understanding of the music" (p. 42). Giving students an opportunity to engage in divergent listening activities allows music educators a glimpse into the hearts and minds of students, giving them a sense of what students know, notice, and value, and who they are as individuals.

One easy way to get a glimpse into the musical minds of students is to allow them to share the music that they value in the context of the music classroom. All students listen to music outside of the classroom, but the music to which they listen on their own time rarely is heard in music classrooms. Each day a student could be asked to share one short piece that is particularly important to him or her. The student could be given five to seven minutes to play a recording and to discuss why that piece is important to him or her and what he or she likes about it, both in terms of its affect and its music content. Clear guidelines would need to be established by the teacher about appropriate content so that the lyrics of a piece would not be inappropriate for classroom use. Otherwise, the requirements should be as open-ended as possible so that the teacher gets a clear sense of what students value musically and why.

Students rarely have an opportunity in the music classroom to engage in discussions of how music makes them feel; yet the "feelingful" components of music often are used as one of the fundamental rationale for including music in education. Perhaps teachers could engage students in informal listening activities with unpacking the emotions elicited by music as an instructional goal. A teacher would play a recording of a work and ask the students how the music makes the students feel as a reminder that effect is an important component of music and music making. This could be enough of an activity, or it could be followed by a discussion of the components of the music that result in those feelings as a way of expanding student's musical vocabulary and helping them understand the link between the elements of music and how those elements combine as a whole and create emotional responses in the listener.

Call charts and listening maps can be used to engage students in convergent music listening, but, if students create those charts and maps themselves, they can engage students in divergent musical thinking. Visual mapping gives teachers insights into what their students hear. They are a good way to investigate students' internal mappings and mental representations of a work (Bamberger, 1994; Barrett, 2004). Students can be asked to create their own visual representations of a work and then present those representations to their class members. With teacher guidance, they can look for and discuss similarities and differences across all of the representations so that students become aware of all of the dimensions that were heard and represented visually by the students. This could result in a deep understanding of the multidimensional nature of music while giving students an opportunity to delve deeply into a musical work with no expectation of "right" answers. The class as a whole will construct a rich understanding of a work through their sharing, comparing, and discussing. With students having access to computers and the internet outside of school, the making of these maps could be completed outside of the classroom to conserve instructional time. Teachers could post a recording of a work so that students could access it from home. Then the visual representations could be shared in class. In an ensemble setting, students could engage in this type of activity before they begin or as they learn to play a work as a means of helping them experience their repertoire more deeply.

Assessment for divergent listening activities, in this case call charts or listening maps, is more difficult than for convergent activities, because there is no correct answer. There is tremendous variation in what an individual visual representation could look like, which makes them difficult to assess. As a result, assessment needs to be more focused on the process than the product. These visual representations could be assessed using multidimensional rubrics that focus on instructional goals that are drawn directly from teacher-developed instructions for the activity. The activity instructions, therefore, would have direct correlates in the rubric with which the students would be evaluated. For example, if the students were asked to draw a visual representation of the work with which they could follow along as they listened to the work, one dimension of the rubric would be designed to measure the extent to which the students were able to follow along with the visuals as they presented them to the class. This could be accomplished through a continuous rating scale representing the dimension as follows:

1. Student had difficulty following the visual representation throughout.
2. Student lost his or her place multiple times but was able to find his or her place again relatively quickly.
3. Student lost his or her place once or twice but generally was able to follow the visual representation well.
4. Student consistently was able to follow the visual representation.

Other dimensions could focus on the quality of the student's explanation of the representation in the oral presentation, the richness of the vocabulary that the student used in his or her explanation, the clarity of the listening map in terms of its visual representation, or many other possibilities, depending upon the focus of the listening activity as articulated in the instructions. Rubrics could be given to the students at the time the activity was assigned to help clarify what was going to be evaluated.

All of the listening activities so far have focused almost entirely on the process of listening and the expression of what was heard in that listening through movement, visual representations, or discussion and description. However, students also could express what they heard through performance. Green (2008) and the teachers in a study by Kastner (2012) engaged students deeply in listening by asking them to perform "covers." Green asked students first to cover popular songs and then to cover a classical piece using popular instruments commonly found in rock bands. Kastner's teachers asked their students to create covers of popular songs using recorders, classroom instruments, and/or their voices. Students accomplished this aurally rather than relying on music notation, although some students in Kastner's study were given copies of the song lyrics to facilitate their learning process. Creating covers of songs and performing them requires that students immerse themselves in a work through listening so that they know not only the melody but also the other voices. They also must be able to replicate those voices in their own performances. This type of activity creates a bridge between music in and outside of school, because students in both studies worked with popular music, which is what most students listen to outside of school. Perhaps more important, though, students learn music in the way that most vernacular musicians learn—by ear or by listening.

In designing these types of activities teachers can decide how open they would like to be in terms of what repertoire their students cover. For example, in Kastner's study, some of the teachers asked students to choose from a list of songs that were currently popular with their students but that they had already vetted in terms of lyrics and technical difficulty. They also can decide how prescriptive they would like to be in terms of the final product. For example, should the cover be as close to the original as possible, or can students change the original song while still maintaining its integrity?

Assessment of "cover" projects could be accomplished through rubrics with several continuous dimensions. Dimensions could relate to quality of the performance, as well as the quality of arrangement of the song. Again, the dimensions should relate directly back to the instructions that the students are given for the activity.

Conclusion

Most students listen to music every day outside of the classroom. Therefore, if music teachers want to make music instruction relevant to their students, helping them develop their listening skills makes sense. Teachers should strive to create listening activities for students that help them learn more about music and experience music more deeply. These activities should be designed taking into consideration what is known about what facilitates effective music listening. They also should be developmentally appropriate and should encourage both convergent and divergent thinking. Through well-designed listening activities, music teachers are empowering their students to engage deeply and knowledgeably in the world of music listening both in and outside of the classroom and throughout their entire lives.

Citations

Bamberger, J. (1994). Coming to hear in a new way. In R. Aiello & J. Sloboda (Eds.), *Musical perceptions*, (pp. 131–151). New York: Oxford University Press.

Barrett, M. (2004). Thinking about the representation of music: A case study of invented notation. *Bulletin of the Council for Research in Music Education, 161/162*, 19–28.

Blacking, J. (1973). *How musical is man?* Seattle: University of Washington Press.

Boal-Palheiros, G. M., & Hargreaves, D. J. (2001). Listening to music at home and at school. *British Journal of Music Education, 18*(2), 103–116.

Cusano, J. M. (2005). *Music specialists' beliefs and practices in teaching music listening.* Unpublished doctoral dissertation, Indiana University, Bloomington, IN.

Davidson, J. W. (1995). What does the visual information contained in music performances offer the observer? *In Mind and the mind machine: Psychophysiology and the psychopathology of the sense of music,* ed. R. Steinberg, 105–114. Heidelberg: Springer.

Dunn, R. (2011). Contemporary research on music listening: A holistic view. In MENC Handbook of Research on Music Learning Volume 2: Applications. Eds. R. Colwell and P. R. Webster. New York: Oxford University Press.

Dunn, R. (2008). The effects of auditory, visual, or kinesthetic perceptual strengths on music listening. *Contributions to Music Education, 35,* 47–78.

Dunn, R. E. (1997). Creative thinking and music listening. *Research Studies in Music Education, 8*(1), 42–55.

Elliott, E. (1995). *Music matters: A new philosophy of music education.* New York: Oxford University Press.

Fung, C. V., & Gromko, J. E. (2001). The effects of active versus passive listening on the quality of children's invented notations and preferences for two pieces from an unfamiliar culture. *Psychology of Music, 29*(2), 128–138.

Gordon, E. E. (2013). Listening: The critical component for understanding music. *Audia, Spring 2013,* 5–8.

Gordon, E. E. (2012). *Learning sequences in music: A contemporary music learning theory.* Chicago: GIA Publications.

Gordon, E. E. (2001). *Preparatory audiation, audiation, and Music Learning Theory.* Chicago: GIA Publications.

Green, L. (2008). *Music, informal learning and the school: A new classroom pedagogy.* Burlington, VT: Ashgate Publishing.

Gregory, A. H., & Varney, N. (1996). Cross-cultural comparisons in the affective response to music. *Psychology of Music, 24,* 47–52.

Hufstader, R. A. (1977). An investigation of a learning sequence of music listening skills. *Journal of Research in Music Education, 25*(3), 184. Retrieved from http://ezproxy.msu.edu/login?url=http://search.proquest.com/docview/1306757725?accountid=12598

Johnson, D. C. (2006). Listening and thinking. *Visions of Research in Music Education, 7.* Retrieved from http://www-usr.rider.edu/%7Evrme/v7n1/visions/Johnson%20Listening%20and%20Thinking.pdf

Kastner, J. D. (2012). *Exploring informal music pedagogy in a professional development community of elementary music teachers.* (Order No. 3548741, Michigan State University). ProQuest Dissertations and Theses, 351. Retrieved from http://ezproxy. msu.edu/login?url=http://search.proquest.com/docview/128240 4696?accountid=12598. (1282404696).

Kerchner, J. L. (2000). Children's verbal, visual, and kinesthetic responses: Insight into their music listening experience. *Bulletin of the Council for Research in Music Education, 146,* 31–50.

Kinarskaya, D., & Winner, E. (1997). Musical ability in a new key: Exploring the expressive ear for music. *Psychomusicology, 16,* 2–16.

Kjelland, J. M., Kerchner, J. K., & Dura, M. T. (Eds.) (1998). The effects of music performance participation on the music listening experience: A review of literature. *Bulletin of the Council for Research in Music Education, 136*(Spring), 1–55.

Koops, L. H. (2012). "Ñungi noss (They are enjoying)": Enjoyment and socialization in Gambian children's music making. In P. S. Campbell & T. Wiggins (Eds.), *Oxford Handbook of Children's Musical Cultures.* pp. 266–280. New York: Oxford University Press.

Kratus, J. (2014, January 17). *Teaching music listening as a creative activity.* Presentation at the Michigan Music Conference, Grand Rapids, Michigan.

LeBlanc, A., Sims, W. L., Siivola, C., & Obert, M. (1996). Music style preferences of different age listeners. *Journal of Research in Music Education, 44*(1), 49–59. Retrieved from http://ezproxy. msu.edu/login?url=http://search.proquest.com/docview/619353 753?accountid=12598

Madsen, C. K., & Geringer, J. M. (2008). Reflections on Puccini's La Bohème: Investigating a model for listening. *Journal of Research in Music Education, 56*(1), 33–42.

Meyer, L. B. (1956). *Emotion and meaning in music.* Chicago: University of Chicago Press.

Moerk, E. L. (2000). *The guided acquisition of first language skills. advances in applied developmental psychology, 20* Stamford, CT: Ablex Publishing Corporation. Retrieved from http://ezproxy. msu.edu/login?url=http://search.proquest.com/docview/624326 66?accountid=12598

Morrison, C. D. (2009). Music listening as music making. *Journal of Aesthetic Education, 43*(1), 77–91.

Narmour, E. (1990). *The analysis and cognition of basic melodic structures: The implication-realization model.* Chicago: University of Chicago Press.

National Association for Music Education. (2014, July). National core arts standards. Retrieved from http://musiced.nafme.org/ musicstandards/

North, A. C., Hargreaves, D. J., & O'Neill, S. A. (2000). The importance of music to adolescents. *British Journal of Educational Psychology, 70*(2), 255–272.

Peery, J. C., & Peery, I. W. (1986). Effects of exposure to classical music on the musical preferences of preschool children. *Journal of Research in Music Education, 34*(1), 24. Retrieved from http:// ezproxy.msu.edu/login?url=http://search.proquest.com/docview /1306758899?accountid=12598

Peterson, E. M. (2006). Creativity in music listening. *Arts Education Policy Review, 107*(3), 15–21. Retrieved from http://ezproxy. msu.edu/login?url=http://search.proquest.com/docview/621067 09?accountid=12598

Reimer, B. (1967). *The development and trial in a junior and senior high school of a two-year curriculum in general music* (Report Number H-116). Cleveland, OH: U. S. Department of Health, Education, and Welfare. (ERIC Document Reproduction Service No. ED 017 526).

Silverman, M. (2013). A critical ethnography of democratic music listening. *British Journal of Music Education, 30*(1), 7–25. Retrieved from http://ezproxy.msu.edu/login?url=http://search. proquest.com/docview/1373085428?accountid=12598

Sims, W. L. (1991). Effects of instruction and task format on preschool children's ability to demonstrate single and combined music concept discrimination. *Journal of Research in Music Education, 39*(4), 204–221.

Sims, W. L. (2004). What I've learned about research from young children. *Update: Applications of Research in Music Education, 23*(1), 4–13.

Sloboda, J. A. (1990). Music as language. In F. R. Wilson & F. L. Roehmann (Eds.), *Music and child development: The biology of music making* (pp. 28–43). St. Louis, MO: MMB Music.

Temmerman, N. (2000). An investigation of the music activity preferences of preschool children. *British Journal of Music Education, 17*(1), 51–60.

Valerio, W. H., Reynolds, A. M., Bolton, B. M., Taggart, C. C., & Gordon, E. E. (1998). *Music play: The early childhood music curriculum.* Chicago: GIA Publications.

Woody, R. H. (2004). Reality-based music listening in the classroom: Considering students' natural responses to music. *General Music Today, 17*(2), 32–39.

Zangwill, N. (2012). Listening to music together. *British Journal of Aesthetics, 52*(4), 379. Retrieved from http://ezproxy.msu.edu/login?url=http://search.proquest.com/docview/1142609136?accountid=12598

Part Four:
Specific Contexts for Learning and Future Directions

CHAPTER 14

EARLY CHILDHOOD MUSIC CURRICULUM

Alison M. Reynolds
Temple University

Wendy H. Valerio
University of South Carolina

In general, music curriculum seems successful if conceived as a dynamic, breathing entity that, while honoring what individuals bring to the table, offers a predetermined time frame during which those individuals ostensibly are prepared for active engagement in and with skills, knowledge, attitudes, and beliefs required for their "next steps"—or, continued real-world applications of their learning in their musical lives alongside and "after" curriculum. Curriculum acts as a compass, providing direction for individuals as they navigate both the content of the curriculum and their journey through it. In this chapter, we offer considerations for writing and engaging in early childhood music curriculum.

To help frame the contents of this chapter, we define early childhood as the time in a child's life encompassing at least birth to the end of a child's eighth year. Chief among the many valuable outcomes of an early childhood music curriculum: by the time children are eight years old, they organically and consistently live social, playful, music interactions that affirm for them that music not only is a natural part of their play, but also of the world around them. They comfortably and confidently are able to apply initial fluencies with at least singing, chanting, and moving to express and communicate music ideas at least through performing, improvising, and creating. Naturally, then, children can believe that their music instincts, curiosities, and ideas are worth continuing to explore, express, and develop both individually and in community. In sum, we assert that successful early childhood music curriculum situates children for continued successes applying vocal and kinesthetic fluencies with at least tonal and rhythm audiation and expressions to authentic music making contexts in and out of school.

Generally, there is agreement that an early childhood music curriculum serves a different function from an elementary general music curriculum: an early childhood music curriculum primarily focuses on informal music learning contexts and outcomes for children; a typical elementary general music curriculum primarily focuses on formal music learning contexts and outcomes. Both types of curricula require developmentally appropriate practices.[1] Implementing a curriculum that has mindfully integrated specific benchmarks for music development requires an understanding that, like with differences in other types of learning and development, individual children can differ in the extent to which they demonstrate their music learning and development. Some children demonstrate music expressiveness earlier in life than others, illustrating differences between musical age and chronological age. Although children can and do achieve formal music learning objectives in formal music settings before they are nine years old, adults should feel comfortable honoring developmentally appropriate practices for informal music learning throughout early childhood, rather than accommodating a "pushing down" of formal music-learning outcomes when pressured by administrators, colleagues, or already-established formal music learning objectives within PreKindergarten, first, or second grade curricula. And, although most children immersed in music interations emerge from early childhood music curricula having achieved initial music fluencies as described in this and other chapters of this text by age nine, we have found that some children do not. As we present information in this chapter, we have considered that it can be adapted and modified to support the maturation of musical age to align with chronological age for persons nine years of age and older.

---

[1]   See Developmentally Appropriate Practice at http://www.naeyc.org/DAP (The National Association for Music Education, 2009).

We realize there are multiple pathways you can take when writing and implementing an early childhood music curriculum. The pathway you take depends, in part, on answers to numerous, interrelated, context-specific questions. For example,

- What professional development do I need to create, implement, reflect on, and revise early childhood music curriculum?
- What is the setting or broader context in which the curriculum will be implemented (e.g., private, music-education-specific business providing early childhood music classes or contracting teachers who provide music embedded within and located on site at a day care or early childhood education business, private preschool with or without religious affiliations, or subsidized preschool serving as intervention prior to public Kindergarten; or public-school preschool setting in which a certified music teacher is hired by the school district to provide music instruction)?
- Who are the children who will benefit from the curriculum? What are their cultural, language, and family backgrounds?
- What types of music engagement have the children experienced previously?
- What are the children's age ranges? If children's age ranges in this context span across several years, will children be separated by chronological ages, or will groups be mixed-ages during music making?
- In this setting, how can existing spaces and materials (indoors and outdoors) support or inhibit children's musicing[2] and movement? Will the need to acquire additional materials inhibit curriculum creation or implementation?

---

[2] David Elliott uses the spelling of the verb *musicing* as "a contraction of music making . . . most often . . . to mean . . . : performing, improvising, composing, arranging, and conducting" (http://www.davidelliottmusic.com/praxial-music-education/music-and-listening-in-praxial-music/). We have used musicing in this chapter as a collection of music activities supporting audiation, music interactions, music conversations, and music situations in early childhood: listening, moving, singing, chanting, approximating, improvising, creating, imitating, reading music, writing and composing music, interacting.

- What expectations are there for the early childhood music curriculum to fit with the music curriculum children will next encounter?
- Are other adults charged with working alongside you to write and/or implement the curriculum? If so, what are their beliefs about young children and children's music capacities? To what extent do their early childhood music curriculum compasses align with yours?
- Will parents or guardians attend and participate in music with their children? Whether the answer is "yes" or "no," what will be the roles of parents or guardians within the curriculum?
- Will day care providers, early childhood teachers, or parapro-fessionals attend and participate in music with the children? Whether the answer is, "yes" or "no," what will be the roles of the respective adults within the curriculum?"
- What type or combinations of types of music interactions will you and other adults working in the setting prioritize? For example, do the types of interactions occur in music centers, music during routines and/or transitions, as accompaniment to traditions or celebrations, as structured music making during circle time, or co-constructed and informal music play?
- What will be the minimum number of weeks and minimum amount of time allotted for daily or weekly music interactions in the setting?
- How will the curriculum culturally and authentically support children's music making out of school?
- To what extent will children have choice about their music making activities in this setting?
- Are there additional curricular goals for children, or perfor-mance evaluation expectations of adults that all adults will be expected to infuse alongside the early childhood music curric-ulum goals?

- Does the setting require communications about music achievement at certain time frames or in certain formats that affect construction of curriculum?

Because of vast differences and rapid changes among children's physical, motor, cognitive, intellectual, social, emotional, and broad artistic development during the early childhood years, your theoretical and practical understandings of child development, children with special needs, and children with different language learning needs will apply as you answer such questions and create developmentally appropriate practices. Specific understanding of children's music development to guide your work will be of utmost importance. Three resources that combine research-based and practical information have been particularly helpful to our early childhood music curriculum engagement:

1. *A Music Learning Theory for Newborn and Young Children* (Gordon, 2013),
2. *Music in Childhood: From Preschool through the Elementary Grades, 4th Edition* (Campbell & Scott-Kassner, 2014), and
3. *Tools of the Mind: The Vygotskian Approach to Early Childhood Education, 2nd Edition* (Bodrova & Leong, 2007).

Also of tremendous help have been publications about early childhood music education by the National Association for Music Education:

- *Early Childhood Music Education Position Statement* in 1991 (http://musiced.nafme.org/about/position-statements/early-childhood-education/)
- The PreKindergarten Music Standards and elementary grades K through 3 as part of the 1994 *National Standards in Music*
- Subsequent articles referencing them such as *The School Music Program: A New Vision* (http://musiced.nafme.org/resources/the-school-music-program-a-new-vision/), *Opportunity-to-Learn for Music Instruction: Grades PreK–12* (1994) and *Performance Standards for Music Strategies and Benchmarks*

for Assessing Progress Toward the National Standards, Grades PreK–12 (1996)

- Outcomes from the *Early Childhood Summit: Start the Music Strategies Summary Report* (2000) (http://musiced.nafme. org/resources/start-the-music-strategies/start-the-music-a-report-from-the-early-childhood-summit/) and accompanying materials (See http://musiced.nafme.org/resources/start-the-music-strategies/foreword-and-introduction/)

- In 2014, the revised music standards that include PreKindergarten through second grade among the P–12 *National Coalition of Core Arts Standards* (http://nationalartsstandards.org/).

Our perspectives about creating and implementing early childhood music curriculum began with and continue to be informed by our work with Gordon's preparatory audition theory as outlined in *A Music Learning Theory for Newborn and Young Children* (1990, 2013) and applications of an early childhood music curriculum we co-authored, *Music Play: Guide for Parents, Teachers, and Caregivers* (1998).[3] Understanding aspects of our underlying curriculum-writing process and our resulting perspectives of the outcomes as only one example of early childhood music curriculum may be of use to you as you make choices during your own curriculum-writing processes.[4] In the next four paragraphs, we share our process, or journey, with you. After that, we offer seven pillars[5] that have supported our evolving perspectives about early childhood music curriculum since the publication of *Music Play*.

---

[3] In this chapter, we abbreviate remaining references to this title as Music Play. Each abbreviation implies the corresponding citation Valerio, Reynolds, Bolton, Taggart, & Gordon, 1998.

[4] With gratitude we thank each of the teachers, colleagues, students, and children who have contributed to ideas developed in this chapter.

[5] The idea to use the term pillars in this chapter to frame points to consider when creating or implementing early childhood music curriculum stemmed from the Association for Childhood Education International's use of that term in their Ten Pillars of a Good Childhood, which we recommend as a useful resource (http://www.acei.org/programs-initiatives/ten-pillars-of-a-good-childhood-a-finnish-perspective.html).

To develop *Music Play*, we drew on our experiences teaching, learning, and researching in private, early childhood music settings, where Edwin Gordon and graduate school colleagues had been exploring young children's music audiation.[6] In 1990 he completed *A Music Learning Theory for Newborn and Young Children*, a text in which he outlined children's progression through types and stages of preparatory audiation he observed children ideally should engage in as they acquire the initial tonal and rhythm fluencies and comprehension of music in preparation for formal audiation-based music instruction (See Figure 1).

TABLE	STAGE
ACCULTURATION From birth to age 2: each child engages with little consciousness the environment.	1 ABSORPTION - Each child hears and aurally collects the sounds of music in the environment. 2 RANDOM RESPONSE - Each child moves and babbles in response to, but without relation to, the sounds of music in the environment. 3 PURPOSEFUL RESPONSE - Each child tries to relate movement and babble to the sounds of music in the environment.
IMITATION From ages 2–4 to 3–5: each child engages with conscious thought focused primarily on the environment.	4 SHEDDING EGOCENTRICITY - Each child recognizes that his/her movements and babble do not match the sounds of music in the environment. 5 BREAKING THE CODE - Each child imitates sounds of music in the environment, specifically tonal patterns and rhythm patterns, with some precision.
ASSIMILATION Ages 3–5 to 4–6: each child engages with conscious thought focused primarily on him/herself.	6 INTROSPECTION - Each child recognizes his/ her lack of coordination between singing and breathing and between chanting and muscular movement, including breathing. 7 COORDINATION - Each child coordinates singing and chanting with breathing and his/her movement.

Figure 1: *Gordon's summary outline of the Types and Stages of Preparatory Audiation as adapted from* A Music Learning Theory for Newborn and Young Children, *(p. 32). Copyright 2013 GIA Publications. Adapted and reprinted with permission.*

---

[6] For Gordon (2013), "audiation is to music what thought is to language" (p. ix); and audiating is "hearing and comprehending in one's mind the sound of music that is no longer or may never have been physically present" (p. 165).

Gordon asserted that, with ideal, high quality, and frequent music interactions, children could phase through the types and stages by approximately age seven years. In 1993, he and colleagues published repertoire for engaging young children in aspects of the theory in *Experimental Songs & Chants Book One* (Gordon, Bolton, Hicks [Valerio], & Taggart, 1993). In 1997, Gordon issued a second edition of his 1990 text, with relatively few alterations.

Applying our learning from our experiences, those resources, and the then-current edition of *Learning Sequences in Music: Skill Content and Patterns—A Music Learning Theory* (1997), we spearheaded the construction of a curriculum that reflected our understandings of young children's capacities for music learning and development. Specifically, we sought ways to share practical applications of ways to use Gordon's types and stages of preparatory audiation as benchmarks for music development. Broadly, we sought to ensure the curriculum would provide information and example activities to help adults successfully prepare children during their early childhood for smooth transitions into formal instruction in elementary general, choral, or private/group instrumental music settings. We also sought cohesion between *Music Play* and the already-published audiation-based curricula for elementary grades and settings. We worked to ensure that preparation via *Music Play* meant children would pass through their early childhoods having demonstrated playful, social, musical, and joyful shared music experiences; and demonstrate bolstered initial, emerging fluencies associated with musicing through audiation (See Chapters 7–13 in this text).

As does *A Music Learning Theory for Newborn and Young Children*, *Music Play* focuses on initial fluencies underlying tonal, rhythm, and movement expression and audiation, and music interactions common to Western music. We used Gordon's types and stages of preparatory audiation and music responses we had observed to be characteristic of each stage to create a curricular scope and sequence. We additionally organized scope by suggesting music featuring a variety of contexts (i.e., tonalities, meters, and harmonic functions) and content (i.e., tonal functions and rhythm functions); and movement content promoting body awareness, feeling or demonstrating style and expression in music, and coordination among breathing, moving, and musicing. We suggested instructional materials, activities for adults to use as they intentionally and informally guide children's music development, and examples of music patterns and movements to offer, listen for, and encourage during playful, social music interactions. Further, we offered basic considerations surrounding curriculum implementation, such as ways for adults to establish an early childhood music program; prepare themselves and physical spaces prior to offering *Music Play* interactions; make decisions about how to select repertoire and feature repetition, variety, and purposeful silences; understand ways that musical interactions using songs, chants, and patterns without words provide critical opportunities for children's music expression and audiation apart from language learning; and communicate observations of children's music vocalizations and movement.

Interpretations and applications of curriculum as a published document require its stakeholders to ensure it remains dynamic relative to the context in which they are implementing it. Responsively, curriculum breathes when it expands and evolves to integrate teachers' personalities, expertise and music-learning philosophies, and—most important—the children and their broader lives for whom and within which the curriculum ultimately exists. Therefore, we consider that curriculum as a written document relies on persistent self-reflection among adults charged with implementing it. When applying our self-reflection in broad strokes to *Music Play* as written curriculum, we have found that it has worked well as a prototype for persons initially beginning an audiation-based, social-music interaction music curriculum. We have observed, too, ways it has worked well as an initial guide for adults who either have the flexibility to spend extended time with young children and, therefore, can music with them at any time; or who provide or seek specific times during the day or a week to music with children separate from or integrated with other play activities. So far, we note ways the tenets of *Music Play* have been applicable in a wide variety of settings and with a variety of children. *Music Play* also has offered compatibility with broader considerations for children's overall learning and development, such as those related to inclusion for children or special needs or for whom English is not their primary language. We find, with sensitive modifications and adaptations, its tenets are applicable with learners older than nine years, when musicers have not yet demonstrated fluency with singing, chanting, or moving. That Gordon's preparatory audiation theory and *Music Play* tenets were applied in other countries and versions of the curriculum have been published in other languages suggests that their applications cut across multiple cultures (e.g., Valerio et al., 2002, 2004a, 2004b). We note ways in which using tenets has required musicianship-focused professional development, and ways in which our musicianship has expanded as a result of working with its tenets alongside young children.

Reflecting on our journey writing and subsequently implementing variations of *Music Play*, we have identified seven pillars contributing support for early childhood music curriculum engagement. The pillars stem from Gordon's theoretical framework outlined in *A Music Learning Theory for Newborn and Young Children* (2013), our work with colleagues expanding practical applications, and our continued evolving philosophies about musicing with young children. Perhaps you will find the pillars helpful to your curriculum writing and implementation, either for your work specific to early childhood, or when determining ways curriculum for a different age group can be compatible with a life-long music learning and engagement curricular mindset.

Pillar 1. Each child is born ready to audiate and communicate musically.

The auditory system of a typically developing fetus enables the fetus to hear and respond to music during the last 10–12 weeks of gestation.[7] By the time a full-term fetus exits the uterus and enters

---

[7]   Evidence of a fetus's first music acquisition and language acquisition can sound like in utero are featured on the CD produced from Sheila Woodward's research, *Womb Sounds* (Educational Research and Development CC).

the world of humans who are living and breathing separately from them, the newborn already has at least 10–12 weeks' worth of music listening, and an even longer time frame for having moved and felt the mothers' movement vocabularies. Speech and music heard in utero create memory circuits in newborns that affect their language pattern recognition, music pattern recognition, and mood recognition (Graven & Browne, 2008). Further, not long after birth, infants imitate vocalizations and facial movements in one-on-one exchanges with adults (e.g., Kelly & Sutton-Smith, 1987; Papoušek & Papoušek, 1981; Tafuri & Donatella, 2002).

For us, that evidence supports a mindset that, in utero, children are ready to begin to make sense of their worlds through music listening and movement. We consider infants' first dances as occurring in the womb; and at birth, infants' first vocalizations and independent movements as their first song and dance combinations. That mindset underlies our habits of musicing with and for children, beginning with at least newborns and infants and reaching to the oldest children. Described simply here (but in more detail in Pillars 6 and 7), we notice the vocalizations and movements newborns and infants make, interpret them as music and possible invitations for us to join a music conversation through audiation. We play with their ideas musically and through movement during our interactions with them as if they are ready to audiate and communicate musically. We realize that they are not fully audiating; that is, they are not thinking and communicating using music with syntax recognizable in most of our adult music culture. So, we meet them using their music culture—their subjective music syntax—and use aspects of their subjective music culture to guide them toward thinking and communicating through objective music syntax (Gordon, 2013). We do so gently, playfully, and gradually.

The next time you notice a woman who is pregnant, notice music in her environment, and notice her movements. Imagine those as creating music listening and movement environments for the fetus. The next time you are with or near newborns or infants, notice vocalizations and movements they are making, and consider them as music.

Consider how adopting a mindset that children are born ready to audiate and communicate fits with evidence that children are born with music learning potential that lasts throughout their lifespans. Consider ways curriculum can honor the subjective music and movements the very youngest children bring to the table.

Pillar 2. Each child is born with music learning potential, which does not disappear.

The evidence supporting young children's capacities for music engagement in utero and as newborns and infants supports assertions that all persons are born with music learning potential. Gordon (2013) refers to that potential as *music aptitude* (p.11). He asserts that music aptitude, a psychological construct, is the source for one's capacity to audiate (Gordon, 2013). Tonal music aptitude and rhythm music aptitude, and the capacity to audiate underlie one's music achievement associated with music listening, creation, and expression.[8]

Through research, Gordon identified two stages of music aptitude: developmental and stabilized.[9] He has classified children as being in the *developmental music aptitude* stage from at least birth through approximately age nine years. During the developmental music aptitude stages, he asserts that the upper limits of a child's music aptitudes fluctuate naturally; but, the limits fluctuate additionally as influenced by the breadth, depth, quality, type, and frequency of music nurturing in the child's environment. Specifically, the higher the quality and the more frequent the music interactions during the developmental stage, the larger a child's capacity to audiate and achieve musically—to think and communicate musically—once music aptitude stabilizes. When

---

[8] Gordon (2012, pp. 13–24) has described types of audiation as happening when persons interact with music (e.g., listening, reading, writing from dictation, recalling and performing, recalling and writing, creating, or improvising while performing, reading, and writing; creating or improvising while performing, reading and creating or improvising; and composing).

[9] Gordon's 2012 reference, and music aptitude test manuals referenced at the end of this chapter describe music aptitude in more detail, and are the sources from which information for this pillar stems.

music aptitude stabilizes at approximately age nine, the upper limits of a child's music aptitude no longer fluctuate. It is important to realize that a child's music aptitude does not disappear at age nine. On the contrary: the child will continue to draw on his or her music learning potential throughout life, and can continue to reap benefits from high quality and frequent music interactions, potentially achieving increasingly sophisticated music achievement.

Gordon designed three music aptitude tests to learn about tonal and rhythm aspects of children's developmental music aptitude: *Audie* (1989), *Primary Measures of Music Audiation* (1986/1979), and *Intermediate Measures of Music Audiation* (1986/1979). *Audie* is a measure of tonal and rhythm developmental music aptitude for children three and four years old. An adult plays a recording for an individual child. In the form of a game, the child hears a criterion melodic pattern, and subsequently listens to additional melodic patterns. The child has moments of silence after each pattern to tell the adult whether the subsequent melodic patterns are the same as or different from the criterion pattern. The two other developmental aptitude tests, *Primary Measures of Music Audiation,* and *Intermediate Measures of Music Audiation* are suitable for children between five and nine years of age. Adults can administer both tests to groups of children who listen to two tonal patterns and decide whether the two patterns sound the same or different, or to two rhythm patterns and decide whether the two patterns sound the same or different. Each child marks his or her decision on an individual answer sheet the adult scores. Each of the three measures of music aptitude yields scores that adults can interpret relative to individual children's developmental tonal, developmental rhythm, and composite music aptitude. The higher an individual child's accuracy with hearing and comprehending same and different as applied to tonal or rhythm pattern comparisons, the higher that child's score for tonal or rhythm developmental aptitude.

Knowing young children's tonal music aptitude or rhythm aptitude score can guide adults' decisions about creating and implementing curriculum. Noticing differences between children's expressed musicianship, which represents their music achievement, and the same children's developmental music aptitude scores, which represent their *potential* music achievement, can remind adults that children who less frequently express musicing through vocalizations or movements are not necessarily less capable of doing so; and of the importance of nurturing children's expressed music achievement to match higher levels of developmental music aptitude. Based on these tenets, Gordon recommends that children be guided concurrently, yet separately, through tonal preparatory audiation and rhythm preparatory audiation (Gordon, 1989, 1990, 1997a, 1997b, 2003, 2012, 2013).

Early childhood music education curriculum can support children to ensure they are situated to fully realize their audiation powers. As they become lifelong musicians, they can remain free to pursue music as a career or a hobby, recognize ways their music learning achieved through audiation positively differs from music learning achieved through technical prowess alone.

Pillar 3. Authentic music development, skills, and learning are rooted in audiation.

Just as authentic language development and learning are rooted in thought, authentic music development and learning are rooted in audiation. Infants, toddlers, and preschoolers learn to think using the tool of language because, fundamentally, most adults and older children expect them to think, and expect they will use spoken and written language with fluency (e.g., Reynolds, Long, & Valerio, 2007). Somehow most humans naturally understand and act as if learning to communicate with language is a natural, reciprocal process. They accept that the process takes time and playful social interaction for optimum development. The fruits—and the limits—of a child's language development and learning authentically present themselves as the child thoughtfully expresses expanding vocabularies, types of expression, reading skills, writing skills, and comprehension skills. Language interactions and, importantly, language itself both act as tools supporting and connecting the child's internal thinking and external expressions of it.

Both are so critical to the child's learning and development (Bodrova & Leong, 2007) that recently, the American Academy of Pediatrics has adopted new policy that "doctors will tell parents to read aloud to their infants from birth" (Rich, 2014, paragraph 1). The new policy is issued in response to observations that when children's environment lacks language-and-print-rich interactions, children's cognitive and intellectual developments are thwarted, causing children to struggle, particularly once they are in school.

Similarly, we assert that authentic music development and learning are rooted in audiation—music thought. Infants, toddlers, and preschoolers learn to audiate—to think music—using the tool of music because, ideally, adults and other children expect them to audiate, and expect them to music (e.g., create, improvise, sing, chant, move, read, write) with fluency (Reynolds, Long, & Valerio, 2007). Music and movement interactions and, importantly, music and movement themselves, act as tools supporting and connecting children's internal audiation to their external expressions of it. Both are critical to children's music learning and development.[10]

We consider it is never too early to expect a child can use music as a tool, *if* the expectations include unhurried time and ample space for natural, playful, and reciprocal social music interactions (Reynolds, Long, & Valerio, 2007). The fruits—and the limits—of a child's music development and learning authentically present themselves as the child uses music and movement to communicate fluencies with initial, emergent, and expanding audiation vocabularies; styles of music expression; music reading skills; music writing skills; and music comprehension skills (e.g., Reynolds, Long, & Valerio, 2007). Early childhood music curriculum can play critical roles in creating musically rich and diverse, playful, social, and interactive environments.

---

[10] The American Academy of Pediatrics' new policy also recommends that adults sing to infants, as they identify that activity as bolstering infants' acquisition of words (Rich, 2014).

Pillar 4. Young children learn through play.

From the ever-expanding body of literature on play by childhood practitioners, researchers, theorists, and historians, we continue to learn definitions of play, why it is valued, and how adults can best support and engage in children's play relative to the curricular goals particular to a setting (Wisneski & Reifel, 2012). Evidence mounts that play is "linked . . . to [children's] social and emotional development, cognition, creativity, language, and physical growth, [and] to academics, including literacy, mathematics and physical science, and the social studies" (Wisneski & Reifel, 2012, p. 177). Through play, children can practice social skills and emotional regulation, both of which contribute to building strong relationships among music learning partners, and, in turn, a socially-musically interactive community of learners. As adults set up spaces for play, their mindfulness that, rather than considering play "a vehicle for delivering the curriculum" (Rogers, 2010, p. 15), "play should be viewed as the context" (Wisneski & Reifel, 2012, p. 183) that includes space for children's contributions as they, with adults, reflect on curricular goals, strength in their relationships, and ways to share the roles of expert and novice in multiple situations.

There are infinite possibilities for contexts, or settings, of children's play; and, there is sufficient evidence that children make music making during their play, regardless of the context (e.g., Campbell, 2010; Harwood, 1993; Koops, 2010, 2014). Playful music interactions, like jovial conversations, can occur at practically any time and in any space. Be musically ready for music situations to present themselves spontaneously, such as when riding the train or in a car with a child, shopping with a child who is seated in a shopping cart or stroller, or during a worship service! As such, you will reinforce for children that music making is a dynamic and joyful form of expression. Music-play based situations and interactions provide phenomenal glimpses into children's initial, emerging fluencies with musicing and audiation.

Pillar 5. Interactions are critical to audiation and music learning processes.

Gordon's *A Music Learning Theory for Newborn and Young Children* (2013) offers early childhood music facilitators a music-specific theory about ways newborn and young children develop musically. He suggests establishing music contexts with repertoire featuring a variety of tonalities and meters, supported by corresponding, richly varied music content: tonal patterns, rhythm patterns, and movement. The music content, or patterns, he suggests are useful for encouraging music dialogue between individual children and adults. Taking those suggestions, we extensively have considered parallels between language learning processes and music learning processes (Reynolds, Long, & Valerio, 2007). In the next two paragraphs, we offer a summary of the language-learning process. As you read, you might find it helpful to recall situations and conversations you have experienced or overheard that illustrate the parts of the processes.

Typically-developing children learn to speak at least the dominant language in their household. They use that language to express and preserve what they are thinking, and refer to others' spoken and written thoughts. Everyone surrounding them *expects* this—but not immediately at birth, and not typically immediately in sentences or with correct grammatical structure, and clearly articulated and pronounced words (e.g., Cambourne, 1988; Cheng, TED-Ed, & Wooten, 2012; Hirsh-Pasek, Golinkoff, & Eyer, 2003). Simply put, children who become fluent in one or more languages are natural and organic beneficiaries of environments that are language-focused. They are surrounded by spoken and written language. Importantly, if fortunate to grow up in environments that combine language-rich, print-rich, and conversation-rich interactions—both around and with them, they have thousands of conversational demonstrations. They have thousands of invitations from more knowledgeable, responsive language users to engage in one-on-one conversations and conversations in groups. Consequently, they have thousands of opportunities alongside their conversational partners to gain familiarity with how to use words they know and are beginning to know, and ways language works in print relative to the questions, ideas, and thoughts they are expressing. Their interactions mostly are informal, unstructured, and situated firmly within contexts supporting their interactions.

As the more knowledgeable language users encourage and guide children's language use, they engage children meaningfully and intentionally in ways that require children to use critically interrelated skills: thinking, listening, speaking, reading, and writing. As they do so, they interact with children as though they are *thinkers, listeners, speakers, readers,* and *writers.* Along the way, as the children express their language skills—as they think, speak, write, or read, their more knowledgeable partners either assign predicted meaning or ask for clarification or further description when their engagements are not yet clear. The more knowledgeable language users offer sensitively crafted feedback, and guide children toward what they were coming to know through continued language use. In such socially interactive processes of learning, children indeed express themselves as thinkers, speakers, readers, and writers—using combinations of approximations, imitations, and improvisations—sometimes simultaneously. Children gain several competencies: competencies within and fluencies across multiple contexts for conversations, with multiple styles of communicating across multiple language users, and conversing on many topics. They also apply their language competencies and fluencies to their reading and writing. Ideally, throughout, they retain agency to express their own thoughts and initiate creating and interacting with a variety of text and print media. Underlying all of those active experiences, children's expressive language skills enhance their skills associated with relegating language to internal ideas, thoughts, and understandings. In turn, internal ideas, thoughts, and understandings continue to enhance their expressive language skills. All of that represents an environment full of language-rich, print-rich, and high-quality language-based interactions—the type recommended by the American Academy of Pediatrics, preparing children for later success in school (e.g., Hirsh-Pasek, Golinkoff, & Eyer, 2003; Martoccio, Brophy-Herb, & Onaga, 2014).

Considering those observations about language learning, we encourage you to reread the previous two paragraphs, replacing the word *language* with the word *music*, the forms of the verb *thinking* with corresponding forms of the verb *audiating*; and the verb *speaking* with the corresponding forms of the verbs *singing, chanting, creating,* and *improvising.* As you read, imagine music situations and music conversations that illustrate the ideas.

With an expectation (not hurried guidance or accelerated instruction) that children are audiators and musicers, we honor the possibilities that children's vocalizations and movements—from birth—are invitations for musicing. We have made that our habit, but we realize many adults vary regarding what they tune in to regarding children's musicing. That is, they vary in the extent to and ways in which they interpret what they hear and see children doing as being *music* or *music-related* (Reese, 2011; Valerio, et al., 2012). Learning to notice and, ideally, to interpret vocalizations and movements as invitations for musicing can critically shift an adult's mindset about very young children's musicianship and the beginnings of early childhood music curriculum. With that shift, possibilities for increased types and frequencies of music-based interactions with children emerge for the adult. In turn, children's increased expression of music ideas can increase adults' natural and organic opportunities to spur children's music learning process forward. Ultimately, we recommend curriculum that establishes music making among adults and children as music making that takes place alongside colleagues (Filsinger, 2012). Shared roles among collaborators will, no doubt, blur the lines of distinction between who is the expert and the novice, and who is initiating and who is responding to musicing (Reynolds, 2006). As such, adults and children play interactively as audiators: listeners, movers, singers, chanters, readers, and writers who are increasing competencies and fluencies with expressions of music that emphasize vocal tonal, rhythm, and physical movement in a variety of ways across many contexts.

Adults are responsible, ultimately, for shaping the environment to be musically rich. Tapping into their own audiation, adults need to be ready with music ideas and playful ways to start and extend music conversations with the whole group or individual children. When they hear children or one child musicing, adults' understanding of the types and stages of preparatory audiation is a useful map to provide possibilities about where children might go next either naturally or through guided music interaction. Together, adults' and children's collaborations importantly establish joint music attention (McNair, 2010) that deepens their abilities to relegate music to internal *audeas*—music thoughts and understandings—organized, manipulated, initiated, and communicated apart from language. When we prioritize attention to music situations and conversations, children offer amazing examples of their expressive audiation capabilities, like those featured in Figures 2, 3, and 4.

Since interactive music conversations like those can occur in practically any space, any time, we recommend prioritizing time daily for playful, social, and interactive musicing that allows children's music initiations and creations with each other, and with guidance from adults.

Pillar 6. Continually monitoring and adjusting during playful music interactions leads to assessment of music fluencies in music making contexts authentic to early childhood.

Our primary guidance focuses on facilitating individual children's progression through the types and stages of tonal and rhythm preparatory audiation. That, in turn, focuses our primary assessments on individual children's initial expressive music fluencies and audiation. When children are demonstrating their initial expressive music fluencies consistently, they are listening, babbling, approximating, imitating, or imitating with coordination (See Figure 1). Once they have emerged from Stage 7, they are able to coordinate their breathing with their movement and musicing. With their coordinated breathing, they express themselves with singing voice quality and in-tune singing, consistent tempo singing and chanting, and expressive and musical chanting. When they are demonstrating initial audiation skills in music interactions, they evidence their engagement with tonality through singing resting tones, tonal patterns, harmonic functions,

Figure 2: *Toddler and two music teachers in music interaction (Valerio, 2000b). A toddler vocalizes and two adult music teachers interpret the vocalizations as music and the three collaborate rhythmically, tonally, melodically, and harmonically. Lyrics written using the International Phonetic Alphabet. As found in* Listen to Their Voices: Research and Practice in Early Childhood Music, Research to Practice, Vol. III *(p. 219). Copyright 2007 by Canadian Music Educators Association. Reprinted with permission.*

Figure 3: *Toddler and one music teacher in music interaction (Valerio, 1999). A music teacher sings in solo, pauses, and a toddler responds with a tonal pattern. The two musicers collaborate with tonal patterns in meter. Lyrics written using the International Phonetic Alphabet. As found in* Listen to Their Voices: Research and Practice in Early Childhood Music, Research to Practice, Vol. III *(p. 220). Copyright 2007 by Canadian Music Educators Association. Reprinted with permission.*

Figure 4: *Three school-aged children and two music teachers collaborate in melodic improvisation (Valerio, 2000a). A music teacher improvises in solo. Three school-aged children each improvise melodically in solo in succession. A second music teacher improvises and pauses before reaching the resting tone. One student completes the phrase by singing the resting tone, and then the group sings the resting tone. Lyrics written using the International Phonetic Alphabet. As found in* Listen to Their Voices: Research and Practice in Early Childhood Music, Research to Practice, Vol. III *(p. 221). Copyright 2007 by Canadian Music Educators Association. Reprinted with permission.*

and intentionally improvising or echoing; and their engagement with meter through pulsating macrobeat tempo, and chanting expressively when intentionally improvising or echoing rhythm patterns. The prevalence of music composed in major and harmonic minor tonalities and duple and triple meters in Western culture underlies the suggestion that achievement of expression of initial fluencies and audiation means being able to engage in songs, chants, patterns, and movements in at least those tonalities and meters. When children are able to coordinate their breathing, movement (See Figure 1, Stage 7), and singing of major and harmonic minor tonality, and when children are able to coordinate their breathing, movement, and chanting (See Figure 1, Stage 7) of duple and triple meters, those achievements have been considered the minimal demonstration required to have emerged officially from the final informal stage of preparatory audiation, and are considered prepared to engage in the formal stages of audiation.

Although we are confident each child will demonstrate expressive musicianship and evidence of their engagement with audiation, we also expect those demonstrations will, among groups of children, emerge in different ways (including silence and stillness characteristic of children who choose to absorb or listen rather than kinesthetically or vocally participate) and on different days (or weeks or months). Within individual children's demonstrations of tonal, rhythm, and movement fluencies, we expect fluctuations in the frequency and consistency with which a child expresses his or her musical thoughts using one or more of those fluencies. We also expect most children's expressions will demonstrate that they are in a different stage of tonal preparatory audiation than rhythm preparatory audiation, and they are moving through both tonal and rhythm preparatory audiation in a non-linear fashion. Thus, we view assessments as multidimensional, flexible, continual processes of monitoring and adjusting that we cannot hurry or rush. The processes align with techniques associated with informal guidance and an informal music-learning curriculum. Whether charged to engage young children in music curriculum during designated daily or weekly times (e.g., centers, circle time, music class), or in settings in which we interact musically with children at any time, we prefer to employ assessment techniques in ways that preserve the informal, multiple, authentic, playful, and interactive music contexts from which children's musicing emerges. We avoid using language to pressure or solicit children's demonstrations for which to receive a grade.

When we are singing, chanting, and moving, we notice that children use their expressive fluencies, too. Interactivity in the form of dialogue is critical. Through turn taking one-on-one with us, a child shares his or her expressive fluencies to invite us our response, or in response to our music expressions. The silent time in turn taking leaves children space to take in all they have heard and expressed, and possibly to generate new music ideas. We have found, further, that when we offer children a variety of silent times, they demonstrate their music fluencies, and they express *their* music ideas (Hicks, 1993; Reynolds, 1995). We leave silent and stillness between repetitions of songs or chants, pattern interactions, or jam sessions full of improvised harmonies and rhythms. Often, after a song, chant, or jam session format is familiar to children, we will insert purposeful silences in place of expected music. We mindfully include purposeful silences during music interactions for absorption time, and as invitations for children to vocalize or move. We do so with no expectations about particular ways they will respond. Sometimes during our purposeful silences, their absorption silences and stillness are "deafening." Other times, individual children or groups burst into musicing to create a symphony of sounds that can become the basis for the next improvised music interaction. The purposeful silences create child-centered musical moments. Importantly, they provide everyone with time to audiate—and to be present in the moment of music interactions. They also provide useful changes of pace for discreetly charting observations, particularly when more than one adult is facilitating interactions.

We employ a variety of assessment and documentation techniques. As we interact, we continually notice the children. We consider what we hear and see and notice ways children's expressions are relative to the tonality, meter, form, and style of the music serving as the basis for the interactions. We listen and watch for children's fluencies with coordinating their breathing with their moving and singing, and ways their expressive singing provides evidence of initial audiation of tonality through their singing resting tones, and flexibility while echoing and improvising tonal patterns. We equally listen and watch for children's fluencies with coordinating their breathing with their moving and chanting, and ways their expressive chanting provides evidence of initial audiation of meter through the underlying tempo of their movements and chanting or singing, and flexibility while echoing and improvising rhythm patterns. As children offer vocalizations and movements, we encourage each child to listen to their own musicing, to play with those patterns via babble, imitation, and improvisation. We interpret the music content of children's music vocalizations and movements relative to the context (i.e., tonality and meter, style and form) of the musicing to echo, improvise, or create harmonies or rhythmic ostinati. We also interpret the music content relative to the music situation in which the interaction has occurred, such as ways children are coordinating their breathing, moving, and vocalizing; and imitating or improvising. We apply our simultaneous interpretations to split-second decisions about how vocalizations and movements are characteristic of a given stage of tonal or rhythm preparatory audiation, or suggesting a child is transitioning to a higher stage.

We document our interactions to track learning and development and to share achievements with the children, their parents, and other teachers. When we have access to developmental music aptitude scores, we can note discrepancies between music achievement and music potential, and create individual music possibilities to raise both to match at their upper limits. Using a relatively simply form of documentation, through recall, we make written descriptions of the music context (e.g., tonality, meter, style), music content (e.g., resting tone, tonal function such as tonic or dominant, rhythm function such as macrobeat/microbeat or divisions), and quality of children's vocalizations (i.e., evidence of coordination among breathing, moving, and vocalizing as demonstrated via singing voice, chanting voice, and general expression). We chart those relative to stages of tonal or rhythm preparatory audiation.[11] We then use the child's relative position within the stages to consider possibilities for our next music interactions with them.

Because of the spontaneity, complexities, and sheer numbers and types of children's vocal and movement contributions, we have found that capturing music interactions via audio or video recording offers opportunities to review children's contributions repeatedly. More elaborate forms of documentation, borrowed from recommendations by experts in the Reggio Emilia Approach to Early Childhood Education (Infant-toddler Centres and Preschools Istituzione of the Municipality of Reggio Emilia, 2010) and Reggio-Emilia inspired settings include approaching the music learning process as collaborative research, in which adults and children collect music interactions through photographs, audio and video recordings, children's drawings, and notation. The resulting documentation techniques offer music interaction narratives that invite individual children, groups of children, and adults, in community, to revisit music learning processes. Together, adults and children can collaboratively reflect, and generate subsequent music possibilities.[12] We have found that sharing the stage of development and types of musical responses with parents or guardians, other teachers, or administrators often requires sharing the information featured in the pillars of this chapter, as adults sometimes are unfamiliar with what music expressions look and sound like relative to music learning and development in early childhood.

In sum, we use assessments and documentations of individual children's vocalizations and movements to monitor and adjust— in the moment of musically interacting, and after reflection on

---

[11] For examples of ways to document music interactions, see *Music Play* pp. 24–40 and information shared by Marshall and Bailey (2009) in their article referenced at the end of this chapter.

[12] We acknowledge with gratitude colleagues in Japan and the United States who have considered *Music Play* in relation to the co-constructivist tenets of the Reggio Emilia to early childhood education in preschool settings, specifically the children, with Kerry Renzoni (Filsinger), Junko Cancemi, Claire Weston, Barbara Folliett, Karen Chayot, Kathy Goldenberg, Heather Waters, and Emily Westlake.

interactions—to play with subsequent ways to offer music play, music interactions, and music guidance. As you fold assessment into your early childhood music curriculum, realize that the cycle of preparing, interacting, documenting, reflecting/revisiting, and communicating takes continual practice, and—to do it well—a surprising amount of time. However, we predict that, as you revisit documentation of an individual child or group of children, you will hear and see activity you missed in the moment that can help you chart each child's music development and, in turn, can inspire new music and music activities as possibilities for subsequent interactions. Also, we predict that systematic documentation of individual children's progression through the types and stages of preparatory audiation will help prepare you and them for formal music assessments such as the Grade 2 Model Cornerstone Assessments offered by the National Coalition for Core Arts Standards (2014).

Pillar 7. Guiding young children to realize their audiation powers takes culturally-relevant, musical preparation.

Although children are born ready to audiate and to communicate using their natural music learning potential, most children will realize their music potential best when, throughout their early childhoods, they have the benefit of interacting with persons who serve as their more knowledgeable music conversation partners (e.g., mother, parents, guardians, siblings, additional family members, caregivers, teachers, other children). When the more knowledgeable music conversation partners are charged with implementing music curriculum, children will benefit from their partners' understanding how music interactions support music development. We recommend understanding the types and stages of preparatory audiation and their use as benchmarks when preparing for possible music situations, offering specific types of music interactions, scaffolding children's music learning, and assessing their achievements relative to stages of music development.

To prepare ourselves musically for playful, social, music interactions, we continually seek to increase the number, styles, tonalities, and meters of our expressive vocabulary of songs, chants, and patterns. We continually seek ways to understand the home music culture of each child, and integrate their music into the early childhood music setting. We continually ensure we are able to use our bodies and movement flexibly and fluidly to demonstrate coordinated breathing, moving, and musing; tempo and meter; and expression and style in music. We reach into the variety of repertoire or children's musical contributions and play with tonal patterns, rhythm patterns, movements, and purposeful silences and stillness as building blocks for music play and music dialogues. We play with audiation and musing by composing, improvising, harmonizing, notating, and jamming with harmonic, melodic, and rhythmic ostinati. We are mindful of our models of body use, coordinated breathing, and expressive and fluid musing.

We practice noticing ways children move, sing, chant, and play. We practice all of these ideas in the chapter when we are with children, guiding their musing. With them, we have adopted habits of talking less and musing more for and with expectant mothers, newborns, infants, toddlers, preschoolers, and elementary school children. We practice initiating improvisations, compositions, and harmonizing. We practice playing with props, toys, and materials typically available in early childhood or early childhood music settings to discover ways resulting movements support coordination among breathing, moving, and musing. We play with ways to insert purposeful silences within and between songs and rhythm chants. We practice using the silent time to wait for, notice, listen, and watch young children's musing and movements. We practice echoing their musing to acknowledge and reinforce their contributions. We improvise and harmonize with their music ideas to emphasize that music is a dynamic communication tool, and to possibly extend their music play (Reynolds, 2005; Valerio, 2007). In general, we practice using related musing in response to children's vocalizations and movements as feedback to encourage confidence with expression and extensions of children's musing. With practice, we also use musing related to theirs in spontaneous, improvised activities we recognize as *leading activities* (Bodrova &

Leong, 2007) toward further approximations or progression into a new stage of preparatory audiation.

We strive to ensure spaces indoors and outdoors support children's free movement and music making and feature aesthetically pleasing materials and authentic music instruments to support music interactions. If adults are with children for extended time each day, practically any of the materials that support children's free choice, creativity, exploration, and play will support their musicing. Music-specific materials, such as instruments with a variety of timbres, music books, and writing materials focus children on music-specific practices, valuable for their emerging fluencies. With understandings of children who are learning English or have special needs, adults can adapt the physical space and materials and modify activities to continue applying recommendations from this chapter (See Chapter 16).

In general, we practice incorporating what we learn from children and our music interactions into our ever-expanding, social-music, and playful-interaction repertoire. Overall, we find that as our repertoire increases and diversifies, our music interactions with children become more fluid and flexible. We find all of that useful as we seek to build strong and caring relationships with the children and propel their current music learning and development forward.

When reflecting on our own musicianship and listening to other adults reflect on theirs, we note powerfully that, to fill the role of more knowledgeable music conversation partner, adults draw on musicianship that reaches back to their own musical childhoods. Repeatedly, we notice that if they feel they lacked an interactively rich music musical childhood, they generally voice a lack of confidence or regret that they lack a level of comfort with interacting musically. When adults feel they benefitted from rich musically interactive environments during their early childhood, they often voice confidence about making music comfortably. Either way, adults often describe a lack of understanding about music development, or ways interacting musically as described in this chapter differs from performing music or teaching music through direct instruction. We have found that, along with preparing to become musically confident and musically comfortable making music with the youngest children, adults can learn to identify and understand music development constructs, particularly in the moments of interacting with and guiding children. Engagement in professional development that includes musical interactions with children can help ensure adults are able to interact musically with cultural sensitivity, and understand, notice, interact with, and scaffold children's expressive music and moving learning. Coursework, certifications, in-services, and conference workshops are helpful experiences; children are the best teachers. Ultimately, we envision adults acieving cycles of success in which playful, social-music interactions in early childhood translate into continued confidence and comfortability through remaining music curricular options and and musical lives alongside and after music curriculum. Then, when children become parents, teachers, administrators, or policy makers, each adult can successfully become a music conversation partner with future generations of children. Together, adults and children will understand that there are relatively few boundaries to enjoying a lifetime of music situations and conversations.

SUMMARY

Through activities based on pillars described within this chapter and presented in *Music Play*, and through children's music making and movement through play apart from adults, we have noted ways children learn about themselves and each other through their music making. We have noted ways their identities as musicians are affirmed. Perhaps as you have journeyed with us through this chapter, you collected aural and visual images to illustrate the pillars supporting an audiation-based early childhood music curriculum. If you have embedded those images in playful, interactive music scenarios, perhaps you have imagined positive ways music making establishes relationships, builds community, and promotes enjoyable social interactions. We invite you to retain those images and scenarios as we summarize this chapter.

Early childhood music curriculum matters. Use the pillars to breathe life into your social-music interactions with children. Believe children are ready to audiate, and communicate musically. Know that each child has music learning potential. Use music as context to root children's music development skills and learning in their audiation. Continually prepare them for successive realizations of their audiation powers using music. Prepare them using culturally specific content, making sure to use variety, repetition, and purposeful silences. Keep music situations playful and interactive. Listen to the children. Use their vocalizations and movements as springboards for musical conversations. Guide them through the types and stages of preparatory audiation. Continually document and share children's vocalizations and movements.

Adults' and children's vital and symbiotic roles relative to music learning and development matter. Children's interactions with more knowledgeable others guides learning, fostering its internalization. Then, learning "become[s] part of the child's independent developmental achievement" (Vygotsky, 1978, p. 90). Through interactions and cycles of documentation, adults and children breathe life into written curriculum. Together, they focus on building children's emergent music acquisition and comprehension skills, and bolster children's music comfortability with creative musical expression, confident that their musical thoughts do matter.

Applications of the pillars in this chapter matter. As you continue the journey creating early childhood music curriculum, so do we. Applications of *Music Play* will continue to evolve, as should teaching practices and materials. Notions of music curriculum as outlined both in this chapter and throughout this text continue to push early childhood and PreK–12 music curriculum designs outward as well as deeper. Regarding the pillars, we make the following assertions:

- The pillars are portable. Adults can access them at any time, to enjoy music making in practically any location.
- Because one can learn to audiate and achieve musically beyond the early childhood years, the pillars can be applied to audiation guidance at any time along the lifespan.

- The pillars are transferable. Adults and children can apply the pillars flexibly to varied music making situations using multiple means of music expression—including sensitively guided interactions with electronic and digital media—via performances, improvisations, compositions, responses, preferences, purchases, and sharing and organizing electronic files.

- The pillars need to be central in pre-service teaching and professional development models. As a profession, we need to prioritize focused and sustained support for adults' confidence that they understand young children's music development and music learning, can access their own musicianship and music ideas to create music learning settings, are capable music partners for children, and can enjoy playfully and musically interact with them.

- The pillars are compatible with the PreKindergarten through grade 2 standards in the newly revised *National Coalition for Core Arts Standards* (2014), intended for young children two to eight years old.

- The pillars and these assertions offer rich areas for longitudinal research. Although early childhood music researchers reference early childhood music curricula as part of their research designs, to date, only a few researchers have studied the long-term effects early childhood music curriculum and experiences have on music achievement (e.g., Runfola, Etopio, Hamlen, & Rozendal, 2012). Improving practice and learning systematically through research about ways music interactions contribute to children's music and overall development continue to be priorities, but alone likely will be insufficient. To ensure all children's access to high-quality early childhood music interactions, researchers and practitioners need to increase communications with policy makers about why and, specifically, how early childhood music matters.

Each person's contributions to early childhood music and curriculum matter. Children are born ready to make music. There are many ways for the child to make music, be musical, and be considered a musician. During their early childhood years, children will encounter persons who, to generate music interactions with them, rely to some extent on their own musical childhoods. If P–12 music curriculum nourishes persons' music instincts to reinforce musicing and interacting musically with others as perpetual human activities, imagine the effects. The notion that early childhood music education begins in the womb will no longer be astonishing. Each person would comfortably and confidently tap into his or her own rich musical childhood to "pay attention to young children, notice their expressive [musicing], share with them what you like about their [musicing]" (Reynolds et al., 2015, p. 212) and interact musically with them. In closing, we encourage you to consider that, each time you make music with the youngest child, your contributions matter.

References

Bodrova, E., & Leong, D. J. (2007). *Tools of the mind: The Vygotskian approach to early childhood education.* Columbus, OH: Pearson.

Cambourne, B. (1988). *The whole story: Natural learning and the acquisition of language.* Auckland, NZ: Scholastic.

Campbell, P. S. (2010). *Songs in their heads: Music and its meaning in children's lives* (2nd ed.). Oxford: Oxford University Press.

Campbell, P. S., & Scott-Kassner, C. (2014). *Music in childhood: From preschool through the elementary grades* (4th ed.). Boston: Schirmer Cengage Learning.

Cheng, A., TED-Ed., & Wooten, V. (2012). *Music as a language* [Video file]. Retrieved from http://ed.ted.com/lessons/ victor-wooten-music-as-a-language

Elliott, D. J. (2013). *Musicing and listening in paraxial music.* Retrieved from http://www.davidelliottmusic.com/ praxial-music-education/music-and-listening-in-praxial-music/

Filsinger, K. B. (2012). *Webs of interactions: International perspectives on cultural music mediation among adults and young children* (Dissertation). Available from ProQuest Dissertations and Theses database (UMI No. 3564808)

Gordon, E. E. (1986/1979). *Manual: Primary Measures of Music Audiation and the Intermediate Measures of Music Audiation.* Chicago: GIA.

Gordon, E. E. (1989). *Audie: A game for understanding your child's music potential.* Chicago: GIA.

Gordon, E. E. (1997b). *Learning sequences in music, skill, content, patterns: A music learning theory.* Chicago: GIA.

Gordon, E. E. (2012). *Learning sequences in music: A contemporary music learning theory.* Chicago: GIA.

Gordon, E. E. (2013/1997b/1990). *A music learning theory for newborn and young children.* Chicago: GIA.

Gordon, E. E., Bolton, B. M., Valerio (Hicks), W. K., & Taggart, C. C. (1993). *Experimental songs and chants, book one.* Chicago: GIA.

Graven, S. N., & Browne, J. V. (2008). Auditory development in the fetus and infant. *Newborn and Infant Nursing Reviews, 8*(4) 187–193.

Harwood, E. E. (1993). Content and context in children's playground songs. *UPDATE: Applications of Research in Music Education, 12*(1), 4–8.

Hicks, W. K. (1993). *An investigation of the initial stages of preparatory audiation* (Dissertation). Available from ProQuest Dissertations and Theses (UMI No. 9316493)

Hirsh-Pasek, K., Golinkoff, R. M., & Eyer, D. (2003). *Einstein never used flash cards: How our children really learn—and why they need to play more and memorize less.* USA: Rodale.

Infant-toddler Centres and Preschools Istituzione of the Municipality of Reggio Emilia (2010). *Indications: Preschools and infant-toddler centres of the municipality of Reggio Emilia.* Reggio Emilia, Italy: Reggio Children.

Kelly, L., & Sutton-Smith, B. (1987). A study of infant musical productivity. In J. C. Peery, I. W. Peery, & T. W. Draper (Eds.), *Music and child development* (pp. 96–106). New York: Springer-Verlag.

Koops, L. H. (2010). "Deñuy jàngal seen bopp" (They teach themselves): Children's music learning in The Gambia. *Journal of Research in Music Education, 58*(1), 20–36.

Koops, L. H. (2014) Songs from the car seat: Exploring the early childhood music-making place of the family vehicle. *Journal of Research in Music Education, 62*(1), 52–65.

Marshall, H. D., & Bailey, J. M. (2009). Observing and communicating early childhood music and movement development. *Perspectives: Journal of the Early Childhood & Movement Association 4*(2), 1–8. Retrieved from http://www.ecmma.org/perspectives/

Martoccio, T. L., Brophy-Herb, H. E., & Onaga, E. E. (2014). Road to readiness: Pathways from low-income children's early interactions to school readiness skills. *Infants & Young Children, 27*(3), 193–206.

McNair, A. A. (2010). *Joint music attention between toddlers and a music teacher* (Dissertation). Available from ProQuest Dissertations and Theses database (UMI No. 3433168)

National Coalition for Core Arts Standards, PK–8 General Music Standards. (2014). Retrieved from http://www.nationalartsstandards.org/

Papoušek, M., & Papoušek, H. (1981). Musical elements in the infant's vocalizations: Their significance for communication, cognition and creativity. In L. P. Lipsitt (Ed.), *Advances in infancy research, Vol. 1* (pp. 163–224). Norwood, NJ: Albex.

Reese, J. A. (2011). *Adult identification of meaningful and intentional music behaviors demonstrated by young children* (Dissertation). Available from ProQuest Dissertations and Theses database (UMI No. 3457936)

Reynolds, A. M. (1995). *An investigation of the movement responses performed by children 18 months to three years of age and their caregivers to rhythm chants in duple and triple meters* (Dissertation). Available from ProQuest Dissertations and Theses database (UMI No. 3457936)

Reynolds, A. M. (2005). Guiding early childhood music development: A moving experience. In M. Runfola & C. C. Taggart (Eds.), *The development and practical application of music learning theory* (pp. 87–100). Chicago: GIA.

Reynolds, A. M. (2006, Spring). Vocal interactions during informal music classes. *Bulletin of the Council for Research in Music Education, 168*, 35–49.

Reynolds, A. M., Renzoni, K., Turowski, P. L., & Waters, H. D. (2015). "Pssst . . . ! Over here! Young children shaping the future of early childhood music education. In C. Randles (Ed.), *Music education: Navigating the future* (pp. 201–214). New York: Routledge.

Rich, M. (2014, June 24). Pediatrics group to recommend reading aloud from birth to children. *New York Times*. Retrieved from http://www.nytimes.com/2014/06/24/us/pediatrics-group-to-recommend-reading-aloud-to-children-from-birth.html?module=Search&mabReward=relbias%3Aw

Rogers, S. (Ed.) (2010). *Rethinking play and pedagogy in early childhood education: Concepts, context, and cultures*. New York: Routledge.

Runfola, M., Etopio, E., Hamlen, K., & Rozendal, M. (2012). Effect of music instruction on preschoolers' music achievement and emergent literacy achievement. *Bulletin of the Council for Research in Music Education, 192*, 7–27.

Tafuri, J., & Donatella, V. (2002). Musical elements in the vocalizations of infants ages 2–8 months. *British Journal of Music Education, 19*(1), 73–78.

Valerio, W. H., Reynolds, A. M., Bolton, B. M., Taggart, C. C., & Gordon, E. E. (1998). *Music play: The early childhood music curriculum guide for parents, teachers, and caregivers*. Chicago: GIA.

Valerio, W. H., Reynolds, A. M., Bolton, B. M., Taggart, C. C., & Gordon, E. E. (2002). *Music Play*. (H. K. Yi, trans.). Hanam-city, Korea: IEC Music English.

Valerio, W. H., Reynolds, A. M., Bolton, B. M., Taggart, C. C., & Gordon, E. E. (2004a). *Muzikos z˘aismas* [Music play], R. Poškutė-Gruen (Ed.). Lithuania: Kronta.

Valerio, W. H., Reynolds, A. M., Bolton, B. M., Taggart, C. C., & Gordon, E. E. (2004b). *Yinyue youxi* [Music play], translated by G. Wang and H. Liu. Beijing: China Translation and Publishing Corporation.

Valerio, W. H., Reynolds, A. M., Morgan, G., & McNair, A. A. (2012). Construct validity of the parent-completed Children's Music-Related Behavior Questionnaire. *Journal of Research in Music Education 60*(2), 186–200.

Valerio, W. H., Seaman, M. A., Yap, C. C., Santucci, P. M., & Tu, M. (2006). Vocal evidence of toddler music syntax acquisition: A case study. *Bulletin of the Council for Research in Music Education, 170*, 33–46.

Vygotsky, L. S. (1978). *Mind in society: The development of higher psychological processes* (M. Cole, V. John-Steiner, S. Scribner, & E. Souberman, Eds. & Trans.). Cambridge, MA: Harvard University Press (Original work published 1930, 1933, 1935).

Wisneski, D. B., & Reifel, S. (2012). The place of play in early childhood curriculum. In N. File, J. J. Mueller & D. B. Wisneski (Eds.), *Curriculum in early childhood education: Re-examined, rediscovered, renewed* (pp. 175–187). New York: Routledge.

CHAPTER 15

ADULT MUSIC TEACHING AND LEARNING

Scott N. Edgar
Lake Forest College

Linda A. Hartley
University of Dayton

After teaching music to children in elementary, middle, and high school for 10 years, I felt that I was starting to become an effective teacher. I had worked with youth from varied backgrounds and at different ability levels. I felt I could teach beginning or advanced students. Even with this experience, when Matt, a 75-year-old beginning trumpet player asked me to give him lessons, I was forced to teach in a way I never had before! It was completely different and a challenge. (Scott Edgar reflection)

Each week I have the opportunity to work with adult music learners, not only college-level students, but also with those primarily over 50-years-old. Holding the perspective of teaching elementary through high school-age students for many years, I thought that the transition I would need to make in my instructional methods would be minimal—not true. Exploring and understanding the differences in adult music education has been fundamental to providing meaningful instruction and musical rewards for participants. (Linda Hartley reflection)

The majority of this text is dedicated to instruction of music to students in P–12 schools and undergraduate colleges and universities. Curriculum and assessment of music in schools is essential; however, these students graduate and active music making is often left behind. Even if students are receiving a quality music education in schools, it may not carry past their graduation day. What are we doing as music educators to prepare students for a *lifetime* of music?

While the term *adult* could apply to anyone past the age of 18, we are focusing this chapter on young adults after they leave formal education (including undergraduate education) through adults in retirement, ages 55 and higher. There are plentiful opportunities for formal music education and music making while in school (P–16); however, it is when these opportunities cease to be easily accessible that many who once classified themselves as musicians discontinue making music. Additionally, many adults may have not participated in formal high school music programs and may wish to later in life (Elpus & Abril, 2011). In this chapter, we will discuss the importance of teaching music to adults regardless of past experience. Exemplary practices for teaching adults, curriculum for adults[1], and assessment strategies for adult learning will be included.

Andragogy

For the first time in our society adults outnumber youth. The number of adults in the United States over the age of 85 is expected to grow to 20 million by the year 2050 (U.S. Bureau of the Census, 2004). In contrast to pedagogy (teaching youth), andragogy refers to the study of adult education and learning strategies (Knowles, 1970). With the rise in the number of adults, increased attention to andragogy is warranted. There are several theories underpinning the andragogical model that are different from the traditional pedagogical model. Knowles, Holton & Swanson (2012) provide core principles for adult learning as established much earlier by Knowles. Holton and Swanson stress that there will be a variety of other factors affecting

---

[1] While the term *curriculum* is often associated with formal schooling, we broaden the definition for this chapter to include both formal and informal adult music making opportunities.

adult learning, which may or may not align closely with these principles. The authors of this chapter note assumptions marked with an asterisk (*) which could especially be considered narrow in perspective. These assumptions may present a falsely dichotomous view of pedagogy versus andragogy[2]:

Assumption	Pedagogy	Andragogy
The need to know	Learners need to know only that they must learn what the teacher teaches to pass and get promoted.	Adults need to know why they need to learn something before undertaking to learn it.
The learners' self-concept	The teachers' concept of the learner is that of a dependent personality; therefore the learner becomes a dependent personality.	Adults have a self-concept of being responsible for their own decisions, for their own lives.
The role of the learners' prior experiences	The learners' experience is of little worth as a resource for learning. What counts is the experience of the teacher, and resource materials.*	Adults come into an educational activity with both a greater volume and a different quality of experience from that of youths.
Readiness to learn	Learners become ready to learn what the teacher tells them they must learn if they want to pass and get promoted.	Adults become ready to learn those things they need to know and be able to do in order to cope effectively with their real-life situations.
Orientation to learning	Learners have a subject-centered orientation to learning; they see learning as acquired subject matter content.	Adults are life-centered in their orientation to learning.
Motivation to learn	Learners are motivated to learn by external motivators (grades, teachers' approval or disapproval, parental pressures).*	Adults are responsive to some external motivators (jobs, promotions), but the most potent motivators are internal pressure (self-esteem, quality of life).

Figure 3: *Pedagogical and Andragogical Assumptions* (Knowles et al., 2012, pp. 60–67, abbreviated by the authors of this chapter)

---

[2] For further details regarding pedagogy, andragogy, and critiques of these assumptions, see Kruse, 2007.

The ability of an adult to articulate self-directed objectives and draw from their life experience positions them in a different situation than a ten-year-old learning violin for the first time; however, there are certainly overlapping similarities. Self-direction, as with all of these objectives, could also be viewed as a goal rather than a natural characteristic of adults and their learning. Knowledge of adult learning strategies aid in teaching children, and comprehensive pedagogical skills can enhance adult musical learning. For example, adults learning something new often need step-by-step instruction provided by an expert, and young children will often benefit from relevance. Good teaching is good teaching—sometimes children benefit from andragogical approaches and adults benefit from pedagogical approaches.

These assumptions underpinning andragogy can provide guidance in the creation and successful implementation of adult music curriculum. Due to the differences highlighted above, music educators accustomed to teaching youth may need to adjust their philosophy and instruction to meet the needs of adults. Educators are urged to adapt instruction as needed to fit the uniqueness of the individual and situation, just as we do with youth. In the next section we offer select examples of adult music making curricula that have been influenced by the above assumptions.

Adult Music Curriculum

Over the years, especially in my adulthood, people have expressed dismay at the number of hours I volunteer to singing in choruses, both for rehearsals and performances, without any form of monetary compensation. For me the answer is simple: I do it because I love it, and because of the 'magic' that happens in an ensemble when a group of singers come together to make music.
(Stephanie, adult choir participant)

A survey of opportunities for adults to learn and make music is an important initial step for them to continue music making past formal schooling. These opportunities can be found in churches, neighborhoods, schools, and community centers. Adult music education commonly takes the form of large ensembles (band, choir, orchestra), small ensembles (church groups, folk groups, chamber ensembles), community musical theatre, or informal groups (garage bands, jam sessions, individual exploration). One organization advocating for adult and community music-making opportunities is the National Guild for Community Arts Education. They have articulated three separate goals differentiating the types of curriculum available: (a) performance; (b) education; and (c) social enjoyment (National Guild for Community Arts Education, 2011). Regardless of the goal, the voluntary nature of the music making is one attractive element for adults.

Community Ensembles

Community music ensembles take many forms and can be found formally and informally in both secular and sacred settings.

Community bands, choirs, and orchestras. Community ensembles are one of the most common practices of adult music making found in the United States. In its heyday, every city and town had its own band, choir, or orchestra. They have maintained their popularity but have adapted into several different forms. Some are "come one, come all" groups where the priority is community engagement and provides an outlet for musicians of all musical levels to continue music making. There is rarely an entrance procedure and auditions are seldom required. The typical literature for this type of ensemble is popular in nature and includes audience favorites such as movie music, holiday tunes, and marches.

Other community ensembles have developed into elite ensembles requiring an audition and focus on performing a very high difficulty level of literature, performing high-profile concerts, and producing recordings. Literature chosen for this ensemble, while still audience friendly, is often more varied and includes a more sophisticated level of music. Current or retired music educators who have gained some level of renown in the area direct most of these ensembles. Participants are usually professional musicians and/or music educators looking for a performance outlet. Musical success is the principle goal of these ensembles.

Objectives and goals vary greatly for middle and high school ensembles; however, most directors focus on performance and expanding the musical knowledge and skills of their members. These goals can be similar for community ensembles, depending on their objectives. One objective for community ensembles is entertainment for the community it serves. This greatly impacts literature selection, rehearsal strategies, and performance opportunities to meet the musical needs of the *community*. While preparing for a concert or contest may be of importance for school ensembles, preparing for the Fourth of July concert filled with Sousa marches may be the priority for community ensembles. While this would facilitate an entertaining concert, this might be a limited repertoire for school ensembles.

Church choirs and instrumental ensembles. Another common ensemble is the church choir and instrumental accompaniment. This often requires little rehearsal and time commitment but gives participants an opportunity to perform and engage in social and cultural (faith) interaction. These ensembles are frequently associated with varied faiths and provide music for worship services. The musical level of these ensembles is wide-ranging, and roles, such as soloist or cantor, are often assigned according to ability. Instrumental participation differs based on the particular congregation's needs and whether it provides a traditional or contemporary worship service. Traditionally focused congregations rely on a solo organist/pianist who is usually a paid professional. More contemporary congregations often have larger instrumental ensembles that could include multiple keyboards, guitar, bass guitar, brass, woodwinds, percussion, and may possibly resemble a rock band. Members in church choirs/ensembles can have a deep connection with the music, their community, and their faith.

Church choirs focus on the needs of the congregation. This may or may not meet the musical needs of the performers. Leaders of church choirs aim to foster musical excellence; however, this purpose is for the end goal of quality music for the congregation. This is similar to the historical context for the creation of school music education in the United States—to facilitate better musicians to sing in church choirs.

Semi-professional organizations. There are also collaborative music programs with organizations such as professional ensembles and colleges or universities. Many professional orchestras have community choruses to accompany them. These ensembles commonly have a performance-based emphasis and could include entrance requirements, such as an audition and résumé submission. The level of musicianship required to participate in most of these ensembles require a substantial musical background and expertise. Many are composed of music educators who are looking for a performance outlet in addition to their teaching responsibilities.

Popular and vernacular music. Popular and vernacular music, or music with which the musician associates, offers opportunities for adult musicians. Commonly informal, these can take the form of rock, folk, or other popular music ensembles and offer opportunities for adult musicians to perform music that resonates with them. For example, many adults now are from the baby boomer generation. Rock 'n' Roll was a genre of music that was wildly popular with them; therefore, performing as part of a rock band could be attractive. Most of these ensembles are self-created and require initiative on the part of the participants to create, rehearse, and perform. Other ensembles discussed above, in contrast, are usually existing and open for participants to join. Other types of vernacular music ensembles that might be attractive are fiddle bands, mariachi bands, steel drum ensembles, African drumming ensembles, barbershop quartets/choruses, and Celtic music ensembles, among many others.

Music education in the United States has made strides to include these types of opportunity for P–12 students; however, this curriculum still remains limited in scope and implementation as the traditional ensembles of band, choir, and orchestra still dominate. Expanding both opportunities for P–12 students and adults to engage in alternative ensembles could contribute to a broader definition of music education and facilitate unique opportunities for intergenerational learning and musical expertise.

Community ensembles provide opportunities for adults of all ages. Multiple generations can collaborate in a single ensemble, offering an additional level of benefit for participants. Some curricula, however, are designed to specifically cater to those of particular age groups.

New Horizons International Music Association

All of my kids got to enjoy playing in the band when they were in school. Now it's my turn! (Bill, New Horizons Music participant, age 68)

New Horizons Music (NHM), later becoming the New Horizons International Music Association, was founded by Dr. Roy Ernst (professor emeritus, Eastman School of Music) in 1991 and was designed for the older adult population (age 50 and up) to enter or re-enter ensemble music making (Ernst, 2001). NHM differs from typical community music ensembles where all participants are expected to read music and be somewhat accomplished on their instrument or voice. Focusing on beginners and providing a re-entry point for those who had left music making for a number of years, NHM programs offer a relaxed and welcoming instructional environment for those interested in music making with others. Initially only involving wind and percussion instruction, NHM expanded to include strings, chorus, and chamber ensembles such as jazz bands. Currently there are more than 200 NHM organizations throughout the United States, Canada, and several other countries, serving more than 9,500 participants (NHIMA, 2014). NHM ensembles often perform at community outreach events such as fairs, charity events, senior centers, and festivals. Typically, NHM programs welcome three distinct levels of participants: the adult beginner, re-entries, and extenders.

The adult beginner.

I didn't know what I was going to do in retirement until I heard about the New Horizons Band. I can't thank you enough for giving me a purpose. (Russ, beginning clarinetist, New Horizons Music member, age 65)

Only 20 percent of adults in the United States participated in formal school music education programs while in high school (Elpus & Abril, 2011). With the premise of "it's never too late to start," the NHM program opened doors for thousands of older adults (the other 80 percent) providing them the opportunity to learn to play an instrument or sing in a group for the first time. Independent older adults can choose their destiny, as they are more likely able to afford needed musical equipment that may not have been available to them at an early age. The life- and self-centered motivations Knowles, et al. (2012) presented are central to why the adult beginner may want to explore music making.

For the adult learner, trying something new can be intimidating, mainly because, as adults, we can be self-conscious about making mistakes. But in a *group* of adult beginners, learning through making these mistakes becomes less intimidating and can be fun. From an instructor standpoint, one can quickly see their pride in progress and the amazement of performing even the simplest of phrases.

Adults who classify themselves as beginners, are generally claiming no formal training on a particular instrument or voice. Because these adults actively seek knowledge (Knowles, et al., 2012), and their parents are not forcing them to take up something new, their motivation to learn as well as the process for learning will differ from school-aged children. Instructors for adult music learning must provide curricular materials and sequenced guidelines for learning that will facilitate the development of skills as well as knowledge. For example, most adult beginners are genuinely interested in learning to read music immediately, and therefore may be frustrated with a Suzuki or Music Learning Theory approach that stress aural skills first. While aural skill development is essential, be prepared to move more quickly to reading notation.

Utilizing standard method books for beginning instrumental instruction can be just as successful for adults, even though these publications were primarily developed for school-aged children. It is recommended to supplement these standard method books with beginning-level appropriate familiar selections that interest the particular age group of adult learners.

Additionally, group learning can enhance the experience for the adult learner. Beginners will become frustrated more quickly than children because adults are accustomed to doing many things well. Learning in a group will help fulfill the social and emotional connections needed to move past the feelings of frustration. Everyone making mistakes together, celebrating individual and group progress, and accomplishing goals they never thought possible, are essential components when designing the adult music learning experience.

Re-entries.

I played the French horn in high school, but never owned one myself. At age 70 I purchased my first horn and love playing it in the band every week! (Jean, New Horizons Band member, age 81)

Lifelong learning can take many forms, not necessarily following a specific or predictable path. While many adults become active listeners and supporters of music, active music making can easily take a back seat. After high school or college graduation, adults find several reasons to stop music participation. Careers and family tend to top the list, not being able to justify extra time to sing in choirs or practice their instruments. But once the children are grown and retirement is in the foreseeable future, those who fondly recall their earlier music making days might be tempted to dust off those instruments or reignite those vocal chords.

The majority of NHM members are "re-entries," which may speak to P–12 music education success. A recent national survey (Hartley, 2012) showed that high school ensemble enjoyment was a strong motivator for initially joining NHM programs. NHM brings together those with similar school experiences who fondly recall the summer camps, bus rides, festivals, and most importantly, making music. Re-entries would find it difficult and somewhat intimidating to take up their instruments/voices right where they left off 40 or 50 years ago and jump right into a community band, choir, or orchestra. NHM provides a re-entry point to rekindle these skills, and encouragement to do so.

Extenders.

> *My goal is to learn to play every wind instrument in the band.* (Shirley, New Horizons Music participant, retired school orchestra director and cellist, age 79)

NHM programs also attract seasoned musicians wanting try something new. An accomplished clarinetist, for example, may have always wanted to play in a jazz band and can now learn to play the saxophone. Many professional and military career musicians find New Horizons a great fit for their retirement—not too much pressure, and focused on the process of learning versus the end product. Membership in a NHM program allows senior adults to extend their prior experiences, continuing their quest for learning and music making. "Extenders" tend to become valuable resources for their fellow peers in the ensemble, as well as to the instructors.

While their personal goal might be to learn something new, they may flip their role on occasion and become mentors/instructors, benefitting all involved. Utilizing musical knowledge of the extenders not only validates their prior life experience and expertise (a valued element of andragogy), but also can add to the musical development of other group members. It is not uncommon to assign extenders to teach other small groups or individuals, and even to rehearse the entire ensemble.

The New Horizons International Music Association provides start-up information and planning materials through their website[3].

---

[3]   http://www.newhorizonsmusic.org/nhima/membership_planning.html

Included in these materials are concept and philosophy, resources needed, steps in starting an ensemble, public relations, how to hold an information meeting, information for teachers, developing the organization, and helpful forms and samples for the organization.

Feeder program.

Just as an elementary school band, choir, and orchestra develops student musicians to move forward into middle school and eventually high school, NHM programs can serve as "feeders" to area community music organizations. While many NHM programs provide a variety of levels of ensembles (beginners, intermediate, advanced), some NHM members begin looking for more challenge, such as auditioning for a local music organization. Conceivably they could play first violin in NHM, and second violin in the local community orchestra. NHM focuses on the process of learning and provides instruction, while community groups have the expectation of proficiency on your instrument or voice.

There are certainly side benefits to this concept of feeder programs. Audience numbers at concerts can rise, as members from each organization tend to support each other through concert attendance. While competition for members could be an issue, directors can take an alternative approach and be proud of members wishing to seek more challenge, knowing they had a part in the musical development of that NHM member. Additionally, purposefully performing combined concerts with local community ensembles adds an amiable factor carrying through to the membership of all ensembles.

Adult Music Camps

In addition to local community music organizations and NHM programs, a growing number of adult music camps are offered annually throughout the United States and abroad. Music camps for "grownups" can provide a renewed interest in music making, exposure to new repertoire, and new friends for a lifetime. The New Horizons International Music Association website offers a planning guide for hosting New Horizons Music camps which includes suggestions on resources and facilities[4].

Administration of Adult Music Ensembles

Recruitment, literature selection, and teaching strategies are three of the most important elements P–12 music educators face on a daily basis. While strategies used to successfully navigate these elements may differ somewhat from P–12 curricula to adult curricula, exemplary practices can inform teaching students of any age. In the following sections we offer insight as to how one might navigate these important elements of teaching, specifically focusing on processes for adult populations.

Recruitment and Advertising

Attracting adults desiring to actively participate in music making organizations can be a challenge. For most community bands, choirs, and orchestras, expectations are that members can read music and have had experience singing or playing an instrument. In alternative community ensembles such as rock bands, ukulele or banjo groups, and multicultural ensembles, reading music may not be a prerequisite, although some form of experience is usually necessary. Conversely, NHM programs seek to attract those with little or no musical experience.

Defining the purpose of an adult music program is essential for recruiting potential participants. Adult music ensembles' goals can vary widely. While some programs exhibit product goals such as performances and competitive events, others may be focused more intently on the process of learning. Certainly there are adult music programs that combine process as well as product. Some adult ensembles focus on performing for specific events, such as parades, funerals, special holidays, or festivals. Determining the purpose of the ensemble will also dictate the style of music studied and performed. Community adult music ensembles can emphasize particular cultures or genres,

---

[4]   http://www.newhorizonsmusic.org/camps_events/documents.html

such as Scottish bagpipe, Javanese gamelan, Dixieland band, and Renaissance ensemble.

Once the purpose of the musical organization is ascertained, recruitment can begin. Reputable and established ensembles' main method of recruitment tends to be word-of-mouth and through encouragement of family and friends who are already members. However, this would not be possible for a new group trying to recruit initial membership. Local media are usually willing to assist through publishing articles and advertisements, but targeting specific populations focused on purpose of the organization also needs to occur. Starting a barbershop-style chorus, for example, may include recruitment strategies such as contacting local church choirs, and offering training sessions on barbershop style singing. Adults who enjoy music but not actively making music are usually consumers of music and music events. Placing strategic ads in local theatre and symphony concert programs help publicize new adult music learning opportunities to those who regularly support live music. Local music stores are excellent connections where frequently private lessons are offered and are intricately involved in the P–12 schools. Adults who take up instruments or sing for the first time tend to begin with private lessons. Once they progress to a certain level of accomplishment, playing in a group is a likely next step for their development as a musician.

Some community ensembles hold auditions due to the purpose of their group, and others do not. Auditioned ensembles will tend to attract more serious and accomplished musicians and cause others to hesitate, looking for a more inclusive music making experience. Again, the purpose of the organization defines the types of recruitment activities and must focus on attracting members who will be comfortable in the learning environment established. Those interested in starting a NHM group may utilize detailed start up and planning information found on the New Horizons International Music Association website[5]. Specific recruitment materials include sample fliers, strategies for

---

5   http://www.newhorizonsmusic.org/promotional_tools/growing.html

media, information sessions, and recruitment performances. Utilizing the objectives outlined by Knowles, et al. (2012) in recruitment could be beneficial. Specific elements could include acknowledging potential participants' life experience, highlighting opportunities for self-exploration, and answering "why" questions instead of just "what."

Literature Selection (Curriculum)

Choosing literature for adults versus school ensembles deserves careful thought. Because adult ensembles usually perform for community audiences and special events, music selection differ from middle school, high school, and collegiate ensembles. For example, performing a medley of armed forces songs will touch adult individuals in multiple and meaningful ways. Due to a collective history of life experiences, Frank Ticheli's beautiful rendition of *Amazing Grace* could draw not only more expression from an adult community band than a school band, but instill motivation and urgency to improve tone quality, intonation, phrasing, balance, blend, and an increased desire to practice to do justice to this selection. However, the goals of musical growth and satisfaction through the process of rehearsal and performance of the literature are often similar between young ensembles and adult groups. Therefore, time spent searching for high quality compositions and arrangements is always worthwhile.

Rohwer (2005) surveyed NHM directors and found that the need for familiarity was a key factor in choosing literature. In her study, directors cited the most common musical styles chosen for New Horizons Bands, which included jazz (swing and standards), marches, musical medleys, light classical, and patriotic. Because New Horizons generally has a focused age group (50 and up), recognizable and memorable compositions can be somewhat easier to find versus choosing familiar selections for a typical adult community ensemble comprised of a wider age group.

Directors of adult bands, choirs, and orchestra need to be cognizant of rehearsal time when selecting literature. Often, directors of adult music ensembles are current or former school music teachers accustomed to rehearsing their school ensembles daily. Because most adult ensembles meet only once a week, there may be just a handful of rehearsals between performances. Additionally, rehearsing once a week begs for review of previous rehearsal progress. Choosing music with the allotted rehearsal time in mind is essential.

Though school music ensembles tend to be comprised of students with similar musical achievement skills, adult music ensembles may include a wider variety of abilities. Fortunately, there are published musical arrangements specifically designed for ensembles with varying levels of proficiency that will challenge more accomplished musicians and not frustrate those who are developing.

Unique to adult music ensembles, as compared to typical school ensembles, members may participate for an unlimited number of years. School music ensemble members eventually graduate and no longer participate in communal music making, but most community ensembles do not impose age limitations. This notion must be considered when choosing literature. Exploring new literature is a vital component of musical growth and can also affect retention. Directors of adult music groups should cogitate rotating favorites and including a gentle mix of newer literature.

Teaching Strategies

Principles of andragogy (see Figure 1) are central when designing appropriate teaching strategies and curriculum for adult music learning. Particularly when teaching individuals something new, such as learning to play an instrument for the first time as an older adult, the concept of self-directed learning is necessary to consider. Because adult students come pre-packaged with life experiences, they often have an idea of what they would like to learn, and when they are ready for new information. While receptive to expert instruction, an adult will be inclined to interject self-assessment. Music lessons can be viewed as a team-approach to reaching progress and goals versus a teacher-learner method. The teacher must shift gears from "disseminator" to "facilitator."

The chapters in Part 2 of this book outline exemplary practices for teaching individual musical elements. These strategies work well with populations of any age; however, they should be tempered by the assumptions of andragogy and keeping the following elements, unique to teaching adults, in mind.

Elements Affecting Teaching Music to Older Adults

There are biological variables associated with aging that music teachers need to consider when teaching adults. Visual and aural difficulties can arise making traditional instruction from the podium and note reading difficult for the adult learner. Adaptations would need to be made, such as vocal amplification, larger print music, or increased room lighting. There are also physical limitations associated with aging. For example, arthritis could make it difficult to play a string instrument. An awareness of physical ability would need to be considered when providing instruction and feedback. Instructing some to listen, when they are struggling to physically do so, would not be a teaching technique appreciated by adult learners who may be navigating their disability. These situations need to be handled delicately and respectfully as adults could take offense to being told they need glasses or hearing aids. Memory capacity can also become an issue as adults age. Sensitivity to these situations needs to be present as adults may be struggling due to a variable completely out of their control.

Social benefits are a critical reason why many adults choose to participate. Depending on the purpose of the ensemble, expecting adults to sit quietly and focus on musical advancement during a rehearsal may not be the best approach. Music directors need to provide their adult musicians the opportunity to socialize and interact in the rehearsal. Many adult musicians can learn and teach on their own. This independent learning and social engagement should be nurtured—learning the music cannot be the singular goal of rehearsals. Meeting the ensemble members' social needs also should be considered. Adults seek new learning opportunities for a variety of reasons. Some adults are goal-oriented and wish to pursue a life-long dream of playing or singing in an ensemble. Older adults, especially those who are retired, may be looking for social activities to meet new friends and feel an integral part of a group, and fill the void of their previous job or career. And still others may realize the physical, social, and emotional benefits of active music making and take needed steps to maintain and improve their health.

Musical benefits are only part of what participants in adult music making can experience. Many of the participants are retired, craving social interaction. Especially in the United States, people commonly use their employment community to populate their social base. When retirement arrives, losing this socialization can be difficult. Communal music making can offer an opportunity for socialization as well as music making. Emotionally, senior adults can struggle finding a new identity after retirement. Recreating themselves as a musician can offer an emotional outlet for these feelings. It can be frustrating for an adult, used to feeling successful with their endeavors, to have to face the challenges of learning to read music or play an instrument from the beginning. Participating with like-aged people in a similar position can help with this.

The Process Model

When designing rehearsals for adult music groups, the director should consider that adults tend to be more motivated to learn if they are provided a purpose for particular rehearsal strategies (Knowles, et al., 2012). Learning to play a chromatic scale with correct alternate fingerings, for example, will be more meaningful if they see an immediate application in a selection of music that is being prepared. Explaining why you are subdividing during a specific measure is just as important as showing how you are conducting this measure. In Coffman's (2009) survey of New Horizons band and orchestra directors, one respondent noted, "adults more often question changes in teaching approach, but usually are willing to try anything after discussion/explanation" (p. 234).

Not only do adult musicians want to focus on improving their musical skills, but they also enjoy expanding their musical knowledge. Adults appreciate information about the composer and the music they are performing, and frequently will add their own life experiences to these discussions. Incorporating opportunities to glean factual knowledge not only enhances the progress of the participants, but also can also heighten their experiences in the adult learning environment. A central characteristic of adult learning is for adults to view themselves as learners (Brookfield, 1986). The authors recognize that these suggestions represent good teaching at any level, but note that adults outwardly appreciate learning more than reading the notes.

Teaching strategies can differ between teaching adults and teaching younger students. Knowles developed an andragogical process model (Knowles, Holton, & Swanson, 2012) in contrast to a content model: "the content model is concerned with transmitting information and skills, whereas the process model is concerned with providing procedures and resources for helping learners acquire information and skills" (p. 114). When teaching adults, the teacher becomes much more of a facilitator for learning. The director of an adult music ensemble needs to prepare rehearsals to involve the learners versus solely disseminating knowledge. Knowles, Holton and Swanton provide the following list of elements to include when utilizing the process model: (1) prepare the learner; (2) establish a climate conducive to learning; (3) create a mechanism for mutual planning; (4) diagnose the needs for learning; (5) formulate program objectives (content) that will satisfy these needs; (6) design a pattern of learning experiences; (7) conduct these learning experiences with suitable techniques and materials; and (8) evaluate the learning outcomes and re-diagnose learning needs. This process model focuses on a proactive versus reactive approach to learning and highlights andragogical philosophies. This process model could be beneficial for P–12 music educators as well.

Coffman (2009) provides an excellent point when comparing teaching adults to teaching younger students. In his study surveying directors of community bands and orchestras with experience teaching K–12, he noted consistent comments from directors about their positive experiences teaching adults, with one director stating, "Adult community bands are the ultimate reward to a long teaching career." (p. 236) Coffman wonders if we should be reconsidering the way youth are taught, perhaps utilizing some aspects of andragogical principles. (See Appendix for resources following the eight tenets of Knowles' process model for adult music learners.)

Life Experience and Self-directed Learning

The adults' life experience is the greatest asset they bring to the learning environment. Music education is an apprenticeship-model profession; we teach how we were taught. Adult students learn how they have their entire lives, and learn based on how they have engaged in education in other contexts. Acknowledging adult learners' prior knowledge and experience is critical for instructors to effectively teach new concepts and to understand existing adult student preconceived ideas and beliefs. The adult musician may be a beginner playing an instrument or reading music, but they are not a beginner in life. Adult music educators must treat their adult students with the respect and dignity they deserve.

Given their life experience, adult learners are usually more independent than youth—their instruction must reflect this need for self-direction. Teachers of adults must assume the role of mentor and guide instead of imparter of knowledge. While an adult might not have ever played an instrument before, their experience will likely facilitate a much faster learning curve. It is more important that the teacher help the adult learner "plan, carry out, and evaluate their own learning" (Merriam et al., 2007, p. 107), than to dictate specific learning objectives that the teacher designs. Adult learners can accomplish a great deal outside of the learning environment. Practice techniques are much more important than fundamentals—they can teach themselves.

This technique can be difficult for music educators accustomed to teaching youth. Opportunities for adults to explore and figure it out on their own are necessary to be included in rehearsals. For adults, it is more than just the literature; it is about giving them the skills to teach themselves. This self-efficacy is necessary for the adults to be successful musically, and satisfied emotionally.

Assessment

Unlike assessing musical progress for youth, assessing adults' progress toward musical goals necessarily differs. The nature of self-directed learning tells us that adults are better equipped to provide their own evaluation of a particular musical passage or concept, or to provide their assessment of progress over a period of time. A young student learning to play the saxophone may not necessarily know how her tone should sound, needing specific guidance from the instructor. In contrast, an adult learning to play the saxophone is more likely to instantly realize that the first tones produced do not represent the ideal tone of the saxophone and is motivated to make the necessary adjustments for good tone production. Adult beginners will often seek guidance of the instructor based upon their own evaluation. Adult music learners can thrive on progress, encouragement, and motivation, just as younger learners do. But the types of structured evaluation for individual adult learners can be much more informal due to adults' ability for self-evaluation.

Teachers of adult musicians and especially those directing adult music ensembles should, however, systematically assess program goals on a regular basis. Program goals should be realistic and based upon adult learning goals, which may considerably differ from those of school music ensembles. Depending upon the purpose of the adult music ensemble, program goals may include: membership retention; winning or placing in festivals or competitions; increasing membership; performing more challenging repertoire; attracting more beginners; group travel; performance opportunities; providing opportunities for social interaction; promoting an enjoyable, nurturing, respectful and non-threatening learning environment; and attracting a diverse membership. Larger adult music groups may have a structure of leadership where volunteers or elected members assist the director to meet program goals. Member leadership could effectively develop, assist, or lead program assessment. The three purposes of adult music making articulated above by the National Guild for Community Arts Education (performance; education; and social enjoyment) will dictate the type of program assessment necessary.

Intergenerational Curriculum

Intergenerational experiences can be heightened through music making. All ages can sing together and play instruments together. Differences as well as similarities between pedagogy and andragogy can affect the learning process, but end results can produce a positive impact on participants and audiences alike. One of the most powerful outcomes of intergenerational experiences is witnessing lifelong learning in action. Groups of musicians performing together demonstrate that music is one of those activities that can be appreciated throughout a lifetime, and can be enjoyed by multiple generations. Routinely designing intergenerational experiences for music making will enhance participants' understanding of musical styles, learning differences, and appreciation for multiple age groups.

Conclusion

The concept of teaching adults and adolescents music at first seems quite similar; however, after taking a closer look, profound differences emerge. Adults bring wonderful life experience to their learning that must be capitalized upon. The necessary objectives for adult learners are much less standardized than those present for P–12 students, therefore the assessment must follow suit. The true purpose of assessment is to measure a student's growth and to direct future teaching. It is with this mindset that assessing adult learners should be approached—not to rate, grade, or place. Adults are *choosing* to learn for their own benefit and assessment and motivational techniques should reflect this. When designing and implementing curriculum for adult musicians principals of andragogy can provide guidance. Music educators accustomed to teaching youth should continue to utilize the teaching methods they have found to work, tweaking them by implementing tools such as the process model. Due to the thoughtfulness required to successfully teach adults, expanding teaching expertise to include this population will strengthen your own teaching. Exploring the curricular opportunities for teaching adult music making could be a rewarding experience. See the following websites for a list of existing ensembles:

- New Horizons Music Ensembles: http://www.newhorizons-music.org/music_groups/groups.html
- Community Band and Orchestras: http://www.community-music.info/groups.html
- Community Choirs: http://www.choralnet.org/list/choir/556

With the ultimate goal of music education being to engender a *lifelong* love for and engagement with music, we as music educators cannot ignore the importance of teaching music to adults. We encourage you to look for opportunities to get involved in adult music education. As we have found it can provide a different insight into teaching music and be richly rewarding. Music education should not end after high school and it is never too late to begin, re-enter, or extend!

Acknowledgments

We would like to thank Nathan Kruse, Will Dabback, and Kay Wert Minardi for their feedback and assistance with this chapter.

References

Brookfield, S. (1986). *Understand and facilitating adult learning.* San Francisco, CA: Jossey-Bass.

Coffman, D. D. (2009). Learning from our elders: survey of New Horizons International Music Association band and orchestra directors. *International Journal of Community Music*, Vol. 2, no. 2 & 3. doi: 10.1386/ijcm.2.2&3.227/1

Elpus, K., & Abril, C.R. (2011). High school music ensemble students in the United States: A demographic profile. *Journal of Research in Music Education, 59*, 128–145.

Ernst, R. (2001). Music for life. *Music Educators Journal, 88*(1), 47–51.

Hartley, L. (2012). Survey of New Horizons Music participants. Music and Lifelong Learning Symposium presentation, Columbia, SC. October 14, 2013.

Knowles, M. S. (1970). *The modern practice of adult education: Andragogy versus pedagogy.* New York, NY: Cambridge Books.

Knowles, M. S., Holton, E. F., & Swanson, R. A. (2012). *The Adult Leaner* (7th ed.). New York, NY: Routledge.

Kruse, N. B. (2007). *Andragogy and music: Canadian and American models of music learning among adults.* Unpublished doctoral dissertation, Lansing, MI: Michigan State University.

Merriam, S. B., Caffarella, R. S., & Baumgartner, L. M. (2007). *Learning in adulthood: A comprehensive guide* (3rd ed.). San Francisco, CA: Jossey-Bass.

National Guild for Community Arts Education (2011). Retrieved July 8, 2014 from: http://www.nationalguild.org/About.aspx.

New Horizons International Music Association (2014). Retrieved March 1, 2014 from: http://www.newhorizonsmusic.org/music_groups/groups.html.

Rohwer, D. (2005). Teaching the adult beginning instrumentalist: Ideas from practitioners. *International Journal of Music Education.* 23: 37 DOI: 10.1177/0255761405050929. Retreived from: http://ijm.sagepub.com/content/23/1/37

U.S. Bureau of the Census. (2004). *U.S. Interim projections by age, sex, race, and Hispanic origin.* Retrieved from http://www.census.gov/ipc/www/usinterimproj

APPENDIX

Sample Ensemble Rehearsal Planning Guide and Supplemental Materials for the Adult Music Learner Based on the Process Model

Prepare the Learner

Preliminary musical instruction for the next rehearsal should be electronically distributed *several days* ahead.

Example:

We will focus on tempo transitions and ensemble blend and balance.

The following selections will be rehearsed in this order:

- Dixieland Spectacular (arr. Jennings)
- Barnum and Bailey's Favorite March (King/arr. Brubaker)
- Mountain Thyme (Hazo)
- American River Songs (LaPlante)
- You're A Grand Old Flag (Cohan/arr. Story)

Changes from routine need to be communicated in advance. For example, if ensemble seating is to be adjusted in any way, it is suggested that ensemble members have a copy of the new seating chart before they come to rehearsal.

Establish a Climate Conducive for Adult Learning

Choose rehearsal space wisely. An organized rehearsal room will aid adults getting to their seats safely with an established routine. Adult members tend to arrive early for rehearsal and carefully prepare their instruments and equipment for rehearsal. The following are suggested guidelines to establish a conducive climate:

- Conductors should assign rehearsal set up to trusted ensemble members to pre-arrange seating and other needed equipment for rehearsal, long before the rehearsal start time.

- Visibly include the rehearsal order so that members can see it from their seat.
- Provide a space for instrument cases and other gear to be stored during rehearsal.
- Make sure appropriate lighting is available.
- Temperature and ventilation must be controlled and comfortable.
- Only rehearse in a space where appropriate acoustics are available, and not detrimental to the auditory health of the ensemble members.
- Handicap access and easy access to restrooms is essential.
- If available, utilize technology resources to enhance learning, such as listening and playback tools.

Create a Mechanism for Mutual Planning

Just like middle school and high school music ensembles, adult ensembles need organizational and leadership structure to ensure contributions by all members. Mutual planning helps ensure commitment, responsibility, and a sense of belonging. Be sure to include time during rehearsal for committee leadership to communicate to the membership. The following is an excerpt from the NHM New Group Planning Guide:

Committee Signup

Please look over the following and return this form with your choices if you are able to take on a volunteer assignment. Do not feel guilty if you are not able to volunteer at this time. We will arrange all the committees so that the amount of work and responsibility is not a burden. Working on committees will give you a chance to get to know people better. We can change committee assignments every year (or semester), so you will get to know more people and do different things. Each committee will be co-chaired. If we involve more people in committees, we can have many more enjoyable events.

Mark your preference for the following by using these indications: VI for very interested, I for Interested, N for neutral, and NI for not interested.

1. Steering Committee _____
2. Music Library Committee _____
3. Social Arrangements Committees _____
    Coffee _____
    Party Committee _____
    Coordinator _____
4. Concert Coordinator _____
5. Telephone Network _____
6. Attendance _____
7. Facilities /Equipment _____
8. Treasurer _____
9. Gig Scheduling _____

If you are willing to help any place that help is needed, please check here. _____

Name _____

Instrument _____

Additionally, it is suggested that an evaluative survey periodically be administered so that participants may contribute to future programming and goals of the ensemble.

Evaluation Form

Please take a few minutes to help us by giving us your evaluation. The evaluations will be carefully considered in planning for the future. Circle your response. Add comments wherever you wish to do so.

1. Do you plan to continue? Yes   No

2. Did your accomplishments this semester meet your expectations, fall short of your expectations, or exceed your expectations?
   Meet   Fall short   Exceed

3. What are your most satisfying accomplishments so far? Check all that apply.

   _____ Playing a new instrument

   _____ Reading music

   _____ Writing music

   _____ Playing in small ensembles

   _____ Playing in the band

   _____ Playing by ear

   _____ Improvising

   _____ Starting a new area of learning and recreation

   _____ Expanding your social activities

   _____ Other:

4. What would you like to accomplish next?

5. What do you want to spend more time on?

6. What would you like to spend less time on?

7. Check ways in which your music listening has changed:

   _____ Have gone to more live performances

   _____ Enjoy listening to recordings and radio music more

   _____ Other:

8. List any health problems that may have developed as a result of your participation:

9. List any ways in which your physical and mental health may have improved as a result of your participation:

10. Where did you obtain your instrument?

    _____Already owned it

    _____It belonged to someone else in my family

    _____Found it through a want ad

    _____I purchased it at a music store

    If so, what store? _____

    Reasons for selecting that store: _____

    _____

    Did you purchase from the store from which you rented?

    Yes   No

    If no, why? _____

11. Please list music and accessory items that you have purchased since September:

12. Please give us your general comments. What did you like best? Least? What suggestions do you have for making improvements? Sign your name at the end if you would like to, or remain anonymous.

Diagnose the Needs for Learning

Based upon the purpose of the adult music ensemble, the director should determine primary learning goals for the participants. Because adults are able to voice their learning needs, membership input is vital to assess the needs of individuals as well as the ensemble. An evaluative tool such as the sample survey listed above will be helpful as the ensemble progresses each year. Of course, the instructors will possess the expertise to determine realistic learning goals for the ensemble.

Ability and achievement levels may differ widely in adult, non-auditioned music ensembles. Alternative instruction should be provided for those who have the desire and ability to progress more rapidly than the entire ensemble as a whole. Conversely, alternative instruction should also be provided for those who are not yet ready to perform at the level of the large ensemble.

Formulate Program Objectives Satisfying These Needs

In the P–12 setting, instructors traditionally set objectives for their students, testing them periodically to see if these objectives have been accomplished; however, objectives for adult music ensembles must be formulated from a different perspective. Objectives tend to emerge through individual as well as ensemble needs. Relevancy is key, and objectives should not be solely musical. With regard to learning objectives, "…according to andragogical theory, the learner is likely to resist unless he or she freely chooses them as being relevant to his or her self-diagnosed needs" (Knowles, Holton, & Swanson, 2012).

Design a Pattern of Learning Experiences

Over a period of time, adult music ensemble participants should expect a particular routine of learning experiences that focus on the development of musical attributes. Thoughtful, sequential instruction is a model that holds up well with adult music learning. Instruction with a clear purpose is seen as a means to reach individual musical goals. Typical rehearsal structure as one might traditionally find in the school setting can work very well with adults. But because most adult ensembles do not meet daily (contrary to most school music ensembles), careful planning must occur to include individual and ensemble musical objectives.

An example of a typical adult music ensemble rehearsal could include:

- Welcome/announcements
- Warm up and tuning exercises
- Work on a familiar selection to reach higher performance goals

- Sight reading and/or a less-familiar selection
- A special performance by a professional musician
- Listening to a portion of a rehearsal, providing analysis input and new performance goals
- Ending with a selection that the group can perform successfully.

Rehearsals with a social structure built, such as refreshments after rehearsal, helps satisfy the adult need for friendship building. Participants appreciate starting and ending rehearsals on time.

Conduct These Learning Experiences with Suitable Techniques and Materials

Instructors must be chosen carefully in order to meet the needs of adult music learners. Ensemble members charged with finding new instructors must understand that subject-matter experts must also possess attributes that will be conducive to adult music learning. The following suggested job description, found in the NHM Group Planning Guide, indicates desired qualities of an adult music ensemble instructor:

Adult Band or Orchestra Director Job Description

Education and Experience

- Degree in music education and teaching experience.
- Experience in teaching all of the woodwind, brass, and percussion instruments for band directors, and all of the string instruments for orchestra directors.
- Familiarity with method books and ensemble repertoire for all levels.
- Experience in group instruction, especially for mixed instrument groups.
- Experience in programming for general audiences. If in doubt, ask to see programs the candidate has conducted.
- Good standing with music teachers and music dealers who know his or her work.

Personal Qualities

- Good sense of humor.
- Must value creating a group that is inclusive rather than exclusive.
- While everyone enjoys the accomplishment of performing as well as possible, excluding players or using methods that are intimidating or stressful to accomplish that goal is not acceptable.
- Must be comfortable with including others in decision making, and responsive to the likes and dislikes of the musicians, both musical and non-musical.
- Should value turning much of the operation of the ensemble over to volunteer members of the ensemble. This is especially important in consideration of the valuable experience of members.

Responsibilities

- Conduct rehearsals and work cooperatively with teachers of smaller groups (sectionals, chamber music ensembles, etc.).
- Select instructional books and music repertoire that members will enjoy. Periodically ask players which items and pieces they like and dislike.
- Teach in a supportive and positive manner with good humor. A good guide is "Your best is good enough."
- The main goal of a New Horizons Band or Orchestra is to continually create entry points to music making for adults with no musical background and those with music making far in the past. It is essential for the director to make this a top priority.
- The director should be comfortable sharing conducting responsibilities with other directors. This benefits the directors by providing flexibility to miss rehearsals or performances when necessary. Ensembles usually enjoy having more than one personality and teaching style.
- Be available to conduct performances in the community one or two times per month on average.
- Communicate with the national New Horizons organization.

We have found that enthusiastic adult learners may have particular music selections in mind, some even purchasing arrangements for the ensemble to play without the understanding of difficulty level or particular needs for the ensemble. While music selection input is encouraged, instructors must guide members in sequential instruction and musical arrangements that will encourage members to continue performing.

Much different than the school setting, adults are more likely to be able to afford and make decisions on purchasing their individual instruments. It is important that directors communicate to ensemble members that they would like to provide guidance prior to purchase. We have found that because adults are accustomed to making their own decisions, that often times they will do so with major purchases such as a musical instrument. A beginner should be encouraged to rent or borrow an instrument until he/she demonstrates a secure interest and progress.

Evaluate the Learning Outcomes and Re-diagnose Learning Needs

Utilizing a program evaluation survey as listed earlier in this appendix is central to determining learning outcomes, membership satisfaction, and future needs. Additionally, gathering data on aspects such as rehearsal attendance, membership sustainability, and growth will provide an indication on the health of the organization. Musical progress can be assessed through rehearsal and performance recordings. We do not recommend formal individual assessments, as we typically would provide in a school ensemble setting. Adults and adult music ensembles possess different needs than young students, and the purpose of adult music ensembles can be much different than that of school groups.

CHAPTER 16

MODIFICATIONS OF MUSIC CURRICULUM AND ASSESSMENT FOR ENGLISH LANGUAGE LEARNERS

John Eros

California State University, East Bay

Introduction

The music students of today represent a remarkable diversity of languages and cultures. This fact was driven home to me when, amongst twelve students in a graduate class that I taught, nine languages were spoken: Italian, Korean, Tagalog, Mandarin, Cantonese, Taiwanese, Arabic, Farsi, and English. Granted that I teach in a particularly diverse metropolitan area, the evidence that linguistic diversity in school settings in the contemporary United States remains incontrovertible. All music educators may encounter English Language Learners (ELLs), regardless of the level (P–12 or college) or the setting. While one might at first associate ELLs with large urban areas, as in my example, ELL students may be found in any school setting: urban, suburban, rural, etc.

The purpose of this chapter is to address the issues inherent in considering music curriculum and assessment as they pertain to English Language Learners (ELLs). The chapter begins by considering the overall topics and issues that face music educators as they work with English Language Learners. Subsequent sections include a discussion of how curricula can be structured to take students' language backgrounds into account, and how assessment might be designed and implemented.

Understanding the Language of Languages

A word on nomenclature is warranted before continuing this discussion, as terminology evolves, often rapidly. For quite some time, *ESL*, or *English as a Second Language*, was the term most commonly used to describe students who came to school with a limited (or perhaps no) knowledge of English. Even in today's discussions in music education, ESL is a commonly used term. The term *ESOL*, or *English for Speakers of Other Languages* is another term that music educators may encounter. In current discussions, however, the terms *ELLs* (English Language Learners) and *ELs* (English Learners) are used more often. Also, and most significantly, given today's linguistic diversity, English Learners (ELs) often speak multiple languages before they begin to learn English. The National Board for Professional Teaching Standards awards national certification in English as a New Language, indicating among other things that our students may come to us already speaking a second, or third or fourth, language. To them, English is a *new* language, but it is not their second language. For that reason, I will use the term *English Learners* (or *ELs*), in this chapter.

Related Literature

Abril (2003) brought this issue to the fore in his article: *No Hablo Inglés: Breaking the Language Barrier in Music Education,* which appeared in the Music Educators Journal in 2003 (pgs 38–43). In addition to discussing issues of English Language Learning in general and in music education, Abril's discussion focused specifically on Hispanic children for purposes of outlining instructional strategies and curricular content. Abril identified three fundamental components that should be considered when teaching English Learners:

- Show Respect
- Get Student Involved
- Study the Culture

Although the article is focused on Hispanic students specifically, Abril's discussion resonates with any situation in which music teachers are working with ELs. Moreover, Abril identifies the crucial fact that, in addition to language issues, music teachers must develop an awareness of their EL students' cultures.

Additional research into the musical education of ELs has focused on music listening (Abril & Flowers, 2007; Brittin, 2014), often via students' preferences for listening to music in both English and in their home language. This research also often discusses the relationship of culture to music listening. Abril and Flowers (2007) suggest that, "Listeners approach music from their unique cultural purview and make judgments about it based on both musical and extra-musical elements" (p. 205). Within the context of this chapter, then, it is important to note that music students are reacting not only to the language that they hear in music, but also their own connections to that language and the culture that it represents. To a Mexican-American student, the fact that a song is in Spanish is more significant than simply being able to understand the Spanish lyrics.

Brittin (2014) studied 4th-grade to 6th-grade students' listening preferences amongst a variety of instrumental and vocal, including popular, musical selections. The students self-identified their culture through several factors, including the degrees to which they felt they identified with Spanish/Hispanic/Latino cultures and Asian cultures. Among other findings, there was some correlation between cultural identification and preference for the four pop music selections in the study. Brittin cautions against selecting listening material based on cultural identification alone:

> From a practical standpoint, a teacher would be advised to include music recorded by artists of diverse cultural backgrounds; it appears students from those cultures likely may find the selections appealing. ...teachers should consider the population of their classes as they make curricular decisions. Clearly it is too simplistic to assume all material by Hispanic artists should be presented in Spanish or that students who speak only English always will prefer the English version of a song. (p. 424)

It is also important to realize that contemporary P–12 schools are home to a myriad of languages, sharing a variety of linguistic characteristics. For example, recent research has examined specific connections between music and tonal languages (such as Mandarin and Cantonese). Bidelman, Hutka, and Moreno (2013) studied English-speaking and Cantonese-speaking adult musicians for possible differences in the participants' music perception, among other topics. The evidence pointed towards tonal language speakers having a more accurate sense of pitch difference and pitch memory.

A final factor to be considered is the entering age of the ELs. Entering high school ELs face different issues than elementary ELs. In addition to these differing issues, social and otherwise, inherent in the various levels (elementary, middle, and high school), high school age students do not have the same amount of time to build the language proficiency required for academic settings as do the younger students, putting them at a significant disadvantage. Carlow (2006) studied EL students in high school choral settings, exploring how those students told their particular stories through the use of dialogue journals. These journals provided a way for EL students to express their feelings regarding their experiences, musical and otherwise, through one-on-one (rather than in front of the entire group) communication. As a result, the students gained more confidence in speaking and writing in English, and teachers were able to build crucial relationships with students from other cultures.

Use of Music in EL Instruction

A brief note about the use of music in English language instruction is warranted. Music is frequently used as part of English language instruction, as documented in numerous studies and articles (Berman, 2014; Li & Brand, 2011), although this research typically uses the term *ESL* rather than *EL*. Li and Brand (2011) observe that, "Teachers of English as a Second Language (ESL) from around the globe enthusiastically report about their successful use of music and associated song lyrics with ESL students" (73–74).

It should be noted, however, that this and other research and discussion typically occur from within the setting of an ESL classroom rather than a music classroom, which asks the question of how music plays a role in ESL instruction from within its own educational space. I would suggest that music educators should be careful about allowing music instruction to be assimilated exclusively into English language instruction, such that music becomes one educational approach within another discipline, rather than standing independently as its own discipline. While music instruction does have something to contribute, its sole purpose is not to aid in language instruction.

More Than Language

Students who are English Learners often bring more to the classroom than linguistic differences. They bring cultural differences as well. These may take the form of expectations regarding classroom (or school) culture, teacher-student interaction and perception, verbal/ non-verbal communication, and generational differences. For that reason, music educators should not only be knowledgeable about which language(s) might be spoken in the classroom; they should do a bit of research into the larger picture of how school is perceived in students' lives.

It is not uncommon for EL students, who are recent arrivals to the United States, to come from very different academic backgrounds. Students at the elementary level may have had very little formal education at all or, conversely, be at a more advanced academic level then their peers at the same grade level (in a native language, rather than English, however). Additionally, the role and perception of a teacher within a society may differ from expectations in the United States. For example, EL students might be accustomed to automatically standing when the teacher enters the room. As part of their preparation for EL students, whether as preservice teachers or as inservice teachers who are changing/schools/assignments, these cultural differences are important for music educators to know.

The "Musical Mother Tongue"

Continuing with the larger concept of culture, in addition to language, many students will bring with them an already formed musical background that differs in some way from the western classical cannon. The concept of students having a native musical tradition, or a "musical mother tongue" has been a powerful force in the development of pedagogies for choral, instrumental, and general music for decades. Hungarian composer, linguist, and music educator Zoltán Kodály based his philosophy of music education in large part on the concept that all students have a musical "mother tongue," or home language comprised of the music that is native to the culture with which they identify. In his case, it was the authentic music of the Hungarian culture.

What "musical mother tongue" might your ELs bring with them? What are its musical characteristics (i.e., scales, meters, rhythms, instruments, performance settings, etc.)? And what impact might having their musical culture recognized have on your students, from the perspective of building a classroom environment that is comfortable and welcoming to all students? As Abril and Flowers (2007) observe: "Children may take comfort in listening to familiar music because they understand it or can identify with it" (p. 205). ELs may, in turn, be able to share elements of this musical mother tongue with the rest of the students. From the larger classroom perspective, then, having such a primary source will be of great benefit to all of your students. It is up to music educators to do a bit of research into the authentic musical resources potentially present in their own classrooms. This research can also involve the students themselves, as Carlow (2006) describes, via the use of students' journals.

Curricular Modifications

In order to plan curricular modifications, music educators need to know some basic information about their students. The following questions should be answered:

1. Which language(s) do students speak?
2. Are different dialects present, within a language (i.e., Mexican Spanish and Puerto Rican Spanish)? If so, which dialects are present among your students?
3. What is the student's current level of spoken and written language proficiency, in both English and his/her native language?
4. When did the students and their families come to the United States? Which "generation" are the students?
5. What language(s) are spoken at home? How much English do students speak when not at school?
6. What other language instruction are the students receiving?
7. What support is available at your school in terms of training and resources?
8. Does your school or district have an English Learner Specialist?
9. Are fluent speakers of your students' languages present at school, i.e., bilingual teachers or aides, for purposes of translating materials or communicating more fluently with students and families?

Depending on the number of EL students with which music educators work, an easily-accessible record-keeping system for this information would prove particularly useful (see Appendix).

Music teachers might work with language specialists to gain knowledge of district and state ELD (English Language Development) standards. Then, they will be able to seek out ways to translate those standards into music education. California has ELD standards, passed in 2012, which are aligned to the Common Core State Standards (CCSS). These might be compared to state and national standards in music education in the development of curricular materials.

When assembling curricular materials, music educators should research and consider using culturally authentic music (as represented by their EL students) in terms of musical elements (rhythms, scales, instruments):

- Choose material, such as folk songs, that includes characteristic musical elements from diverse communities. These might be tonal, such as particular scales or harmonies, or rhythmic, such as characteristic rhythms or beat groupings. Specific examples might be a focus on odd meters, or the use of *la-* or *re*-based pentatonic scales rather than the *do* pentatonic scale that is more common in the folk music of the United States.
- Focus on timbres and instruments. These also make excellent opportunities to engage EL family members, who might be able to come in to school to perform authentic music on authentic instruments.
- Consider the element of movement, as well. Explore the use of folk dance, as well as folk song (pitch and rhythm).

Popular Music

Popular music can also play a role in students' music education. With the move in recent years towards popular music playing a greater role in school music education, music educators should consider the added significance of American popular music as it impacts ELs' learning experiences. The aural component of popular music pedagogy is a natural fit for students whose learning modality is geared more towards the aural than the visual.

Additionally, research has indicated that students' listening preferences for popular music increase as they grow older. In fact, it is quite likely that students will be interested in listening to popular music in English, even more than culturally-authentic music. In this way, popular music might be utilized to a greater degree in planning lessons, as a gateway to building familiarity as well as English knowledge amongst ELs. As with the selection of any curricular materials, of course, music educators should pay careful attention to musical (particularly lyric) content in choosing materials, as there is an added significance to lyrics with EL students.

Moreover, there may be cultural benefits to the study of popular music for new arrival students. Knowledge of American popular music can facilitate a feeling of "fitting in" for newly-arrived students. To extend the value of popular music, it should be noted that there are popular musical forms that, in one form or another, are nearly ubiquitous among countries and cultures. Hip hop, for example, has developed into a global genre.

In fact, recently-arrived students might be able to bring the popular music of their native countries/cultures to the music classroom. This is an opportunity to reverse the popular music-based curriculum, and to actually place EL students in the role of the authority. Film music, in particular, presents one such opportunity. Film music, as both concert music and as movie soundtracks, is very well known to students in the United States. Many of the most prominent composers in the western classical canon have also written music for films, e.g. Copland, Prokofiev, and Shostakovich, as have other more recent composers, such as John Williams, James Horner, and Danny Elfman. However, as one example, recent arrivals from the Indian subcontinent might be able to bring a greater immediacy to the study of popular music through presenting the film music of India. As Sarrazin noted in 2006:

> Is it possible that the most popular music in the world has been left out of most American music classes? While many in the United States have never heard of it, the Indian film industry [commonly known as "Bollywood"] is the largest film industry in the world, with an output nearly three times that of Hollywood. (p. 26)

Through the inclusion of popular musics from around the world, multiple curricular objectives can be easily addressed.

Instructional Strategies

First of all, realize that it is not necessary to speak every student's language(s) fluently in order to provide a high-quality music education. It will, however, require thoughtful and careful planning. From the music teacher's perspective, over reliance on spoken English can be problematic. What exactly, then, is the role of language in the delivery of instruction? A concrete example illustrates this point well. In an anecdote regarding the use of spoken English, Cooper and Grim-Anderson (2007) describe the following teaching example in regards to teaching a song to elementary age students using the phrase-by-phrase method:

> Blank looks on children's faces when I asked them to echo me made me stop and assess my teaching and its effectiveness. My students were eager to learn but did not have any idea what I wanted them to do. Teaching a song echo style to my kindergarten students was pointless. They did not understand the words echo me and looked at me with glazed expressions on their faces. Most of them could not even understand when I asked them their name, let alone echo songs or even short phrases. (p. 20)

What is most important initially is that this teacher realized that, rather than simply repeating the same approach and almost certainly leading to frustration for both teacher and students, there was a more fundamental problem that needed to be addressed. In this example, EL students did not understand the spoken English direction echo me. The solution in a situation of this sort, then, is to drop the use of the spoken phrase. Rather, with a combination of singing and gesturing back and forth between students and teacher, the expectation can be clearly communicated and the musical objective achieved.

I have employed several strategies as a general music teacher. Over time, I expanded my use of non-verbal signals, i.e., using rhythmic patterns, either clapped or played on instruments, rather than asking for attention. I have also used student interpreters; that is, having a student standing next to me and interpreting for the class. While that technique may work in small conversations, I was not satisfied with it in a classroom setting due to the delay. On the smaller scale, however, in an ensemble setting for example, ELs might be paired with students who are able to provide additional support. Those might be students with knowledge of that particular language (or more advanced ELs), or students who have demonstrated an ability/disposition to provide one-on-one support.

In instrumental music, the "sound before sight" approach should be given careful consideration. In beginning instrumental music, students are first presented with aural models, in both listening and performance. As in the Kodály prepare-present-practice approach, instrumental students would perform numerous examples of a given concept (as drills, exercises, and pieces) before the concept is identified by name.

Written English, as opposed to spoken English, should also be considered. Research indicates that students understand spoken and written English before developing the capacity for speaking fluently. Therefore, the development of written materials must take into account students' levels of written English proficiency. Consultation with language experts and other teachers at the school will prove helpful here. Teachers might even be able to obtain bilingual materials, such as tests or worksheets with directions in both English and another language. Bilingual educational materials are becoming more and more available, although this is certainly not exhaustive. Translation of materials can take time, however, so music teachers should be prepared in advance. Additionally, however, music teachers should be careful to retain all of these translated instructional materials for future classes. Electronic files, written materials, etc., should be stored safely for future classes. The internet can provide freely available resources, as well.

A few general rules to employ are:

- Speak slowly and clearly, leaving appropriate spaces in between words.
- Be particularly aware of American idioms and slang. It's remarkable how many common metaphors are focused on

sports, particularly baseball, basketball, and (American) football. Hip hop might be global but baseball is not.

- Become aware of different meanings for the same terms. For example, the terms "high" and "low" can be used to denote both pitch and volume. Make sure that students are clear on what you mean when referring to high notes in a piece.
- Provide aural examples. In an ensemble setting sing the phrasing and articulation that you want.
- Use gestures where they are helpful.
- The musical terms, as well as pitch and rhythmic figures, that you have posted on your walls become even more significant. Refer to them.

The following vignette was written by Mr. Bryan Holbrook, an instrumental music teacher in Hayward Unified School District (HUSD) in Hayward, CA:

Javier arrived atop the narrow, creaky stairs and raced past the small sea of musicians. He was both excited and hesitant about today's lesson: beginning clarinet embouchure. I reassured the students that no sound is a bad sound and that they were all in a safe classroom. The beginning clarinetists prepared their embouchures and, with a welcoming smile, I told them: "blow into the mouthpiece." Javier enthusiastically followed my direction… and produced a sound that drew laughter from the others. I gave the students a calm, accepting look and gave Javier a reassuring pat on the shoulder.

I quickly realized that the problem was both technical and verbal. Javier's abrupt change in body language told me that he didn't understand my directions or objectives, despite receiving translations and encouragement from his classmates.

After assessing the problem, I modified my approach to working with Javier. Rather than relying on musical terminology and using American slang, I demonstrated visually how to place lips, teeth, and tongue to achieve the desired result. In other words, I "acted out" the process. I continued this procedure, patiently, until the remaining members of the class were able to apply this visually odd—but can't-look-away—facial distortion and to achieve the desired results, instantaneously bringing forth a celebration of cheers and chants in the students' own native language.

HUSD's demographics, as reported in 2014, are:

Hispanic or Latino of any race	12,519	60%
American Indian or Alaska Native, not Hispanic	95	0%
Asian, not Hispanic	1,585	8%
Filipino, not Hispanic	760	4%
African American, not Hispanic	1,392	7%
White, not Hispanic	2,602	13%
Two or more race, not Hispanic	1315	6%
Not reported	387	2%
TOTAL	**20,729**	**100%**

Source: http://www.husd.k12.ca.us/Demographics

Whose Culture Is It?

In some ways, you may know more about the students' cultures than they will themselves. My Mexican students (all newly arrived or 1st generation) had not heard of Mexican composer Silvestre Revueltas when I first introduced them to the composer and to his music. Although they may have found his orchestral composition *Sensemayá* to be a bit difficult at first, they were nonetheless excited to know of a Mexican composer of orchestral ("classical") music. And what a fantastic way to begin the study of odd meter! As many approaches to music curriculum place a heavy emphasis on repertoire, teachers would be well-advised to consider students' linguistic and cultural backgrounds. For example, when studying music from the Baroque era, music teachers might include the music of Mexican composer Manuel de Zumaya (1678–1756), a contemporary of Johann Sebastian Bach (1685–1750).

Moreover, as mentioned earlier, be aware of cultural differences within languages, such as regional or national variants. During my teaching, I became aware of the differences between Mexican Spanish and Puerto Rican Spanish, as reported by students and teachers at my school, both in terms of vocabulary (words and expressions) and differences in pronunciation and cadence of speech. These differences are also expressed through culture-specific musical forms. In specific reference to Hispanic students, Abril (2003) speaks to this point:

> Integrating students' cultures into instruction is an effective way of motivating ELL children to learn. Consider including aspects of the Hispanic culture in the curriculum. Select Spanish-language songs that respectfully depict the cultures. Be aware that each Hispanic culture has a unique body of music that is as diverse as the people who create it. The *criolla* of Cuba is very different from the Mexican *corrido*, which is different from the *tango* of Argentina. (p. 41)

Music educators should be aware of these differences for two reasons:

1. To expand the range of musics with which they are familiar. As Abril points out the music of Hispanic culture (as one example) includes a tremendously varied group of genres and sub-genres of music.
2. To be aware of assumptions/generalizations regarding music of a particular culture.

In the case of my own teaching, it was important for me to be aware that my students were approximately 60% Mexican and 30% Puerto

Rican, with the remaining 10% composed of black and white students, as well as Cuban and Ecuadorian students (two additional Hispanic cultures). This became apparent to me over time when a Mexican-American student spoke Spanish and only half of the class understood.

My Puerto Rican students might not have reacted well if I began a unit on Mariachi music and presented it as a music representative of all Spanish-speaking cultures. That is not to say that a music educator should teach Mariachi music in an all-Mexican or Mexican-American class only. Rather, the music educator must be aware to present the music as one form of music from a Hispanic culture, while also acknowledging (or studying) musics of other cultures present. What is most important is that we know who is in our classes. In this case, the elements of culture and language make it even more important.

Language Tendencies

In particular, when considering diction, choral directors should become aware of students' home language pronunciation and speech tendencies. Choral directors might investigate what these tendencies are amongst their students' home languages. What sounds are or are not present? Indeed, ELs might not perceive what diction is being given to them. For example, Latino students might have difficulty distinguishing b's and v's in spoken English, and certain Asian students might have difficulty with l's and r's.

Comparing notes with other choral directors, or speaking with other teachers or staff are good ways to learn more about the specific issue(s) in a given situation. Music educators might also pair ELs with native, or proficient, English speakers. By the same token, however, EL students can be a tremendously valuable resource for choral programs. An entire ensemble may benefit from being coached on their diction by students who are native speakers of a given text that is being performed.

Families

EL students bring another potentially substantial resource to the music classroom: their families. Consider in what ways the students' families can be involved in your curriculum. Begin by doing what you can to make contact with students' families. These families might have musical/cultural contributions that they can make. Students' families might come in to your classes to model authentic music and/or movement, also modeling appropriate styles and perhaps performing on authentic instruments, such as a Chinese bamboo flute or a Mexican guitarrón. This can be a way of expanding all students' knowledge of repertoire, as well as their knowledge of instrumental/vocal timbres and performance techniques presented in a truly authentic manner. Realize, however, that communication with home might be somewhat problematic for teachers not fluent in the language in question. Particularly in the case of recent arrivals, there may be no one in the home (students included, of course) with a good command of spoken English. So, an interpreter might be needed for written and spoken communication.

Assessment

As has been discussed elsewhere in this text, assessment strategies and techniques are numerous. How, then, are these practices impacted when different levels of English learning become an additional factor? Regardless of format selected, as with any student, English Learners must be clear on the topics on which they are being assessed, as well as the criteria by which they are being evaluated. Learning outcomes must be made clear.

Furthermore, what is perhaps most important regarding these assessment expectations and learning outcomes is that they remain consistent across all students in a class or ensemble. There might be a tendency, conscious or unconscious, to hold different expectations for English Learners. Within the specific context of Hispanic students, Abril (2003) cautions against this, and recommends that music educators be wary:

> Maintain high expectations for Hispanic children despite their
> limited English proficiency. It may be tempting to set lower

standards for Hispanic ELL children; we recognize that simultaneously learning a new language and new content in a new context is quite complex. However, a teacher's expectations can have a profound impact on the child. Low expectations can lead to minimal effort and low achievement. (p. 41)

The same is certainly true of speakers of any language.

Given the topic of this chapter, one of the primary elements of this section is that teachers must be aware of the amount, and format (spoken or written), of English used in their classes, curricula, and assessments. How often and in what ways is English used in generating assessment? What phrases are used? How complex are the sentences? Through trial and error, music educators should develop a sensitivity to the utilization of English in their instruction and assessment. This is certainly not to say that music classrooms should abandon all written and spoken English when ELs are present. Rather, that music teachers should simply be aware of the language that they are using, perhaps even more so than they are already.

Performance-Based Assessment

Performance-based assessment might in some cases remain relatively unchanged. It depends, however, on the level of interaction within the assessment device. One major scale is just the same as any other. However, providing spoken feedback, or asking for particular sections of a passage or exercise to be repeated might be somewhat problematic. Therefore, music educators should have a way of communicating these requests to students, such as a student interpreter, or through specifically defined passages. Clear rubrics, perhaps even in the students' native languages as well as English, may facilitate the process.

Including a physical element to performance-based assessment can be of immediate benefit to ELs. Students might demonstrate knowledge of time signature via conducting, or knowledge of pitch with Curwen hand signs. These assessment devices are appropriate for all students, but may have additional benefit in music classes including

EL students. Music educators should remember that, historically in the United States, particularly in the early and middle 20th century and even through the present time, a language barrier has existed between conductors and ensembles in the United States. Maestros who were themselves English Learners directed professional ensembles composed of a great diversity of performers, many with a very limited command of English but a great command of their instruments. As the recordings tell us, this language barrier was certainly not an impediment to the performance of music of the highest caliber.

Written Assessment

Written assessment, depending on its format, might be challenging. Therefore, assessment with a written component should be considered carefully. Written assessments that rely strictly on English, such as forced-choice tests or essays will be problematic. Written assessment that is more symbolic in nature, however, need not be as difficult to use. Assessment based on conventional notation, such as pitch identification or error detection, can be used with little modification beyond making sure that all students are clear on parameters. Different forms of conventional notation, such as the stick notation commonly found in Kodály-based classes, could also be used. Other written artifacts, such as formal diagrams or listening maps might be excellent forms of assessment. Aural forms of assessment, such as melodic or rhythmic dictation, might also be utilized.

Composition

Musical composition is another area of music education that provides great potential for curricular and assessment materials. All students are capable of creating music. The amount of resources for musical composition is substantial at the present time, and the creation of new music is an excellent way to engage ELs. Composition also provides a perfect vehicle for EL students to showcase their own musical contributions. These might be things such as:

1. The use of home language

2. Setting a text in the student's first (or second) language

3. Mixing languages in a text

4. Using representative scales or harmonies (e.g., pentatonic, alternate tunings)

5. Using representative rhythms or meters (e.g., odd meters, characteristic figures)

6. Using representative forms, such as various folk dances

7. Using authentic instruments alone or in combination with western instruments. These might be pitched (e.g., Mexican *guitarrón*) or unpitched (e.g., Indian *mridingam*)

8. Performance formats (e.g., shadow puppets)

Returning to Kodály's concept of the musical mother tongue, it is in a compositional setting that an ELs musical culture might really shine through when, for example, using the pitches of *la* pentatonic rather than the more common (in the United States) *do* pentatonic.

Peer Assessment

An excellent instructional strategy for classes involving ELs is to form students into cooperative groups. Groups should contain both ELs and non-ELs. Within their cooperative groups, students will both collaborate to achieve their musical objectives and also provide feedback to one another throughout the process. Cooperative group activities that might be well-suited to ELs include:

- Performances of chamber music (vocal or instrumental)
- Composition/Arranging
- Improvisation

Cooperative groups are an approach already familiar to music educators. In the case of working with ELs, the pedagogical benefits of cooperative groups become even greater.

Technology

The ever-changing element of technology offers a number of resources for EL instruction in the music classroom. This might take the form of desktop, laptop, or tablet-based notation programs. Resources in languages other than English, as well as applications and programs facilitating translation provide additional resources for music education. As they continue their professional development, music educators should maintain an awareness of resources for music teaching that will be of particular value to EL students. In particular, programs with a focus on symbol/notation and aural-based learning will be valuable. Music educators working with ELs should be aware of the music technology resources available to them (see chapter 20 in this text for additional discussion).

Preservice Music Teachers

Preservice must be considered in this discussion, as well (see chapter 18). As a profession, we should consider language backgrounds among the relevant skill sets that teacher candidates bring to the preservice programs. We should also realize that our preservice teachers might themselves bring a diversity of languages, without having consciously realized how these backgrounds can be utilized in K–12 teaching situations. I teach in a large metropolitan area, with an extremely diverse student body at my school. Several years ago, I had three non-native English speakers amongst my nine student teachers. In my discussions with them, I discovered the multiple ways in which their experiences were impacted by being ELs themselves, such as in their interactions with students both in and out of class. Calls for a culturally diverse teaching force are plentiful in music education. The fact, however, is that the music teaching profession is getting more diverse, and these culturally and linguistically diverse preservice teachers have a tremendous amount to offer today's P–12 students.

Conclusion

We are fortunate to live in a time of great, and ever-increasing, diversity in the modern United States. Although not every area of the country is as diverse as mine (a large urban area on the west coast), the fact that students representing diverse communities and diverse language backgrounds are gaining a greater presence is incontrovertible. While this may present us with challenges as music educators, it is to be viewed for what it is: an incredible opportunity to build our students' musical knowledge, as well as our own. Moreover, as more and more new music teachers join the music teaching profession, we will find that the teaching force itself is also becoming more diverse. A few short years ago, three English Learner music teachers, two native Spanish speakers and one native Cantonese speaker, began K–12 teaching careers in California. Diversity exists on both sides of the podium.

As I reflect on my graduate class of several years ago, as well as my earlier days teaching elementary and middle school music in Hispanic schools, I am reminded that among my objectives was simply for my students to leave my class saying, regardless of language, "I love music."

References

Abril, C. R. (2003). No hablo inglés: Breaking the language barrier in music instruction. *Music Educators Journal 89*(5), 38–43.

Abril, C. R., & Flowers, P. J. (2007). Attention, preference, and identity in music listening by middle school students of different linguistic backgrounds. *Journal of Research in Music Education 55*, 204–219.

Berman, A. S. (2014). Music as a second language. *Teaching Music 21*(4), 36–39.

Bidelman, G. M., Hutka, S., & Moreno, S. (2013). Retrieved from
http://memphis.edu/acnl/pdfs/plosone2013.pdf on May 23, 2014.

Brittin, R. V. (2014). Young listeners' music style preferences: Patterns
related to cultural identification and language use. *Journal of
Research in Music Education 61*, 415–430.

California ELD standards: http://www.cde.ca.gov/sp/el/er/documents/
sbeoverviewpld.pdf retrieved from http://www.cde.ca.gov/sp/el/
er/eldstandards.asp on February 13, 2014.

Carlow, R. (2006). Building *confianza*: Using dialogue journals with
English-language learners in urban schools. In C. Frierson-
Campbell (Ed.) Teaching music in the urban classroom: *A guide
to leadership, teacher education, and reform* (Vol. 1, pp. 25–34).
Lanham, MD: Rowman & Littlefield.

Cooper, S. & Grimm-Anderson, S. (2007). *General Music Today 20*,
20–24. http://www.husd.k12.ca.us/Demographics retrieved on
July 23, 2014.

Li, X., & Brand, M. (2001). Effectiveness of music on vocabulary
acquisition, language usage, and meaning for Mainland Chinese
ESL Learners. *Contributions to Music Education 36*(1), 73–84.

Sarrazin, N. (2006). India's Music: Popular Film Songs in the Classroom.
Music Educators Journal 93(1), 26–32.

Appendix

This form is intended to serve as a model of an information record such as a music teacher might keep for EL students in music:

English Learner Information

Name/Preferred Name:

Grade:

Class(es) (i.e., general music, wind ensemble, chamber orchestra, treble choir, etc.):

Primary Language (other than English):

Other Languages Spoken (if any):

Specific Country/Culture:

Language Spoken at Home:

English Proficiencies:

Oral Comprehension: None   Somewhat   Basic   Good   Fluent

Spoken: None   Somewhat   Basic   Good   Fluent

Written: None   Somewhat   Basic   Good   Fluent

Years of formal English instruction:

Cultural Music Background

Instruments played:

Familiar Styles/Genres:

Performance Background:

Musical Experiences (formal and informal):

Family

Musicians in the Family:

Instrument(s) played:

Styles:

Other arts (i.e., dance):

Notes:

Chapter 17

Traversing the Terrain of Music Competition: Curricular Mapping with Adjudicated Events in Mind

Jared R. Rawlings
University of Michigan

Attending adjudicated events is an important part of the learning process with school ensembles. However, many challenges (musical and non-musical) exist with preparing for and participating in adjudicated events in the United States. This book chapter explains how ensemble directors fit adjudicated event preparation into the curricular framework of a music ensemble course. Following a brief historical account of adjudicated events, musical and non-musical challenges are examined. The second half of the chapter is devoted to curricular decision making and recommendations for participating in adjudicated events.

Introduction

Adjudicated events have fascinated and engaged music teachers in lively debate over the past century. This debate can be found in articles, empirical research, or even every day discussions amongst music colleagues. Whether the discussion of adjudicated events is in a formal or informal setting, it has permeated the musical discourse and become a part of the curricular fabric of secondary school music programs. This section includes a brief historical account of the rich dialogue over the past one hundred years and will serve as a backdrop for understanding the current curricular challenges with adjudicated events.

History of Adjudicated Events

Discussions about instrumental and choral music adjudicated events have been a topic of concern among music teachers since the Great Depression (Wilson, 1926). The concern centers on the value of adjudicated events in school music programs and how they serve a student's musical education. There are multiple reasons cited in past literature, which explain why music educators may advocate for the inclusion of adjudicated events in the music education process. Advocates contend adjudicated events: (a) prepare students for life-long skills; (b) teach students how to control nervous energy; (c) set high standards and recognize outstanding effort for secondary school music making; (d) advocate for state-level policy to include music education programs; and (e) offer a chance for unbiased feedback of musical performance. Music teachers opposing adjudicated events as a part of the music education process prefer a modified experience of the traditional *snapshot* competitive music contest to a more comprehensive, learner-centered approach. Opponents against competitive adjudicated events argue that the events promote: (a) overconcentration on two or three pieces of music to the exclusion of the reading and study of greater quantities of music; (b) excessive absences from classes because of travel; (c) a tendency to rely on scoring mechanism to evaluate music teachers; and (d) centering the year's music program on the adjudicated event.

Dialogue about Adjudicated Events

Discussion about adjudicated events is still unclear how music teachers are able to balance the curricular preparation and implementation necessary for attending adjudicated events with the yearly curricular outcomes of the music program. In her dissertation, Stoll (2008) investigated adjudicated events and curricular preparations. Stoll investigated the relationship of curricular and assessment decisions made by high school band directors to rating outcomes from large group adjudicated events. She found that the relationship between frequency of assessment type and performance rating was not statistically significant. The most common types of assessment used by band directors in this study were class participation and students performing individually because of reported time constraints with instructional time. This combination of performance-based and participation-based assessments was reported as the most common method of assessment used by ensemble directors in preparing an ensemble for an adjudicated event. In an article appearing in the *Music Educators Journal*, Stegman (2009) documented a shift of music teacher philosophy from the historical advocacy/public relation outcomes associated with participating in adjudicated events to supporting student musical learning outcomes. These examples of scholarship represent a current interest in adjudicated events; however, what are the musical considerations directors must make with choosing how to implement a curriculum, which supports attending these adjudicated events? In the next section, the musical challenges associated with attending adjudicated events are explained so that the reader may consider how to navigate the terrain for curricular planning.

Musical Challenges

"History is written by the victors."
–Winston Churchill

Before ensemble directors prepare their musical groups to participate in adjudicated events, there are several musical challenges to consider when making curricular decisions for student learning. From a national perspective, musical challenges that appear in this section of the chapter include: (a) required music lists; (b) the notion of selecting the "right music"; and (c) ensemble instrumentation and voicing.

Required Music Lists

Statewide music or activity organizations, which organize adjudicated events, typically provide a statement or policy about the music required for performance at large group adjudicated events. For instance, most states use a required music list with a myriad of policies guiding the use of the music list. Issuing a required music list accomplishes multiple missions with imposing a statewide curricular philosophy. The first mission of these lists may be to unify the difficulty of repertoire being performed in school music programs. Repertoire selection is mostly associated with a school classification system based on geographic region or school/music program population. School or music programs across the nation ranked higher on a classification system (e.g., A versus C or 6A versus 2A) are required to perform repertoire, which is more technically challenging than music programs with less population. Although this is a common policy for adjudicated events, state music or activity organizations may have a procedure where directors of instrumental ensembles may petition to perform repertoire not listed at their required achievement level. Often, directors who elect to perform music not on their requisite list will not be rated or ranked and given "comments only."

Another mission of required music lists may be to streamline the adjudication process and adjudicator training. For instance, a few states have a yearly rotation of a few pieces from which directors of instrumental and choral ensembles may choose to perform at the adjudicated event. This allows all ensembles to perform similar repertoire in order for the adjudication process to be valid and consistent. Musical notation can vary in technical and musical ways. By selecting only a few pieces on the repertoire rotation, the adjudicators have an opportunity to judge consistently.

Professor Emeritus and former Director of Bands at the University of Michigan, H. Robert Reynolds, wrote an article for the *Music Educators Journal* entitled "Repertoire Is the Curriculum." In that article, Reynolds (2000) focused on repertoire selection as a means of enabling music educators to grow as teachers. However, if music educators have music that is selected for them, then how are they to grow as teachers? I consider part of the creativity of what we teach as curriculum is how we teach the music beyond the notation. The musical challenge with required music lists is that a state music or activity organization selects the repertoire vis-à-vis the curriculum for the ensemble directors. Whose curricular decisions are guiding the teams or person who selects this music? What are their ethical obligations to select the very best music? These questions are not answered in this chapter; however, it does lead to a discussion about selecting the "right music" for performances at adjudicated events.

Selecting the "Right Music" for Adjudicated Events

Most states have required music lists for participating ensembles directors; however, as music educators who lead ensembles in performance at adjudicated events, I have heard anecdotes from experienced music educators discussing the phenomenon of selecting the "right music." Even though there are required music lists, these experienced music teachers still discuss the process of selecting repertoire for adjudicated events. The state organizations have selected the repertoire (i.e., curriculum) for directors of performing ensembles, but why is this phenomenon still interesting to music educators? By inferring that there is the "right music" for adjudicated events, logic says that there is the "wrong music" as well.

Because of the range of technical and musical difficulties that exist within works of music, there are inherent benefits and challenges to selecting one work over another for adjudicated events. Careful consideration is given by ensemble directors to these benefits and challenges as to position the ensemble in succeeding or "winning" at adjudicated events. This is where the notion of selecting the "right music" intersects with curricular decisions. By selecting the right repertoire for ensembles to succeed at adjudicated events, what curricular outcomes are promoted and furthermore, is student musical learning stunted as a result of privileging the right music for adjudicated events? When ensemble directors choose repertoire for adjudicated events, two considerations relate to the technical and musical difficulties of the repertoire.

Discussions of technical difficulties with selecting the "right music" are focused on the notation of the repertoire. The "right music" is considered repertoire that does not put the ensemble at risk for failure at executing the notation. For example, string ensembles may avoid tonal key areas that require advanced technique for successful execution of the notation. Likewise, wind bands may avoid thinly orchestrated notation for adjudicated event performances. The curricular decision of selecting repertoire based on the musical notation is commonplace for most music ensemble directors. There is a strong practice of showcasing the technical strengths of student musicians while protecting the void(s) in technical knowledge that an ensemble director has to negotiate when selecting repertoire for performance at adjudicated events. Factors that ensemble directors take into consideration include: (a) ensemble instrumentation; (b) ensemble size; (c) rehearsal times; (d) school or music program resources for additional instructional support (e.g., personnel, clinicians, technology, instruments); and (e) depth of technical and musical facility amongst student musicians. Furthermore, ensemble directors may reflect on the successes and shortcomings of historical programming choices when selecting the "right music" for their ensemble. This negotiation of selecting the repertoire based on the technical and musical difficulty also connects to the musical decisions ensemble directors must make when performing at adjudicated events.

Musical difficulties with selecting and performing the "right music" deals with how the repertoire is taught. When music educators think about how curricular content is taught, especially with ensemble performance, five factors of musicianship are considered. These five factors are: (a) ensemble tone; (b) ensemble intonation; (c) ensemble articulation; (d) ensemble musicianship (e.g., musical style, dynamic contour, musical phrasing); and (e) ensemble rhythm and pulse. What makes these factors a musical challenge for ensemble directors is that these are subjective to the hearing and interpretation of the adjudicator. For example, the curricular decision to program a Mozart symphony for an adjudicated event presents many challenges to string ensemble directors. Mozart may be a challenge because of the interpretation of musical style beyond the notation on the page. Music curricular content goes deeper than just objective written notation. This makes selecting the "right music" for adjudicated events a bit of a moving target because of the panel of judges and how they hear the instrumental ensemble's execution of appropriate classical treatment (i.e., Mozart) of rhythm and filigree.

Even though ensemble directors may select the "right music," *how* do they know what that is? This process of selecting the repertoire, as curriculum, is a unique musical challenge for ensemble directors to consider because of the vulnerability it places with the stakeholders (e.g., student musicians, parents of musicians, music program, school, community) in ensemble music making. In the case of Mozart symphonies being performed at adjudicated events, despite their representation on state required music lists, I would doubt that many are performed at adjudicated events because of the risk the ensemble directors make with not interpreting classical style the same way as the adjudicators. By not choosing to program Mozart for performance at adjudicated events, I wonder what other (classical) composers are not being selected to be a part of the student's musical education.

Habits of Directors Who Select the "Right Music"

1. *Know every student's musical ability* – Teachers must know the abilities of their students. In musical ensembles, it is easy for students to "hide" behind a section of people performing a similar part.

   Suggestion: Regularly scheduled sectionals or small group lessons reveal much needed information for ensemble directors to plan and implement curriculum.

2. *Listen to your students perform individually* – Students need to perform by themselves for instructors of ensembles. Not only

can a teacher assess the fundamentals of musicianship (i.e., tone, intonation, articulation, etc.), but also they can assess reading ability. Moreover, hearing a student perform individually may inform the ensemble director about the student's *readiness* for solo passages in repertoire. For example, if an ensemble director does not have a student musician who can perform a solo passage, avoid programming that work for adjudicated events.

Suggestion: Playing exams are an easy way to track individual progress. The teacher can structure these exams to be in person, recorded, or submitted electronically via a music software program.

3. *Motivate and Regulate* – Regulating rehearsal and practice expectations for steady musical improvement takes careful planning. Motivating students can come from extrinsic or intrinsic places; however, if the practice expectations are designed in a reasonable manner, students will comply. Students meet our expectations, if they are reasonable.

   Suggestion: Consider creating a long-term plan for studying a piece of music (from sight-reading to performance) and sharing it with the students. Included are performance goals, assessments, guest clinicians, etc.

4. *Planning is Year 'Round* – Teachers admit to planning for adjudicated events year 'round. Even though selecting the "right music" can be a bit of a moving target, if a teacher has an idea of what will be programmed for the adjudicated event, then the requisite technique can be taught leading up to the event. Also, the repertoire can be performed in the Fall/Winter concerts that teach similar concepts to those of the pieces being performed for adjudication.

   Suggestions:
   a. Know the required music list and both the technical and musical demands of the musical selections. Keep a running list or chart of these demands with any special

considerations (e.g., English horn solo, flugelhorn, muted brass, crotales) for easy access.

b.   Keep an up-to-date listening library with music from the required list and other music that you may program for adjudicated events.

c.   Visit your music merchants and peruse scores as a professional development opportunity.

d.   Imagine your ensemble instrumentation and project whom may be seated in your ensemble. From here consider, how much endurance it will take to perform the selections for adjudicated events? Are members of the ensemble engaged and challenged in appropriate ways?

Ensemble Instrumentation and Voicing

A fascinating debate has entered the discourse amongst ensemble directors regarding ensemble instrumentation and voicing. Deeply grounded in philosophical values, decisions about the ethics of ensemble instrumentation and voicing are made every day across the United States. These decisions begin with recruiting practices of music educators and lead to student motivation of continuing ensemble participation through grade school and ultimately reach a secondary experience. Moreover, the decisions throughout a student musician's trajectory in school music programs may be centered on the "greater good" of the ensemble program rather than the needs of the individual. What is the motivation behind the instrumentation and voicing decisions of ensemble directors?

When connected to adjudicated events, ensemble instrumentation and voicing may be seen as a musical challenge for music educators. The challenge is two-fold. First, the notion of performing at adjudicated events with incomplete instrumentation (e.g., missing instruments or voice parts from the written notation) and second, substituting instruments or rewriting the notation to accommodate the ensemble's needs. State music or activity associations who write policies about participating in adjudicated events may have procedures for such modifications of presenting the musical notation; however, given the philosophy of the adjudicated event, some events are able to accommodate these modifications and some are not. For example, some states allow for ensemble directors to modify the score by adding, deleting, or changing the tonal center of the notation. However, some states do not allow these modifications. This musical challenge is a point of contention amongst all music educators (including those in higher education), but what is most important is knowledge about these policies.

The student experience is paramount when making repertoire decisions for adjudicated events. In addition to the constraints of a required music list and understanding how to pick the "right music," the ensemble instrumentation and voicing are potential challenges. Not having complete instrumentation or appropriate voicing to perform a piece of music does not necessarily exclude the piece from the curriculum, but a few diagnostic questions must be answered:

1. What aspect about this piece of music is necessary for this particular ensemble, right now in the curricular sequence?
2. Is there another piece that can serve the same purpose?
3. Does performing this piece of music serve the students and meet their curricular needs?

Sometimes there is flexibility with programming music and as directors of these ensembles, we must be flexible and keep in mind the overall student experience.

Curricular Connections

Musical challenges exist with preparing for and attending adjudicated events. Since our repertoire is the curriculum, music educators need to be aware of the curricular implications of the decision to attend these events. Peer music educators may select the repertoire to program at these adjudicated events without knowing school district curricula. Assumptions can be made at the state-level; however, the committees, people, or person who select the repertoire also assume that an individual district's music curriculum mirror the state's music curricular outcomes. The quote by Winston Churchill at the beginning of this section reminds music educators that the "victors" are deciding what curriculum is and is not taught. It is possible and likely the voices of the real musical pioneers are silenced. Instead, ensemble directors are left with the remnants of those who have selected the music perhaps out of their own conviction as opposed to those who advocate for a system which privileges musical innovation.

A situation not yet mentioned is how curriculum is enacted with multiple ensembles in a music program. For example, how does a choral director account for multiple choirs when attending adjudicated events? If the ensemble director has the ability to select which student is enrolled in different choirs, then who is selected for each choir, and what music does each choir perform? This nuanced reality precipitates a number of philosophical discussions about adjudicated events, which choir(s) perform at adjudicated events, and how curriculum is enacted; however, it is beyond scope of this chapter to present answers to these individualized situations. Rather, the principles outlined in the second section of this chapter may help guide the reader answer the questions associated with multiple ensembles.

This section has discussed the musical challenges with preparing and attending adjudicated events and how they interact with music educator's curricular decisions. Instrumental and choral music educators have unique challenges associated with having the opportunity to select the repertoire in order to meet district-level curricular outcomes; however, music challenges are not the only challenges that exist. In the next section of the chapter, I will discuss the non-musical challenges associated with preparing for and attending adjudicated events.

Questions

1. What limitations have you experienced with the musical challenges of attending adjudicated events?
2. How have these limitations influenced your planning and implementation of curriculum?

3. Looking ahead, what other ways will you address the musical challenges of adjudicated event preparation with curricular planning?

Non-musical Challenges

There are several non-musical challenges to consider when making curricular decisions. Non-musical challenges included in this section of the chapter are: (a) adjudicator reliability; (b) extra-musical influences; and (c) logistical challenges.

Adjudicator Reliability

Receiving unbiased feedback from an adjudicator with advanced content knowledge is a benefit of attending adjudicated events. One challenge with adjudicated events that has received national attention takes issue with organizing a reliable and valid adjudication experience for students (Brakel, 2006; Hash, 2013). Unpacking the issues of validity and reliability with adjudicated events is complicated. The issues of validity relate to how adjudicators (e.g., judges) are required to measure the success of an ensemble's performance in a "snapshot" format. National-, state-, or local-level music organizations have evaluation rubrics for adjudicated events and the adjudicator is required to award a ranking, point value, or rating designation. Despite the national trend of having more than one adjudicator at the performance, sometimes adjudicators do not agree on the outcome of the ensemble's performance. For example, we have heard of the "spectrum" or "rainbow" effect. An ensemble may perform and receive a division rating of a I (or superior), a II (or excellent), and a III (or good) respectively from the three judges.

There are many ways adjudicators are selected to work adjudication locations. Regulations or restrictions on geographic location, context expertise, and performance medium may be challenges to select an appropriate panel of adjudicators. Most states require adjudicators be trained to adjudicate ensembles; however, some states do not require such training. For example, particular mediums or age groups of performing ensembles are privileged by having trained adjudicators. Meanwhile, other ensembles may not have trained adjudicators at their performance site. An experienced orchestra teacher discusses this challenge in the first vignette.

Vignette 1

> There is no judge's training in my state. I judge in a neighboring state quite a bit and I have to go through a training session when I judge. However, the training session is more of how to set a standard of musicianship. Basically, the group walks in with a III (or good) and they go up or down from there. So, I give mostly threes when I go to judge. However, in my state there is not the same musical standard and most ensembles receive a I (or superior) or a II (or excellent). Obviously it is in tune or out of tune, the rhythms are correct or incorrect. When you are subjectively judging an art, one judge hears a one, superior performance, and one judge hears an average performance.

This experienced music teacher understands the challenge of not having adequately trained adjudicators because he is also a trained adjudicator in a neighboring state. The challenge of adjudicator reliability is compounded by not having adjudicator training.

Extra-musical influences

Extra-musical influences are defined as those influences, which manifest with implementation of the day or with the performance location. Directors or students typically do not have control over these influences and can interrupt concentration with the task at hand. Three extra-musical influences have been discussed on a national level (Bergee, 2006; Rickels, 2012). First, is the time of day adjudicated events are held. Most states do not privilege geographic location with event time slots (e.g., those having to travel the furthest will not have an 8:00 am time slot); however, some organizers of events do privilege geographic location or district requests. Adjudicated events occur at many different times during the academic year and occasionally, conflicts with district-level events can and do occur.

The second influence is the schedule of ensembles for the adjudicated event. The lore of when an ensemble performs at adjudicated event is a real concern for music educators (Bergee, 2006). There are times of the day that can be a challenge. For example, performing before or after a scheduled break for the adjudicators during the day. The interruption in the flow of adjudication has been known to worry ensemble directors because of possible adjudicator fatigue. Also, performing after an ensemble from a "well-resourced" school district has been known to be an extra-musical influence. Finally, sharing students between ensembles can be stressful on the day of an adjudicated event. This can be particularly challenging if students are scheduled at different performance sites (e.g., choirs and orchestras are at the home site and bands are at an alternative site). Despite the schedule of ensembles for the adjudicated event, other pressures exist that are beyond the control of directors and students.

The last influence is the performance location. Adjudicated events typically have rules about equipment and space usage. Debate among athletic band directors has been the use of electro-acoustical music for marching band performances and performance site limitations sometimes prohibit the use of particular pieces of equipment. Choirs, bands, and orchestras occasionally are influenced by the performance space limitations. These site limitations manifest themselves with allowing soloists ample space to perform and equipment malfunctions. Ensemble directors proactively address performance site influences with site visitations and bringing their own equipment (e.g., percussion, audio, risers, platforms).

Logistical Challenges

Immediately connected to extramusical influences are the myriad of logistical non-musical challenges associated with the events. It is impossible to acknowledge all of the logistical challenges; however, there are a few that are necessary considerations for curricular planning and implementing adjudicated events. The resources necessary to travel to the adjudicated event need to be scheduled with the school district. This process takes time and much advanced planning (in the next section of the chapter, I suggest a timeline for implementing adjudicated events). Most school districts have paperwork or electronic requests for student transportation, equipment trucks, ordering music, and permission slips. It is ultimately up to the ensemble director to facilitate travel to the performance site of the adjudicated event. Occasionally, issues with ensemble personnel can arise. Student eligibility may be regulated at the building level for secondary students and affect ensemble membership. For example, if a student is not passing X number of classes, then they are not eligible to travel. It is a bit of a paradox that one curricular subject would take precedent over another; however, school districts have policies for a reason and knowing them in reference to the possible logistical challenges may help structure adjudicated event preparation in to the curricular decision-making.

Curricular Connections

In order for music teaching and learning to take place, valid and reliable assessment of the curricular outcomes is needed. Assessment is an expected part of the academic curricular process. Adjudicated events provide one avenue of offering an authentic assessment for student musicians; however, the validity of the measure and reliability of the person using the measure are concerns for attaining curricular benchmarks. There is a danger with adjudicated events serving as a formal assessment to capture student learning and growth for district-level curriculum (Hash, 2013).

Music curricula have been written with performance-based outcomes and benchmarks in mind; however, music teachers know that assessments for music teaching and learning need to be balanced and provide a wide variety of opportunities for students to demonstrate learning in different ways. Since adjudicated events do have challenges, these evaluations may be used as a part of the learning process, rather than as a definitive, evaluative experience. Quality performance assessments in music need to be: (a) directly related to the curriculum content and structure; (b) varied in type; (c) frequent in nature; and (d) clear and definable. Evaluations of performance at adjudicated events do not meet the requirements of quality performance assessments and therefore music teachers must look past the "snapshot" model of adjudicated event participation and consider it as only a part of a more robust curricular assessment plan. The organization, planning, and participation associated with attending adjudicated events are additional considerations that will be taken up in the next section of the chapter.

Questions

1. What context-specific limitations have you experienced with attending adjudicated events?
2. How have these limitations influenced your planning and implementation of the curriculum?
3. Looking ahead, what other ways will you address the non-musical challenges of adjudicated event preparation with curricular planning?
4. How have the organizations, which plan and execute adjudicated events, addressed issues of inter-judge reliability?
5. If there were no challenges (musical or non-musical) associated with preparing for and attending adjudicated events, what would the ideal experience look like? What events would be available? How would the experience be organized? What are the considerations to organizing adjudicated events? Are there any adjudicated events that meet curricular outcomes? If so, why or why not?

Curricular Design and Implementation with Adjudicated Events in Mind

Challenges of adjudicated events do present barriers to achieving curricular outcomes and benchmarks. Given these challenges, many directors value the experience and insist on linking the experience as a curricular outcome. Yet, some directors find other learning experiences to help students meet the curricular outcomes and benchmarks. These learning opportunities meet the district-level curricular outcomes and do not present some of the challenges outlined above.

Despite the challenges of preparing for and attending adjudicated events, the benefits outweigh the challenges for some music teachers. The experience of adjudicated event for student musical learning is valued as an important part of the learning process. This section of the chapter outlines promising practices describing how teachers fit adjudicated event preparation into the curricular framework of an ensemble music course.

Definitions

Language may vary from district to district; however, for the purposes of this chapter a shared understanding of the terminology is important to the comprehension of the content below.

Curricular Outcomes – This is a general statement that describes what students should know and be able to do.

Objectives – These are smaller divisions of curricular outcomes. Objectives are specific, observable, and measureable. Usually, objectives are written to include a targeted percentage of achievement by individuals or class-wide.

Indicators – The smallest division of an objective, which lists the specific behavior a student needs to demonstrate.

Benchmarks – These are beginning points that specifically describe knowledge and skills.

Milestones – These are mid-points that describe the student acquisition of knowledge and skills.

Capstones – These are final points that describe the student acquisition of knowledge and skills.

Level 1 – This refers to the lowest level of rigor as an outcome, benchmark, or indicator is approached.

Level 2 - This refers to the middle level of rigor as an outcome, benchmark, or indicator is approached.

Level 3 - This refers to the highest level of rigor as an outcome, benchmark, or indicator is approached.

Introductory – Beginning stage of working toward a skill (novice).

Targeted – Understanding and working toward mastery of a skill (in progress).

Mastery – What is expected at grade level (proficient).

Least Priority	Level of Achievement	Level or Rigor	Scope and Sequence
	Introductory	Level 1	Outcome
	Targeted	Level 2	Benchmark
	Mastery	Level 3	Indicator
Most Priority			

Table 1: *Seriation of terminology used in this chapter.*

First Steps

(*This section is for readers with no experience in curriculum alignment. If you have experience, please proceed to "Planning with the End in Mind."*)

Most important to planning for an adjudicated event experience is to know what are the curricular outcomes and benchmarks and how the outcomes fit into the curricular scope and sequence. Sometimes this information is available from a district-level administrator who is charged with monitoring the curriculum. Ideally, the music department chair or administrator will have this information at the building-level and can locate it in a timely manner. Sometimes the document is streamlined electronically and is available on a district-level faculty portal. Rarely this information is open access to the parents and community.

Once the document has been located, it is important to understand the contents. In a simplified manner, take notes about your observations. As you examine the document, ask the following questions:

1. When was the document last updated?
2. How detailed is the document?
3. Is there a scope and sequence?
4. Does the document offer enough descriptive information for providing a clear picture as to how the course is to be constructed?
5. Are assessments provided as a part of the document?

Once the document has been located and scanned, questions should be answered by seeking out the expertise of the administration before beginning the planning stage of incorporating adjudicated events into the fabric of the curriculum.

Planning with the End in Mind

Understanding by Design (UbD) is a way of thinking purposefully about curricular planning, assessment and school reform. The UbD model aims to provide teachers with the tools to structure their curriculum around understanding, and provide a means to communicate with colleagues and students about the development of understanding in the learning environment (See Chapter by Forrester for more information about UbD).

By selecting adjudicated events as an experience or what Wiggins and McTighe (2008) call the "big idea," the process of backwards planning may begin. The adjudicated event experience must fundamentally meet curricular outcomes. Since most curricular outcomes are performance based, this should not be a problem. For example, if a district has adopted state-level outcomes and benchmarks for the district music courses, it is safe to assume that performing is an outcome. The performing outcome directly connects to the experience at adjudicated events. Some curricula specify how performing should take place. The performing may be in a group or individually. Both large group and solo & ensemble adjudicated event experiences would meet these curricular outcomes. Depending on the medium of ensemble (e.g., choir, orchestra, band, jazz ensemble, marching band), other curricular outcomes may be selected. Reading notation and singing are additional curricular outcomes, which are accomplished by attending adjudicated events.

Once these outcomes have been identified, other decisions need to be considered (See Table 2 for a synthesized sequence). Begin by selecting which outcomes, benchmarks, or indicators truly capture the essence behind the adjudicated event. These outcomes must be objective, measurable, and specific enough so that an assessment may be constructed to inform the music teaching and learning process. Rank the outcomes, benchmarks, or indicators at their most specific level. For example, some districts have chosen to list indicators of behavior and other districts have chosen to list benchmarks (See Table 1). The most desired step in the planning process is to know the curriculum at the most specific level and use those outcomes, benchmarks, and/or indicators during the prioritization process.

Now that the prioritization process is finished, the next step is to decide what level of achievement (e.g., introductory, targeted, mastery) of the curricular outcomes is needed for the student musicians. Occasionally, this information is decided for the teachers and is located in the scope and sequence. If not, this step in the process will need to be completed. This may only be accurate if the ensemble director has prior knowledge of the student achievement in the ensemble. Not all outcomes need to be mastered in secondary ensembles. Some outcomes are introduced, while others are intended to be targeted leading toward mastery.

The final step in this process of beginning with the end in mind is to decide the level of rigor the outcome will receive. This is much like deciding how intense or privileged an outcome will be as the preparation for adjudicated events begins. For example, levels 1–3 were selected for this chapter; however, districts may choose other terminology to represent levels of rigor. This concept is a matter of value and priority. Some curricular outcomes need to have direction. This language provides vocabulary for that direction.

What?	How?
Locate the curriculum.	Ask your administrator (e.g., building-level or district-level curriculum supervisor).
Scan the curricular documents.	This may be done by photocopying it and working from a draft copy. Take notes about questions you may have as you read the document.
Ask questions.	Seek out expert opinions from music and curriculum writers.
Identify the curricular outcomes that fit adjudicated events.	As you read the curricular document, note those benchmarks or indicators that may relate to adjudicated events.
Prioritize the outcomes.	List which outcomes, benchmarks, or indicators, truly capture the essence behind the adjudicated event. There may be primary outcomes and secondary outcomes.
Level of achievement	Decide if your primary and secondary outcomes are all intended for student mastery. This may be described in the scope and sequence.
Level of rigor	Decide how intense the outcomes will be focused on during lessons.

Table 2: Sequence of Preparing for Curricular Decisions

	Level of Achievement	Level of Rigor
Outcome 1 *Students will demonstrate technical proficiency through the entire practical range of their instruments or voice.*	Mastery	Level 3
Outcome 2 *Students will demonstrate performance competency on required scales and arpeggios. All scales will be memorized.*	Targeted	Level 2
Outcome 3 *Students will demonstrate a representative tone quality at all dynamic levels throughout the range of their instruments or voice.*	Targeted	Level 3
Outcome 4 *Students will demonstrate their ability to perform alone.*	Introductory	Level 2
Outcome 5 *Students will sight read music in all major and minor keys.*	Introductory	Level 1

Outcome 1 is an example of an outcome that can be connected to adjudicated events. The combination of "Mastery" level of achievement and "Level 3" level of rigor makes this outcome a high priority in the music classroom. Outcome 5 is an example of an outcome that can be connected to adjudicated events, if the event has an opportunity for sight-reading notation. The combination of "Introductory" level of achievement and "Level 1" level of rigor makes this outcome a low priority for achieving in the music classroom.

Table 3: *Sample Diagram for Curricular Decision Making*

In summary, the process of planning with the end in mind is much like planning a structured journey. Knowing that attending adjudicated events is the goal, beginning with the goal in mind for planning will ensure that the destination is reached. In the next section of the chapter, the process of planning for adjudicated events is unpacked and examined.

Process of Planning for Adjudicated Events

Now that the curricular outcomes, benchmarks, and indicators have been identified and prioritized, the process of backward planning may begin. The curricular outcomes that ensemble directors select directly relate the experiences that mirror or support adjudicated events. Building authentic assessments that are frequent in nature and mirror the adjudicated event process is imperative to the adjudicated event being a robust learning opportunity for students. Depending on the adjudicated event experience that ensemble directors elect to attend, the experiences will be different. These experiences may include: (a) additional specialized instruction from professional musicians; (b) pre-festival concert night; (c) guest ensemble clinicians; and (d) pre-festival adjudication night. These experiences are considered promising practices from experienced music teachers who regularly attend adjudicated events. These experiences are each presented in a separate vignette.

Vignette 2

Hiring additional specialized instruction from professional musicians to facilitate preparation for the adjudication event is a common experience for secondary performing ensembles. Joe hires professional musicians as guests to coach student musicians. Years ago, his program established a partnership with a local symphony orchestra. This partnership allows for professional musicians to coach students taking small ensemble and solo events to adjudicated events. Joe remarked, "...Many times music ensembles are understaffed for the number of learning differences and musical ability which exist in an ensemble setting." This is the main reason he hires additional specialized instruction. Ensemble membership varies across the nation; however, rarely are music classroom teachers held the same teacher-to-student ratio calculated for STEM subjects. The individualized instruction with the students is valued by the experienced music teachers because more students are able to receive personalized instruction as they prepare for the adjudicated event experience. In Joe's particular program, the professional musicians are weekly visitors to the music classroom as they help students set goals and regulate a practice regiment leading toward a concert experience and the adjudicated event.

Vignette 3

Marla holds a pre-festival concert night as an opportunity for student musicians to perform in front of an audience. She is one of many experienced music teachers who know the power of planning a pre-festival concert night prior to the adjudicated event. There are many strategies to planning the date of the concert. Marla prefers to have the concert within a week of the adjudicated event as to make sure the ensemble is playing at peak performance, while her colleagues across the district prefer to have the concert a few weeks ahead of the adjudicated event so students have time to reflect on the concert experience and improve their performance level leading up to the event. In a neighboring city, a few ensemble directors turn this concert night into a fundraiser for the music program. For example, one ensemble director (Amy) combines a catered dinner and silent auction with school ensembles (large group and small ensembles) as a way of providing additional performance opportunities for the student musicians. Another idea comes from one ensemble director (Jim) who has a solo and ensemble concert for all students participating in these events. Each ensemble is scheduled for a performance location and the audience members rotate every ten to fifteen minutes. This way each ensemble has multiple opportunities to practice the process of performing for different crowds. Despite how Marla, Amy, or Jim schedule this pre-festival concert nights, they see the value in strategically planning these experiences to maximize student learning.

Vignette 4

Guest clinicians offer a wealth of information for all learners as they prepare to attend adjudicated events. Regularly scheduling guest clinicians or teachers, who have expertise in the medium of performance (e.g., choir, orchestra, band), is a promising practice of experienced music teachers. All of the experienced music teachers mentioned above invited current adjudicators for an authentic contest experience. Amy believes in the notion of having a guest clinician(s) work with an ensemble, thereby demystifying the scoring mechanism (e.g., performance rubric) and offering valuable information related to setting goals for continuous learning. Jim discussed the additional peer mentoring from the clinician to him as an added benefit of this practice. Joe and Marla schedule multiple clinicians because of the added expertise in content knowledge; however, other directors (not mentioned in this book chapter) only schedule one visit as to avoid the "too many cooks in the kitchen" mentality (i.e., possible conflicting interpretive information about the music notation).

Vignette 5

A pre-festival adjudication night offers an authentic, simulated adjudicated event experience. This final promising practice synthesizes the prior practices to involve a panel of clinicians. For the large group ensemble, Dara and Chris ask trained adjudicators to simulate the adjudication experience (this experience may vary depending on regional context) with an evaluation of the ensemble associated with this experience. For example, multiple large ensembles are scheduled in three locations: listening to a performing ensemble, warm-up room, or performing space. Dara reported that "…Occasionally, there is an opportunity for a clinic immediately following the performance." The performing ensembles during this experience are adjudicated by a panel of adjudicators (the number of the adjudicators mirrors the adjudicated event experience). Chris added that "…the scoring mechanism needs to be the same tool as used at the adjudicated event. Recording the ensemble's performance and judge's comments needs to be a part of the process." Some directors choose to involve the audience by allowing them to score the ensemble as well. This process educates the audience as to the criteria for earning a rating or score at adjudicated events. Dara and Chris also mentioned having a guest adjudicator speak to the audience about the process as a way of informing about how to use the mechanism. Although educating your audience in this way may help build advocacy for the program, Dara and Chris are careful not to consult the audience as adjudicators. Simply put, the audience does not get a say in what or how the curriculum is being delivered to the students.

Mapping out the Terrain

The metaphor of mapping is a useful image for understanding the learning process in curricular planning with adjudicated events.

Incorporating all of the promising practices into a timeline may be done eventually; however, gradually adding one or two promising practice(s) at a time is recommended.

Suggested Sequence for Incorporation

1. Hiring Additional Specialized Personnel (Vignette 2)
2. Guest Clinicians (Vignette 4)
3. Pre-festival Concert Night (Vignette 3)
4. Pre-festival Adjudication Night (Vignette 5)

There are many sources of information to consider when ensemble directors map out the terrain of their curriculum. The suggested sequence below needs to be context specific and therefore, the model timeline provided (See Table 4) assumes a specific medium or context.

Suggested Sequence of Gathering Information Prior to Mapping

Summer Prior to the Academic Year

1. Locate the school and district calendar and record all days off from school or non-instructional days.
2. Record all known sporting events or school activities, which may impact your performing ensembles onto your calendar.
3. Construct a performing arts calendar or request performance dates from the department and transfer these dates to the calendar.
4. Record dates for requesting transportation, entrance fees, or music purchases from the district- or building-level on the calendar.
5. Plan time during the summer to peruse scores or directed listening for concert planning and adjudicated event music selection.
6. Be sure that planned concerts are not double- or triple-booked with sport or school activities.

	What	**Considerations**
Summer	• Planning Adjudicated Event (AE) program • Secure transportation. • Secure funding. • Invite clinicians. • Organize Pre-festival Concert Night.	• District timeline for completion of resource requests • Clinician schedules • School and district calendar
Seven months	• Athletic Band Performances • Order Music for Concerts 1, 2, and AE program.	• Department musical rehearsals
Six months	• Begin Concert 2 repertoire.	• Sports and athletic band performances • Department musical performance
Five months	• Concert 2 leading to AE program	• Sports and athletic band performances
Four months	• Begin Concert 3 repertoire.	• New semester • Inclement weather days
Three months	• Concert 3 leading to AE program • Register for the AE.	• Inclement weather days
Two months	• Begin AE program. • Schedule sectionals with professional musicians or clinicians. • Ensemble Camp or Lock-in	
One month	• Pre-festival Concert • Schedule a guest clinician to work with a full ensemble. • Confirm buses and if AE payment has been processed.	• Concert programs • PSATs, ACTs, SATs • Clinician compensation
Two weeks	• Pre-festival Adjudication Night • Judge's score copies prepared; measures numbered • Bus list sign-up or assigned • Listen to the judge's comments in class with the students. • Create a logical plan, which addresses the comments from the performance.	• Meet and Greet with the clinicians • Clinician compensation • Concert programs, materials for adjudication (taped comments, pencils, etc.) • Advertising
One Week	• Detailed practice without many complete run-throughs as to delay the peak of the ensemble • Perform for a student population (e.g., performing arts, general). • Perform for a faculty meeting.	• Sectionals
Day before the AE	• Pack up the judges' scores/packets. • Bring extra music, instrument accessories, instrument repair kit, tuners, etc. • Snacks or necessary personal care items • Bus lists and numbered signs • Rosters for chaperones	• AE score policy – no photocopies are allowed. • How will you transport the materials?
Day of the AE	• Enjoy the event! Everything is done.	• Be sure to follow district policies for curricular field experiences. • Permission slips, chaperones, attendance procedures, medical forms, etc.

Table 4: *Suggested Timeline for Academic Year*

By attending to this sequence, the ensemble director is ready for the next step in the planning stages.

Selecting music for the adjudicated event is a monumental task and prior knowledge of the student's musical achievement is required. By consulting the musical challenges at the beginning of the chapter, ensemble directors know where the hurdles are associated with the adjudicated experience. Begin by selecting the repertoire in the music library and possibly issue new music that fits the instrumentation of the ensemble(s). If you do not have violas in the orchestra, do not pick music that has a prominent viola part, rather that may offer a third violin part instead of a viola part. Similarly, do not program Hindemith's March from *Symphonic Metamorphosis* if you have only one horn performer. Being realistic at this stage of the planning process will structure students for success.

Next, be sure you select a variety of repertoire that aligns with the requirements of the adjudicated events. Each event is different. Time requirements, style of notation, and technical facility are all considerations. Reduce the list of repertoire to these limitations and begin looking at the scores and listening to recordings. Once you find an "anchor piece" for your adjudicated event then consider what pairings may fulfill the requirements and be an appropriate sonic match to the "anchor piece." What about featuring an all-state musician(s) with a solo section or duet? What about considering the unique acoustical properties of the venue the performance will be held in?

Once the program(s) for adjudicated events have been selected, the next step is to list the necessary technical and musical requirements of the notation. Technical requirements are known as objective skills (e.g., the tonal key area or key changes, slurring-tonguing combinations, rhythmic content, range, and tessitura demands), which are presented in the musical score. Musical requirements are known as *subjective skills*, which are beyond the musical notation. For example, articulation choice, tone production, balance issues, and blending considerations. As a way of building a rationale for attending the adjudicated events, all of these requirements can be linked to the curricular outcomes. Once a thorough list of the requirements have been made, prepare supporting repertoire that will lead to the adjudicated event program. More specifically, select repertoire that will address similar technical and musical requirements to the adjudicated events program as to help reinforce the concepts necessary for that program.

In a study conducted during the 2013–2014 academic year, I examined experienced music teachers' insights about adjudicated events. These teachers agreed that the supporting repertoire should be focused on the technical and musical requirements leading up the adjudicated event. All of the considerations in planning repertoire require careful thought. There is wisdom from experienced music teachers which suggested that the support repertoire is more advanced than the adjudicated event program. By using this philosophy of planning repertoire, students may focus on the musical requirements of the piece rather than the technical. There is also wisdom from experienced music teachers, which suggest that adjudication repertoire may not be given to the students at the beginning of the academic year. This model promotes an approach that does not promote musical fluency and perhaps contradicts the curricular outcomes. The graphic representation of the academic year below is a suggested sequence of timing the promising practices with a large group adjudicated event in April situated in a secondary band program.

When setting up a graphic representation of the academic year, it is also important to think about the level of achievement and rigor that repertoire is approached during the sequence of instruction and timing. Systematic planning by acknowledging when repertoire needs to be introduced, targeted, and mastered are necessary for long-term planning to be relevant. As the chart above gives a global overview of the academic year, more specified planning needs to be considered. For each concert series, what level of achievement does repertoire need to be after a week of rehearsals? Two weeks after rehearsals? Three weeks after rehearsals? How many minutes of music has been programmed versus the amount of minutes of rehearsal?

Conclusion

Adjudicated events will always be on the minds and tongues of music educators. A rich history of dialogue explaining the benefits and challenges of adjudicated events exist and looking forward to future years of adjudicated events, will new benefits and challenges emerge (See Chapter 4 by Schuler and Chapter 6 by Siebert)? Musical challenges associated with adjudicated events are present; however, the best way to navigate these challenges is to be a sensitive musician (See Chapter 12 by Shaw). When aligning curricular outcomes to adjudicated events, the procedures outlined in this chapter are suggestions and because of the reader's context may need modification. The opportunity to attend adjudicated events can be a fantastic experience for students as their musicianship matures and for teachers to inform their pedagogy. H. Robert Reynolds was right! The repertoire is our curriculum and it takes effort on the part of music educators to demonstrate that fact through curricular alignment.

References

Bergee, M. J. (2006). Validation of a model of extramusical influences on solo and small-ensemble festival ratings. *Journal of Research in Music Education, 54*(3), 244–256. doi:10.2307/4151345

Brakel, T. D. (2006). Inter-judge reliability of the Indiana State School Music Association High School Instrumental Festival. *Journal of Band Research, 42*(1), 59–69.

Hash, P. M. (2012). An analysis of the ratings and inter-rater reliability of high school band contests. *Journal of Research in Music Education, 60*(1), 81–100. doi:10.1177/0022429411434932

Hash, P. M. (2013). Large-group contest ratings and music teacher evaluation: Issues and recommendations. *Arts Education Policy Review, 114*(4), 163–169. doi:10.1080/10632913.2013.826035

Reynolds, H. R. (2000). Repertoire is the curriculum. *Music Educators Journal, 87*(1), 31. doi:10.2307/3399675

Rickels, D. (2012). Nonperformance variables as predictors of marching band contest results. *Bulletin of the Council for Research in Music Education*, (194). doi:10.5406/bulcouresmusedu.194.0053

Stegman, S. F. (2009). Michigan state adjudicated choral festivals: Revising the adjudication process. *Music Educators Journal*, 95(4), 62–65. doi:10.2307/30219240

Stoll, J. L. (2008). *The relationship of high school band directors' assessment practices to ratings at a large group adjudicated event* (Ph.D.). Kent State University, Ohio. Retrieved from http://search.proquest.com.proxy.lib.umich.edu/dissertations/docview/304565057/abstract/13E00530ED854558228/5?accountid=14667

Wilson, G. V. (1926). Making the most of contests. *Music Supervisors' Journal*, 13(2), 11–65. doi:10.2307/3382639

CHAPTER 18

CURRICULUM AND ASSESSMENT IN PRESERVICE MUSIC TEACHER EDUCATION

J. Si Millican and Kristen Pellegrino
The University of Texas at San Antonio

When preservice teachers begin the formal path of becoming professional educators, they often visualize themselves working with musical ensembles much like the ones they participated in as student musicians. Perhaps they envision themselves standing in front of their high school ensemble or returning after graduation to lead their former elementary school music program. Rarely, however, do these future music teachers consider the important roles of curriculum and assessment in their teaching careers. In this chapter, we discuss how we guide preservice music teachers' understanding and development of (a) broad concepts of curriculum, (b) their own teaching philosophy, (c) goals, benchmarks, and standards; (d) lesson plans; and (e) assessment tools.

Broad Concepts of Curriculum

One metaphor we like to share with our preservice teachers when we begin to explore curriculum, lesson planning, and assessment is that of planning a family vacation. In this metaphor, we think of the broad planning that takes place when visualizing the vacation as the "curriculum." Where do we want to go on our trip? How long will we take to get there? What special stops do we want to make on the way? Benchmarks might be represented by goals we set for ourselves on our family road trip: Where should we be by the end of the first day? What will be the best place to fuel up the car? Should we stop for lunch in a small town or travel on to a big city on the third night? The detailed itinerary for the day or a step-by-step guided tour at a national monument might be representative of lesson planning. Assessment of our road trip might be made up of the informal evaluations about how our trip is progressing as we move down the road: Are we making good time? How are my fellow travelers feeling about the schedule? We might engage in more formal assessments such as: What kind of gas mileage are we getting? Does it match our plans for stopping for fuel? And perhaps our most important assessment question: how do we know when we've arrived at our destination? In the next few sections, we'll consider how the curriculum and philosophical development interact with the important tasks of long- and short-range planning and how preservice music educators can develop their own knowledge, skills, and attitudes related to these topics.

Curriculum can be visualized broadly using a wide view, which we call "macro" level in this chapter. At this level, we explore ways in which we help our preservice teachers develop philosophical frameworks so that they begin to work through problems associated with developing goals and objectives. These macro-level decisions have a significant impact on teachers' micro-level decisions as they put their philosophies into action by developing unit, weekly, and daily lesson plans. Next we look at ways in which we might define *curriculum*. We conclude with ways in which preservice teachers might develop a familiarity with the process of planning individual lessons and activities at the micro level of curriculum development.

We ascribe to Bruner's (1966) "spiral" approach when acclimating our preservice teachers to the intricacies of working with curriculum and assessment. We are fortunate to have our students in classes as early as their second semester of their university coursework, and we are able to introduce concepts in these initial stages of their time with us as preservice teachers and then revisit topics in more depth throughout the rest of their professional preparation. In our case, we work with preservice teachers in classes such as string techniques; wind, string, or choral pedagogy; wind, string, or choral literature; and two semesters of Curriculum and Instruction classes, which preservice music teachers take during the two semesters before they student teach. Many of our string specialists also teach in our String Project. We hope that they will continue that development by spiraling back to the same topics and have conversations with their supervisors, mentors, and peers as they develop as young teachers after they leave our program. What we present in the next few sections is not meant to be an all-encompassing guide to teaching curriculum, and we certainly would not present these methods as one-shot prescriptions to address the complexities of developing curriculum in the real-world work of music teaching. Instead, we present the following sections in the hopes that other music-teacher educators might recognize both familiar and new ways to present these topics to help preservice teachers develop the skills, knowledge, and attitudes necessary to begin their journeys as curriculum and assessment writers at the micro and macro levels.

Developing a Music Teaching Philosophy

What do you love most about music making? Why do you want to be a music teacher? What kind of music teacher do you want to be for your future students and why? What are your beliefs about how students learn best and what role do you play in their learning? These are key questions to consider when developing a music teaching philosophy. Allowing preservice music teachers to address their own beliefs about music, teaching, and learning will help them clarify their own goals and assist them in developing systematic, sequenced ways to teach that include long-term (macro level) and short-term (micro level) goals.

As with lesson planning, activities only make sense in relation to one's overall objectives. Devising goals, objectives, benchmarks, and assessment tools is directly related to each teacher's philosophy. The importance of a philosophy as a starting point becomes clear when comparing established models based on methods and approaches such as Kodály, Orff, Gordon, Suzuki, Dalcroze, and Comprehensive Musicianship. Although all of these models began with the premise that music is for everyone, their mission statements often emphasize different aspects of what each designer believes to be most important. For example, who would object to goals such as promoting universal music literacy, aesthetic and creative experiences, developing audiation skills, or music as expression and connection to other arts? While most music teachers would say that these are all valuable goals, promoting universal music literacy is part of Organization of American Kodály Educators' mission statement, "awakening aesthetic responsiveness" and inspiring creativity is associated with Orff-Schulwerk approach (American Orff-Schulwerk Association, 2014; Banks, 1982), audiation with Gordon's Music Learning Theory (Gordon Institute for Music Learning, 2014), and music as expression and connection to other arts with Dalcroze's approach (Dalcroze Society of America, 2014). Choosing one's top music-learning priorities is a difficult task. We believe that these priorities influence curricular decisions at all levels, so we feel that it is important for each preservice teacher to understand the origin of their beliefs and decisions, as well as to consider additional options.

We often begin this exploration by asking our preservice teachers to engage in the following type of conversation:

> Understanding that all great music teachers do not teach alike, consider whether it is more important TO YOU to teach about music as *expression*, music as *creativity*, music as music *literacy*, music as *audiation*, music as being *connected to other arts*, music as *representative of different cultures*, or some *other orientation*. All are worthy goals, but curricula designed to address any one of these ideas as a top priority will greatly differ. Similarly, if any one of these ideas is left out, this will drastically affect one's curriculum.

Kristen's music teaching philosophy

My (Kristen's) music teaching philosophy includes helping students develop musically, individually, and socially. I work to help create an environment conducive to learning and try to challenge all students without overwhelming anyone. I also want students to experience the joys of music making and to understand that their music making can be an outlet of expression, a way to improve their own well being, and a way to help them form a sense of identity through feelings of success and belonging (Pellegrino & Millican, in press; Pellegrino, 2010, 2014). How I arrived at this is included below. In my dissertation, I wrote:

> "I consider myself a string teacher because I love helping others make music on their string instruments. I love helping students discover themselves and their voices through interacting with the music, their stringed instrument, themselves, and me... I became a string teacher in order to contribute to the creation of an orchestra family—a community of people who made meaningful, moving music together. The string orchestra room was a place where we worked long and hard, socialized, supported each other, and became the best versions of ourselves through the inspiration of the music and the manner in which we interacted. I could help my students on their musical, personal, and social journeys.
>
> For me, being a string teacher is interwoven with me as music-maker...I always felt that, in order to show my students how to love music making, I needed to show them that I was a music-maker and that I myself love making music!
>
> Making music on my violin is a way for me to feel centered, connected, inspired, and whole. Music making is intertwined with my sense of self, family, and spirituality. It is personal, pedagogical, and magical." (Pellegrino, 2010, pp. 4–5)

This philosophy guided me as a teacher and was evident in my curricular choices on both the macro level of developing overall goals, standards, and benchmarks, as well as at the micro level of developing units, weekly goals, lesson plans, and specific activities.

Millican (2013) poses several questions designed to help preservice music teachers begin to develop their own music teacher philosophy, including:

> What is music? What is "good" music? Which music should be taught in schools? Before you answer "all kinds of music," do you really mean that? What about popular music...rap music...(and/or) mariachi music? "Who should teach music? Who should study music? Before you answer "everybody," really think through this answer. When can a person begin to learn an instrument? Why should music be taught in schools? Why not after school? Why not in professional studios? How should music be taught? How is music learned most efficiently? (p. 247)

Thinking through these types of questions and having these types of conversations often challenges preservice teachers to reflect upon their own experiences and frequently leads them to think about their own orientations to music learning and teaching. This is an important first step in helping them to frame their own ideas about curriculum and assessment.

Defining Curriculum and Developing Goals, Benchmarks, and Standards

When preservice teachers begin thinking about curriculum, they often retain their focus on performance skills or on specific repertoire. Within this performance orientation, they consider questions such as "What should my students be able to play, create, or comprehend?" or "What pieces will my ensembles perform?" One of our first concerns after our music education students begin developing philosophical orientations is helping them start to define and expand what *curriculum* means. Raiber and Teachout (2014, pp. 116–120) present several different ways of defining *curriculum*. They argue that curriculum might be viewed in multiple ways: (a) as a body of knowledge in which students demonstrate understanding and skill within musical elements such as tonal, temporal (rhythmic), expressive, and structural (formal) components; (b) elements representing students' musical independence and interdependence in performance may make up a curriculum; or (c) expression and creativity or interdisciplinary and multicultural learning as central components of a curriculum. Certainly, no one approach is all-encompassing when it comes do defining *curriculum*, and many state curriculum frameworks and the National Core Arts Standards combine elements from each of these areas. The point is that we can help expand preservice teachers' thinking to consider other views of curriculum rather than just a list of technical skills and definitions we need to teach our students in order to be successful, and we can help these future educators become familiar with a broader view of curriculum beyond performance skills. In this section, we explain how we preservice music teachers develop goals, benchmarks, and standards; and develop outcomes and objectives.

Goals, Benchmarks, and Standards – Curriculum at the Macro Level

While we believe that a curriculum should be contextualized to the environment in which it is practiced, it is helpful to understand knowledge, skills, and attitudes of learning music at the macro level through an investigation of state and national standards. Goals and benchmarks are not curriculum—they are merely lists of things that people should learn. However, broad guidelines such as these can provide a good starting point to develop one's own views on what people can and should learn in music. In this section, we discuss unpacking national and state standards and creating goals and benchmarks.

Unpacking national and state standards. Often preservice teachers lack a context for what is developmentally appropriate for students at various levels. State and national standards and local curriculum guides and standards can help them solidify their knowledge about what their students need to know and be able to do or understand. Feldman and Contzius (2010) highlight three areas of the 1994 version of the National Music Standards: declarative learning (what students should know), procedural learning (what students should be able to do), and conceptual understanding (what students should be able to understand). The revised National Core Arts Standards include the four artistic processes of creating, presenting/performing/producing, responding, and connecting (National Coalition for Core Arts Standards, 2014).

After they become familiar with some of the frameworks at the state and national levels, future music educators can begin to develop specific goals and benchmarks for various grade levels, ensembles, and teaching situations. Understanding the basic elements of performance (1994 National Standards 1, 2, and 5), creativity (3 and 4), response (6 and 7), and making connections between other arts and subjects outside of the arts (standards 8 and 9) is a fundamental step in broadening the misconception that some preservice teachers hold that musical standards are primarily performance-based. The new National Core Music Standards emphasize this orientation to include the areas of creating and responding in addition to performing (National Coalition for Core Arts Standards, 2014).

While many music education students might easily relate to the performance-based standards, they may need help understanding and conceptualizing the creativity, response, and relationships standards. Raiber and Teachout (2014) emphasize that writing, improvising and creating music, as well as criticizing and describing music, are just as significant indicators of accomplishment in music as reading and performing music. Allowing preservice music teachers the opportunities to explore ways in which their students might express their musicianship through creating and responding to music is an important task for the music teacher educator. One way we help preservice music teachers become familiar with state and national standards as they relate to curriculum development is adopted from Raiber and Teachout (2014, p. 218). Students randomly select slips of paper with three different music content standards written on them and choose a teaching specialization (band, choir, orchestra, general music) and a piece of music. Students then design an activity that would address all selected content standards.

Goals and benchmarks: What do students need to know and do? Some people make a solid distinction between goals and benchmarks. Benchmarks are often formal or informal checkpoints practitioners or other stakeholders create in order to measure their students' progress. Developing their own benchmarks allows future teachers to begin to consider the long- and short-term goals and expectations they will set for their students. These goals and benchmarks also interact with their music teaching philosophies as well as the construction of lesson plans at the macro (unit, semester) and micro (lesson and activity) levels. Preservice teachers can develop their own lists of developmentally appropriate goals and benchmarks for what their students need to know and be able to do by considering two organizing frameworks.

One framework that may be more familiar to those preservice teachers operating within the ensemble performance mode may be one in which concerts and festivals drive the curricular calendar. In this application, preservice teachers develop goals and benchmarks by carefully analyzing the typical performance calendars of secondary-level performing groups. Making a list of performances and activities that occur throughout the year might stimulate concrete thinking about the knowledge, skills, and attitudes needed to perform successfully at these events. Students might even analyze adjudication sheets from state festivals to see the component performance skills that might be added to a list of goals and benchmarks. Beginning with this admittedly limited view of performance skills allows us as faculty to introduce other student learning goals such as creativity, evaluation, and response.

Duke (2009) proposes a broader view of goals and benchmarks present in a well-thought-out list of the "skills for intelligent musicianship" for students in areas of performance, subject matter knowledge, and music appreciation (pp. 37–47). Duke's presentation intentionally omits skill-level specificity so that each item in his list can be applied as appropriate based on the students' developmental needs and experience level. For example, Duke presents performing "successive tones in congruity with a steady pulse" as a learning goal (p. 38). This goal could be applied appropriately to an all-state percussionist performing an etude or a pre-kindergarten maraca player equally. Starting with a well-developed framework like this can help preservice teachers begin to consider the specific skill and knowledge components that each student should begin to develop. In the next sections, we'll look at ways in which these frameworks can be used to further develop a more focused curriculum at the middle and micro levels.

The *ASTA Curriculum Guide* (Benham et al. 2011) is an incredible resource. We have our preservice string teachers create a curriculum document over eight class homework assignments using the ASTA Curriculum Guide as a resource. For the first assignment, preservice teachers choose and describe a teaching context: (a) urban, suburban, rural; (b) socioeconomic status; (c) teaching level and where they are in their development; (d) how often you work with students a week and for how long. Over the next seven assignments, students consider different portions of the curriculum and write out the most relevant parts that are related to their chosen teaching context, including specific language and assessment tools related to that teaching context.

Developing Outcomes and Objectives – Mid-level Curriculum Development

After music education students become familiar working with and thinking about goals and benchmarks generally, they are ready to dig deeper into developing the mid-level curricular decisions involved with designing outcomes and objectives for specific activities, pieces, and events. These types of plans might involve periods of time as short as a week or two up to as long as six weeks or longer. In the case of performing groups, this involves a careful analysis of the knowledge, skills, and attitudes that are necessary to perform a particular set of pieces at a particular time in a particular venue. In addition, there may be learning goals and benchmarks that are not necessarily tied to a particular performance. Elementary and general music classes and those with fewer public performances might divide goals and objectives into logical "units" of study. Whatever the motivation or organizational paradigm you explore for dividing up the smaller units of study, there are a few different ways to organize this level of planning.

One way to engage preservice teachers in planning mid-level curriculum is to have them complete a thorough analysis of the literature to be performed by creating a knowledge and skill inventory of the pieces. For example, if an elementary music methods class devises a unit on Samba drumming, then they can analyze the component knowledge and skills needed to perform these pieces. Secondary band and orchestra methods students might adopt a *Comprehensive Musicianship Through Performance* (CMP) model like ones presented in Patricia O'Toole's (2003) *Shaping Sound Musicians* or Robert Garofalo's (1983) *Blueprint for Band*. Both of these resources stress the significance of using the performance of great literature as a vehicle to teach musical skills and concepts; the emphasis is to teach about music through performing, analyzing, composing, and discussing the music to be performed. This starts with teachers becoming very familiar with the music through careful analysis of performance pieces in order to develop learning inventories, outcomes, teaching strategies, and effective assessments. The *Teaching Music Through Performance* series published by GIA Publications provides some examples of this type of analysis for bands, choirs, and orchestras using pieces at varying levels of difficulty (GIA Publications, 2014). Figure 1 on page 468 is an example of an analysis tool that we use in our literature classes.

Overview

Title:_____ Composer:_____ Grade:_____

Category/Genre:_____ Dates:_____ State Contest List: 5 4 3 2 1 no

Length of Piece:_____ Key(s):_____ Meter(s):_____

Evaluation:_____ Form:_____

Objectives:_____

Relate to State/National Standards:_____

Purchasing Info:_____ Listening Info:_____

1. This piece is a great choice because of its intrinsic musical value.

    1 strongly disagree   2 disagree   3 neutral   4 agree   5 strongly agree

2. This piece is a great choice because of its pedagogical value.

    1 strongly disagree   2 disagree   3 neutral   4 agree   5 strongly agree

3. This piece is a great choice because of its technical level.

    1 strongly disagree   2 disagree   3 neutral   4 agree   5 strongly agree

4. Summary of the chart below:

Score Divisions	First Violin	Second Violin	Third Violin/ Viola	Cello	Bass	Other (Harp, Percussion, etc.)
Melodic Interest (measure #s)						
Rhythmic Interest (measure #s + define)						
Technical Challenges (measure #s + define)						
Positions						
Bowing Challenges (measure #s + define)						
Harmonic Challenges (measure #s + define)						
Other Challenges (e.g. - tempi changes)						
Overall Assessment						

Prior knowledge: Left Hand Demands:

Information/Historical background: Formal Design:

Musical Demands: Conducting Thoughts:

Right Hand Demands: Creative Rehearsal Strategies:

Figure 1: Analysis Worksheet

As preservice teachers develop these lists of "things you could teach" with each piece of music through their analysis, they should continue to connect the learning outcomes and activities to the national and state standards. For example, if preservice teachers develop knowledge, skill, and aesthetic outcomes, they should also list the specific national standard and/or state standard that apply to each. Many school districts ask their teachers to specify the learning goals or state curriculum standards that are being applied in teachers' lesson plans.

We have found that using Bloom's Taxonomy (Bloom & Krathwohl, 1956) as a framing device helps preservice teachers write more meaningful and clear mid-level goals and objectives. By asking preservice teachers to write knowledge, skill, and affective outcomes focusing at the highest levels of evaluation, synthesis, and analysis levels (or perhaps using Anderson and Krathwohl's (2001) revised higher thinking skills of creating, evaluating, and analyzing), we help ensure that the areas of creativity, responsiveness, and cross-curricular modes of artistic expression are more likely to be addressed. O'Toole (2003, pp. 32–5) outlines some ways in which teachers write outcomes that address the higher-order thinking skills used in the top levels of the taxonomy. After a thoughtful knowledge and skill inventories are completed for the mid-level curriculum planning, more in-depth planning at the micro level can be completed.

Lesson Planning – Curriculum at the Micro Level

Lesson planning is where curriculum thinking is moved to action; sticking with our metaphor, this is the time when we get in the car, start the engine, and begin our trip. This can be viewed as the culmination of our work on developing philosophical orientations, crafting goals and benchmarks, and carefully analyzing the teaching materials and repertoire in order to create learning experiences for our students. We ask our preservice music teachers to write lesson plans that are often much more detailed than in-service teachers might write, but we feel that having our music education students express their thoughts and plans in very specific language accomplishes two major learning goals. First, it helps preservice teachers begin to think of all of the necessary elements to execute the activities they have in mind. A less-experienced music education student might write an elementary music teaching activity as simply "Sing through *Little Liza Jane*." We ask them to more clearly visualize what the students and teachers are doing during the activity: *How fast? What tonality? Will you tonicize before singing? Will you take a whole, part, whole approach or something else? How might you break that folk song into chunks? How will your students be arranged in the classroom for this activity?* Developing this type of clarity of thought and attention to detail helps preservice teachers formulate a clear vision in their mind of exactly how they want the lesson to go.

The second benefit of writing plans in this type of detail is that it allows us as music-teacher educators to peer into the minds and thought processes of our students. By describing all of the elements of their lesson plans in detail—with objectives clearly stated using observable terms, connections clearly made with state and national learning standards, with each step of the activities presented precisely, and incorporating specific and related student assessments—we are able to better trace the preservice teachers' comprehension and application of the theory and practice of planning and organizing instruction. While we acknowledge that in-service teachers often do not put all of this information into writing when they create their daily lesson plans, we feel that truly effective teachers do participate in this type of specific, thoughtful planning and examination of beliefs.

Initially in our program, we ask our freshman-level students to present short (5-minute) micro teaching lessons (Raiber & Teachout, 2014, pp. 56–7). In these early teaching episodes, we require our students to engage in very rudimentary planning asking broad questions such as "What will you teach? How will you teach? How might [the students] learn best?" (Raiber & Teachout, 2014, p. 56). Later in the semester, we begin to talk about structuring these questions into more formal planning. In these second micro teaching episodes, the preservice teachers begin to look into how they might create specific objectives, assessments, and activities to structure learning (Millican, 2012, pp. 253–256). An important part of this process is having preservice teachers reflect upon the impact of planning on the effectiveness and efficiency of their micro teaching lessons. They are often quick to recognize the effect of careful planning (or lack thereof!) upon the flow and success of their lessons.

As our preservice teachers continue to develop, they are often given specific micro teaching opportunities in various courses. For example, they might be asked to teach rest position and playing position as if it was the first day of violin class, develop a "default warm-up," or teach a customized warm-up that relates to one objective in a piece they are conducting. After preservice teachers have experience designing lesson plans for these small segments, then they are assigned longer teaching assignments, such as teaching a rote tune or conducting a 10- or 20-minute rehearsal or even presenting a full rehearsal of a particular piece. Because of time restrictions and course enrollment issues, opportunities to plan a full lesson from beginning to end occur most regularly in String Project and during student teaching placements.

There are many different possible approaches to planning a full lesson. West (in press) suggested addressing elements of the "The Big 5" in every lesson: rhythmic ability, tonal ability, executive skills, notation-reading ability, and creativity. Robert Culver suggested to his students at the University of Michigan that every lesson (a) begin in review, (b) extend students' technique and knowledge, and (c) finish class on a high, which might include playing through a composition that you had deconstructed, playing through a favorite piece, or playing a musical game. Culver named this progression the "Energy Profile," which also included meeting students at their current energy, bringing the energy level lower while you extend their knowledge, and leaving students with high energy, which, in turn, makes students more excited to go home and practice and to come back to class the next day.

In Figure 2 on page 472 we present questions for consideration before beginning to lesson plan. Preservice teachers need to develop two fundamental abilities when constructing specific lesson activities. First, they must be able to deconstruct skills to the point where they teach a new skill beginning with something everyone can do successfully. Since they have already developed knowledge and skill inventories for each piece and they are clear about the benchmarks, preservice teachers can plan backwards as to what skills need the most time to develop as well as which skills set the foundation for further skills.

1. **What are your procedures for beginning class?**
   What should students do when they enter the class? What are they responsible for? (Tuning, getting music in order according to what is written on the board, respond to the music playing as they entered the room, write a reflection about what they learned in their practice session yesterday, continue working on a composition project, warm-up stretches, and so forth. You could vary this according to day of the week or keep it consistent.)

2. **What kind of default warm-up might you design to help students address foundational issues such as posture, position, tone, intonation, and/or rhythm?**
   Beginning each class the same way helps students focus and leave everything else behind. It also gives them time to set their technical and musical thoughts and to perform something successfully. If you create a beautiful warm-up (chorale, folk tune with bass line, scales in canon, and so forth), it reminds students why they love music and music making and gets them excited to play.

3. **Have you developed a specific warm-up to teach curricular goals?**
   Teach an important concept or technique that can be applied immediately to the musical selection you are rehearsing.

4. **How will you apply your warm-up to the music literature?**
   Apply concepts or techniques from the specific warm-up to parts of the piece. Remember the teaching cycle: State the goal, have students play, and then evaluate what they did well and what needs improvement. First, address the stated goal. If the students have done well, you can move on. If not, offer specific suggestions for improvement or ask students to evaluate and offer specific suggestions and play again.

5. **How often will you remind students about foundational skills throughout the lesson?**
   I suggest repeating yourself often, finding fun ways or code words to use as reminders, and layering on the reminders after students have played something; i.e., "Excellent pulse/lilt! now let's play it again and keep that sense of lilt but lengthen your posture and play with a beautiful tone!"

6. **How long do you estimate each activity will take in minutes?**
   If you have estimated too little time, how important is it that you finish that activity as opposed to other activities you have planned? Sometimes, it is important to finish your activity but sometimes, it is important to move on and revisit it next class.

7. **How can you limit teacher talk and find clearer, more concise ways to teach?**
   Introduce concepts through sound and have students be active by performing by performing (vocally and instrumentally). "I sing, you sing. I play, you play." Sound before sight; experience, then label. This approach helps students understand concepts better than explainig and then applying.

8. **What are your ultimate goals for the day?**
   - Have you designed experiences that promote the joy of music making?
   - Do you help students realize that music making should evoke an intellectual (storyline) or emotional response in audience members and in themselves?
   - Do students understand the objectives for each activity?
   - Are students inspired and motivated to improve?
   - Do students experience aspects of the "Big 5" (rhythmic ability, tonal ability, executive skills, notation reading ability, and creativity) every day? If not,what are your top five goals?

Figure 2: *Ideas for lesson Plan Construction*

Then, as Duke (2009) suggests, they inch forward by adding one new skill component at a time.

We like to provide templates for our preservice teachers to help remind them of the elements of a detailed and effective lesson plan. These templates change depending on the developmental level of the preservice teachers and the specific course application. For example, in our introduction to music education class, the music education students are just becoming familiar with writing objectives, assessing those objectives, and then developing activities for their lessons (see Figure 3).

> **Teacher Names:**
>
> **Student-centered learning goal(s):**
> *What will your students be able to do at the end of your lesson?*
>
> **Learning activities:**
> *List step-by-step in great detail. Hint - write this so someone else could use your plan to teach this lesson.*
>
> **Teacher feedback or assessment activities:**
> *How will you know your students can complete your learning goal(s)?*
>
> *What special arrangements or concerns will you keep in mind to account for individual learning differences or situational factors in your lesson?*

Figure 3: *Lesson Plan Template One - Intro to Music Education*

More advanced string pedagogy students use a template that includes space to include important elements such as specific warm-ups designed to teach skills performers would need to know and be able to do in order to be successful. This template also includes reminders about the teaching cycle (see Figure 4 and Figure 6).

Teaching Context *Target audience/grade level, time in the year, what students already know, etc.*

Long Term Goals *Connected to National and State Standards*

Objectives

Procedures *List step-by-step description of activities in the boxes below. HINT: Write these so that another person could teach the lesson based on your plans* *Warm-up: Make objectives clear ALWAYS REVIEW - Posture, Position, Tone, Intonation, Rhythm, Balance, Style* *Reminder: Complete teaching cycles! Give specific feedback about Posture, Position, Tone, Intonation, Rhythm, Balance, Style, etc.*
Activities: State goals and review or teach necessary skills to be successful (add more boxes if necessary)
Relate activities above to a specific place in the music being rehearsed:
Activities: State goals and review or teach necessary skills to be successful:
Relate activities above to a specific place in the music being rehearsed:

End With Fun! *End with a fun activity, play through a favorite piece/section, or play through a large chunk of music that they have been working on and can play successfully*

Summarize *At the end of the lesson, recap for the students what they learned*

Evaluation Materials *How do you know if the students learned what you intended for them to learn?* *Include a checklist, rating scale, rubric, or assessment activity such as playing alone or with others a portion of the music*

Figure 4: *Lesson Plan Template Two*

Working with Assessment

Asmus (1999) wrote that "from a teaching perspective, assessment involves not only objectively measuring acquired knowledge and skill over time in order to assign a fair grade, but also identifying appropriate future learning experiences that the teacher may offer to enhance student learning" (p. 19). Although people in the education field commonly use assessment terms, many preservice teachers fail to recognize that assessment is a process by which evidence is collected, analyzed, and interpreted for the purpose of evaluation so that information gathered may be used *to make educational decisions.* As an example, imagine that an elementary music teacher observes that his students consistently miss a particular interval when singing several different songs. Using this informal assessment, the teacher makes the educational decision to develop a series of warm up exercises isolating and developing the skills to perform this interval more accurately. This teacher may devise a formal assessment of his students' progress on improving their skill in performing this interval. The teacher may or may not include a formal grade attached with that assessment. The teacher may give students additional attempts to complete the skill. Whatever the teacher decides in this case, he is using formal and informal assessment to drive what happens in the classroom. In this way, assessment is a part of the normal teaching cycle (see Figure 6) and a normal part of the teaching process presented by O'Toole (2003) in which teachers design instruction, collect evidence of student learning, and make a judgment about the collected evidence in an ongoing cycle.

Some music education students' confusion about the nature of assessment may be traced in part to connections between assessment and state festivals ratings, the SAT, and other formal assessments and how the scores are actually used. Linking "assessment" scores and admissions requirements, teacher evaluations, student evaluations, funding, and school ratings puts the emphasis of assessment on evaluation and the buzz word in this political climate, "accountability." Even though it is important to understand the original intent of assessment tools, it is also important to understand how student assessment is used for various purposes.

Reliability and Validity

Students are also sometimes unfamiliar with or misunderstand common terms related to reliability and validity. Evaluating whether an assessment instrument is reliable and valid involves asking questions such as "Will the instrument yield consistent results," and "Does the instrument measure what I want it to measure?" For example, if you use a scale for weighing food, you expect it to be reliable. Six ounces of chicken today is the same as six ounces of chicken in a week. Similarly, if you use a recipe to cook, it should yield consistent results if you measure the ingredients carefully. You know what to expect and you expect that various measurements and combinations of ingredients will work consistently and reliably. Let's say a middle-school teacher wanted to assess her students playing the G major scale in tune. This teacher might design an assessment in which students played a whole-note scale while the teacher marked variations in pitch on a sheet while the teacher monitored a strobe tuner. This would be a reliable and valid test because it measures what it is designed to measure (valid) and would be accurate each time the test was given (reliable). Conversely, if this teacher chose to test the intonation of the scale by asking her students to write the key signature and notes on the staff for a G major, this test would not be a valid measurement. This does not mean that paper and pencil tests are irrelevant; only that this test format would not assess whether students could hear the G major scale in their minds and produce it vocally or on their instruments in tune.

Creating Grading Policies

When teaching preservice music teachers about assessment, we first discuss findings from Russell and Austin's (2010) survey of secondary music teachers who taught in the southwest region of the country. They found that student grades were determined by both non-achievement and achievement criteria, with non-achievement criteria, such as attendance, attitude, and practice charts, receiving greater weight (60 percent). However, Russell and Austin suggest teachers do not base grades only on achievement criteria. After discussing this article, we brainstorm possible achievement criteria (playing tests, narrative descriptions of music, creating compositions, projects, papers, tests, etc.) and grading policies. Then, we ask preservice music teachers to debate whether teachers should grade students on improvement, ability, or both (Millican, 2012).

We offer an example of a grading policy Kristen designed for her high school orchestra students for preservice teachers to critique and consider. The grading policy in Figure 5 represents a particular philosophy and set of values, just as the grading policies that preservice

35% **Playing Tests** (Every seven school days during the first quarter; every 14 days for the rest of the year)
Rubric includes 20 points each for:
* Posture/Position
* Tone
* Intonation
* Rhythm
* Speed and Style/Interpretation/Musicality/Technical Facility

25 - 35% **Improvement over the grading period** (underclassmen 35%; upperclassmen 25%)
20 - 30% **Projects** (underclassmen - 2; upperclassmen - 3)
10 % **Other** (Written reflections, analysis of performances, tests, papers, etc.)

Expected: **Develop Orchestral dispositions** - Contribute to a positive orchestral experience
Responsible - Bring music, pencil, accessories, $ and forms, organize rides, keep parents informed, comes prepared to rehearse and learn, etc.)
Actively Engaged - participate in discussions, demonstrate connections, write in bowings, fingerings,and musical directions, listen to other sections, etc.)
Attendance - Punctuality counts! Points may be deducted from overall grade for excessive absences or tardies. See Orchestra Handbook for policy.
Leadership, Ethics, and Good Citizenship - Responsibilities as an orchestra and community member (school and larger community)

Projects: *The three categories below are suggestions of possible projects but is not an exclusive list. Students propose projects at the beginning of each quarter to be approved by teacher.*

A. Improving Level of Musicianship
1. Improve your own playing and musicianship
   Private lessons, chamber music, youth orchestra, all-state orchestra member, summer camps, solo & ensemble festival, etc.
2. Help others improve their playing
   Teach privately, mentor peer(s), orchestra buddy, all-city elementary orchestra mentor/assistant conductor
3. Compose or arrange pieces for orchestra or quartet

B. Contribute to Orchestra Community
Orchestra officer or librarian, chair a fundraiser, help prepare program/program cover, publicity, decorate auditorium, set up/tear down before/after concerts, etc.

C. Bring Music into the Community
Perform weekly at places of worship
Perform at nursing homes, hospitals, prisons, local businesses, etc.
Perform at charity events, political events, sporting events, etc.
Perform at parties, weddings, etc.

Figure 5: *Sample Grading Policy*

music teachers create should represent their philosophy and values. After preservice music teachers know what they want to include in their grading policy and what kind of achievement criteria they will assess, then they can begin understanding different types of assessment and begin to develop assessment tools.

Informal and Formal Assessment

We reiterate to our preservice music teachers that assessing students is something that is a part of the teaching process and therefore is something that they will be doing all the time. When students play, teachers should be assessing students' playing. After this assessment, effective teachers share with their students what they did well and what they can do to improve. This is part of what Raiber and Teachout (2014, p. 250) call the teaching cycle.

The teaching cycle begins with a set in which the instructor gives some type of direct instruction to the students. The set may be verbal or non-verbal or could even include modeling or demonstrating musical ideas or skills. After the set has been given, the students are allowed to follow through by demonstrating the particular skills or knowledge the teacher asked for in the set. After the students' follow through, the teacher assesses how the students did, and then gives appropriate feedback in the response portion of the cycle. In layman's terms, the teacher asks the students to do something (set), then the students try it out (follow through), and then the teacher gives the students feedback on how they did (response). The informal assessment occurs during the follow-through portion of the cycle. The students' response in the follow-through portion of the cycle guides the teacher in selecting his or her next course of action. If the students executed the instruction successfully, he or she may acknowledge that accomplishment in the *affirm* portion of the cycle. If however, the students were not immediately successful, the teacher has the option of initiating a *reset* (Let's try that one more time), modifying the set (This time try….), or by *releasing* the students from the cycle (We'll work more on that next time).

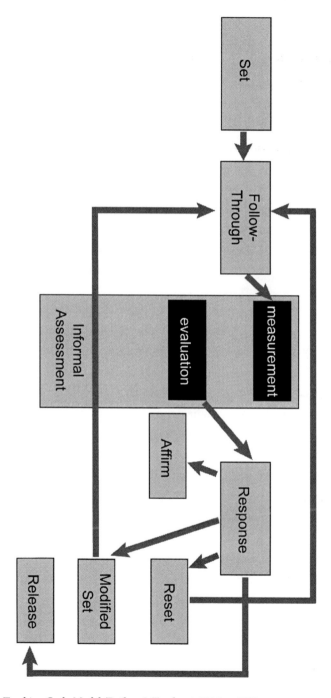

Figure 6: *Teaching Cycle Model (Raiber & Teachout, 2014, p. 250)*

We have found that using the teaching cycle allows our preservice teachers to focus their instruction as well as their assessment and feedback in ways that truly improve their teaching. Using the cycle effectively requires music education students to have a specific objective for improvement during a cycle rather than just giving general praise or vague critiques. The teaching cycle also helps preservice teachers focus their attention on one particular performance element thereby allowing them to filter out some of the information that they receive on the podium or in front of a large classroom. Students often complain that they are bombarded with so many different sounds and details coming at them when standing in front of a large ensemble for the first time; giving a specific set allows these teachers to focus their ears on one particular performance problem in order to assess how their students are performing on one aspect of their playing.

Informal assessments such as these should be happening often throughout every class to check on student progress and decide if students need more support in order to be successful or if they have internalized and automated musical skills and knowledge. Teachers may also ask questions to assess whether the students know and understand concepts or employ learning games or exercises. For example, string preservice teachers might utilize bow games to assess whether students have a relaxed, rounded bow hold and open and close their elbow hinge. Wind and percussion preservice teachers might have students perform breathing exercises to assess air flow.

Formal assessments should be designed to document and guide student learning and understanding. Assessments are also useful in collecting information for achievement criteria for which to base a formal grade and to address "accountability" to stakeholders such as students, parents, administrators, and state officials. Students most often have advanced knowledge of the upcoming formal assessment, and they can prioritize studying, practicing, analyzing, or creating for the particular assessment. Students work to prepare for the assessment so they can successfully perform a specific section or skill, complete a composition, write a response, analysis, or music history paper in the manner that the teacher has prescribed.

Evaluating and Creating Assessment Tools

Various assessment tools are designed not only to measure student performance but also to help guide teachers in their educational decision-making. These tools may include but are not limited to rubrics, checklists, rating scales, journals, portfolios, self-evaluations, or other formal and informal assessments. In order to help preservice teachers develop familiarity with various assessment tools, we show them how the same knowledge and skills may be measured differently (See Figure 7 on page 482). Then, they develop categories that they want to assess and deconstruct it to fit the way they teach.

We ask preservice music teachers to work in small groups to evaluate and create different types of assessment tools. First, they evaluate the advantages and disadvantages of each assessment instrument provided in the example, and then they work to develop tools of their own that reflect their teaching approach. For example, for violinists and violists, Kristen teaches students that the second knuckle of the index, middle, and ring fingers sit on top of stick above the frog and that, from the second knuckle of the pointer, middle, and ring fingers should be straight all the way to the elbow. However, this is not what everyone teaches. Many string teachers prefer that the right hand be pronated toward the body, the knuckle placement is different, and fingers are not always directly above the frog. Also, many string teachers play with curved wrists. Therefore, individual teachers' assessment tools should reflect what individual teachers emphasize so that students understand what is expected before the formal assessment is administered. The examples provided are not inclusive of all types of assessment tools. Other types of assessment tools to consider are self-assessments, portfolios, journals, and external assessments such as adjudication sheets, teacher evaluations, etc.

We sometimes have our preservice teachers develop their own assessment tools to evaluate their micro-teaching episodes. They

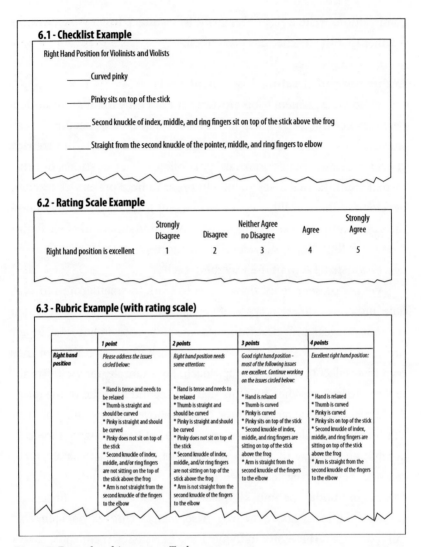

Figure 7: *Examples of Assessment Tools*

select criteria based on background material they read and work with throughout the semester to develop checklists, rating scales, or rubrics that allow the instructor as well as their peers evaluate the elements of teaching, conducting, and musicianship that they feel are the most important. For example, they may choose gesture and baton techniques from their conducting materials, teaching and presentation techniques from another text, and ensemble pedagogy from a different source to include in their assessment materials. This allows the students to feel some autonomy in how they are evaluated, but it also allows them to put the instructional materials for their undergraduate courses into action.

Conclusion

As preservice teachers move from visualizing themselves as music students to music teachers, they need to engage thoughtfully in an examination of their own beliefs about teaching and learning as well as to learn about the broader professional beliefs in order to develop philosophical orientations that will help them craft goals, benchmarks, and outcomes to create meaningful learning experiences. If our future music educators can develop clear orientations in which their students have the opportunities to learn to be creative, responsive, and productive musicians, then the curriculum and assessment tools they develop will reflect those philosophical bearings. Emphasizing the interconnectedness of music teaching philosophy, curriculum development (long term goals or macro level), lessons plans (short term goals or micro level), grading policies, and assessment tools is one approach to helping preservice music teachers develop a curriculum and assessment skills. We hope that you find the ideas, assignments, and templates that we use with our preservice music teachers helpful in stimulating your own visions of how these issues might work for you.

References

American Orff-Schulwerk Association. (2014). About AOSA. *American Orff-Schulwerk Association*. Retrieved May 13, 2014, from http://aosa.org/about/about-aosa/

Anderson, L. W., & Krathwohl, D. R. (2001). *A taxonomy for learning, teaching, and assessing: a revision of Bloom's taxonomy of educational objectives*. New York: Longman.

Asmus, E. P. (1999). Music Assessment Concepts. *Music Educators Journal, 86*(2), 19–24. doi:10.2307/3399585

Banks, S. (1982). Orff-Schulwerk teaches musical responsiveness. *Music Educators Journal, 68*(7), 42–43.

Benham, S. J., Wagner, M. L., Aten, J. L., Evans, J. P., Odegaard, D., & Lieberman, J. L. (2011). *ASTA String Curriculum 2011 Edition.* Alfred Music.

Bloom, B. S., & Krathwohl, D. R. (1956). *Taxonomy of Educational Objectives: The Classification of Educational Goals, by a committee of college and university examiners. Handbook I: Cognitive Domain.* New York, NY: Green.

Bruner, J. S. (1966). *Toward a theory of instruction.* Cambridge, Mass.: Belknap Press of Harvard University.

Dalcroze Society of America. (2014). What is Dalcroze? *What is Dalcroze?* Retrieved from http://www.dalcrozeusa.org/about-us/history/

Duke, R. A. (2009). *Intelligent music teaching: Essays on the core principles of effective instruction.* Austin, TX: Learning and Behavior Resources.

Feldman, E., & Contzius, A. (2010). *Instrumental Music Education: Teaching with the Musical and Practical in Harmony* (Pap/Com edition.). Routledge.

Garofalo, R. J. (1983). *Blueprint for band: a guide to teaching comprehensive musicianship through school band performance.* Ft. Lauderdale, Fla.: Meredith Music.

GIA Publications. (2014). Teaching Music Series. *Teaching Music Series.* Retrieved from http://www.giamusic.com/music_education/ teaching_music.cfm

Gordon Institute for Music Learning. (2014). Audiation. *GIML - The Gordon Institute for Music Learning.* Retrieved from http://giml. org/mlt/audiation/

Millican, J. S. (2012). *Starting out right: Beginning-band pedagogy.* Lanham, MD: Scarecrow Press.

Millican, J. S. (2013). Describing wind instrument teachers' thinking: Implications for understanding pedagogical content knowledge.

Update: Applications of Research in Music Education, 31(2), 45–53.

National Coalition for Core Arts Standards. (2014). PreK–12 arts standards. Retrieved from https://nccas.wikispaces.com

O' Toole, P. O. (2003). *Shaping Sound Musicians/G5739*. GIA Publications.

Pellegrino, K. (2010). *The meanings and values of music-making in the lives of string teachers: Exploring the intersections of music-making and teaching* (Doctoral dissertation). University of Michigan, United States—Michigan. Retrieved from http://search.proquest.com/pqdtft/docview/761661197/

Pellegrino, K., & Millican, J. S. (in press). Influences on string teachers' career decisions.

Raiber, M., & Teachout, D. (2014). *From music student to teacher*. New York, NY: Routledge.

Russell, J. A., & Austin, J. R. (2010). Assessment Practices of Secondary Music Teachers. *Journal of Research in Music Education, 58*, 37–54. doi:10.1177/0022429409360062

West, C. (in press). Developing internal musicianship in beginning band through teaching the "Big 5." *Music Educators Journal.*

CHAPTER 19

CURRICULUM AND TEACHER PROFESSIONAL DEVELOPMENT: SEEKING POSSIBILITIES AND SOLVING PROBLEMS

Ann Marie Stanley

Eastman School of Music

The intersection between curriculum and teacher professional development is an important one. Music teachers are expected to create, implement, and assess curricula as part of their professional practice. To do so effectively, they will likely need targeted support from colleagues, school district personnel, and their professional organizations. Professional development is one important mechanism for supporting teachers in their work on music curricula and related projects. Positive, meaningful professional development is also vital for teachers' growth, well-being, and productivity.

Researchers in teacher learning, including myself, have written about how some of the richest, most fulfilling professional development for teachers effectively taps and builds upon the immense body of wisdom already held collectively by any group of teachers (e.g., Horn, 2005; Little, 2003; Robbins, 1995; Stanley, 2012). Professional development does not necessarily mean the process of teachers being "trained" or "re-trained" by outside experts. Rather, professional development that uses and honors music teacher expertise allows teachers working in groups to have a large degree of autonomy and control over their self-initiated projects. This sort of collaborative professional development can be a place to uncover the exciting, creative possibilities in curriculum evaluation and use. Groups of teachers who come together to work on curricular issues often find the process re-energizing and meaningful.

In addition to being personally rewarding to teachers, professional development should be a learning experience. Guskey (2000) defined professional development as any participation in a process to improve teaching. Whatever the format—the typical 50-minute clinic at state music education conferences, mandated attendance at district-level in-service day workshops, or a teacher learning community—professional development should result in movement along one's individual trajectory toward fully understanding and refining one's own teaching practice. Curricular work with colleagues can be one medium for this learning, and therefore one of music teachers' most important professional development efforts. What could be more crucial to improving one's teaching practice than identifying and interrogating one's intentions about what is to be taught, i.e., the curriculum? I characterize collaborative work on music curricula as one of the most essential learning experiences teachers may encounter throughout their career.

However, music teachers in many places seem to have similar questions about initiating and sustaining professional development experiences about the creation and use of music curricula. This is because typically, the process of working together on curriculum is not a straightforward or easy one. There are many challenges teachers and professional development providers encounter as they work together on curricular issues, including the need to value and reconcile various beliefs and viewpoints about music teaching and learning. In this chapter, I examine typical roadblocks to successful professional development experiences in curricular creation and usage, provide possible solutions to these problems, and suggest practical ideas and tips for making curriculum meetings productive and rewarding opportunities for teacher development, based on my experience working with groups of music teachers.

I receive inquiries like the following three communications many times a year, from teachers who are stymied in one way or another from using curriculum work as professional growth opportunities. Consider these questions, below, and think about what these uncertainties indicate about teachers' professional development needs vis-à-vis curricula.

1. *Meeting About the Curriculum*

Workshop question, January 2014:

> "We have a terrible time aligning our music curriculum, P–12, mostly because we don't get to meet as a group, ever. I had to come 95 miles to this [the state music conference] to see my colleague who teaches two blocks away! She's sitting over there… [*laughs and waves*]. Truthfully we all just teach our own thing: we don't have an 'official' curriculum. Coming together and organizing everything is just too overwhelming without regular music staff meetings. Do you have any suggestions?"

2. *Writing or Evaluating the Curriculum*

Email, November 2013:

> "We found your name online as someone who has done curriculum workshops with music teachers. Our district wants us to meet and use backwards design to construct and re-write units for P–12 music. Can you help us?"

3. *Using the Curriculum*

Visit to local school, February 2014:

> "Here's our district curriculum. It's in these six binders. We got them at the start of this school year at our teacher professional

development day. [*lifts one off shelf*]. Oof! These are heavy. Sorry about the dust, I haven't opened it for a while! Should we be using these on a daily basis?"

I get questions like the ones above frequently, as I travel from district to district and state conference to state conference doing music teacher professional development clinics and workshops. These three queries in particular represent the complexity of interaction between curriculum development, the use of a curriculum, and teacher professional development.

It is often assumed by school district personnel that the following steps will happen, seamlessly and in order: 1) district music teachers meet to evaluate, write, or evaluate and re-write a curriculum; 2) district music teachers return to classrooms and use said curriculum to plan and organize their teaching; 3) students progress from year-to-year in the district, accumulating skills through the curriculum in a well-sequenced way. In my experience—as music education professor, curriculum facilitator, professional development provider, and K–5 classroom music teacher—the process can, and often does, break down at each point. It is important to examine each part of the process individually to anticipate potential problems and solutions. Therefore, the purpose of this chapter is to identify typical music curricular development and implementation issues within three phases: *I. Meeting About the Curriculum*, *II. Writing or Evaluating the Curriculum*, and *III. Using the Curriculum*. I will discuss ways in which targeted, specific music teacher professional development efforts can identify and repair any interruptions in the curricular creation and usage cycle.

I. Meeting about the Curriculum

Many efforts to reform, create, or evaluate a curriculum break down as early as the meeting or planning stage. Even in school districts where music teachers meet as a group regularly, it can be hard to carve out time in the agenda to work on curricular matters. Many districts do not regularly require or expect the music teachers to meet as a group; some large districts' numbers make music staff meetings unwieldy and nearly impossible. Teachers also report the following matters contribute to difficulty scheduling and holding curriculum-related meetings:

- Finding a leader
- Finding times to meet and creating a reasonable and productive meeting agenda
- Convincing district administration to offer tangible support for music staff meetings
- Managing conflict and disagreement within meetings
- Structuring staff meetings in ways appropriate for adult learning
- Reconciling the needs and desires of various stakeholders to participate, or not.

In the following sections, I suggest possible solutions to these and other problems.

No one wants to be in charge. The difficulties inherent in just trying to schedule curriculum meetings can feel insurmountable, and many times the biggest hill to climb is finding someone to lead the process. In my experience, things simply don't get done without someone at least temporarily in charge: that one individual with a great deal of initiative and motivation to instigate a process. Usually the person most interested in carrying out curricular work (perhaps it's you, reading this chapter?) is the logical one to start the process. However, it is important that people be able to take on a leadership role for a short period of time; leadership need not feel like a lifetime commitment. Even reluctant leaders can often be persuaded to serve a limited term, if the duties rotate. Plan from the start to switch leadership after six weeks, or two months, or at winter break. This prevents burnout and keeps everyone feeling ownership of the project. One issue with curricula is that they are often imposed from the "top-down." Rotating leadership promotes more buy-in from all. I have written before about the "sense of symmetry" (Stanley, 2011, p. 75) that derives from the collective feeling that each member of a committee or group will act as a leader and as a follower at various times; this ability to participate within various, changing roles equalizes power within the group and assures that no person has to be "the expert" or "the one in charge" all the time.

There's no time to meet as a group. Many districts routinely schedule curriculum meetings the week before school starts in the fall: sandwiched somewhere within the crush of in-service training, class scheduling, and district-wide informational sessions. This may work for some subject areas, but typically the week before school is in session is extremely difficult for music teachers. We often have to set up several large classrooms while preparing to encounter multiple grade levels and hundreds of students. For this reason, I recommend steering away from intense discussions of curriculum in the few days before the students arrive. Music teachers will feel too pushed for time and often this stress produces unnecessary tensions.

This conflict necessitates creatively finding other times. I recommend teachers try to meet more frequently throughout the year for shorter durations. A three-hour meeting once a month sounds great, but if everyone is on time, 45 minutes two or three times a month can be just as productive. Once momentum and interest in meetings gets going, you can always add more or longer sessions. I suggest using technology to assist in finding meeting times: there are apps and online software that will do most of the work for you and minimize emails and phone calls. For example, Doodle.com allows meeting participants to log on at a convenient time and check whether various possible meeting times work for many or only a few. Plan for the long term, understanding that professional development works best as a sustained process over many months and that your approach will evolve and change as the tone and tenor of your group goals emerge. Task orientation is good; "get it done quick, no matter what" is not as productive.

Realize that people will approach meetings and curriculum-related projects with varying degrees of interest and motivation. Some teachers may not choose to prioritize the meetings in their schedule. Keep in mind it is not an all-or-nothing proposition. If only three or four teachers want to or can attend a given meeting, perhaps those are just the three or four that are best suited to this task at any given time. Nobel prize-winning author Doris Lessing was quoted in *The Guardian* newspaper: "Whatever you're meant to do, do it now. The conditions are always impossible." (Theguardian.com, November 18, 2013). Even if attendance is not 100, or even 50 percent, it is still better to start and maintain discussions rather than waiting for perfection. Sometimes part of meeting is just learning how to meet and how to work together; this places emphasis on the *process* of getting together and communicating—not necessarily the product. That is a good thing for people trying to establish norms of collaboration.

Meeting attendance can flag due to teachers feeling their time is wasted. Establish a timekeeper for meetings, and another person who can keep detailed minutes of the meeting to be posted on a secure webpage (more about that later). Record in the minutes how long was spent on each topic/agenda item; this can be a tool to uncover where discussions bog down and go off-topic. Also, don't forget to consider virtual meetings. Teachers sometimes find it most convenient to meet online in groups of two or three using Skype or Google hangout. Webinar software (available by subscription for a fairly nominal rate) like GoToMeeting.com can be used to enable online discussions for larger groups.

Our meetings seem to go nowhere. Approach all curriculum-oriented meetings from a task-oriented standpoint. Free-form brain-storming and discussion is fun for only about the first 15 minutes and quickly veers off-topic. Have small, manageable goals in the form of questions to answer, specific problems to strategize about solving, or fact-finding about a certain topic. Make sure the goals for each meeting are posted somewhere visible to all attendees. For groups of five or more, always divide into smaller groups for more personal, quieter discussion. Consider having participants write down their thoughts privately before sharing even in small groups; many people are reluctant to share openly in larger settings about innocuous as well as potentially divisive topics.

Large group tasks are usually awkward and difficult to complete, so meeting leaders should delegate tasks to smaller groups to work on simultaneously. Honor teachers for their expertise and willingness to attend and work on curriculum matters. Look for teachers' hidden talents—for example: note-keeping, technological wizardry, ability to summarize others' viewpoints, creative solutions, organization— and delegate appropriate tasks to those people. Teachers like to lead others, and people appreciate being recognized for their individual abilities and strengths.

I recommend all teacher groups who meet regularly establish an online, secure, password-protected record (perhaps a shared folder in a Google drive). When projects and tasks are created, give participants the ability to sign on and add a little at a time to a shared document, commenting on others' additions at the same time. A shared Google document is perfect for this purpose; maintaining a secret group on a social media site may also work. Think of an online presence for your committee as a way to a) record your activities and progress and plan for future projects and tasks; b) get work accomplished in between meetings, bit by bit, at teachers' convenience; and c) provide a virtual "parking lot" for important, or even trivial, matters and considerations that aren't necessarily pertinent at the time but that you don't want to forget.

Our district doesn't support us. Music supervisors or department heads can be effective allies and go-betweens that bridge the needs of the music teachers with the awareness of central administration. However, many districts have no formal leadership within the music staff: no supervisor, chair, or department head. In that case, delegate two or three music teachers to try to get a meeting with the appropriate district-level stakeholder. It may be the director of curriculum, the assistant superintendent for instructional services, or the superintendent. Explain your needs and desires as a music staff in a short and concise way, and have your specific curricular goals ready to talk about. Bring a list of requests, including the need for stipends, district professional development credit, release time and substitute replacements, meeting space, etc. It is possible district administration may not have even *thought* about the unique curricular needs of music teachers. Give them the benefit of the doubt and expect that they will come forth with resources throughout the year, and especially on in-service or parent-teacher conference days. Some music teachers have been particularly successful in investigating other sources of support for meetings, in terms of meeting space, meeting facilitation, tech support, or even providing meeting refreshments. Consider your local arts organizations, university music education departments, PTAs, band boosters groups, and go to them with specific requests.

Our meetings aren't productive, because we disagree. I often think about Karly, a music teacher participant in a research project I did on collaborative teacher study groups. She said she hated her departmental music meetings, because she felt isolated and frustrated with what passed for serious discussion of music education. She said when her department meetings moved from superficial topics to more important issues, things got uncomfortable:

> It's been, "Oh I have an idea!" "Oh, I have a cute idea too!" ...
> And you know, when we finally talk about something great, we
> end up in a catfight, and so we keep [meetings] about "cute."
> (Stanley, 2012, p. 61)

This disagreement, when talking about meaningful issues of music teaching practice, is a common and difficult problem for music teachers. It is easier to keep discussions superficial and light; to dwell in the realm of "cute" Karly referred to above. Our isolation and uniqueness within schools breed autonomy and independence, which are hard-won and valuable attributes for many of us. Music teachers are sometimes included with librarians, physical education teachers, and art instructors as "The Specials"; we relish our specialness and enjoy working on our own, using the methods which work best for us and our students. Teaching in general is subject to the occupational norms of congeniality, non-interference, conservatism, and privacy (Curry, 2008) and it seems as though music teachers often hold these values dear.

Much awkwardness can be avoided by goal-setting and the task-oriented nature of meetings I advocate above. However, consensus is not necessarily the endpoint. Consider Feiman-Nemser's (2001) words on the difference between teacher meetings oriented toward idea-sharing and politeness, and teacher meetings oriented toward learning:

> The kind of conversation that promotes teacher learning differs from usual modes of teacher talk which feature personal anecdotes and opinions and are governed by norms of politeness and consensus. Professional discourse involves rich descriptions of practice, attention to evidence, examination of alternative interpretations, and possibilities. (p. 1043)

Your curriculum meetings may be the only place to ask the hard questions and have the disagreements that are opportunities to share and clarify your beliefs about music teaching practice and philosophy. These tough conversations are not to be shied away from. According to researchers in teacher workgroups: "pseudo-community" is the friendly consensus that arises at the expense of real growth (Grossman, Wineburg, & Woolworth, 2000). Often convening a group of teachers who have worked together before is more difficult than bringing together a group of strangers. Long histories of conflict, competition, or misunderstanding can color any attempts to work toward common goals. So, expect conflict, just be prepared with ways to mediate it. Establishing a habit of purpose-driven meetings is best; and keep public records of discord. Even just recording in the minutes the amount of time spent on disagreements can have an after-the-fact calming effect as attendees read the notes from the meeting and realize how discord affected the group's productivity. Make certain the team leader has a mechanism—perhaps sticky notes, a file on a computer, a section of the shared document in the cloud—to record disagreements that seem unsolvable at the moment. Often just the act of documenting people's thoughts, emotions, and beliefs makes contributors feel heard and valued, when they realize their contributions are not going to be discounted or forgotten.

Finally, researchers in motivation theory have found that people are more proactive, engaged, and ready to work and learn when their circumstances enable them to be self-determined, rather than passive. Ryan and Deci (2000) in their well-known overview of Self-Determination Theory stated, "Three basic needs yield self-motivation, achievement, and satisfaction: competence, autonomy, and relatedness." (p. 68) If members of the group seem alienated, consider whether they need tasks that support their competence, or their ability to feel that they are working at an endeavor that is coherent with their strengths, that they can actually complete with success. Perhaps autonomy is an issue; often group members can feel that they are not free to interact and support the group's work at will. Enabling participation along various roles and in different goals as delineated above can remedy this. Relatedness refers to participants' connections and feeling of belonging and attachment to one another. Ryan and Deci explained, "the degree to which any of these three psychological needs is unsupported or thwarted within a social context will have a robust detrimental impact on wellness in that setting" (retrieved from http://www.selfdeterminationtheory.org/theory/ May 1, 2014) so it behooves us to consider whether the tenor of meetings is optimal for participants' competence, autonomy, and relatedness. If not, examine which element may be missing, and consider how to strengthen it.

II. Writing or Evaluating the Curriculum

Curriculum evaluation or writing can be, in and of itself, a profound means of collaborative professional development, and the teacher learning that results from the experience can be meaningful. However, this makes curriculum work less of a "point-A-to-point-B" neat, orderly process. Learning is more messy, arduous, and unpredictable! Whenever I teach curriculum seminar on the graduate level, or facilitate curriculum work with a group of music teachers, people ask me to provide a template or a method for writing a curriculum. Unfortunately there is no "one-size-fits-all" easy method for curricular creation. Each district and locale is so different in terms of student contact time, teacher-student ratio, division of grade levels between sites, variety of musical course offerings, and community needs. There are a host of characteristics unique to each context, which make templates fairly useless. An online search for sample music education curricula will provide you with plenty of examples of formatting, organization, and personalization for particular, local needs. Rather than belaboring the format of the eventual product, it is most helpful to get going with a process of identifying the needs and goals within your community of schools. Once you discuss the strengths and weaknesses of any existing curriculum, as well as the qualities and characteristics that make your musical community unique, you will come to a fuller understanding of how a curriculum might be put together in a way that works for current and future music teachers in your district. Therefore, a full discussion of how to write and evaluate a curriculum is outside of this chapter, but readers may be greatly helped by the information in Chapters 4 (Forrester) and 6 (Siebert) in this volume.

It is most helpful to begin work by deciding exactly which endeavor you will take on in your district: writing a curriculum or evaluating a curriculum, and for which grade level and subject. Realize that it may be helpful to start small; many committees try to accomplish too much in limited time. Writing a P–12 curriculum for Music is a gargantuan task. Working on one age level and subject, say, eighth grade orchestra, or kindergarten general music, may be a helpful beginning in developing your group's "ways of working" together. Again, remember to value the process of learning to come together in shared curricular goals, rather than just seeking an end product: a written curriculum or other document.

Nowak (2012, p. 33–34) delineates five categories of curriculum examination. You can begin to sort out your work by deciding which of the topics on the following page is most appropriate for your needs.

Understanding the destination, and talking about the journey. Deconstructing the term *curriculum* is interesting: it derives from the Latin, *currere*, for *course*. We routinely refer to a curriculum as a "course of study"; when we write our "curriculum vitae" we are recording our

Curriculum Evaluation or Curriculum Review	An examination of the curriculum structure, content, and outcomes, intended to reveal if the curriculum is efficiently meeting the stated district goals.
Curriculum Auditing	An evaluation or review, but an external consultant or organization completes the review.
Curriculum Development	The process of performing a curriculum evaluation and improving the curriculum as a result. Can refer to either writing a new curriculum or improving a pre-existing one. Often implies the inclusion of other variables such as professional development.
Curriculum Writing	The creation of a new curriculum or related documents where one(s) did not previously exist.
Program Review/Evaluation	An examination of the variables that support music instruction but do not directly pertain to improving achievement. Examples include budget, facilities, staffing, schedule, etc.

"course of life." Keeping the idea of a course as a preplanned journey, imagine the kindergarteners entering our school districts for the next thirteen years of music instruction. When our students start this journey at age five, where might they end up? How much of their course is planned, scribed, and organized, and what part of it is student choice, teacher choice, and serendipity? Most important, how can we as teachers talk effectively and meaningfully about the road and the destination?

I always recommend beginning with conversations about the big picture. (See Forrester on *Understanding By Design*, this volume). One quote I have found helpful in working with groups of teachers is from Covey's book *The Seven Habits of Highly Effective People: Powerful Lessons in Personal Change*:

> To begin with the end in mind means to start with a clear understanding of your destination. It means to know where you're going so that you better understand where you are now and so that the steps you take are always in the right direction. (2013, p. 105).

I suggest the following activities as good discussion-starters for getting teachers to think and talk about a K–12 curriculum as a road, a journey, and an eventual destination.

Concentric Circles. A fun and meaningful activity to get people thinking about their end goals for K–12 education, is adapted from Wiggins and McTighe's (2005) *Understanding By Design* (p.10). First ask teachers to write their three favorite things to teach on three sticky notes. Then draw three large concentric circles on a white board or chart paper, labeled: (figure 1)

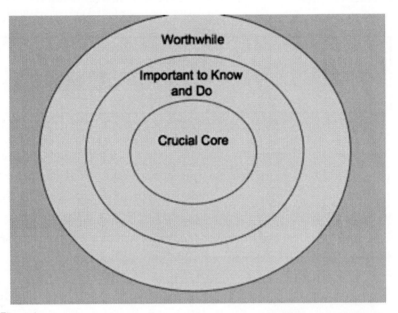

Figure 1.

Ask teachers to place their sticky notes according to where they place the concept on the hierarchy of circles. This often uncovers the fact that the objective of some of our most enjoyable lesson plans is worthwhile, but not crucial to students' destination along the curricular road.

When I recently did this activity with a group of P–12 educators, this was their first placement of their sticky notes.

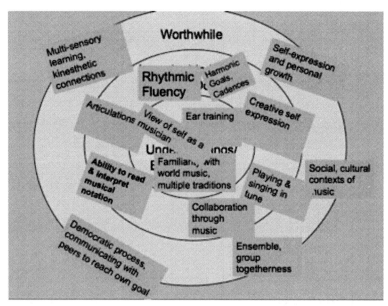

Figure 2.

After the teachers discussed, debated, and voted on the placement of sticky notes they made the following changes:

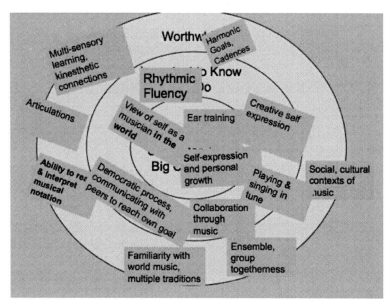

Figure 3.

- "Harmonic goals, cadences," "Articulations," and "Ability to read/interpret musical notation" all moved out one level from "Important to know and do" to "Worthwhile"
- "Familiarity with world music, multiple traditions" went out two levels. Instead, the teachers added three words to a sticky note placed in the "Crucial Core" circle: they changed "view of self as a musician" to "view of self as a musician *in the world*."
- "Democratic process, communicating with peers to reach own goal" was upgraded one level: from "Worthwhile" to "Important to know and do."
- "Self-expression, personal growth" moved in two levels: from "Worthwhile" to "Crucial Core."

Then I asked them to reword the central core goals (Figure 4) as a view of what students might be able to know and do at the end of the P–12 destination: This teacher group ended up agreeing that what they want for their students is a deep understanding of music—particular, hard-won

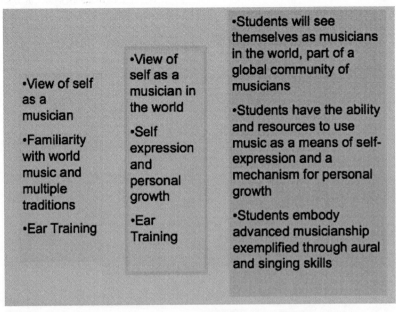

Figure 4.

insights into music as a result of cleaving together disparate, discrete bits of information and multiple experiences—versus merely learning a series of isolated, facts & skills. It is a view of knowledge embedded in the student's self, as students learn to see themselves as musical thinkers who make their musical thinking visible in a number of ways.

Interact with a quote. Ask teachers to act out a skit depicting, write their reactions to, or simply discuss, the classroom application of a quote. I have used these two to great results:

1. Video games teach children what computers are beginning to teach adults—that some forms of learning are fast-paced, immensely compelling, and rewarding. The fact that they are enormously demanding of one's time and require new ways of thinking remains a small price to pay (and is perhaps even an advantage) to be vaulted into the future. Not surprisingly, by comparison school strikes many young people as slow, boring, and frankly out of touch. (Papert, 1993, p. 5)

2. At the center of the reform-minded teacher's work is a profound commitment to student learning informed by the continual adjustment, invention, and reconstruction of the teacher's beliefs and practices. Reform-mindedness is characterized as a "deeply ingrained and habitual dedication to improvement on the part of teachers" (Thiessen and Barrett, 2002, p. 762). Further, teachers are motivated toward improvement on multiple fronts, which can be portrayed as three overlapping realms of work: in the classroom, in the corridor, and as part of other communities. (Barrett, 2006, p. 21)

Buzz words. Ask the group to list all the curriculum jargon and terms they can think of. Chart them on a white board, and try to come to consensus on how each of the terms are used or enacted (or not) in your district. Here is the list one group of teachers I worked with devised:

- backwards design
- standards-based
- student-centered
- benchmarks
- essential questions
- inquiry-based
- lesson plans
- template
- sequence
- spiral design
- data-driven
- performance-based
- authentic assessment
- common assessment
- value-added measurement

Likes and dislikes. Share freely and record (without judgment or commentary) answers to questions like the following: (a) What makes a curriculum plan ineffective or less usable? and (b) What would make a curriculum desirable and easy to work with?

Here are responses from one group to (a) What makes a curriculum plan ineffective or less usable?

- too general
- goals that are too easy or too difficult, unrealistic goals ("keep a steady beat")
- not student-centered; students aren't kept in mind
- fails to take into account population you are dealing with
- it's the higher authority's idea; sometimes they just want something, anything, done
- administrators are sometimes oriented toward a pre-existing framework that doesn't work for the situation
- not musical enough (written by administrators who aren't music teachers)
- placed on an arbitrary schedule
- too hard to deviate from and come back to
- inflexible
- geared toward competitions, accomplishing very specific tasks
- written in fiefdoms—silos of isolation—that exist independently. Doesn't work for all the music teachers in all the classrooms.

- overarching philosophy doesn't represent a unification between programs
- incoherent
- there are goals but no information on how to correlate them with materials teachers have
- sometimes the curriculum just lists arrival points, without the "how" and that is not too helpful
- what is the point of a curriculum anyway? I'd rather have a really broad document anyway—will let me do what I want
- assessment should be done by people who understand the curriculum

And the same group's responses to question (b): What would make a curriculum desirable and easy to work with?

- teachers' understanding of how elements function within the document, not a list of specific tasks
- not "Students will find a steady beat" but "Students to understand steady beat as a function that is meaningful in music?"
- values process over performance
- one that caters to student readiness and not specific date
- having flexibility to grab the teachable moments
- acknowledging the multiple ways students enact "knowing" in music
- goals and marking points relate to materials teachers already have and use
- enables flexibility and teacher choice
- contains ways to assess movement through the curriculum. Some classes don't get as far as others.
- one that lets us examine "what is learned" versus "what has been taught"

The last point—teachers' desire to use a curriculum to guide student *learning*, as opposed to merely governing their *delivery* of material—is where teacher professional development is crucial. Many of us have not had the time or space to consider what students have really gotten out of our well-constructed lesson plans, our carefully organized units, and our year-long pacing and scheduling efforts. Professional development can provide an important space for this inquiry, and in the next section of the chapter, I make suggestions for these sorts of activities.

III. Using the Curriculum

Unfortunately, many district curricular efforts end with the distribution of binders of the printed curriculum to teachers. Teachers may find it difficult to implement new curricular ideas, no matter how exciting or meaningful the changes may be, when no one around them offers practical, context-specific help for how to make things work in their school, with their students. Professional development in collaboration with others from the same district or school helps teachers find ways to improve curricular implementation in particular groups of students and communities.

While most teachers make an effort to consult the document, it's easy to imagine how teachers might find it easier or more comforting to retreat into their usual practice rather than make substantial alterations. In fact, many researchers, including me, have found it is almost impossible for teachers to implement curricular change, one-by-one, alone in their classrooms (Penuel, Fishman, Yamaguchi, & Gallagher, 2007). Efforts to change teaching practice often fail when there is a lack of support on site (Stanley, Snell, & Stringham, 2013). This is why I am a strong advocate of continual professional development that has collaboration at its core, and the following seven characteristics as structural features.

Collaborative professional development: Collaborative PD for music teachers has the following seven characteristics (Stanley, Snell, & Edgar 2013):

- It is musical, and organized around music content-specific skills and strategies for particular genres of music education (band, choir, general music, orchestra, alternative ensembles).

- It is a sustained, long-term, effort: a semester, a year, or several years.
- It is voluntary, with elements of teacher choice and control over their own learning.
- It honors teacher wisdom and builds on teachers' collective knowledge base.
- It is full of opportunities for reflection, during and after the experience.
- It is geared toward providing site-specific support.
- It is a way for teachers to experience meaningful mentoring.

Some of these characteristics have been addressed in the section about scheduling and organizing meetings. In this section I will comment explicitly about how group curriculum work can exemplify each of these characteristics, and finally, discuss how the curriculum may be housed in a flexible, living way.

Collaborative Professional Development Is Musical. Professional development that encourages teachers to be musical and make music themselves is a great way to break the ice between colleagues and remind everyone what we have in common: musicianship. Pellegrino (2009) wrote,

> Music teachers are, ideally, integrated people who bring meaningful musical experiences with them into the classrooms. These experiences may inform and influence teachers personally and professionally and their students' learning. (p. 50)

Because personally meaningful music making is often what most interests and sustains teachers in our profession, why not make it a more central part of our professional development activities? I recommend having each group member take a turn starting the meetings with a fun, musical warm-up. When talking about and writing a curriculum, take the time to actually enact the musical activity under discussion. Keep a playful, non-critical attitude toward making music, and stay open to different ways and means of making musicality visible within the group.

Sustained and Voluntary Participation. The next two characteristics are strongly related in curriculum work. As I previously discussed in this chapter, curriculum work is not a quick and easy task. The propensity for school districts, however, toward wanting to see completion in the form of a finished document cannot be discounted. I recommend that curriculum be evaluated, edited, and created in a fluid form (more details about that later). Having the curriculum be a living document that is readily changeable and malleable—yet accessible to all district personnel at all times—mediates possible conflict between the need to keep working on it over the long term, and the need to see tangible progress toward product.

Along the same lines, voluntary participation is necessary to allow teachers to feel that they have choice over what they need to grow and benefit from a professional development process. It is possible the people who participate in curriculum work in September are not the same who are working on it in June. The more people who come into contact with the work, the more who will feel ownership of it; forcing people to continue along a schedule or a path that is not coherent with their own needs does no one any good.

Honoring Teacher Wisdom, and Building on It. Teachers often cite frustration with professional development that assumes they need to be retrained. Collaborative sharing of knowledge creates a collective sense of expertise and confidence in the group's body of professional practice. This is quite different than the experience of being led into new ideas by an outside expert. However, it is sometimes tricky not to let the idea-sharing process devolve into turf wars, superficiality, complaining, or even retreat. Some strategies I have found that work well are techniques from the *Looking at Student Work (LASW)* movement. (Please see *The facilitator's book of questions: Tools for looking together at student and teacher work* (Allen & Blythe, 2004) for specific ideas and instructions, as well as the website: www.lasw.org for a more complete look at this concept than I can provide here.)

LASW centers around structured conversation about *student work*: "[c]ollegial conversation, particularly when guided by protocols, offers a learning environment with unique features, and therefore unique opportunities, for the growth of understanding and professional skill and judgment" (Allen & Blythe, 2004, p. 26). While the *LASW* procedures provide for many different sorts of meetings, one commonality is that they all involve looking at samples of student work. In music, student work takes a variety of forms: perhaps a composition, an audio file of a performance assessment, or videos of students at work in a music class. In curriculum efforts, *LASW* is phenomenally helpful for getting to the difference between (a) what is being taught, or covered, or rehearsed by the teacher (the written curriculum) and (b) what is actually being learned, and exhibited in tangible form, by the students. It is a non-threatening way of taking the focus off the teacher's actions and allowing a group of teachers the luxury of examining what students are actually doing in class—often things you do not and cannot notice in the heat of the moment.

Reflection. Curriculum work and reflection can be natural partners in teacher learning. Taking the time to think and reflect about what one planned, taught, assessed, and will change for next time is almost a luxury for music teachers. With high student-teacher ratios averaging 475:1 (Parsad & Spiegelman, 2011), music teachers lead extraordinarily fast-paced teaching schedules with little time for contemplation, despite its importance. The opportunity for reflection is a key to teacher learning (Merriam, Caffarella, & Baumgartner, 2007), which results in teachers who understand their own practice and how to incorporate new concepts. Professional development providers have experimented successfully with such reflective tools as written and oral responses to prompts, completing evaluation forms after each meeting, and maintaining written and online reflection repositories like wikis or blogs (Stanley, Snell, & Edgar, 2013). If teachers who naturally gravitate toward reflective practice can model it as a source of motivation and inspiration for curricular work, others may follow suit.

Site-Specific Support and Meaningful Mentoring. Curricular innovation can lose momentum quickly if teachers have no support in implementation. Both mentor and mentee can learn profound things about teaching if the relationship is strong and effective. But members of curriculum work groups often find it hard to sustain communication and support between meetings, so how can teachers help one another in their own individual contexts? I suggest the answer is mutual observation (either live, virtually, or via video), the idea of which deserves a bigger discussion than just about the role it may play in curriculum work.

Music teachers value their privacy and autonomy. These tendencies are reinforced by the literal and figurative isolation many music teachers face. We are not used to having other music teachers around, or watching us teach. Inviting others into our classroom, either in real time or through video, may be threatening. But seeing real teachers instructing real students is the only basis for pragmatic, rational conversations about music education curriculum. Any discussion of "here's what happened in my classroom when I tried to teach to that curricular objective" becomes vague in the retelling. We can't provide an objective recounting because we were such an integral part of the lesson and our perspective colors any description.

Many benefits might accrue to teachers who are allowed to visit one another's classrooms on a regular basis. Teachers will be eventually relieved and reassured by breaking down the strong barrier of privacy and allowing others in. At a recent workshop I conducted, a young teacher told me afterward she feels like "a fraud" because others assume she is doing brilliantly in the classroom, by virtue of her resume. However, alone with the students, she struggles to incorporate the district's learning objectives in her plans. She said she has told others about her problems but the quick fixes suggested by others did not work, which further compounded her feelings of inadequacy. If sharing of video or real-time visits were a regular feature in a professional community for this teacher, she would understand that not only do the same problems she faces recur everywhere, they have been dealt with in many effective ways. She might feel relief from not having to hide her uncertainty.

However, I stress that this sort of transformative view—when a teacher learns to see herself as part of a sharing profession— can only be obtained through the use of video or visits; merely getting together in collegial groups to talk about realities of teaching will not have the same impact. Only by seeing what actually goes on in music classes will we strengthen our basis of professional knowledge of curriculum in action, on which we can build improvements in music teaching and learning. Many efforts to create a cohesive curriculum flounder because districts consist of many individual programs, built by individual teachers. These range from unsuccessful to unremarkable to outstanding; the reasons for their success or failure are often only theoretical, rumored, or legendary. We often do not know why a teacher is said to have an outstanding program, because usually we see only the product—the concerts, the musicals, the graduates— and we never glimpse the daily progress in the classroom. I believe transparency and openness across schools and programs would help build our understanding of the ways curricula are used and enacted across a district. And mentoring about curriculum matters should be conducted in ways that are not onerous, not connected to formal evaluations, but rather, are intended to develop and enhance teaching practice in a way only possible through frank and candid talk.

Assessing Teacher Growth through Professional Development. Papert (1993) wrote about when he finally identified what was troubling him about a teacher workshop on computer code he was teaching:

> The discordant element had been a sense I couldn't yet articulate that the participants thought of themselves as teachers-in-training rather than as learners. Their awareness of being teachers was preventing them from giving themselves over fully to experiencing what they were doing as intellectually exciting and joyful in its own right, for what it could bring them as private individuals. The major obstacle in the way of teachers becoming learners is inhibition about learning. (p. 72)

As Papert implies, assessing the benefit of teacher professional development first depends on the teachers being able to see themselves as alive, energized learners themselves. But measuring the learning is

difficult if not impossible, as teachers' experiences within a professional development effort will of course vary widely. Our profession is
just beginning to think about how to assess professional growth and its
impact on student musical achievement; there is not as yet any satis-
factory way to do so that captures all the subtleties of the multifac-
eted teaching-learning relationship. One concept, however, that I have
found useful in assessing the value of various professional development experiences is the idea of catalytic validity. In the *Encyclopedia of
Curriculum Studies* (Kridel, 2010), *catalytic validity* is defined as how
much an "endeavor intended to spur personal and social transformation
serves as a catalyst for that transformation" (p. 921). If the professional
development around curriculum creation, development, or evaluation is long-term and collaborative, teachers are likely to be frank and
vocal about whether your work together spurs them to make transformative, meaningful change in teaching practice. The key to relating
your work to the change that may occur in individual teachers' classrooms, one-by-one, when doors are closed, is to have regular, tangible
processes for commenting on, altering, and adjusting the curricular
document as necessary. In other words: if teachers are using, editing,
and annotating the curricular ideas created by your work group with
information about corresponding changes in the musical achievement
of students, then it's likely to have a high degree of catalytic validity in
its purpose. However, for this to happen, any curricular documents
need to be fluid, changeable, and able to accommodate input and read-
justment on regular, formal and informal, bases. In the next section, I
write about ways to keep your curriculum from being too static.

The Curriculum: It's Alive! In conclusion, I encourage you to make
curricular work a regular and constant part of staff development.
Rather than finishing a polished document and calling in quits, your
goal might be to constantly evaluate how students are progressing
on their curricular "course" in the thirteen years of music education. What sort of travels are they encountering, and can the course
be altered mid-way to be more efficient, more student-centered, or
simply more musical? In his research on curriculum development

and implementation processes, Nowak (2012) found that some music supervisors advocate for the curriculum to be a living, breathing document. He interviewed a music administrator on this subject, who said:

> I think that sometimes people get too carried away with wanting to have a finite document that encompasses everything and forget that curriculum development is a daily process, and that you need to have flexibility built into your own process so that you can make it a living document as opposed to an "every half-a-dozen years" document. (p. 162)

Binders and hard copies are one way to ensure a dead document. A three-ring binder is likely the worst format for it, as this construction seems to sit solidly on the shelf more often than not. Electronic versions that are easily collapsible into an overview, or expandable for more detail, make the document easy to transport, locate, refer to, and look at from either the macro- or micro-viewpoint. I suggest the curriculum be housed on an interactive web page for teachers to weekly post updates, comments, and lesson plans. The curriculum should be an exciting, interesting, and helpful aspect of music teaching; not a dry, dusty tome of impossible or impractical objectives. In all stages—meeting about, writing, evaluating, or implementing—teachers should be encouraged to make the curriculum a useful and creative construct that aids them in their professional development—in their quest to improve their teaching practice—and as a result, the musical achievement of their students.

References

Allen, D., & Blythe, T. (2004). *The facilitator's book of questions: Tools for looking together at student and teacher work.* New York: Teachers College Press.

Barrett, J. R. (2006). Recasting professional development for teachers in an era of reform. *Arts Education Policy Review, 107*(6), 19–28.

Covey, S. (2013). *The seven habits of highly effective people: Powerful lessons in personal change.* New York: Simon & Schuster.

Curry, M. (2008). Critical friends groups: The possibilities and limitations embedded in teacher professional communities aimed at instructional improvement and school reform. *Teachers College Record, 110*(4): 733–74.

Feiman-Nemser, S. (2001). From preparation to practice: Designing a continuum to strengthen and sustain teaching. *Teachers College Record 103*(6): 1013–55.

Grossman, P., Wineburg, S., and Woolworth, S. (2000). What makes teacher community different from a gathering of teachers? Seattle: University of Washington Center for the Study of Teaching and Policy.

Guskey, T. R. (2000). *Evaluating professional development.* Thousand Oaks, CA:

Horn, I. S. (2005). Learning on the job: A situated account of teacher learning in high school mathematics departments. *Cognition and Instruction, 23*(2), 207–236. Corwin Press.

Kridel, C., Ed. (2010). *Encyclopedia of curriculum studies.* Thousand Oaks, CA: Sage Publications.

Little, J. W. (2003). Inside teacher community: Representations of classroom practice. *Teachers College Record, 105*(6), 913–945.

Merriam, S. B., Caffarella, R. S., & Baumgartner, L. M. (2007). *Learning in adulthood: A comprehensive guide (3rd Ed.).* San Francisco: Jossey Bass.

Nowak, T.E. (2012). *Procedures for evaluating public school music curricula.* (Unpublished master's thesis). University of Rochester, Eastman School of Music.

Papert, S. (1993). *The children's machine: Rethinking school in the age of the computer.* New York: BasicBooks.

Parsad, B., & Spiegelman, M. (2011). A snapshot of arts education in public elementary and secondary schools: 2009-10 (NCES 2011-078). Washington, DC: National Center for Education Statistics, Institute of Education Sciences, United States Department of Education.

Pellegrino, K. (2009). Connections between performer and teacher identities in music teachers: Setting an agenda for research. *Journal of Music Teacher Education, 19*(1), 39–55.

Penuel, W. R., Fishman, B. J., Yamaguchi, R., & Gallagher, L. P. (2007). What makes professional development effective? Strategies that foster curriculum implementation. *American Educational Research Journal, 44*(4), 921–958.

Robbins, J. (1995). Levels of learning in Orff SPIEL. *Bulletin of the Council for Research in Music Education, 123,* 47–53.

Ryan, R. M., & Deci, E. L. (2000). Self-determination theory and the facilitation of intrinsic motivation, social development, and well-being. *American Psychologist, 55*(1), 68–78.

Stanley, A.M. (2011). Professional development within collaborative teacher study groups: Pitfalls and promises. *Arts Education Policy Review. 112*(2), 71–78.

Stanley, A.M. (2012). What is collaboration in elementary music education? A social constructivist inquiry within a collaborative teacher study group (CTSG). *Bulletin of the Council for Research in Music Education, 192,* 53–74.

Stanley, A. M., Snell, A., & Edgar, S. (2013). Collaboration as effective music professional development: Success stories from the field. *Journal of Music Teacher Education.* DOI: 10.1177/1057083713502731

Thiessen, D., and Barrett, J. R. (2002). Reform-minded music teachers: A more comprehensive image of teaching for music teacher education. In R. Colwell and C. Richardson, Eds., *New handbook of research on music teaching and learning,* pp. 759–85. New York: Oxford University Press.

Wiggins, G., & McTighe, J. (1998). *Understanding by design.* Alexandria, VA: Association for Supervision and Curriculum Development.

Chapter 20

Music Curriculum and Assessment: The Role of Technology

William I. Bauer

University of Florida

Today's world is infused with technology. Technology allows us to instantaneously access information about nearly any topic via the Internet. It enables us to easily communicate with others around the globe by voice, text, and video. Computers are embedded in many common household appliances to assist us with mundane, daily tasks. Cars have computers that monitor their operation and often include integrated GPS units to help guide us to our destinations. In numerous ways, technology has become deeply integrated into our lives.

Technology has also become increasingly prominent in today's schools. Both governmental entities (U. S. Department of Education, 2010) and professional organizations (International Society for Technology in Education, 2014) urge teachers to integrate technology into the teaching/learning process. Music teachers, too, are finding ways that technology can facilitate the development of their students' musicianship (Bauer, 2014). But understanding how to best utilize technology in music classes and rehearsals can be challenging. This chapter will discuss the applications of technology to music curricula and assessment.

Technology and the Curriculum

A Model for Technology Integration

When considering ways to include technology in school curricula, a frequent approach has been to start with the technology itself. Teachers and administrators often learn about a new technology, become intrigued with its features, and seek to discover ways it can be put to use in the classroom. Papert (1987) refers to this mode of thinking as *technocentric*, making an analogy to the egocentric stage in Piaget's model of child development.[1]

> Egocentrism for Piaget does not, of course, mean "selfishness"—it means that the child has difficulty understanding anything independently of the self. Technocentrism refers to the tendency to give a similar centrality to a technical object—for example, computers or Logo. This tendency shows up in questions like "What is THE effect of THE computer on cognitive development?" or "Does Logo work?" Of course such questions might be used innocently as shorthand for more complex assertions, so the diagnosis of technocentrism must be confirmed by careful examination of the arguments in which they are embedded. However, such turns of phrase often betray a tendency to think of "computers" and of "Logo" as agents that act directly on thinking and learning; they betray a tendency to reduce what are really the most important components of educational situations—people and cultures—to a secondary, facilitating role. (Papert, 1987, p. 23)

For technology to be effectively integrated into student learning experiences, there is more involved than just the technology itself. Instructional planning in music that includes technology should not be technocentric.

---

[1] In this passage, Papert refers to *Logo*, an educational, computer-programming language that he and others developed in 1967.

Technological Pedagogical and Content Knowledge

In the spirit of Papert and building on Shulman's (1987) theory of pedagogical content knowledge, Mishra and Koehler (2006) developed a model for conceptualizing the integration of technology into educational settings called Technological Pedagogical and Content Knowledge (TPACK). Shulman believed that all teachers need a deep knowledge of their disciplinary content and of general approaches to teaching and learning. However, he recognized that when the content of a particular subject area and pedagogical practices intersect, a type of pedagogical understanding that is unique to that specific discipline, pedagogical content knowledge, occurs. Thus, pedagogical content knowledge differs for each teaching discipline, resulting in teachers having individualized expertise on what teaching approaches work best when helping students to learn specific content. For example, the science teacher, physical education instructor, elementary general music educator, and marching band director will all scaffold[2] (Vygotsky, 1978) a class differently due to the nature of the content they are teaching, as well as the context in which they are teaching it.

Mishra and Koehler (2006) added a technology component to the pedagogical content knowledge model, resulting in Technological Pedagogical and Content Knowledge (see Figure 1). TPACK provides a conceptual framework for the teacher knowledge that is essential to the effective use of technology for learning. It involves a complex interaction among technology, pedagogy, and content, all within the context of a particular learning environment. Table 1 further describes the various components of the TPACK model.

---

[2] Scaffolding "refers to a variety of instructional techniques used to move students progressively toward stronger understanding and, ultimately, greater independence in the learning process. The term itself offers the relevant descriptive metaphor: teachers provide successive levels of temporary support that help students reach higher levels of comprehension and skill acquisition that they would not be able to achieve without assistance. Like physical scaffolding, the supportive strategies are incrementally removed when they are no longer needed, and the teacher gradually shifts more responsibility over the learning process to the student." [http://edglossary.org/scaffolding/]

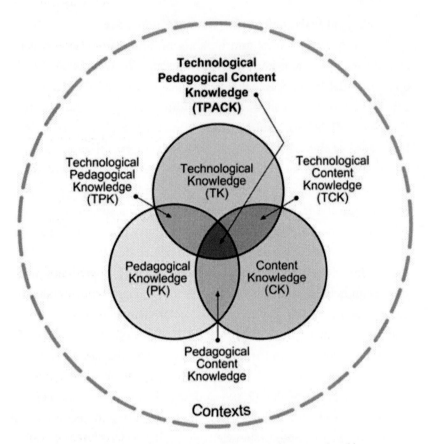

Figure 1: *Technological Pedagogical and Content Knowledge. Reproduced by permission,* © 2014 [http://www.matt-koehler.com/tpack/using-the-tpack-image/].

The educator with well-developed TPACK has an expertise that goes beyond subject matter, pedagogical, and technological knowledge, possessing the ability to consider the varying relationships among these areas and how they may impact student learning within a particular teaching context. Importantly, TPACK is not technocentric, focusing on disciplinary outcomes and ways in which pedagogy and technology can support achievement of those outcomes. Thus, the TPACK model can serve as a guide for curricular development that includes technology.

Component	Description
Technological Knowledge (TK)	General technological literacy that may include knowing how to operate a computer; how to use common software like web browsers, word processors, and spreadsheets; and how to search for information on the Internet.
Pedagogical Knowledge (PK)	General principles of teaching and learning that are common among all teaching disciplines (e.g., learning theories, general assessment principles, and strategies for managing a classroom).
Content Knowledge (CK)	Knowledge of disciplinary content. In music this would include an understanding of creating, performing, and responding to music.[3]
Pedagogical Content Knowledge (PCK)	The intersection and interaction of content and pedagogical knowledge. A teacher with strong PCK can select and use teaching approaches that are best suited to helping students learn specific disciplinary content (e.g., Knowing how to scaffold an ensemble rehearsal is a different form of PCK than that required to structure and sequence a more traditional academic class such as social studies).
Technological Content Knowledge (TCK)	How technology is used in a content area outside of the school setting as well as how the content area may be impacted by the technology (e.g., The digitization of audio has had a profound impact on the recording industry).
Technological Pedagogical Knowledge (TPK)	The combination and interaction of technological knowledge and pedagogical knowledge. An understanding of the affordances and constraints of using common technologies (e.g., interactive whiteboards) for teaching and learning across disciplines.
Technological Pedagogical and Content Knowledge (TPACK)	The central point of the model. All three areas—technological, pedagogical, and content knowledge—interact with and influence each other to create a unique form of teacher knowledge that affects a teacher's choices regarding the use of specific technologies and pedagogies, and even the precise content to be taught.
Context	The teaching/learning environment impacts how technology may be used. It includes the physical nature of the classroom and school, the technologies available, the support for technology in the school, scheduling, socioeconomic factors, and so on.

---

[3]   Creating, performing, and responding to music are the three primary musical processes in which humans engage (Ernst & Gary, 1965; MENC Task Force for National Standards in the Arts. (1994); Shuler & Connealy, 1998) and serve as the organizing principles for the National Core Music Standards [see http://www.nationalartsstandards.org].

Curricular Development

Like other approaches to instructional design, the consideration of how technology might be utilized in the development of music curricula should begin with the desired learning outcomes for students. What is it that students should know and be able to do in regards to creating, performing, and responding to music? Once that has been determined, appropriate technologies and pedagogical approaches that may enhance or even transform the learning process can be considered. It is essential that the initial focus be on musical content—cognitive, affective, and psychomotor outcomes. Curricular approaches in music that include technology should not be technocentric, driven by specific technologies. Technology is merely a tool to facilitate student experiences with music.

A document that can assist music educators in the process of instructional design that includes technology is the *Music Learning Activity Types* (Bauer, Harris, & Hofer, 2012). Researchers (John, 2006; Yinger, 1979) have found that when teachers plan, they often think in terms of types of learning activities that will help students achieve curricular outcomes. In general education these activities are things like discussion, reading, role-playing, and so on. In music, learning approaches might include singing, playing an instrument, listening, or composing. What many teachers who are inexperienced with technology don't know is how common learning activities can be enhanced with, or possibly even transformed by, technology. The *Music Learning Activity Types* align common learning activities related to creating, performing, and responding to music with corresponding pedagogical approaches and supporting technologies (Bauer, Hofer, & Harris, 2012). Examples of the Music Learning Activity Types can be seen in Table 2 on the following page.

Technology Infused Curricula

Technology can be included in music curricula designed for several types of instructional settings—face-to-face classes and rehearsals, courses that are offered completely online, or blended class

Creating Music		
Activity Type	*Brief Description*	*Possible Technologies*
Compose a melodic variation	Students create a variation on a given melody. They can explore alterations of musical elements (e.g., pitch, duration, timbre). The SCAMPER technique: http://goo.gl/sYCW4 is an approach that has been found effective.	Acoustic, electronic and/or digital instruments; music notation software; music production software; mobile apps
Performing Music		
Activity Type	*Brief Description*	*Possible Technologies*
Play with technical accuracy	Play music with precision (pitch/rhythmic accuracy, unified attacks and releases, balance, blend, and intonation). Technology can be used to monitor and provide self-, peer-, and/or instructor feedback.	Audio recording software, audio recorders, auto-accompaniment software, tuners, metronomes
Responding to Music		
Activity Type	*Brief Description*	*Possible Technologies*
Discuss the lives of musicians throughout history, including the social and political events that impacted them.	Students use digital and nondigital technologies to access information about musical composers, conductors, and/or performers and document the understanding that they are building.	Audio/video recordings, audio/video sharing sites, presentation software, Web sites, wikis, e-books, interactive whiteboards, discussion forums

Table 2: *Examples of Music Learning Activity Types*

Note. The complete Music Learning Activity Types are available under a Creative Commons license at http://activitytypes.wmwikis.net/Music

environments (part of the learning experience is face-to-face, part is online). Students and teachers may use technology in a variety of ways, such as described in the Music Learning Activity Types, when learning in face-to-face classes. Online music classes are becoming increasingly common, especially at the collegiate level, and provide certain affordances that include flexibility in learning at a time and place that is convenient to the learner. Here, technology is essential to the learning experience itself, facilitating the delivery of content and, when done well, meaningful interaction among students and the teacher. Blended learning may offer the best of both face-to-face and online worlds.

Researchers have found that blended learning experiences result in superior student achievement when compared to face-to-face or online-only learning environments (Means et al, 2010). Providing online resources to supplement and enhance traditional face-to-face classes can be a relatively easy way to begin integrating technology in a manner that may prove beneficial to student learning outcomes.

When developing any type of technology assisted learning experience, the principles of Universal Design (CAST, 2014) should be kept in mind.

> Universal Design for Learning is a research-based set of principles that together form a practical framework for using technology to maximize learning opportunities for every student. UDL principles draw on brain and media research to help educators reach all students by setting appropriate learning goals, choosing and developing effective methods and materials, and developing accurate and fair ways to assess students' progress. (Rose & Meyer, 2002).

While the principles of Universal Design for Learning are not completely dependent on technology, technology offers affordances in terms of differentiating instruction for all students and providing assistance to students with disabilities. Because technology can present material in a variety of forms—text, graphics, audio, and video—it can be a means to differentiate instruction, providing alternate ways in which students can access and interact with content in a manner that adapts to their readiness, interests, and other learning needs.

In addition, assistive technologies can allow individuals with disabilities to perform tasks that they otherwise could not. Kelker and Holt (1997) describe assistive technology devices as

> mechanical aids which substitute for or enhance the function of some physical or mental ability that is impaired. Assistive technology can be anything homemade, purchased off the shelf, modified, or commercially available, which is used to

help an individual perform some task of daily living. The term assistive technology encompasses a broad range of devices from "low tech" (e.g., pencil grips, splints, paper stabilizers) to "high tech" (e.g., computers, voice synthesizers, braille readers). These devices include the entire range of supportive tools and equipment from adapted spoons to wheelchairs and computer systems for environmental control. (p. 2)

Watson (2014) discusses a number of assistive technologies for music teaching and learning and Hammel and Hourigan (2011) describe ways in which technology can facilitate special needs students' performance of music.

Technology can provide affordances to traditional music classes and ensembles, however it also has the potential to facilitate new curricular approaches to music learning. How technology is used can be conceptualized on a continuum from primarily teacher-centered (e.g., the teacher lectures using a slide-based presentation program with embedded media) to mostly student-centered (e.g., each student uses a music notation program to compose an original composition). Whether learning experiences with technology are student-centered, teacher-centered, or at some point between these two extremes will depend on a number of factors. The desired learning outcomes, the developmental level of students, the availability of necessary technologies, and other contextual factors will all impact instructional design decisions.

New technology-based music courses are growing in popularity (Williams & Dammers, 2014), especially for non-traditional music students. Williams (2011) describes non-traditional music students as individuals who aren't involved in the music programs typically found in secondary schools, programs that frequently consist primarily, if not exclusively, of performance ensembles. These non-traditional music students may comprise as much as 80 percent of the student population of secondary schools. Williams and Dammers (2014) provide profiles of numerous schools that are offering technology-based music courses that include performing, recording, and composing. The non-traditional students enrolled in these programs, many who would not otherwise be participants in school music classes, appear to find these courses engaging.

Integrating Technology

When considering how to begin utilizing technology in the music curriculum, the SAMR model of technology integration can provide guidance (see Figure 2). SAMR stands for *substitution, augmentation, modification*, and *redefinition*. It provides a way to think about the integration of a technology along a continuum from simple to advanced, from enhancement to transformation. As an example, consider how the design of student music listening experiences might be informed by the SAMR framework.

At the *substitution* level, a new technology directly replaces a traditional means of accomplishing a task. For classroom music listening experiences, teachers at one time used records, which were replaced by compact discs, and which now have often been replaced by digital audio files on an MP3 player, computer, smartphone, or tablet. The ultimate objective, being able to listen to a recording, remained essentially unchanged. It has, however, been accomplished with newer types of technology that have substituted for the old.   .

Technology integration at the *augmentation* level not only replaces what was used before, but also provides additional functionality. The teacher who creates playlists of music to use in class using a software program such as iTunes[4] makes it possible to easily and quickly access the music for a lesson, eliminating the necessity of having to swap compact discs in and out of a CD player. A playlist of musical selections makes the act of accessing listening examples more efficient. In addition, for music teachers who travel from room to room, or even from school to school, having all of the digital music files they plan to use available on a single, portable device (computer, MP3 player, smartphone, or tablet) that can be plugged into portable speakers or

---

4   https://www.apple.com/itunes/

the sound system in a room, also simplifies the logistics of transporting and having easy access to the materials necessary for learning. Used this way, digital audio files and the associated software and hardware used to play them have augmented the design and instruction of music listening experiences.

When conceived at the *modification* level, technology allows for a new design to a learning task. While the outcome remains similar, technology enables the process to be enhanced. With free, cloud-based[5] music services such as Spotify[6], teachers and their students have access to a multitude of types, styles, and genres of music from anywhere they have access to the Internet. No longer are the selections available for listening limited by what has been purchased by the school or teacher. Streaming music services allow teachers and students to effortlessly obtain different versions of a musical composition to compare and contrast, and to easily explore many different types of music and musical artists with which they may be unfamiliar. It also enables music that the teacher hadn't planned to be included in a lesson to be immediately accessed should it come up in the course of the class or suddenly be pertinent as an example to illustrate a musical concept. When used in a manner such as described here, the technology has afforded a modified way to approach music listening activities.

Finally, the *redefinition* level of the SAMR model implies that the technology allows for completely new approaches that were not previously possible. Another feature of streaming music services is the ability to create and share playlists of music online. Both teachers and students can create such playlists as activities related to a variety of musical outcomes. For example, ensemble teachers could create playlists of repertoire being performed and studied for students to listen to outside of class. Students could create playlists of music to represent

---

[5]   Cloud-based refers to data that is stored on a remote computer server that can be accessed at any time over the Internet. In this case, the musical data is not stored on the computing device, but rather "in the cloud" that is the Internet.

[6]   Spotify is one of a number of streaming music services. Many aspects of Spotify can be used for free (with advertisements), with more advanced features (and no advertisements) available for a monthly subscription fee. See http://www.spotify.com

their understanding of style, genre, or exemplar performances of compositions written for their instrument. The ability to share music online could be further expanded by combining the playlists with a discussion forum in a learning management system[7] or other service such as a Google+ community.[8] Students could also create a listening blog where they reflect on music to which they listen, creating hyperlinks to specific recordings and other resources that may, for instance, be related to the composer, performer, style, genre, and historical and cultural aspects of the music. These approaches are examples of how music listening experiences can be redefined through technology to include easy sharing of musical selections, discussions about that music both in and outside of the classroom, synthesis of relevant resources, and critical thinking about musical concepts.

SAMR Model of Technology Integration

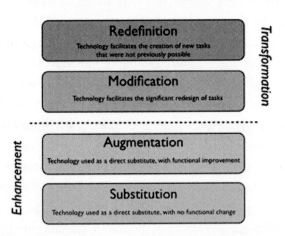

Figure 2: *The continuum of SAMR: Substitution, Augmentation, Modification, and Redefinition*

---

7   "A learning management system (LMS) is a software application for the administration, documentation, tracking, reporting and delivery of e-learning education courses or training programs." [http://en.wikipedia.org/wiki/Learning_management_system]. Common LMS platforms are Blackboard [http://www.blackboard.com], Edmodo [https://www.edmodo.com], and Moodle [https://moodle.org].

8   See http://www.google.com/+/learnmore/communities/

In summary, music curricula can be enhanced, and even transformed, with the appropriate integration of technology. Such integration should not be approached technocentrically. Instructional design that includes technology must start with student music learning outcomes. Then, the affordances and constraints of potential technologies, and the alignment of content, pedagogy, and technology within a particular teaching-learning context may be considered. For further discussion and ideas regarding the integration of technology into music teaching and learning, please see Bauer (2014).

Technology and Assessment

Assessment is an essential aspect of the teaching and learning cycle (see Figure 3). Teachers plan learning experiences, teach to implement those plans, assess whether students have learned, reflect on those assessment results, and then begin the cycle again by planning new lessons if outcomes have been achieved or developing remediation strategies if they have not. Often when the word assessment is used it is associated with grading. However, music educators engage in a variety

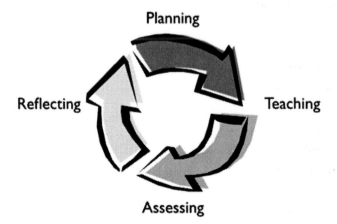

The Teaching-Learning Cycle

Planning

Reflecting

Teaching

Assessing

Figure 3: *The Teaching-Learning Cycle*

of formal and informal student assessments that go far beyond the assignment of grades. Two major types of assessment, formative, feedback for students during instruction to improve learning, and summative, determining a student's level of achievement at the conclusion of an assignment, unit, grading period, etc., will be the focus here.

Technology may be useful in formative and summative assessment of cognitive, affective, and psychomotor learning outcomes. It is capable of enhancing traditional assessment practices, improving their efficiency and effectiveness. Some technologies also offer the possibility of new, alternative types of assessment tasks and processes. Finally, technology can assist music educators in the management of assessment processes and data. When thinking about the assessment of musical outcomes, it may be useful to consider the SAMR model described previously. How might technology be used to enhance (substitute and augment) and possibly transform (modify and redefine) assessment practices and procedures? The examples that follow are not meant to be all-inclusive. Rather, they are presented to suggest some potential affordances of technology to assessment. Readers are encouraged to exercise their TPACK to develop additional approaches that are well suited for their students, curricula, and teaching-learning context.

Enhancing Traditional Assessment Practices

Traditionally, both written and performance-based assessments have been used in music education. Written tests are best suited for the assessment of cognitive understanding. Performance-based measures provide a means to examine psychomotor skills and products that are the outcome of musical activities. Word processors are helpful to develop both written tests and performance-based assessment instruments such as checklists, rating scales, and rubrics. When these materials are saved as a word processing document they can be easily modified and printed on demand as needed. In addition, music notation programs can be used to develop musical examples to insert in the word-processed tests. Cloud-based word processing applications such as Google Docs[9] provide the opportunity to synchronously or asynchronously collaborate online with other teachers in the development of assessment instruments. Rubrics and other performance-based instruments hosted in Google Drive[10] can also be shared with students and their parents prior to a test so that they better understand the criteria to be used in the assessment, allowing students to prepare appropriately.

Traditional written and performance-based assessments can also be administered electronically. There are numerous programs[11] available to create electronic quizzes. Most learning management systems have a quiz component to them. Google Forms[12] may also be used to create assessments that use a variety of item-types (e.g., multiple choice, short answer, essay) and can include images, videos, and audio.[13] Depending on their design, assessments in Google Forms can be automatically graded using a free add-on called Flubaroo.[14] Performance-based assessments created in Google Forms can be displayed and completed on a computing device (computer, smartphone, tablet) with the resulting data automatically flowing to a spreadsheet for access by the teacher at a later point in time.

Music teachers have traditionally utilized audio recordings for formative and summative assessment of musical performance. Both students and teachers can access free software such as Audacity,[15] a program to create and edit digital audio recordings. Free and inexpensive apps for smartphones and tablets, along with dedicated digital audio recorders, are other ways to easily create audio recordings. Students can record themselves and self-assess their strengths and

---

9 See http://en.wikipedia.org/wiki/Google_Docs
10 See http://drive.google.com
11 These include commercial products such as SurveyMonkey [https://www.survey-monkey.com] and Qualtrics [http://www.qualtrics.com], as well as LimeSurvey [http://www.limesurvey.org/en/], an open-source solution.
12 http://goo.gl/2g1DVE
13 At the time this chapter was written, including audio in a Google Form requires a little bit of a workaround. One possibility is to post audio as a YouTube video and then insert that video into the quiz.
14 http://www.flubaroo.com
15 http://audacity.sourceforge.net

weaknesses, and also exchange recordings with each other, engaging in peer-assessment. Of course, students may also record themselves and submit it to the teacher for a summative assessment. This can be done at home or the teacher could provide opportunities for students to record themselves at school—before or after the school day, or during class time. Having students listen to rehearsal and performance recordings to analyze their ensemble's progress is another effective formative assessment strategy. Digital video can be used in a similar manner to digital audio, with the added benefit of being able to view and provide feedback on things that can be observed visually such as posture, embouchure, instrument holding position, performance demeanor, and so on. Like digital audio, a variety of free, inexpensive, and sophisticated commercial software, mobile apps, and hardware are available for teachers and students who would like to explore the capabilities of digital video as an assessment tool.

Finally, a less common but sometimes used form of musical assessment has involved the use of student portfolios. Portfolios are a collection of purposefully selected samples of student work. Depending on the purpose of the portfolio, this work could be chosen to demonstrate development over time or a current level of achievement. Traditional portfolios have been assembled using a variety of containers such as file folders, binders, or even cardboard boxes. More recently, electronic portfolios have grown in popularity. Electronic portfolios can be created using proprietary software programs, blogs, or a variety of web-based platforms.[16] One of their affordances is being able to combine all types of media—text, images, audio, and video—in one seamless package to better portray the full extent of a student's strengths and weaknesses. Electronic portfolios may also be easier to store than bulky analog portfolios. Finally, when set up properly, various stakeholders (students, teachers, parents, etc.) in the educational process may easily access and weigh in on electronic portfolios.

---

[16] Dr. Helen Barrett's website is a rich source of information about electronic portfolios – http://electronicportfolios.org

New Assessment Tasks and Processes

Technology has also made it feasible for teachers to use a variety of innovative formative and summative assessments and assessment tasks, and for students to create new types of artifacts that provide evidence of their knowledge and skill in creating, performing, and responding to music. Music educators have sometimes struggled to address creative musical outcomes such as composing and improvising music. The availability of easy-to-use music notation programs, music production software, and software that automatically creates musical accompaniments in various genres and styles have made a great impact in this area. Notation software and music production software like GarageBand,[17] Mixcraft,[18] and Soundation[19] provide students with tools to compose, arrange, and remix music. The products resulting from the use of these tools become indicators of students' understanding and skill. Likewise, accompaniment software such as Band-in-a-Box[20] and iReal Pro[21] enable students to practice and perform individual improvisations that can also be assessed using appropriate criteria.

In music performance, a plethora of tuners and metronomes available as standalone devices, on websites, and as smartphone and tablet apps are available. These are often free and allow nearly anyone to have access to these tools that are able to provide formative assessment of rhythm and pitch. An influential new technology that has a number of features that can impact the teaching and assessment of music performance is SmartMusic.[22] SmartMusic will provide immediate formative assessment of pitch & rhythm accuracy to students. It also allows students to record themselves and upload the recording to their teacher's online, virtual classroom. The teacher can access student submissions to grade them and provide additional feedback.

---

[17] https://www.apple.com/mac/garageband/
[18] http://www.acoustica.com/mixcraft/
[19] http://soundation.com
[20] http://www.pgmusic.com
[21] http://irealpro.com
[22] http://www.smartmusic.com

Student response systems, commonly known as *clickers*, empower teachers to assess students' musical understanding, preference, attitudes, and other responses to music in the moment, during instruction. The teacher provides a prompt with (usually) several response options, much like a multiple-choice test. Students then select a response using their clicker and the system aggregates the data provided by the entire class, allowing the instructor to gauge the level of student understanding, perceptions, attitudes, agreement or whatever is of interest. While commercial versions of these tools can be purchased, free, online[23] versions that use computers, smartphones, and tablets as the "clicker," are also available. Some forms of these systems allow individual students to be tracked, making them useful for both formative and summative assessments.

Other technological tools such as slide programs, wikis, websites, blogs, and mind-mapping software can also be used for students to create products to provide evidence of their cognitive knowledge and affective response to musical stimuli. As an example, students could be asked to keep a daily listening blog describing all of the music to which they listen during a week. In the blog they might describe the music and its salient features, why they chose to listen to it, the situation(s)/ environments where they typically listen to this kind of music, and so on. Because blogs allow for the inclusion of various media, students could represent their experience of music listening with text, pictures, video, and sound. One way the teacher can assess the musical products created with technologies such as those mentioned here is through the use of screen capture software. By using programs that will capture video of what is seen on the computer screen when viewing a student project, while simultaneously recording the teacher's real time verbal feedback on the project, rich, nuanced feedback can be provided to students on their work.[24]

---

23 For example, see http://www.polleverywhere.com and http://www.socrative.com
24 Two free programs like this are http://www.screencast-o-matic.com and http://www.techsmith.com/download/jing/

Managing Assessments and Assessment Data

A final area where technology can help with musical assessment is in the management of assessment processes and data. Music teachers often work with large numbers of students, and assessing and providing appropriate individual feedback to each child can be challenging. Spreadsheets are excellent ways to track, manage, and analyze all forms of numerical data. Some teachers use spreadsheets as a grade book. Mentioned previously, learning management systems (LMS) typically have quiz tools and grade books built in to them. Usually, when a student takes a quiz in a LMS their grade will automatically flow to the associated grade book. Other grades can be entered manually. In addition, some learning management systems have built in rubric tools[25] that, when completed, also automatically update the grade book.

Many school systems provide an online electronic tool for teachers to communicate with students and their parents about grades and other important matters. This may be part of an LMS or a separate entity.[26] Through these tools both summative grades and formative text-based messages can be provided. If a teacher does not have access to an electronic grade book tool that allows for this type of communication, free and commercial products are available. Engrade[27] is a free, online grade book with many valuable features.

Summary

Assessment is an essential part of the teaching cycle. Music teachers can use technology to enhance traditional assessment practices including the development and administration of cognitive tests and performance-based assessment instruments, the incorporation of audio in the assessment process, and the construction and management of student portfolios that demonstrate development and/or

---

[25] For instance, see http://www.rcampus.com/indexrubric.cfm
[26] For example, see ProgressBook [http://www.software-answers.com/Solutions/Pages/ProgressBook-Suite.aspx]
[27] https://www.engrade.com

achievement. Technology also affords the possibility of new types of assessment tasks and processes such as formative and summative assessment of musical performance using a tool like SmartMusic, student response systems to check for student understanding, and tools for students to create products that provide evidence of their cognitive knowledge and affective response to musical stimuli. Finally, spreadsheets, learning management systems, and electronic grade books are beneficial tools to manage assessments and their resulting data.

Conclusions

The development and implementation of the many and varied types of curricula and assessments in music education is among the most important jobs of the music teacher. In our 21st century world, technology has a role to play in both curriculum and assessment. The focus, however, must not be on the technology itself but rather on learning outcomes and the ways in which technology might be leveraged to assist students in achieving those outcomes. By utilizing technology as a tool that can support, enhance, and potentially transform teaching, learning, and assessment, music educators will benefit both their students and themselves.

References

Bauer, W. I. (2014). *Music learning today: Digital pedagogy for creating, performing, and responding to music.* New York: Oxford University Press.

Bauer, W. I., Harris, J., & Hofer, M. (2012, June). *Music learning activity types.* Retrieved from http://activitytypes.wmwikis.net/Music

Bauer, W. I., Hofer, M., & Harris, J. (2012). *"Grounded" technology integration using K–12 music learning activity types. Learning and Leading with Technology, 40*(3), 30–32.

CAST. (2014). CAST: Center for Applied Special Technology. Retrieved from http://www.cast.org/

Ernst, K.D. & Gary, C. L. (1965). *Music in general education*. Washington, D. C.: Music Educators National Conference.

Hammel, A. M., & Hourigan, R. M. (2011). *Teaching music to students with special needs: A label-free approach*. New York: Oxford University Press.

International Society for Technology in Education. (2014). *ISTE standards*. Retrieved from http://www.iste.org/STANDARDS

John, P. D. (2006). Lesson planning and the student teacher: Re-thinking the dominant model. *Journal of Curriculum Studies, 38*(4), 483–498.

Kelker, K. A., & Holt, R. (1997). *Family guide to assistive technology*. Billings, MT: Parents, Let's Unite for Kids. Retrieved from http://www.pluk.org/Pubs/PLUK_ATguide_269K.pdf.

Means, B., Toyama, Y., Murphy, R., Bakia, M., & Jones, K. (2010). Evaluation of evidence-based practices in online learning: A meta-analysis and review of online learning. Center for Technology in Learning, U.S. Department of Education. Available: http://www2.ed.gov/rschstat/eval/tech/evidence-based-practices/finalreport.pdf

MENC Task Force for National Standards in the Arts. (1994). *The school music program: A new vision*. Reston, VA: Music Educators National Conference.

Mishra, P., & Koehler, M. J. (2006). Technological Pedagogical Content Knowledge: A framework for teacher knowledge. *Teachers College Record, 108*(6), 1017–1054.

Papert, S. (1987). Computer criticism vs. technocentric thinking. *Educational Researcher, 16*(1), 22–30.

Rose, D. H., & Meyer, A. (2002). *Teaching every student in the digital age: Universal design for learning*. Alexandria, VA: Association for Supervision and Curriculum Development.

Shuler, S., & Connealy, S. (1998). The evolution of state arts assessment: From Sisyphus to stone soup. *Arts Education Policy Review, 100*(1), 12.

Shulman, L. S. (1987). Knowledge and teaching: Foundations of the new reform. *Harvard Educational Review, 57*(1), 1–22.

U. S. Department of Education. (2010). *Transforming American education: Learning powered by technology.* Retrieved from https://www.ed.gov/technology/netp-2010

Vygotsky, L. S. (1978). *Mind in society: The development of higher psychological processes.* Cambridge, MA: Harvard University Press.

Watson, S. (2014). *Technology in Music Ed for Diverse Learners.* Retrieved from http://watsonmusic.wikispaces.com/Technology+in+Music+Ed+for+Diverse+Learners

Williams, D. B. (2011). The non-traditional music student in secondary schools of the United States: Engaging non-participant students in creative music activities through technology. *Journal of Music, Technology and Education, 4*(2+3), 131–147.

Williams, D. B., & Dammers, R. J. (2014). *Music creativity through technology.* Retrieved from http://www.musiccreativity.org

Yinger, R. (1979). Routines in teacher planning. *Theory Into Practice, 18*(3), 163–169.

Chapter 21

Challenges to Musicianship-Focused Curriculum and Assessment

Colleen Conway
University of Michigan

The authors in the previous 20 chapters of this book have provided many suggestions, strategies, and new ways to think about structuring and assessing music teaching and learning. However, no change in curricula happens easily. This final chapter is devoted to a discussion of the many roadblocks to music education curriculum development, implementation, and evaluation including: (a) defining musicianship and agreeing upon core goals for music students; (b) performance pressure in music classes; (c) context-specific nature of curriculum work; (d) meeting individual learning needs; (e) lack of time and expertise to implement musicianship-focused curricula; (f) co-curricular and extra-curricular status of music classes; and (g) current teacher evaluation policies.

Curriculum Reform

In his chapter on curriculum implementation and sustainability in the *Sage Handbook of Curriculum and Instruction* (2008), noted school reform scholar Michael Fullan suggested that school reform research has shifted from documenting how particular innovations were implemented in schools to instead considering "how curriculum change can be seen as part and parcel of system reform" (p. 113). He stated curriculum change cannot focus solely on a new and improved strategy for the classroom and that:

> ...the long term solution to implementation and sustainability is not improving an external-in strategy, but changing the strategy itself. Not to an inside-out approach, but rather to how whole system reform can take place. (p. 119)

If we as music educators are interested in true music education curriculum reform we must move away from trying to find the perfect innovation—the perfect lesson, perfect method book, perfect repertoire, or perfect sequence. We must instead focus on what it is we are trying to accomplish. Authors in this volume have focused on an individual learner-centered and comprehensive musicianship approach that encourages active music making through moving, singing, playing, improvising, composing, reading, and listening to music. They have encouraged readers to pay attention to issues of context and to meet students' individual learning needs.

However, for many teachers who may be working in performance-only school music environments there will be a great need for preservice and inservice teacher education in order for them to learn the strategies needed for learner-centered comprehensive musicianship. Fullan (2008) suggested that teachers lacking understanding about innovation need sustained engagement in professional development, rather than "one- shot" workshops. He recommends what he refers to as the three "Ps" inside the classroom: " ...personalization (addressing each child's learning needs), precision (tailoring the instruction to the needs without getting prescriptive) and professional learning (where each and every teacher learns every day)" (p. 121).

Chapter 5 on Universal Designs for Learning (Hourigan) and Chapter 16 on English Language Learners (Eros) both address personalization. All of the chapters in Part III focus on precision as well as personalization. Chapter 3 on the study of curriculum and assessment (Conway, Edgar, and West), Chapter 18 on preservice education (Millican and Pellegrino), Chapter 19 on inservice education (Stanley) and Chapter 20 on the role of technology (Bauer) all address professional learning and the need for reform in teacher preservice and inservice development.

Fullan closed his chapter by stating that most of the work on curriculum reform has been done at the elementary level and there is very little known about curriculum change at the secondary level. What researchers do know is that curriculum reform is difficult and that small pilot projects rarely lead to large-scale change. There is even less known about curriculum reform in areas such as music education. The Conway, Edgar and West chapter (Chapter 3) encourages music teachers to document their curriculum reform experiences so that we can begin to build a stronger base for understanding change.

Music Education Challenges and Opportunities

Although the general school reform literature discussed above presents a somewhat bleak picture of school reform and systemic change, challenges can also provide opportunities for music educators to move the profession forward. In this section, I will discuss seven specific challenges to musicianship-focused curriculum reform as well as opportunities presented by each challenge for pushing music education ahead.

Defining Musicianship and Agreeing upon Core Goals for Music Students

Challenges. Although the new National Core Arts Standards (National Coalition for Core Arts Standards, 2014) provide solid recommendations for ways in which students should be engaged in creating, performing, responding to and connecting with music, coming to agreement among music teachers on the core goals for specific students and classrooms is challenging. Teachers often do not have appropriate collaborative planning time to spend with one another in order to work through differences in philosophy and approach. It is sometimes hard for music teachers to separate their own musical interests (i.e., to conduct a large ensemble work) from appropriate musical goals for students. Finally, professional development for music teachers does not always provide ample time for teachers to process new ideas and share them with one another.

Opportunities. Although consensus is difficult for music teachers, the new National Core Arts Standards provide an opportunity to focus the profession on comprehensive musicianship by encouraging that all students experience music through creating, performing, responding, and connecting to music. Diverse teacher opinions regarding how to do this should be valued in schools. Part III of this book provides many suggestions for keeping the focus of music classes on musicianship. With so much focus on testing in math and reading in schools it is important for music students and teachers to celebrate the uniqueness of our discipline.

Performance Pressure in Music Classes

Challenges. The pressure of performance is mentioned throughout the book and specifically in the philosophy and advocacy chapter (West), the Universal Designs for Learning chapter (Hourigan), the English language learners chapter (Eros) and the chapter on adjudicated events (Rawlings). School districts and communities want their music ensembles to participate in contests, competitions, and festivals and music teachers are challenged to address this demand while still providing sequential music instruction. If we look carefully at the recommendations for sequential music instruction in the new National Core Arts Standards we see that only two of the four anchor standards focus on performance (creating music, performing music) while the others are more "about" music (responding and connecting). I believe that all the authors in this text would suggest that creating and performing are potentially more important musical areas than responding and connecting (such that not all of the four anchor standards are equal). However, the need to attend to creating music as well as performing in addition to responding and connecting makes the performance pressures even greater.

Finally, the primary concern with performance-only classrooms is that they are often very teacher-directed learning environments. Teachers choose the music, prepare the instruction, and rehearse for performance. Authors throughout this text have suggested learner-centered approaches to music teaching and learning which allow students more ownership and involvement in their learning.

Opportunities. There is certainly a place for performance and active music making in a comprehensive music curriculum. Learner-centered teaching strategies can be incorporated into these already powerful learning contexts. There is a tremendous opportunity to showcase our students and the power of music through public performance. Chapter 17 on curriculum and adjudicated events (Rawlings) provides many strategies for balancing these performances with sequential curriculum.

Context-Specific Nature of Curriculum Work

Challenges. All of the authors in Parts III and IV of this volume address the requirement to adapt instruction to the needs of the learners in individual contexts. Issues of individual context include: scheduling, instructional space, financial resources, English language learners, persons with disabilities, time for instruction, administrative and community priorities, and the list goes on. Due to these issues of context it is impossible to provide a template for music education curriculum. The authors in Part II (Understanding by Design, Universal Designs for Learning, and 21st Century Skills and the Common Core State Standards Initiative) share some models that may be of use. However, it is difficult to plan for curriculum and assessment when contexts for the teaching and learning of music are so varied. Some states have strong state policy that support instructional time (e.g., a mandate for general music in K–5 or a requirement for one course in the arts at 9–12) but many states have no detailed requirements.

Opportunities. Although the need for adapting to contexts is challenging it also offers music educators the opportunity to creatively develop responses to these challenges. Darling-Hammond and Bransford (2005) discussed the need to develop adaptive expertise for teachers and suggested:

> The goal for preservice preparation, then, is to provide teachers with the core ideas and broad understanding of teaching and learning that give them traction on their later development. This perspective views teachers' capacity not as a fixed store-house of facts and ideas but as a "source and creator of knowledge and skills needed for instruction" (Cohen and Ball, 1999, p. 6). An important goal of this volume [referring to the text *Preparing Teachers for a Changing World*] is to help teachers become "adaptive experts" who are prepared for effective lifelong learning that allows them to continuously add to the knowledge and skills. (p. 3)

Whether music educators are teaching band, orchestra, choir, or general music, they have core activities to be addressed in all contexts (i.e., performing, composing, creating, listening). Helping teachers to understand these core activities regardless of the specific music-teaching context may help them to develop the skills needed for career-long success as a music teacher. Hammerness et. al. (2005) discussed the need for teachers to learn and continue to adapt throughout their careers:

> ...it is important to help people [teacher] understand that "letting go" of previously learned ideas and routines or incorporating new information into their practice—choosing what to abandon and what to keep or modify—is a big part of what it means to be a lifelong learner and an adaptive expert (Hammerness et al., p. 363)

Meeting Individual Learning Needs

Challenges. Chapters 5 (Universal Designs for Learning by Hourigan), 14 (Early Childhood Curriculum Matters by Alison

Reynolds and Wendy Valerio), 15 (Adult Music Learning by Scott Edgar and Linda Hartley), and 16 (Modifications of Music Curriculum and Assessment for English Language Learners by John Eros) focus specifically on meeting individual learning needs. All musical contexts require a focus on individual students. With changing demographics as well as larger class sizes, music teachers must constantly focus on meeting students where they are and bringing them to the next level of musical learning, which can be a challenge due to limited resources and professional development.

The heavy ensemble performance focus of our music classrooms can also contribute to the challenge of teaching to individual differences. Teachers must often make difficult instructional choices when deciding whether to really address the individual learning needs of students or to quickly "fix" the musical problem of the group.

Opportunities. The authors of Vision 20/20 (Madsen, 2000) encouraged music educators to look beyond school music to both early childhood and adult learners: "Music educators must join with others in providing opportunities for meaningful music instruction for all people beginning at the earliest possible age and continuing throughout life" (Barrett, 2009, p. 101). In addition to the chapters in this book devoted to early childhood (Chapter 14) and adult learners (Chapter 15), all of the authors in Part III have tried to sequence their content in a way that helps teachers to consider how to adjust instruction to meet individual student learning needs. Many of these authors included discussion of music aptitude as a necessary understanding for teaching to student individual differences.

Lack of Time and Expertise to Implement Musicianship-Focused Curricula

Challenges. One of the biggest challenges for music educators is lack of instructional time. As mentioned before, some states have policy to support minimum hours of music-specialist instructional time, but many states do not. The need for music teachers to have a tremendous amount of personal musicianship is also a challenge. Many preservice music education program (college programs) focus exclusively on skill on the primary instrument or voice. However, the musicianship skills needed by the music educator include singing, playing harmonic accompaniment instruments, composing, and improvising in addition to skills on primary instruments.

Opportunities. Music educators can work to balance community interests with curricular needs in the effort to secure time for music instruction. The more the community supports the program, the more time will be allotted for music instruction. Chapter 20 (Bauer) suggests ways in which technology can save time so that more music instruction can occur.

With regard to preparation for musicianship-focused curricula, music education programs in colleges and universities can and should work to attract the best musicians (those who can move, sing, improvise, compose, and play instruments) into music education. As mentioned in Chapters 18 and 19 preservice and inservice education are continuing to focus on the comprehensive musicianship skills needed by music teachers.

Co-curricular and Extra-curricular Status of Music Classes

Challenges. It is unclear as to whether the untested subject of music is really considered a curricular subject in most schools. In places where music is considered more "co-curricular" or "extra-curricular" it is certainly harder to advocate for policy, time, resources, and teachers. It is even more challenging to help administrators, other teachers, and community members understand the need for sequential curriculum and individual student assessment in these environments.

Opportunities. However, the very same issues which make our status challenging might also be considered opportunities. As a nontested subject most music teachers have a great deal of autonomy over their curriculum and as long as communities are supportive, teachers can teach what they want. In addition, the visibility of the music program often creates a positive environment for community advocacy of the music program.

Teacher Evaluation Policies

Challenges. The recent policy focus on connecting student achievement to teacher evaluation through value-added measures is a challenge to learner-centered and musicianship-focused music education curriculum and assessment. Hash (2013) wrote:

> The Race to the Top program, initiated in 2009 by US president Barack Obama, has resulted in new laws governing teacher evaluation, retention, and compensation. In many states, teachers' contributions to students' academic growth will account for up to 50 percent of their evaluations and serve as a basis for decisions regarding retention and pay. (p. 163)

With so much focus on academic area test scores, many music teachers struggle to secure time with students and focus on individual musicianship. Hash (2013) goes on to discuss the notion of utilizing large-ensemble contest and festival ratings as part of teacher evaluation, which would provide another challenge to individual, musicianship-focused curriculum and assessment. The new National Core Arts Standards (National Coalition for Core Arts Standards, 2014) for music encourage curriculum and assessment in the areas of creating music, performing music, responding to music, and connecting music to other subjects. I am concerned that the areas of responding to music and connecting music to other subjects which require cognitive skills rather than musical skills may be easier to assess and thus, will find a stronger place in the curriculum than creating and performing music, which are both musical skills.

Opportunities. Teachers of all subject areas are struggling with teacher evaluation. The hands-on and in-the-moment nature of music making provides us an opportunity to lead the field in developing appropriate and authentic measures of student achievement in our content. The aesthetic nature of our work also provides an opportunity to lead and teach others about that which may be difficult to assess.

Conclusions

Lehman (2009) outlined six conditions that needed to be met before a goal of curricular change in music education is possible. I am encouraged as I consider ways in which the authors in *Musicianship-Focused Curriculum and Assessment* have addressed these conditions.

Lehman's first condition was a need for a "Curriculum that is truly balanced and comprehensive" (Barrett, p. 25). All of the authors in this text have focused on balance, depth, and breadth of content. Lehman then outlined his second condition: "A rationale for music in schools that is short, simple, and convincing" (p. 26) which is addressed directly in this text through Chapter 2, West's "Philosophy, Advocacy, Curriculum, and Assessment." Condition three for Lehman was "In the high school, a diversity of course offerings that attract large numbers of students" (p. 28) which is reflected throughout this text as authors have considered individual student learning needs, curriculum beyond large ensemble, students with special learning needs, and the general notion of musicianship. The West chapter also addressed Lehman's fourth condition ("A public familiar with the content of the music program" on page 29). The notion of a "More supportive professional environment" (Condition number 5 on p. 30) is carefully discussed in this volume in the preservice and inservice professional development chapters (Chapters 18 and 19). Finally, Lehman suggested that there is a need for "a place for music educators at the table when educational issues are discussed" (p. 31) as his sixth condition for improvement. Chapter 6 on 21st Century Skills and the Common Core State Standards Initiative is directly related to being a part of this "table." The two chapters that present specific curricular frameworks (Chapter 4 on Understanding by Design and Chapter 5 on Universal Designs for Learning) both model the type of place at the table that I believe Lehman had in mind. So, in response to Lehman, we may not be there yet, but we are progressing.

The authors in this volume have worked hard to provide practical suggestions for the development, implementation, and evaluation of music teaching and learning. Although there are many challenges to this work, I believe the resources provided will assist music educators in continuing to advocate for, provide, and celebrate music making in early childhood, K–12, higher education and adult learning situations.

References

Cohen, D. K., & Ball, D. L. (1999). *Instruction, capacity, and improvement: CPRE Research Report Series*. Philadelphia, PA: Consortium for Policy Research in Education.

Darling-Hammond, L., & Bransford, J. (Eds.). (2005). *Preparing teachers for a changing world*. San Francisco, CA: Jossey-Bass.

Fullan, M. (2008). Curriculum implementation and sustainability. In F. M. Connelly (Ed.). *The Sage handbook of curriculum and instruction* (pp. 113–122). Thousand Oaks, CA: Sage.

Hammerness, K., Darling-Hammond, L., Bransford, J., Berliner, D., Cochran-Smith, M., McDonald, M., & Zeichner, K. (2005). How teachers learn and develop. In L. Darling-Hammond & J. Bransford (Eds.). *Preparing teachers for a changing world* (pp. 358–389). San Francisco, CA: Jossey-Bass.

Hash, P. (2013). Large-group contest ratings and music teacher evaluation: Issues and recommendations. *Arts Education Policy Review 114*, 163–169.

Lehman, P. (2009). Are we there yet? Why no? In J. Barrett *Music education at a crossroads*, (pp. 25–34). New York, NY: Rowman & Littlefield Education.

Madsen, C. K. (Ed.). (2000). Vision 20/20: The Housewright symposium on the future of music education. http://musiced.nafme.org/resources/vision-2020-the-housewright-symposium-on-the-future-of-music-education/

National Coalition for Core Arts Standards (2014). www.nationalartsstandards.org